Death and Bereavement:
A Halakhic Guide

by

Rabbi Abner Weiss

The Union of Orthodox Jewish
Congregations of America
New York

DEATH AND BEREAVEMENT
© *Copyright 1991* by **ABNER WEISS**
Published by Union of Orthodox Jewish Congregations of America
333 Seventh Avenue / New York, NY 10001 / (212) 563-4000

Distributed by
MESORAH PUBLICATIONS, LTD.
4401 Second Avenue / Brooklyn, N.Y 11232

Distributed in Europe by
J. LEHMANN HEBREW BOOKSELLERS
20 Cambridge Terrace
Gateshead, Tyne and Wear
England NE8 1RP

Distributed in Israel by
SIFRIATI / A. GITLER
10 Hashomer Street
Bnei Brak 51361

Distributed in Australia and New Zealand by
GOLDS BOOK & GIFT SHOP
36 William Street
Balaclava 3183, Vic., Australia

Distributed in South Africa by
KOLLEL BOOKSHOP
Shop 8A Norwood Hypermarket
Norwood 2196, Johannesburg, South Africa

Library of Congress Cataloging-in Publication Data

Weiss, Abner.
    Death and bereavement : a halakhic guide / by Abner Weiss.
    p.   cm.
    ISBN 1-57819-544-6 (hard cover)   1-57819-545-4 (paperback)
    1. Mourning customs, Jewish. 2. Death—Religious aspects—
—Judaism. 3. Funeral sermons, Jewish. 4. Homiletical
illustrations, Jewish.   1. Title.
    BM12.Y64 1990
    296.4 45—dc20

90-30907
CIP

Printed in the United States of America by Noble Book Press Corp.
Bound by Sefercraft, Quality Bookbinders, Ltd., Brooklyn N.Y. 11232

In tribute to my great teachers

Rabbi Dr. Joseph B. Soloveitchik ז״ל
Rabbi Dr. Alter Hilewitz ז״ל
Rabbi Chaim Goldvicht ז״ל
Rabbi Dr. Louis I. Rabinowitz ז״ל
Rabbi Dr. Salo Rappaport ז״ל

CONTENTS

PART TWO

CONTENTS

HALAKHIC

CHAPTER SEVEN

BETWEEN DEATH AND BURIAL:
TREATMENT OF THE DECEASED

CHAPTER EIGHT

CHAPTER NINE

CHAPTER TEN

CHAPTER ELEVEN

CONTENTS

MATERIALS FOR STUDY AND EULOGIES

MISHNAH ANTHOLOGY:
STUDY SESSIONS IN THE SHIV'AH HOUSE

Preface

WHY WE NEED A NEW BOOK ON MOURNING

There is no shortage of books on the Jewish attitude to death and on the responses of the Jewish tradition to the pain of bereavement. This is not surprising. Death is the most universal of human experiences. Its intrusion into our lives is usually traumatic. It terrifies us, confuses us, and often paralyzes us. We grope our way through the valley of the shadow, desperately in need of a compass, of clear guidelines to help us make a healthy adjustment to our new situation. Manuals on death and bereavement are produced to satisfy this need.

Most of the published works on the subject fall into one of two categories. Some are designed to be codes of Jewish practice. They either elaborate or summarize the Halakhah, and are either scholarly or popular. Others deal with the philosophical, theological, and psychological questions which are raised by our encounter with death. They seek to explain and rationalize the Jewish laws and customs which surround the loss of a dear one.

The reader may therefore legitimately ask: If most, if not all, of the bases are already covered elsewhere, why do we need yet another book on the subject? The truth is that *not* all the bases *are* covered. Most works in the field do not cover some very practical aspects of the subject. They do not include the documents that the bereaved may require. They do not provide all the special prayers, formulas, and readings that are used prior to death, during the preparations for the funeral, at the interment, and in the house of mourning. Passages from rabbinic literature are customarily studied in the house of mourning, but this volume is the first to provide an anthology of suitable texts accompanied by a simple commentary, structured to help the survivors apply the lessons of Judaism to their understanding of the life of the deceased, and to enable the presenter to use them as a means of comforting the bereaved.

1

Because of the wide range of material it contains in addition to the rabbinic texts and commentaries, this book is not only a halakhic manual on death and mourning but also a philosophical and psychological guide for the bereaved. To enhance its utility, and for the convenience of readers, different typefaces and layout are used to separate its main component elements. All in all, this volume represents an entirely new approach to the literature on death, and will be, I hope, eminently useful to mourners and the bereaved—a group to which all of us will belong at one time or another.

HOW TO USE THIS BOOK

As a Halakhic Manual

In a sense, this volume is really three books in one. It provides a fairly detailed summary of the *practices*, the laws and customs which govern our encounter with death and bereavement. These practices are carefully and logically structured under main headings, subheadings, sub-subheadings, and side-headings. Each section is presented concisely, step-by-step and point-by-point, without burdening the reader with an elaborate scholarly apparatus.

The summaries of appropriate practice derive from the *Shulchan Arukh* and its standard commentaries, from the classical *Ma'avar Yabok* by Rabbi Aharon Berakhyah ben Moshe of Modena, and from more recent authoritative works on the subject, notably the seminal *Gesher ha-Chayyim* by Rabbi Yechiel Mikhel Tuketchinsky, the *Kol Bo Al Aveilut* by Rabbi Yekutiel Yehudah Greenwald, and *Yesodei Smochos* by Rabbi Aaron Felder, and the sources they cite. Rabbi Felder's work was particularly useful for its citations of often unpublished decisions of *the* halakhic authority of our generation, Rabbi Moshe Feinstein, of blessed memory.

For the sake of simplicity and readability, I have omitted footnotes and the give-and-take of halakhic debate on the various topics. Those who are acquainted with the field will realize my great indebtedness to my predecessors. There is a fairly wide consensus on most halakhic questions on our topic. On some, however, there is a great deal of dispute. In such instances, I have generally used my own judgment, rather than merely restate the various viewpoints to avoid the responsibility of taking a stand. This approach may well be controversial. For the purposes of this volume, it was unavoidable.

The halakhic summaries are set apart from the rest of the text by the use of blocks of different typeface. They are also listed in detail in a separate Table of Contents. They constitute an independent book which can be used as a separate unit for quick reference on a particular subject, or in conjunction with the philosophical, psychological, and theological background and explanatory materials.

The Jewish Worldview

The second part of this volume contains the main body of the text. It presents a complete treatment of various questions relating to death: What happens to our souls after we die? What is the status of our bodies after death? How can we deal with our feelings about the deceased and ourselves, with our losses and with our guilts? How shall we relate to God? How can we resume our normal way of life? And so on. The main body of the text is both explanatory and therapeutic, thought-provoking and consoling.

It can be read alone—by skipping the blocks of halakhic summary—or in conjunction with those guidelines, depending upon the mood, disposition, and purposes of the reader. To facilitate both possibilities, the main Table of Contents lists both the background materials (in detail, by subheading) and the halakhic summaries (in general).

Documents and Texts

Section Two of this book is really the third volume and contains lists of things to do to reduce the turmoil and confusion of our encounter with death. The documents, prayers, formulas, and readings are provided with concise instructions as to use, and are listed in a separate Table of Contents. They are linked to Section One by cross-references.

As indicated, the anthology of Mishnah selections is a radical departure from previous presentations. The selections are catalogued according to the most appropriate circumstances for their use. Thus, texts have been chosen for families which mourn leaders of the community, or scholars, or synagogue members, young children, or Holocaust survivors, and so on. These texts are presented in the original Hebrew and in English translation, accompanied by a simple commentary. Guidelines are presented for personalizing the texts and applying them to the deceased and to the bereaved, adding the element of eulogy to the theme of Torah study. *The treatment of the texts is simple enough to permit any lay person to conduct a study session in a house of mourning.*

The texts are structured to be used as a *resource in the preparation of eulogies* for funerals. The eulogies are "ready-made." But since these talks may easily be personalized, they will carry the stamp of the speaker's style and personality, and apply directly and very personally to the deceased and to the bereaved family.

The texts and topics are listed in the Table of Contents, which can be used as a quick reference.

ACKNOWLEDGMENTS AND THANKS

This volume reflects some twenty-seven years of pastoral experience, and relates to the problems raised by my beloved congregants in Durban, South Africa; Riverdale, New York; and Beverly Hills, California. They have given me infinitely more than I have given them, and I am grateful to them for their love and for helping me grow.

The formal stimulus for my actually sitting down to translate my reading and experience into book form was the persistent urging of the members of the *chevra kadisha* of the Riverdale Jewish Center for written guidelines. I am grateful to the Riverdale Jewish Center for allowing me the time to research and write the first draft. I am also deeply appreciative of the courtesy of my secretary in Riverdale, Ilene Kittay Acevedo, and to Sharon Bar David, a member of the congregation, for typing the first draft. My most recent community, Beth Jacob Congregation of Beverly Hills, has an important share in this book. I have used the members of the daily *minyan* as a sounding-board for its contents, by making it the text for our daily class in Halakhah. Their comments have been most valuable, and have raised issues which were ignored or overlooked in the initial draft. The President, Jack

Slomovic, encouraged me to complete the project, and allowed as much time off as I requested. Flora and Romy Rosman allowed me to use their beautiful home in Rancho Mirage as a "retreat" for research and writing. I am grateful to them all for their friendship. The final draft was typed by Gita Fuchs, my Executive Assistant at Beth Jacob Congregation, and by Vivian Lurie and Stephanie Abrams. I am grateful to them for their contribution.

I owe a great deal to my colleagues and teachers. Rabbi Dr. Alter Hilewitz of Jerusalem researched and produced the Deed of Sale that is included in Section Two, and has been my teacher and mentor for nearly thirty years. The documents, notes, and explanation of the issues relating to preparing a halakhically valid bequest are the work of Rabbi Ezriel Tauber of Mechon Hahoyroa of Monsey, New York. His generosity in making these materials available for this publication is greatly appreciated. Rabbi Gershon Bess and Elchanan Tauber of the Lakewood Kollel in Los Angeles read the draft and helped me correct errors in the halakhic summaries. I am most grateful to Rabbi Tzvi Flaum for his meticulous reading of the text. A number of important revisions were made on the basis of his comments. Although I gratefully acknowledge their generous assistance, I claim full responsibility for any errors that may remain.

Grateful acknowledgement is made to the Singer's Prayer Book Publication Committee (London) for permission to use extracts from the *Authorized Daily Prayer Book.*

I am grateful to Rabbi Raphael B. Butler and Rabbi Moshe Krupka of the Orthodox Union, and to my editor, Dr. Yaakov Elman, for his invaluable assistance. My thanks go to Els Bendheim for her comments as well. The first edition of this volume, with its variety of typefaces and novel layout, reflects the professionalism of Ktav Publishing House, Inc.

Acharon, acharon chaviv — my last acknowledgments are by far the most important. They are, in the first instance, to my dear wife and family. Shifra's insightful comments, constructive criticisms, love, forbearance, tolerance, and expertise at proofreading have make this book, and everything else in my adult life, possible. I dedicate it to her. My son, Rabbi Avram Reuven Weiss, used the rough text in preparing for a rabbinical qualifying examination on our subject, and offered me valuable criticisms. Deena, Chana, and

Yakir contributed to its conclusion in various ways. My love and gratitude to my family defy adequate articulation.

A final comment: The first draft was written in a frenzy, during a fateful summer away from New York. It was written in anticipation of serious coronary bypass surgery, with the perhaps not so unconscious fear that I might not have much further opportunity to work on the project. I have made every effort to check my sources; I have already mentioned the learned colleagues who assisted me in that task. However, it is inevitable that we may have overlooked various important points or even allowed erroneous statements to stand. I shall be grateful to readers who bring such errors to my attention. Hopefully, the second edition will reflect their comments.

I thank the Almighty for having granted me the opportunity of completing this work in good health, and for *all* His abundant blessings.

Abner Weiss

Beverly Hills, California

Part One

CHAPTER ONE

Confronting Death
Before Death Confronts Us

OUR FEAR OF DEATH

Therefore choose life (Deuteronomy 30:19). Judaism is a life-affirming faith. Life on earth, and its benefits, are regarded as divine blessings. Their legitimate enjoyment is not only permitted but mandated. Asceticism and otherworldliness are not in keeping with the mainstream of Jewish thought and tradition.

Our joyful affirmation of the pleasures, challenges, and responsibilities of our earthly existence makes the inevitability of death the more difficult to confront. Frankly, most of us are afraid of death.

In the first place, our fear stems from our terror of the unknown—and nothing is more unknown than "the valley of the shadow of death." We cannot imagine our own death. Our mind is incapable of portraying the emptiness, the absence of existence which some of us imagine death to be—and of identifying ourselves with that nothingness. We do not know what death is, but we are intuitively certain that it will deprive us of the companionship of those we love, and of everything we cherish and enjoy. We block it out completely. We are simply unable to confront our own death.

In the second place, our fear of death relates not only to our own demise, but to the passing of those we love. Our contemplation of their passing, and of thus being deprived of those with whom our lives are inextricably bound, is frightening in itself. Our lives will

9

have to continue in the void created by the loss of their companionship, their love, and the reassuring security of their physical presence. Because our contemplation of their passing makes us increasingly aware of *our* vulnerability, we often refuse to confront the inevitable.

Our refusal to confront the fact of death is both wrong and irresponsible.

FIVE REASONS FOR CONFRONTING THE REALITY OF DEATH

1. Death is inevitable and cannot simply be wished away. Sometimes it announces its coming in long illness; sometimes it comes unannounced, with shattering, unexpected suddenness. But come it must, and we should be prepared to deal with the havoc it creates—calmly and reasonably.

2. The very *worst* time to deal with death is *after* it occurs. Our thinking processes are then often paralyzed by grief, and we are emotionally vulnerable. We sometimes turn for advice to those who may be unqualified to help us, and whose ignorance of proper procedure may be in inverse proportion to their good intentions.

3. The problems created by the death of a loved one are technical as well as emotional. The Halakhah (Jewish law) instructs us how to conduct ourselves in the presence of a loved one whose death is imminent, and how to handle the situation when death has come. We should, therefore, be aware of appropriate procedures *before* they are required.

4. Burial and preparations for burial can become unnecessarily complicated. Funeral homes and directors serve observant, traditional, secular, and assimilated Jews, and are mandated to cater to all tastes and most lawful requests. Salesmen and counselors are not always familiar with the special requirements of their traditional clients. Therefore, many "options" are offered which may not be halakhically acceptable. Both the dignity of the deceased and the interests of the bereaved are best served by prior knowledge of halakhically correct procedures.

5. The emotional disorientation of the bereaved cannot be overemphasized. How should this frightening situation be handled? What behavior is appropriate prior to the burial? How should one conduct oneself in a *shiv'ah* house? How can emotions be reoriented by traditional mourning practices? What are the differences between *shiv'ah, sheloshim,* and the twelve-month period of mourning for deceased parents?

The aim of this book is to ease our confrontation with death by lessening our ignorance of the laws, customs, and procedures whose purpose is both to dignify the dead and to sustain the living. Its purpose will have been partially fulfilled if its readers are stimulated to further reading, and encouraged to consult their rabbis about questions not directly raised in this work. But its purpose will have been best fulfilled if it contributes to the enhanced adoption of halakhic norms as we pass through the valley of the shadow of death.

CHAPTER TWO

Death and Immortality: Body and Soul

LIFE AFTER DEATH

Our horror of death is compounded by the common conviction that it is utterly final. Seen in this way, death is the ultimate frustration. It mocks life's dreams, goals, and strivings, and shows up the vanity of our imagined accomplishments. If life is perceived as a striving for continuous elevation, death becomes, as it were, the last step on an absurdly designed stairway, leading nowhere.

The Jewish tradition does not share this view of death. Despite its affirmation of the value of earthly life, and its general this-worldly approach to life on earth, belief in the *conscious* immortality of the soul beyond the grave is one of the cardinal tenets of the Jewish faith. Life after death is attested to in the Bible, elaborated upon in rabbinic writings, announced in our prayers, and found in Maimonides' principles of faith.

According to tradition, the human being is made up of both body and soul. The invisible soul is the life-giving force of our earthly existence. Body parts can be removed and even exchanged without causing the demise of the human being. They are merely the vehicle for the soul during its earthly existence. The fact that people speak of "my body" reflects their intuition that their bodies are merely *part* of their being, that one's body belongs to an "I" which transcends the body.

13

Death is defined as the irreversible separation of body and soul. No longer required by the soul, the body degenerates and decays. The soul, however, continues to exist in a nonphysical dimension which we call "heaven." Free of the limitations of the body, but enriched by its earthly experiences, it is conscious of its attainments and earthly associations. Death is merely one's passage into a higher, more meaningful, more spiritual, more satisfying realm of existence.

To be sure, granted our personal lack of experience of that realm, we do not look forward to death. Clearly, nobody gladly anticipates the frightening unknown. But imagine that a child in its mother's womb were to be told of its impending birth. Imagine, also, that it had the ability to compare the safety and security of life in the amniotic sac—its needs taken care of automatically, and seemingly permanently—with the terrifying reality of its perilous, painful passage through the narrow birth canal, and into the fearfully unfamiliar, buzzing, dazzling, dangerous, dry environment at the other end. Would it willingly exchange the womb for the world? Given its limited experience, it surely would not. However, despite its dangers, life lived outside the womb soon comes to be preferred by all but those neurotics, who still hanker after the unconscious, responsibility-free security of the fetal condition.

As birth is the frightening passage of the fetus into the terrifying unknown, so death, too, is the passage of the human into another unknown dimension. Both are stages in our development, part of God's plan for our personal evolution. The notion of life after death for those who have been born is no less reasonable than the notion of life after birth for those who are yet to be born. Indeed, life after death is at least a partial justification for all our struggles and strivings on earth.

Life is not in vain. It is not senselessly, suddenly, irrevocably terminated. Virtue *is* rewarded. We *do* enjoy a conscious existence beyond the grave.

Our belief in our personal immortality robs death of its unmitigated dominion and reduces its terrors.

THE BODY AFTER DEATH

Clearly, the soul is of infinitely greater value than the body, for the body is only important as the soul's earthly vehicle. But its association with the soul lends special, permanent importance to the body, whose relationship to the soul has been compared to that of the ancient Temple to God. The Temple was holy because it was consecrated as the earthly abode of the divine Presence; the body is holy because it is consecrated as the abode of the divine soul. Just as the Temple's ruins retain their sanctity even after it has ceased to function as the divine abode, so, too, does the dead body retain its inviolability even after it ceases to be the abode of the immortal soul. Moreover, the human body is also compared to a Torah scroll. Just as a Torah scroll retains its sanctity even after it becomes ritually unfit, when it no longer serves its original purpose, so too does the human body retain *its* inviolability even when it no longer serves as the vehicle for the immortal soul.

The lasting importance of the human body determines the loving care which is lavished upon it after death, and explains the detailed attention directed by the Halakhah to its dignified disposal—in purity and in holiness.

AUTOPSIES

The Jewish belief in the inviolability of the human body is reflected in its attitude to postmortem examinations. The Talmud (*Sanhedrin* 47a) asserts that the biblical imperative of speedy burial (Deuteronomy 21:22–23) is based upon the prohibition of disgracing a corpse. The scope of this prohibition extends beyond delayed burial. Scripture proscribes the inflicting of *any* form of disgrace upon a corpse. In general, this includes the disfigurement of the body as a result of postmortem dissection (autopsy).

Apart from the *general* prohibition against autopsies, which derives from our abhorrence of bodily disfigurement, there is a *special* prohibition against failure to bury the body in its *entirety*. If, after autopsy, for example, part of the body is excised and not buried, it is as if *no* burial *at all* took place (J.T. *Nazir* 7:1).

The prohibition against the performance of autopsies, however, is not absolute. An exception is made if the autopsy may directly contribute to saving the life of another patient who is currently awaiting treatment. Owing to the speed of contemporary communications, a sufferer elsewhere in the world may be aided almost immediately. Moreover, if the presence of a contagious disease, not diagnosed before death, is suspected, an autopsy may lead to the prevention of a plague. If new medicines were used on the patient, an autopsy can help to determine their life-saving effectiveness. It goes without saying that if a hereditary disease is the suspected cause of death, an autopsy may prevent the deaths of the patient's children, by establishing a preventative medical strategy for them.

Obviously, if postmortem needle biopsies or blood samples or peritoneoscopy would suffice, autopsies should not be performed at all.

However, when an autopsy is necessary, permission to undertake this procedure should be given only if the operation is reduced to a minimum, performed as soon as possible—and in the presence of a rabbi or observant and halakhically knowledgeable physician—and undertaken with reverence. There must be absolute assurance that all parts of the body will be retained for burial.

Because, however, the frequency of autopsies has increased, the danger exists of their becoming mere routine; and because recent studies (particularly the *Journal of the American Medical Association* [vol. 233, 1975, pp. 441–443]) have shown the questionable medical value of routine performance of postmortem dissections, permission should be withheld unless a physician who is sensitive to the Halakhah advises its performance in terms of the criteria for saving life which have been listed above.

CHAPTER THREE

Chevra Kadisha: Duties and Obligations

The loving care of the body, from the moment of death until after burial, is one of the greatest of the *mitzvot*. Because we lavish our attention upon an individual who cannot possibly reciprocate our kindness, our *mitzvah* is an act of the purest altruism. It is completely unselfish.

Although this *mitzvah* is incumbent upon every Jew (apart from *kohanim*, "priests," whose status and functions will be defined below), selfless men and women have, throughout our history, formed special groups specifically for this purpose. These groups are known as the *chevra kadisha* (Jewish Sacred Society), and can be organized in every active community. Membership in the *chevra kadisha* should be regarded as a special privilege.

The role of the *chevra kadisha* is twofold. It serves not only those who have passed on, but their survivors also.

The very presence of the members of the *chevra kadisha* at the moment of passing (wherever possible) serves to reassure and comfort the bereaved. More than that, the members of the *chevra kadisha* lay out the body prior to its transfer to the funeral home, accompany it to the funeral home, arrange for *shomrim* (pious attendants) to remain with the body until it is buried, designate an appropriate casket and shrouds, carry out the *taharah* (ritual purification) of the body, organize a fitting funeral service, and arrange both the final journey of the body to its ultimate resting place and

17

an appropriate burial service. Well-established *chevrot* of active congregations often have a binding contract with a funeral home. This contract provides for standardized caskets, shrouds, funerals, burials, and so forth, for the immediate families of members of the congregation.

The *chevra kadisha* thus serves the newly-bereaved in several ways. It performs its principal act of lovingkindness by removing the responsibility for making funeral arrangements from distraught families. A single phone call to the *chevra* or to the rabbi will usually suffice to effect this transfer of responsibility. It will allow the bereaved to deal with their grief without the added burden of having to attend to details for which they have neither experience nor knowledge—nor the best frame of mind. The value of this free service to congregants by the *chevra kadisha* cannot be overestimated.

Apart from making funeral arrangements, in some communities the *chevra kadisha* will place an obituary notice in the newspaper. It will arrange for the provision of a *se'udat ha-havra'ah* (the meal after returning from the cemetery), and, if necessary, for other meals during the *shiv'ah* period. It will also arrange for *minyanim* (prayer services) at the homes of the bereaved congregants, and provide a Torah scroll, *siddurim* (prayer books), and other items required for these home services. It will ensure (if required) that a person is present who will lead the public study of a section of the Mishnah during these services. Most importantly, it will extend sensitive, compassionate counsel to the bereaved throughout the traumatic period of bereavement. Indeed, its functions sometimes extend beyond this period, for in many congregations the *chevra kadisha* is responsible for the upkeep of the cemetery area.

HOW TO FORM A NEW CHEVRA KADISHA

There Are No Reasons Not to Form a Chevra

Most congregations do not have a *chevra kadisha* of their own, thus missing out on all the advantages its existence provides. I have heard many reasons given for not having a *chevra*, and I think that all of them are quite groundless. Let me give you some examples:

- *"Why should I do this work? What's in it for a young person? Death is easier for old people to handle."* WRONG. Everybody is vulnerable to death's intrusion, young and old alike. And *every-body* feels enriched by the importance of this loving and holy work. Why should such feelings of fulfillment and satisfaction be withheld from the young?

- *Modern, educated, Western people are squeamish and uncom-fortable around the dead.* WRONG. This is only a prejudice. They merely *think* that they will be unable to get used to per-forming this task. After one or two sessions, the initial discomfort and squeamishness will almost always disappear.

- *There is no room in a* chevra kadisha *for a person who genuinely will never be able to do hands-on work with the dead.* WRONG. Members of a *chevra kadisha* have many tasks. Some will merely sit with a gentile driver of the hearse. Some will be in the same room as the deceased, without direct contact, merely "watch-ing." Some, like *kohanim*, will have *no* contact with the dead whatsoever. But they can phone other volunteers, arrange rides to the cemetery, organize the *minyan* in the house of mourning, prepare meals for the bereaved, and help the mourners in all kinds of ways. Everybody can play a useful role as a member of the *chevra kadisha*.

- *Hands-on work with the dead requires pious volunteers who are strictly observant.* WRONG. This is the ideal situation. But if strictly observant volunteers are not available, great merit accrues to all Jewish volunteers.

- *It is better to leave the work to professionals. Ignorant amateurs are bound to make unforgivable mistakes.* WRONG. After a while, the work will come to be quite routine. There are very few unforeseen circumstances. Even if they do arise, you can always call a knowledgeable rabbi. And anyway, who says that even pro-fessionals never make mistakes? We all do, and that is why even the most skilled and experienced *chevra kadishas* ask the deceased for forgiveness in a standard formula after each pre-paration for burial.°

- *Chevra kadisha work is a tradition handed down the generations, through family connections. Outsiders need not apply.* WRONG. There is no mystery or secret lore surrounding the work. The tasks are relatively simple, and can be learned by anybody.

° See below, p. 63.

- *The training is exacting and exceedingly time-consuming.* WRONG. Only one or two orientation sessions and a single demonstration are required. You will be given a printed summary of procedures (or you can use Chapter Seven of this book for that purpose). You will then "learn on the job."
- *The work itself is time-consuming.* WRONG. The preparation of the deceased person for burial takes no more than an hour—much less, as the number of workers increases.
- *"I can't take time off from work to do the necessary tasks."* WRONG. You do not have to. The preparation can be done at night after work, or early in the morning before work.
- *Professional funeral directors will resent the competition, and be less cooperative when we really need them.* WRONG. In my experience, professional funeral directors encourage the formation of *chevra kadishas*. They realize that an educated community knows not to take the services of professionals for granted, and becomes even more sensitive to what the professionals are doing as they come to share the problems.

Ten Steps to Start a New Chevra Kadisha

1. Ask your rabbi to publicize the need for its creation and to motivate potential volunteers. He can use the pulpit and the synagogue bulletin for creating interest.
2. Have the rabbi call and organize an initial meeting of potential volunteers. Specific individuals should be "targeted" on the basis of their potential suitability and invited personally. A good attendance *must* be assured at the first meeting.
3. Invite the leader of a working *chevra kadisha* from another city to address the meeting. Your rabbi will be able to research the available resources. Audiovisual materials are available, and should be used. Easily readable books on the subject, such as *A Plain Pine Box*, by Arnold M. Goodman (Ktav Publishers), should be made available.
4. At the very first meeting, elect your officers. At least *three* responsible, devoted, and motivated people (best primed in advance of the meeting) should be elected—a president, the head of the women's division, and the head of the men's division of the *chevra*.

5. A date should be set at the initial meeting for a study seminar, led either by your rabbi or by an experienced worker from another community. Chapter Seven of this book can be used as the source material for this seminar.

6. At this second meeting, a date for a third—a hands-on demonstration on a mannequin (a hospital often has such models available)—should be set. The guidelines in Chapter Seven will be applied in practice.

7. If the professional funeral director in your town has been providing halakhically approved preparations, arrange for the leaders of the newly formed *chevra* to be called out two or three times to participate and to "learn on the job." If not, arrange for at least two men and two women members of your *chevra*-in-formation to spend a day or two in a city where a good *chevra kadisha* exists. The congregation collectively, or a few sponsors should cover the travel costs.

8. These four individuals will then become the teachers of some of the other volunteers at the local funeral home.

9. The *chevra kadisha* should now formulate its rules, regulations, and standards, specifying the type of caskets, shrouds, and so forth, which will be used. These rules, regulations, and standards should be devised in cooperation with your rabbi and presented to him for subsequent dissemination to the congregation. The *chevra* should purchase the necessary equipment.

10. The rabbi will now announce the availability of the *chevra kadisha* services to the congregation in a sermon, in the synagogue bulletin, and in an interview with the local news media. This information should include the phone numbers of the heads of the *chevra kadisha,* and should urge the community to call upon the *chevra* whenever death intrudes into the life of their family.

HOW TO USE YOUR CHEVRA KADISHA: A PRACTICAL GUIDE

1. To be assured of a halakhically acceptable funeral and burial, congregation members should not make funeral arrangements on their own initiative. These arrangements should be made on

their behalf by representatives of the *chevra kadisha* or by the rabbi.

2. Their telephone numbers should be listed in the checklist in Section Two of this book. They can be contacted at any time of the day or night.

3. Even currently existing arrangements which have been made independently by members and/or their immediate families should be reviewed with the *chevra kadisha* at once.

4. Whenever the need arises, do not hesitate to call the rabbi or an officer of the *chevra kadisha*.

5. As soon as the *chevra kadisha* is contacted, its representatives will, wherever possible, call at the home or hospital room of the individual whose end appears to be drawing close, to render direct assistance to the family and to offer whatever comfort is possible to the dying.

6. When death has occurred, the *chevra kadisha* will contact the funeral home directly, and will get the information necessary to facilitate all arrangements. A standard checklist for the *chevra kadisha* is provided in this book.°

° See below, p. 189.

CHAPTER FOUR

Anticipating the End

RESPONSIBLE PLANNING

The terrible grief and paralyzing sorrow which are likely to follow our passing need not be aggravated by our causing unnecessary pain and hardship to those whom we love most dearly, and who will suffer our passing most severely.

Responsible people take steps to obviate these unnecessary and fully avoidable hardships long before they even suspect that they are seriously ailing, and when they do not even remotely consider that they may soon die.

They make sure that they and their dependents have adequate insurance coverage for hospitalization, medical, and pharmaceutical bills. Tragically, inadequate coverage often impoverishes even those families which have worked hard and have saved conscientiously.

Responsible people have regular medical examinations. The primary purpose of these check-ups is preventative. Early diagnosis of illnesses can often prevent their development to the danger point. Furthermore, such check-ups may enable the physician to assure the medical examiner that an autopsy is unnecessary. He will be able to argue the probable cause of death on the basis of his records, even if he has not examined the patient within seventy-two hours of his or her passing.

Responsible people also ensure that they have adequate life insurance coverage to ease the financial pressure on their dependents.

They have carefully worked-out last wills and testaments for the distribution of their assets to their loved ones and to worthy charities. The absence of a properly prepared will can lead both to probate problems and to tragic disputes among heirs. A halakhically valid version of a last will and testament should become the basis of your personalized document, so as to comply with the mandates of Jewish law and tradition.°

It is both responsible and wise for people to plan for the disposal of their remains by acquiring a burial plot. If their near and dear ones have arrangements with burial societies, they should check out the halakhic standards of those societies by consulting their own rabbi or *chevra kadisha*. If the standards prove to be inadequate, their near and dear ones should be persuaded to cancel their agreements and leave all the arrangements to a reliable *chevra kadisha*.

RESPONSIBLE PLANNING: CHECKLIST

The following should be kept in a family bank vault or safe deposit box and noted in the checklist provided in this book. *A copy should be filed at your synagogue.*

1. Names, addresses, and phone numbers of all family physicians.
2. Names, addresses, and phone numbers of insurance agents.
3. Name, address, and phone number of attorney who has drawn up family wills.
4. Name, address, and phone number of cemetery manager where burial plots are reserved.
5. Insurance policies, wills, burial plot number and location.

WHEN THE END APPROACHES

Death often intrudes into our lives with shattering suddenness, and does not permit us to prepare for its unwelcome advent. Some-

° See below, p. 195.

times, however, it announces its agonizing coming through illness and increasing feebleness, either at home or in the hospital.

When death announces its approach, it is prudent to ensure that the physician examines the patient at least once every three days—not only for the intrinsic curative and palliative purpose of the visit, but also to obviate potential autopsy problems.

When death is imminent, the *chevra kadisha* and the rabbi should be informed. They will give moral support to the family and to the patient by praying with them, and by offering practical counsel and assistance.

The presence of loved ones is an enormous comfort to the dying patient. When we are aware of the approach of our end, we desire the comforting presence of those to whom we gave life, and with whom we shared our precious years.

The family does its best for the loved one's most profound emotional needs at a most frightening time. In addition to the family's making the patient physically comfortable, the psalms and prayers which are recited ease the loved-one's passing.°

Apart from comforting the dying, the presence of family members satisfies an important psychological need of their own. Their final demonstration of love and concern affords the family the assurance that they did all they could to the very end. It enables them to deal with their grief more maturely, uncompounded by imagined guilt.

ANTICIPATING DEATH ON SHABBAT OR YOM TOV

Our comforting presence is sometimes involuntarily precluded. We cannot possibly be with our loved ones every moment of every day and night. Under such circumstances, we should not feel guilty if the patient passes away when we are not present.

Our loved one may be hospitalized and it may not be possible for us to find accommodations close at hand. Other practical reasons may also preclude our physical presence. *On no account should we desecrate the Sabbath or a festival to reach the patient before he/*

° See below, p. 198.

she expires. The end does not justify the means. The patient will understand and appreciate the reasons for our absence—either at once or later, when he/she has reached his/her eternal spiritual destination.

WHEN DEATH IS ANTICIPATED ON A SABBATH OR HOLY DAY: HALAKHIC CHECKLIST

In Hospital

1. The rabbi or *chevra kadisha* should be alerted ahead of time.
2. The rabbi or *chevra kadisha* will supply you with the name and phone number of the individual at the funeral home who will take charge of the arrangements.
3. This information should be supplied by you both to the physician and to the nurse in charge of the patient's section of the hospital.
4. These health care professionals should be asked ahead of time to contact the person at the funeral home when death occurs.
5. If the hospital has a Jewish chaplain, he should be alerted *before* the Sabbath or the festival. He will attempt to ensure that the patient is not left unattended.

At Home

1. The rabbi or *chevra kadisha* should be alerted ahead of time.
2. They will tell you to whose home to walk to pass on the information.
3. Representatives of the *chevra kadisha* will walk over to your home or the home of the deceased immediately and begin *shemirah.*
4. They will contact the funeral home after the Sabbath or festival.

CHAPTER FIVE

When Death Occurs

THE SPECIAL RESTRICTIONS APPLICABLE TO KOHANIM

Death and Bodily Defilement

From the Judaic perspective, ritual purity is related to permanence. What endures is pure. Thus the Psalmist declares: "The fear of the Lord is pure; it endures forever" (Psalm 19:10). The greater a thing's endurance, the greater is the degree of its purity. By definition, therefore, the eternal soul is not susceptible to ritual defilement. Accordingly, the extraordinary treatment accorded to a lifeless body by the *chevra kadisha* reflects our view of what the body *was before death*—the sacred Temple of the soul. As such, it must always be treated with respect. In itself, however, the lifeless body is no longer inherently holy. On the verge of decay and disintegration, the body represents impermanence and impurity.

The ritual impurity of a corpse may be understood on another level also. In keeping with the life-affirming nature of Judaism, the human body becomes the chief source of ritual impurity when it is bereft of life. Its status following death is in direct contrast to its status in life. The greater the sanctity of a body during a person's lifetime, the more pronounced is its ritual impurity following death. Paradoxically, therefore, that body which housed a soul, ennobled by its performance of deeds mandated by God's Torah while alive, becomes the most potent source of ritual defilement after death. Thus the remains of a Jewish person have a greater degree of impurity than those of a gentile.

27

Ritual Defilement

The ritual defilement emanating from a non-Jewish body is trans-mitted only through direct contact with the remains, and also, according to most opinions, by walking on the grave of a gentile. The ritual defilement emanating from the corpse of a Jew is in-finitely greater. It takes on an almost tangible quality. It can best be compared to radiation. Although it is invisible, ritual defilement radiates in all directions from its source, the lifeless body. Ritual impurity actually *fills* the dwelling occupied by the Jewish corpse. In ancient times, this dwelling was called a tent (*ohel*), and the word *ohel* is still used to describe the area suffused by the ritual impurity radiating from a Jewish corpse. An *ohel* need not neces-sarily be a single, well-defined area. Separate rooms connected by open doors or windows, and under a common roof, constitute a single *ohel*, totally suffused by the radiating impurity. Even separ-ate buildings connected in the same way make up a single *ohel*. An *ohel*, moreover, need not be surrounded by walls. Any area which is under the same roof as the corpse is its *ohel*. The roof itself need not be a continuous structural unit. A series of overlapping covers con-stitutes a single roof. Even adjacent covers on different levels—for example, the roof of a building and an awning or balcony protrud-ing from the exterior walls—make up a single roof, and extend the dimensions of the *ohel*. Thus, a covered walkway connecting two buildings extends the *ohel* from the one to the other. Indeed, even the foliage of a tree, beneath which the lifeless body lies, acts as its roof and constitutes an *ohel*. It should be noted that ritual impurity cannot generally penetrate physical barriers, such as solid walls and closed doors and windows. Notwithstanding, the door or window through which the corpse will eventually be moved is considered to be open already, allowing ritual impurity to radiate further, and, if applicable, to extend the *ohel*.

Priests and Ritual Defilement

Any Jew who enters the *ohel* of a lifeless Jewish body is ritually defiled, and, must, thereafter, wash his or her hands. But Jewish priests (*kohanim*), the male descendants of Aaron, the brother of

Moses, are generally forbidden even to *enter* an *ohel*. The reason for this prohibition is both historical and ideological.

Ancient religions were largely death-centered. The primary functions of their priests related to the burial of the dead. Indeed, the scriptures of ancient Egypt were actually called the *Book of the Dead*.

As we have seen, the Jewish attitude to lifeless bodies presents a striking contrast to this morbid view. Essentially life-affirming, Judaism forbade its priests to defile themselves through contact with the dead. Had they entered the *ohel* of a Jewish corpse, they would have been disqualified from the performance of their priestly functions.

The isolation of the priests from death had a further effect. They could never become habituated to death and hardened to the loss of human life.

For all these reasons, the Torah proclaims: "And the Lord said unto Moses: Speak unto the priests, the sons of Aaron, and say unto them: Let none of them be defiled by the dead among his people" (Lev. 21:1–2).

Contemporary Kohanim

It may be argued that nowadays, since there is no Temple in Jerusalem, the priestly functions have been dramatically curtailed. This is true. Apart from conferring the priestly blessing and presiding at the ceremony of the redemption of firstborn sons, contemporary *kohanim* have no formal functions. The role of spiritual leadership has devolved upon the rabbis—and rabbis, for the most part, are not *kohanim*. Nevertheless, we *do* preserve our tradition of religious pedigree. *Kohanim* proudly identify with Aaron and his sons. They are aware of their special spiritual status and of the responsibility that this involves. They lovingly accept the fact that their birth as *kohanim* was preordained by God and is inexorable. By maintaining the priestly tradition, they express their personal faith in the ultimate restoration of ancient priestly functions. By submitting to the limitations imposed upon them by the Torah, contemporary *kohanim* gladly accept the will of God.

Exceptions

Obviously, the Torah is sensitive to extraordinary situations. To prevent a *kohen* from participating in the final rites of his closest kin would impose an unreasonable burden upon him. Accordingly, as we shall see, the Torah delineates those relatives whose death suspends the priestly limitations. Furthermore, because of the life-sustaining role of a physician, a *kohen* who is a practicing medical doctor can attend to the needs of his patients in accordance with the imperative of *piku'ach nefesh*—the preservation of human life. Indeed, owing to the requirement of according every Jew a proper burial, *kohanim* are actually *commanded* to participate in the purification and burial of a *met mitzvh*—a person who has nobody else to take care of his or her purification and interment.

RESTRICTIONS ON KOHANIM: HALAKHIC CHECKLIST

Prohibition of Contact with the Dead

1. A *kohen* is defined as a Jewish male who has been told that he is the natural, halakhically legitimate son of a father who is a *kohen*.
2. The following prohibitions apply to all *kohanim* beyond the age of thirteen. Younger *kohanim*, too, should be encouraged to accept the restrictions from the earliest possible age.
3. *Kohanim* may not enter the *ohel* of a dying Jew (*goses*).
4. *Kohanim* may not touch or carry a corpse or the smallest part of a lifeless body, such as bones, flesh, limbs, and blood which has flowed after death. Teeth, nails, and hair which have been separated from the rest of the body, however, do not transmit ritual impurity.
5. *Kohanim* may not enter a building where there is a Jewish body. They may not enter another building joined to that building by a covered walkway. They should be careful not to pass under a balcony or awning attached to a building in which a Jewish corpse or body parts are located.

They may not pass under a tree whose foliage covers both them and a Jewish body or grave.

6. If a *kohen* has been told that a Jew has died in his apartment house or office building, he should leave the building as soon as possible.
7. A *kohen* in whose presence a Jew has died should leave the *ohel* at once.
8. Outdoors, a *kohen* may not come within six and a half feet of a Jewish body or within six and a half feet of a Jewish grave.

Exceptions to these Prohibitions

1. A *kohen* may come into contact with the following dead relatives: father, mother, son, daughter, brother from the same father, never married sister from the same father, wife (provided that the marriage was halakhically valid).
2. The ۱؎ct that there are other mourners present who are *not kohanim* and who are ready and willing to attend the dead is irrelevant. A *kohen* may, nevertheless, come into contact with the seven closest deceased family members we have just listed.
3. A *kohen* may enter a funeral home in which the remains of one of the seven closest relatives are located, even if other Jewish bodies are also there at the time. He should, however, leave the funeral home as soon as the body of the relative for whose last rites he is present has been removed.
4. A *kohen* may help take care of the funeral needs of a Jew who is not related to him. A minimum number of people is required to attend to the final rites. If, without him, the minimum number is not available, the *kohen* may assist.
5. A *kohen* who is a physician is not subject to the priestly restrictions when he is attending a patient.
6. A *kohen* may come into direct contact with the ashes of a cremated Jew.
7. A *kohen* who is the issue of an adulterous or incestuous relationship (*mamzer*) is not subject to these priestly restrictions. A *chalal* should consult a qualified rabbi as to his various halakhic obligations and status.

8. The pregnant wife of a *kohen* is exempted from these restrictions, even though she may be carrying a male fetus.

CONDUCT IN THE PATIENT'S FINAL MOMENTS

We have already emphasized the great importance of surrounding dying people with the comforting presence of those who love and care for them. However, as important as our mere physical presence is, a number of additional halakhic requirements must also be satisfied. These requirements are not only for the benefit of the patient, but also serve to satisfy our own need to do whatever we can to be of practical assistance at this sad and emotionally difficult time.

CONDUCT IN FINAL MOMENTS: HALAKHIC CHECKLIST

1. Summon the patient's physician. It may be possible to revive the patient and the course of decline arrested and reversed.
2. Contact the rabbi or *chevra kadisha* representative. On Sabbaths and other holy days the telephone may *not* be used for this purpose. If contact cannot be made without desecrating the Sabbath or festival, wait until after the Sabbath or festival before making contact.
3. Do not touch, move, or feed the patient.
4. Do not leave the patient alone.
5. Limit all conversation in the room to the needs of the patient.
6. Recite the special prayers and the psalms appropriate for this occasion. The confession should be said with the patient. If the patient is not conscious or responsive, the confession should be said on his/her behalf.°

WHEN DEATH OCCURS

Widely accepted procedures govern our conduct when we are present at the time of the patient's demise. It should be emphasized

° See below, p. 202.

again that these procedures have two purposes. In the first place, they are designed for the benefit of and out of respect to the deceased. In the second, our adherence to these procedures assures us that we have really done whatever is humanly possible to do for the deceased. We are left with a sense of fulfillment, rather than a feeling of guilt.

Obviously, there are variables which affect the standard procedures. The first set of variables is practical. We function under fewer constraints in a private home than in a hospital or other institution. Such institutions may have inflexible rules which restrict our ability to follow all aspects of the customary tradition. Fortunately, these restrictions do not apply in a private home.

The second set of variables is religious. Procedures appropriate for non-holy days will be different from those in force on a religious festival. On the Sabbath, there are further procedural variations and restrictions.

We should not forget that the preparation of the dead for interment is a great *mitzvah*. It is an essentially religious act. We do not merely dispose of remains. We treat them with respect and consideration. We must remember that they are the remains of a person created in the image of God. As such, the will of God should determine the last rites accorded to those who are in His image—not our personal prejudices and esthetic preferences. It is completely irrelevant whether the deceased was religious or totally irreligious, observant or uncommitted. It is equally irrelevant whether or not *we* are observant. As an expression of our respect for the deceased and for the destiny of his/her immortal soul (which is affected by the manner of preparation for burial and by the interment), we are duty-bound to do what is absolutely right—not what *we* merely think is right or what we consider the deceased would have thought to be adequate.

PRESCRIBED PROCEDURES: HALAKHIC CHECKLIST

Death in a Private Home on a Non-Holy Day

1. Open the outside windows of the room in which the deceased is lying.

2. If the deceased is your parent or one of the other close relatives for whom you are required to mourn, rend your garments and recite the full version of the *Dayyan ha-Emet* blessing.

3. The same procedure is followed if the deceased is not a relative but is an individual of outstanding learning and piety, provided that you feel a great deal of sorrow at your loss.

4. In other cases, you recite the abbreviated version of the blessing.

5. A lighted candle, symbolizing the soul, should be placed at the head of the deceased.

6. As soon as death has been certified (or twenty minutes after the cessation of respiration and pulse), the eyes and mouth of the deceased should be closed. If necessary, a handkerchief may be used to keep the mouth closed. The limbs should be straightened.

7. *Hashkavah*, the laying out, now takes place. A sheet should be placed on the floor. The deceased should be gently lowered onto the floor with feet pointing to the door. The head should be elevated on a pillow. The deceased should be completely covered with a sheet—no other coverings are permitted. A lighted candle should be placed at his/her head.

8. Mirrors, because they reflect our vanity and direct our attention at our own image, should be covered.

9. All drawn water in the home should be poured out.

10. It is forbidden to pray, wear *tefillin*, allow one's *tzitzit* to show, learn Torah, eat, drink, smoke, or exchange greetings in the room where the deceased is lying, or within six and a half feet if he/she is lying in a large, open area.

11. The deceased should be attended by at least one Jew at all times until interment. Those in attendance (*shomrim*) should not indulge in idle conversation or frivolity, but should recite psalms.

12. A Jew (usually a member of the family or *chevra kadisha*, or the driver of the hearse) should be with the deceased on his/her journey to the funeral home.

Death in a Hospital on a Non-Holy Day

1. Ideally, one should follow the same procedure in a hospital as one does in a private home. However, hospital authorities may not permit windows to be opened, candles to be lit, *hashkavah* to be performed, and mirrors to be covered. Obviously, only drawn water in the patient's room or his/her section of the hospital room may be poured out.
2. All the other steps in the procedure outlined above should be followed in the hospital—in their correct order.

Death in a Private Home on the Sabbath

1. Only the most minimal arrangements may be made on the Sabbath. These should be limited to the immediate needs of, and in direct respect to, the deceased.
2. The telephone may be used only to summon the patient's physician, since resuscitation may still be possible. The phone should *not* be used to inform relatives, friends, and the funeral home of the passing of the deceased.
3. The *Dayyan ha-Emet* blessing should be recited, and the windows should be opened.
4. A candle should *not* be lit on the Sabbath.
5. Most authorities hold that, apart from placing his/her head on a pillow and shutting the mouth, the deceased should, under normal circumstances, neither be moved nor even touched by either a Jew or a gentile on the Sabbath.
6. One leading authority, however, disagrees. In his view, *hashkavah* (the laying out of the deceased) is a primary demonstration of one's esteem. The demonstration of this esteem supersedes the prohibition of carrying or touching the deceased. Moreover, straightening the limbs before the onset of rigor mortis is clearly motivated by one's concern for the dignity of the deceased. To be sure, there is a technical problem in moving the body on

the Sabbath. If the clothing worn by the deceased will ultimately be removed, the fact that these clothes, are, in fact, being moved along with the deceased obviates this problem. If the clothing will not be removed, the problem can be avoided by placing a loaf of bread next to the deceased while he/she is lowered onto the floor (*tiltul min ha-tzad*).

7. Even the authorities who forbid *hashkavah* on the Sabbath do agree that the body can be removed if dishonor will result from *not* removing it. Thus, if there is a real likelihood that the body will begin to decompose at an accelerated pace in the present environment, or if it is in danger of destruction by fire, it may be removed by a Jew by means of *tiltul min ha-tzad*, as described above. In extreme circumstances, if the body is to be transported through the public domain, a gentile should be asked to move it.
8. Water should *not* be poured out.
9. One should not pray, eat, or indulge in idle conversation in the presence of the deceased.
10. A Jew should be present with the deceased at all times, preferably reciting psalms.
11. After the termination of the Sabbath, the funeral home should be contacted by a representative of the *chevra kadisha* for the prompt transfer of the remains. The deceased should be accompanied by a Jew.

Death in a Hospital on the Sabbath

1. The rules applicable to a private home also apply to death in a hospital on the Sabbath.
2. However, hospital authorities may not permit the deceased to remain in his/her room until the termination of the Sabbath. If the deceased is moved to the hospital mortuary, a Jew should accompany him/her there, and, if at all possible, remain within sight of the refrigeration unit.
3. The deceased should *not* be transferred to the funeral home before the termination of the Sabbath.

4. Under extreme circumstances—as where the hospital has no mortuary and will not permit the deceased to remain in his/her room until the termination of the Sabbath—a gentile should be asked to contact the funeral home to send a vehicle with a non-Jewish driver to transfer the deceased.

Death on a Festival

1. For the purpose of burial only, the second day of a festival (and the last day of an eight-day festival) is regarded as a weekday.
2. However, to prevent unnecessary desecration of the festival, we do not permit burials on these occasions.
3. Accordingly, to all practical intents and purposes, the rules which obtain on the Sabbath also obtain on festivals.
4. However, the closing of the eyes and mouth and the straightening of the limbs should be done, both at home and in the hospital.
5. *Hashkavah* (the laying out of the deceased) is required on a festival. In a hospital room, if *hashkavah* is not permitted, a sheet should be placed over the deceased— after closing his/her eyes and mouth and straightening the limbs.
6. The candle is kindled from a pre-existing flame.
7. In the absence of extraordinary and exceptional circumstances, the deceased should not be transported to the funeral home before the termination of the festival. If at all possible, *even under exceptional circumstances,* the deceased should not be transferred until after nightfall following the first or seventh day of the festival.

CHAPTER SIX

Between Death and Burial: The Mourners

LEGISLATING MOURNING

Grief is one of our most powerful, complex, confusing, and debilitating emotions. It is an amalgam of frustration, remorse, and a deep sense of loss. We are often angry at our deprivation. We are frustrated at our helplessness in preventing the loss. We are sometimes overcome with remorse at missed opportunities for demonstrating our love and affection.

Our unwillingness to confront the harsh realities of death and bereavement is one of the most striking characteristics of contemporary times. We seek ingenious ways of softening the blow, and of pretending that nothing has changed. And of course we succeed. We give the mourner sedatives to make him or her insensitive to the loss and dull the pain. Cosmeticians restore the features of the deceased to their "pristine" glory. The deceased is dressed in his/her finest clothing and placed on a pillow in a padded casket more closely resembling a luxurious bed than a coffin. The deceased is visited, and the wake becomes a social gathering. Interment is accomplished as painlessly as possible. The mourners are spared the reality of the shovelsful of earth thudding onto the casket. The harshest of harsh realities is thoroughly disguised.

The psychological toll claimed by our refusal to directly confront the realities of death and bereavement is heavy. We lose far more

39

than we gain, because, however well we shield ourselves from death's impact, we cannot shut out its effects permanently. We can do nothing more than pathologically repress them for a time. The death of our loved ones *must* be confronted—sooner or later.

Dr. George Mann, director of the Adult Chemical Dependency Program at Minneapolis's St. Mary's Rehabilitation Center, a leading chemical dependency unit in the United States, addresses the problem from his special viewpoint:

> We also get involved in grief therapy with people whose loss of a loved one actually occurred months earlier or even two years before. It is fairly common practice now when there is a death in the family to medicate survivors, to ease things for them with drugs. Thus, instead of being allowed to go through the grieving process at the proper time, the survivors are totally zonked. They don't even remember the death, the funeral or anything about it. When they try to get off the stuff, they must also deal with the postponed grief.

Our sages understood the therapeutic value of confronting great loss directly, and of accepting the reality of death. Since mourning is our method of acting out our grief, and the process is both confusing and upsetting, we require help in focusing our grief. Our sages knew that most of us are uncertain about our responses to grief. They realized that many of us are worried that we do not seem sad enough, and that some of us, on the contrary, suspect that we grieve *too* intensely. They understood that many of us simply do not know how to *express* our feelings, and that we may, therefore, feel guilty because we suspect that we have not demonstrated our love adequately.

For these reasons, and many more, they ordained the laws and practices which govern the treatment of the dying and the dead, and the bereavement of the mourners. By adhering to these standards, we are sure that our response is an adequate demonstration of love for our departed loved ones, and a proven, healthy way of coming to terms with our grief. Irrational feelings of guilt are removed, and our lot is cast with a noble tradition—which directs us through all of life's phases. We are comforted by the assurance that we *can* come to terms with God, and that we shall, in time, come to terms with ourselves, as we gradually resume the familiar patterns of normal living.

THE RELATIVES FOR WHOM WE MOURN

Obviously, although we suffer a sense of loss whenever someone we know well passes away, our sense of loss is the more acute the closer we are to the person who has passed away. Clearly, also, the closer we are in time to the loss, the more profoundly it is felt. The passage of time does, in fact, blunt the pain of the bereavement.

The Halakhah recognizes these truths by carefully specifying the relatives for whom mourning is most appropriate, and by distinguishing between clearly defined stages in the mourning process.

The Halakhah mandates mourning only for the following seven immediate relatives: *father, mother, son, daughter, brother (or half brother), sister (or half sister), and spouse*. This does not mean that we do not grieve for others also. It means only that we are required to act out our emotions in a halakhically defined manner for the seven closest relatives. If no limits were established, it would become exceedingly difficult to deal with grief.

STAGES IN THE MOURNING PROCESS

These limits apply to the intensity of mourning as well as to the objects of our grief. In the Jewish view, there are at least five well-defined stages in the process of mourning, each succeeding stage further in time from the moment of loss.

1. *Aninut.* The period immediately following the passing of a near one, and preceding the funeral and interment.
2. *Shiv'ah.* The first week of mourning, commencing after the interment.
3. *Sheloshim.* The thirty days following interment. After this period, formal mourning is concluded for all relatives other than parents.
4. *Yud Bet Chodesh.* The twelve-month period of formal mourning for parents.
5. *Yahrzeit.* The anniversary of a person's demise.

Each of these stages has its own rationale and practices.

ANINUT

Aninut, the initial period of bereavement, is frequently the most difficult. The passing of our nearest and dearest leaves us numb, angry, drained, and almost paralyzed with shock, disbelief, and grief. When, from a psychological point of view, we are least able to cope, we are required to arrange the funeral with the *chevra kadisha* and/or the funeral home, to obtain a death certificate from the deceased's physician, and to inform family and friends of the arrangements.

The Halakhah recognizes the difficult nature of *aninut.* It is aware that we wish to demonstrate our feelings of esteem for the deceased in a tangible way by ensuring that an appropriate funeral is arranged. Accordingly, it exempts the *onen/onenet* from the performance of certain routine religious obligations. The Halakhah is sensitive to the trauma which the bereaved may experience, and it enables them to deal with this upheaval by freeing them from many regular religious obligations while forbidding them pleasurable diversions.

ANINUT: HALAKHIC CHECKLIST

Who Is An Onen/Onenet?

1. An *onen/onenet* is one who is preoccupied with the funeral of any of the following close relatives: father, mother, brother, sister, son, daughter, spouse. One does not observe *aninut* for a baby who has not survived more than thirty days. *Aninut* also applies (to a lesser extent, as we shall see) to one who has lost a special teacher of Torah, and at whose loss one feels very hurt.
2. *Aninut* does not apply to minors (those who are under the age of *bar/bat mitzvah*).
3. *Aninut* does not apply to a bride or groom during the first seven days of marriage, since they are exempted from participating in funeral arrangements.
4. *Aninut* does not apply when one's relative is missing in action or lost at sea, and a competent rabbinical tribunal

(*Beth Din*) has declared him/her dead. It does not apply before the formal declaration of death.

5. *Aninut* does not apply if the bereaved have no access to the remains of the deceased—for example, when the authorities have not released the body, and are not expected to do so at a definite time in the very near future.
6. *Aninut* does not apply to the bereaved if he/she cannot become personally involved in the funeral arrangements—for example, if he/she is in prison, abroad, in a distant city, or on military service. However, even in these circumstances, if he/she is the *only* close relative and *could* reach the funeral in time, he/she is considered to be an *onen/onenet*.
7. If relatives in one city transfer the body to relatives in another city for burial, the relatives in the second city become *onenim* only when the transfer arrangements are made.

Duration of Aninut

1. *Aninut* commences with the passing of one of one's seven closest relatives. However, the exceptions listed above apply.
2. *Aninut* ceases when one has no further contact with the body—either because one has ceased to accompany the body to the interment, or when the body is handed over for trans-interment, or when the body is handed over for shipment to Israel (or another city), or when interment is completed.

Aninut Restrictions

1. *Occupational restrictions.* An *onen/onenet* should *not* transact business. To avoid substantial financial loss, however, he/she may conclude a previously commenced transaction, and may sell his/her business to allow it to remain open in his/her absence until the end of *shiv'ah.*°

° See below, p. 205.

He/she should not receive any profit before the end of *shiv'ah*. In a partnership, the *onen/onenet* may sell his/her share of the business until after *shiv'ah*. The other partner may give him/her his/her share of the profits as a gift after the termination of *shiv'ah*.

2. *Personal restrictions.* An *onen/onenet* may not eat meat, drink wine or strong drink, bathe, shave, take a haircut, smell spices, or indulge in marital intimacy.

3. *Social restrictions.* An *onen/onenet* may not exchange greetings, eat at table, participate in social gatherings, partake of festive meals, or attend a wedding.

General Religious Exemptions and Imperatives

1. An *onen* is exempted from certain religious obligations. These exemptions are mandatory. An *onen* should not, on the grounds of personal strictness, voluntarily impose on himself those obligations from which he is exempted.

2. An *onen* is exempted from the performance of such positive *mitzvot* as statutary worship, the recitation of blessings (*berakhot*), participation in a quorum for grace after meals (*zimun*), and the putting on of *tallit* and *tefillin*. An *onen/onenet* should not respond to blessings recited by someone else by saying "Amen."

3. If an *onen* had begun to perform one of these *mitzvot* prior to being informed of the passing of a relative for whom he is required to mourn, he need not be told until its completion. However, should he find out about the death in the midst of his prayers, only the blessing which he happens to be saying should be completed.

4. An *onen* who must undertake a journey to the place where the deceased is to be buried *should* recite the traveler's prayer (*tefillat ha-derekh*).

5. An *onen* who has suffered an additional bereavement should say the *Dayyan ha-Emet* blessing.

6. An *onen* may recite *Kaddish*. He is not normally counted as part of the *minyan*. Notwithstanding, he may be count-

ed as the tenth member of a *minyan* if this will enable him
to say *Kaddish*.

7. An *onen/onenet* must observe all scriptural and rabbinical *prohibitions*. Thus he/she should wash his/her hands
upon awakening, leaving the bathroom, prior to eating—
without, of course, reciting the appropriate accompanying
blessings.

8. An *onen*, when called upon to do so, may serve as a witness.

9. To enable him/her to deal with funeral arrangements
effectively, an *onen/onenet* may sit on a regular chair.

Aninut on the Sabbath

1. If the death occurred late on Friday afternoon, the period
of *aninut* does not commence before the termination of
the Sabbath.

2. *Aninut* which commenced prior to the Sabbath ceases
throughout its duration, since one may not make funeral
arrangements on the Sabbath.

3. An *onen/onenet* should change clothes for the Sabbath,
but should refrain from wearing his/her best Sabbath
clothing.

4. He/she may eat meat and drink wine. If somebody else is
reciting *Kiddush*, he/she should satisfy his/her obligation
by responding *Amen* to the blessing. Otherwise, he/she
may recite the *Kiddush*. The *onen* may be included in the
quorum for grace after meals (*zimun*).

5. Although there is no *aninut* on the Sabbath, one should,
nevertheless, desist from doing those things from which
one would derive great pleasure—as long as one's action
does not attract public attention, since the *public* demonstration of grief is inappropriate on the Sabbath. Accordingly, the *onen/onenet* should not indulge in marital
intercourse or participate in a celebration. There should
be no study of Torah beyond the routine review of the
weekly Torah reading. The *onen* should not be called to
the Torah. He should not serve as *ba'al tefillah* (prayer
leader) or *ba'al kore* (Torah reader) unless there is nobody

else present who can fill these roles. He should move to a
seat at least six and a half feet away from his regular place
of worship in the synagogue. Should the rabbi of the synagogue become an *onen*, he should move to a neighboring
seat.

6. An *onen* does *not* recite the evening prayers at the conclusion of the Sabbath.

7. The *onen* does *not* recite the *Havdallah* blessings at the
conclusion of the Sabbath. If the interment will take place
before sunset on Tuesday, the *Havdallah* is recited over a
glass of wine after the interment.

ANINUT ON FESTIVALS

General Rules

1. The first two and last two days of festivals suspend
aninut—except that the restrictions in force on the Sabbath apply to the festivals also.

2. The mealtime and synagogue norms applicable on the
Sabbath obtain on festivals also.

3. However, on a festival, an *onen* may study Torah—in
addition to the laws of mourning.

4. An *onen* who is a *kohen* should leave the synagogue
before the priestly blessing (*Birkat Kohanim*).

5. The *onen* does not recite *Havdallah* at the termination of
the festivals. If the burial is on the day following the
festival, *Havdallah* is recited over a glass of wine after the
interment.

6. *Aninut* is observed during the intermediate days of festivals (*Chol Ha-mo'ed*).

Pesach

1. An *onen* need not search for *chametz* on the eve of Pesach
if another can do it for him. He himself, however, must
nullify his *chametz* (leaven).

2. An *onen* should keep the *mitzvot* relating to the *seder* but
should not wear a *kittel*. He should not eat in a reclining
position.

Sukkot

1. Although an *onen* is exempt from the *mitzvah* of building a *sukkah* (booth), should he wish to fulfill it, he may do so, providing that he does not, thereby, neglect the funeral arrangements with which he is charged.
2. Although an *onen* may eat outside the *sukkah*, he may, should he so desire, eat in the *sukkah* on the first night. He may even recite the *Kiddush* should no one else be present to whose *Kiddush* he can respond "Amen."
3. An *onen* should not do *hakafot* (join the ceremonial procession) with *lulav* and *etrog* (the four Sukkot species).
4. An *onen* should not accept a *hakafah* on Simchat Torah (the Rejoicing of the Torah), although he may accept *aliyot* (Torah honors) other than *Chatan Torah/Bereishit* (the concluding honor in one Torah scroll, and the initial honor in the second scroll).

Rosh ha-Shanah

The norms generally applicable to festivals obtain on Rosh ha-Shanah (New Year).

Yom Kippur

Aninut is suspended on the Day of Atonement.

Purim

1. In the evening, the *onen/onenet* should hear the reading of the *megillah* (Book of Esther).
2. During the day, the *onen/onenet* should hear the reading of the *megillah after* the burial. If he/she had heard the reading of the *megillah prior* to the burial, he/she should hear the reading again thereafter.
3. During the day, the *onen/onenet* may eat meat and drink wine, reciting the attendant blessings.

Chanukah

1. The *onen/onenet* should not light his/her own candles, but should have somebody else do so on his/her behalf.

2. If nobody is present who can do so, he/she should light the candles *without* reciting the attendant blessings.

Tisha b'Av

1. The *onen/onenet* is required to fast and to refrain from those activities which are forbidden.
2. However, he/she is exempt from attending synagogue services.

Brit Millah

1. The circumcision should not be delayed till after the interment.
2. An *onen* may serve as a *sandek* (hold the baby during the circumcision), since this is a *mitzvah* without an attendant blessing.
3. If the father of the infant is an *onen*, the *sandek* should recite the blessing over the circumcision.

Redemption of the Firstborn

1. The *pidyon ha-ben* usually takes place on the thirty-first day of the life of a firstborn male child, neither of whose parents is of priestly (*kohen*) or levitical (*levi*) descent. The *mitzvah* of redemption falls on the father. If the father is an *onen* on the thirty-first day of his son's life, the burial must precede the redemption. If this cannot be arranged, the redemption is postponed.
2. If the only available *kohen* is an *onen*, he may transact the redemption. However, he should not recite the priestly blessing.

Rosh Chodesh

Musaf (the Additional Service), may be recited in the afternoon, after the burial.

The Day of Burial

Tefillin

> *Tefillin* (phylacteries) are not generally worn by an *onen* until the day following interment, except that (1) a groom should, during the seven festive days, put on *tefillin* after interment, and (2) if the burial were on *Chol Ha-mo'ed*, and one's custom was not to wear *tefillin*, one should first put them on on the first day of *shiv'ah* after *Yom Tov;* and if one's custom was to wear *tefillin*, one should put them on after the interment.

Shacharit

1. If the burial was before the sixth hour of daylight, *shacharit* (morning prayers) should be recited after the interment.
2. If it was after the sixth hour of daylight, the liturgical passages *birkat ha-Torah, shelo asani goy, shelo asani eved, shelo asani ishah (she-asani kirtzono)* should be recited prior to the afternoon worship.

Aninut of Students for Teachers

1. The outstanding students of a rabbi, whose passing has affected them deeply, observe a limited form of *aninut.*
2. They may not eat meat or drink wine, but they are not exempted from the performance of positive *mitzvot.*

CHAPTER SEVEN

Between Death and Burial: Treatment of the Deceased

The kind of treatment we provide for the remains of our loved ones is a clear demonstration of our respect for them.

It is important that we feel good about the decisions we make in this regard. Obviously, we feel best when we are convinced we have made the *right* decisions. But the definition of what is right is sometimes confused, because what we *think* is right may be based upon misinformation and prejudice.

Funeral home professionals serve the entire spectrum of the Jewish community. Some of their clients are completely secular Jews. The funerals they demand reflect popular non-Jewish societal norms. For example, they may request ornate caskets of wood and metal. They may insist on embalming, beautifying and dressing up the deceased. They may invite friends and family to a public viewing of the remains.

Other Jewish clients, without being completely secular may be indifferent to traditional Jewish funeral and burial norms.

Your funeral professional cannot guess what your standards are. He needs to hear from you that you insist on strict adherence to halakhic standards. He is paid to serve you. He will surely wish to do what you believe is right. Indeed, he will find it helpful if you ask your rabbi to spell out your needs to him. In this way there will be no unintentional misinformation from this source.

51

The Halakhah mandates continuous attendance (*shemirah*) upon the remains, the selection of a suitable casket, the ritual cleansing of the body (*taharah*), the selection of shrouds (*takhrikhin*), the dressing of the body (*halbashah*), and its being placed in the casket.

Both to protect bereaved families and to ensure that halakhically mandated procedures are followed, the *chevra kadishas* of some congregations have entered into binding written agreements with funeral homes.

CONTENT OF AGREEMENT WITH FUNERAL HOMES

1. Outline of procedures relating to the transportation of the deceased to the funeral home and to the cemetery. Normally only Jews should touch the deceased. However, when the deceased must be moved on the Sabbath or on Holy Days (where hospital authorities, for example, insist on such removal), non-Jews may touch, move and transport the Jewish deceased.
2. Agreement as to the standard type of shrouds and casket to be used for all members of the congregation.
3. Agreement that a *shomer* (watchman) will always attend the remains.
4. Agreement to make available to the *chevra kadisha* facilities to store its equipment in the funeral home.
5. Agreement to allow the *chevra kadisha* facilities to perform *taharah* (ritual cleansing of the deceased), *halbashah* (the dressing of the deceased), and placing the remains in the casket.
6. Agreement to make every effort to ensure that the funeral take place as soon after death as possible.
7. Agreement to forbid the viewing of the remains.
8. Outline of the standard funeral and burial services and procedures.
9. Agreement for the speedy departure of the hearse from the funeral home, to allow those assembled to follow after it without undue delay.
10. Agreement as to the cost of these standardized procedures.

SHEMIRAH: ATTENDING THE DECEASED

In an earlier chapter we indicated that the body should never be left unattended. The imperative of *shemirah* (attending the deceased) is in force from the moment of death to interment. The remains should not be left alone by day or by night, on weekdays, Sabbaths, or festivals.

SHEMIRAH: HALAKHIC CHECKLIST

1. Any Jewish male may serve as a *shomer* (watchman) for any Jewish deceased person. It is desirable for close relatives of the deceased or students of a deceased teacher to serve as *shomrim*.
2. If the body of the deceased is preserved in a refrigeration unit until *taharah* or the funeral, the *shomer* should be in the same room as the unit, or at least be able to see the door of the unit from outside the room. Otherwise, the *shomer* should be in the same room as the body, or at least able to see the body.
3. Smoking, eating, drinking, and the recitation of blessings and routine prayers are forbidden in the presence of the deceased during *shemirah*. They may do these things in another, closed room. The *shomrim* are exempted from performing other *mitzvot* during *shemirah*. Hence, they do not put on *tefillin* or allow their *tzitzit* to show.
4. Obviously, idle conversation is forbidden during *shemirah*.
5. The *shomer* recites psalms throughout his *shemirah* period.

PROHIBITION AGAINST VIEWING THE REMAINS

How should we remember our beloved departed? As they were in life—full of bodily vigor, creative, thinking, doing? Or as they appear in death—frail, waxen shadows of their former selves—or even worse? The Jewish way is the former. We try to remember those we love in their glory, when their bodies were warm and vital vehicles for their immortal souls. We try not to remember them in lifeless repose in a casket, sometimes broken by injury and withered by lengthy, debilitating illness. We make no virtue of viewing the remains. On the contrary, obsession with mortal remains is a form of necrophilia, the adoration of the dead, which is expresssly forbidden by Jewish law, and which is both pagan and unhealthy. *The wake is not a Jewish custom.* Viewing the remains is prohibited by the Halakhah. It is entirely alien to our tradition. Only those who prepare the deceased for burial are permitted to look at their remains.

THE CASKET

Since every human being is equally created in the divine image, it is wrong to make an ultimate distinction between rich and poor in death.

Accordingly, the simplest, unadorned, unlined, unpadded, plain wooden casket should be used.

True love and respect for one's beloved departed is expressed by one's selection of an approved casket. To do otherwise is to alienate the dead from his/her religious heritage.

PREPARATION OF THE REMAINS FOR BURIAL

The preparation of the remains for burial is the special obligation of the *chevra kadisha*. It is a *chesed shel emet*—a true act of loving-kindness. It includes the ritual cleansing of the remains, the dressing of the deceased in approved shrouds, and the placing of the deceased in the approved casket—with attendant prayers and traditional recitations.

What follows is a detailed description of these procedures. Although it may be of interest to many readers, it is primarily intended as a practical, step-by-step guide for the *chevra kadisha*.

CLEANSING THE REMAINS OF AIDS VICTIMS

These unfortunate people are entitled to a full ritual cleansing. The members of the *chevra kadisha* should perform the *taharah* in rubber gloves and disposable gowns, caps and masks. If they take these precautions they will be in no danger of infection.

MANUAL FOR THE CHEVRA KADISHA

TAHARAH: RITUAL CLEANSING OF THE DEAD

Who Performs the Taharah?

1. The *mitzvah* of the proper preparation of a Jewish body for burial is a *chesed shel emet*—the ultimate act of human benevolence. Most Jews are permitted to perform this *mitzvah*.
2. *Taharah* for deceased Jewish females is performed by Jewish women. No Jewish woman is excluded from this *mitzvah* on ritual grounds. For emotional reasons, however, close relatives of the deceased, such as her daughters, her mother, sister, mother-in-law, etc., may not be present at her *taharah*.
3. *Taharah* for deceased Jewish males is performed by Jewish males. If *really* necessary, and if a competent rabbi so rules, women may perform *taharah* on men (although not vice versa). Only *kohanim* are ritually excluded from the performance of this *mitzvah*, since they cannot be in the *ohel*. For emotional reasons, however, close relatives of the deceased, such as his sons, his father, brothers, father-in-law, etc., may not be present at his *taharah*.

When Taharah is Performed

The *taharah* should take place as close to the time of the funeral service as possible. Ideally, no more than three hours should elapse between the *taharah* and the funeral. However, if there is no alternative, the *taharah* may take place on the previous evening.

Initial Preparations

1. Before the *taharah,* the casket, shrouds, and all other necessary items must be prepared and ready for use, in order to prevent the desecration of the dead. These items include the various utensils and the cloth used for wash-

ing and wiping. It is important to check the casket before-hand to make sure that it contains no metal, or any other type of ornamentation. After everything is ready, the *taharah* may commence.

2. Before commencing the *taharah,* the members of the *chevra kadisha* must wash their hands in the same manner as the ritual washing each morning: the hands, beginning with the right, are alternately washed three times with a container.

3. Members of the *chevra kadisha* then recite the prayer which preceeds the *taharah.*°

Preparations for Washing

1. The body is placed on its back on the *taharah* board. At no time should it be placed face-downwards. Then large containers of lukewarm water (not hot) are to be brought in. The prayer appropriate for the commencement of the washing is now recited.° One member of the *chevra kadisha* takes a small vessel, draws from the larger vessel, and pours water over the body. A second member washes that part of the body with a piece of cloth. This procedure is then continued.

2. In respect for the person and his/her dignity, the private parts of the body are to be covered at all times, except when they must be exposed to be washed. They should, obviously, be covered when scriptural passages are recited.

Recitation During Washing

1. While the body is being washed (see next section for order of washing), verses from the Song of Songs of Solomon are recited. These verses extoll the perfection of the human body, describing the head and hair, the eyes and cheeks,

---

° See below, pp. 210–211.
° See below, p. 212.

the lips and neck, the arms and thighs. The body, the seat of the immortal soul, is regarded as a creation of singular beauty.°

Order of Washing

1. The fingernails and toenails are cleansed, and the hair is combed. Care should be taken that the fingers or other joints of the body do not bend or close. The body is washed completely.

2. The following is the order of the washing of the front of the body:
   a. The entire head.
   b. The neck.
   c. The right upper arm, arm, and hand.
   d. The right upper half of the body.
   e. The private parts.
   f. The right thigh, leg, and foot.
   g. The left upper arm, arm and hand.
   h. The left upper half of the body.
   i. The left thigh, leg and foot.

3. The body is then inclined on its *left* side and the *right* side of the back is washed, starting from the shoulder, to the foot.
4. Care should be taken that the rectum be clean, by checking there with a piece of cloth. If, in the cleansing, blood flows, the rectum is stopped up after the cleansing.
5. The body is inclined on its *right* side and the *left* side of the back is washed, starting from the shoulder, to the foot.
6. Blood which flows at the time of death may not be washed away. When there is *other* blood on the body, which flowed during the lifetime of the deceased (from wounds or as the result of an operation) the washing and the *taharah* are *theoretically* performed in the usual manner. In *practice*, however, it is sometimes difficult to deter-

---

° See below, p. 213.

mine when the flow of blood occurred. It is customary to wash away all the blood on the body of the deceased and to place the cloth used for this purpose in the casket for burial.

7. When only *part* of the body was injured and covered with blood, and it is possible to perform a *taharah* on the remainder, it should be performed.

8. When blood flows continually after death and cannot be stopped, the source of the flow must be covered. Under these circumstances the body cannot be washed. The clothes or cloth which contain blood which flowed after death are to be placed in the casket at the feet of the deceased.

9. If the deceased has been operated upon and the cut closed by a plaster or bandage, if the removal of the bandage or plaster will not cause bleeding, it should be removed before the washing. Otherwise it should be left in place.

The Nine Kabin

1. Nine *kabin* (24 quarts—or at least 18 quarts) of cold fresh water from the tap are placed in a pail.

2. After the body has been thoroughly washed and cleansed, two or three pitchers of water are filled from the pail. *No more than three pitchers are to be used.*

3. The water from the pitchers is poured over the body in such a way that before the first vessel is emptied, water is poured from the second, and before the second pitcher is emptied, water is poured from the third. The first pitcher has, in the meantime, been refilled from the pail. Before the third pitcher has been emptied, water is poured from the first. This continues until all nine *kabin* have been poured over the entire body (as in item 5, below). Should the continual flow of water from the pitchers be interrupted, the nine *kabin* should be poured a second time.

4. While the nine *kabin* are poured, all the participants recite the following formula:

For a deceased male: "*Tahor hu, Tahor hu*—he is pure, he is pure."

For a deceased female: "*Tehorah hee, Tehorah hee*— she is pure, she is pure."

5. Ideally, the body should be raised to stand vertically on some straw or wood on the ground, and the nine *kabin* poured over the head—to flow over the entire body. If such a procedure cannot be managed, the following may be substituted:

a. Water is poured onto the board.

b. The body is placed onto its side, and the pouring of the nine *kabin* commences—starting at the head.

c. The body is placed onto its other side and the pouring of the nine *kabin* is completed.

6. The *taharah* board should be dried, and a clean dry white sheet spread over it.

7. The body, which has by now had the nine *kabin* poured over it should be placed on the board. It should be wiped around until it is completely dry.

HALBASHAH: DRESSING THE DECEASED

The Shrouds

1. The shrouds should be made of white linen. They are to be sewn by hand (not by machine) by pious women past the age of menopause. The shrouds may not contain any pockets. They should also have no knots, neither in the garments nor in the threads.

2. The shrouds must be clean. If they have become soiled, they must be washed before use. The *chevra kadisha* should have several sets of shrouds on hand for emergencies, especially on *Erev Shabbat* and *Erev Yom Tov*, when time is short.

3. According to tradition, the shrouds consist of the following garments:

Mitznefet. A headdress, which is to cover the head, the face, and the back of the head to the neck.

K'tonet. A shirt with sleeves, which covers the entire body and the hands. At the neckline, a cloth band is drawn through, with which the shirt is tied at the time of dressing.

Mikhnasayim. Trousers. They should be large enough to reach the belly. They are usually sewn closed at the feet. Should they have pull-through bands, however, the bottoms of the trousers are tied at the ankle.

Kittel. An upper garment, made like the shirt (*k'tonet*). It may remain open at the neck or be tied with bands in the same manner as the *k'tonet.* The *kittel* should reach the knees.

Veil. It is customary to make the veil from the same material as the shrouds. This article is used for a deceased woman.

Avnet. A belt, which is wound around the body over the *kittel.*

Sovev. A linen sheet, with which the dressed body is wrapped.

Tallit. In the case of a male, his four-fringed prayer garment, from which all ornaments have been removed, and from which one of the fringes (*tzitziyot*) has been cut.

4. A child of less than one year is wrapped in four swaddling cloths.
5. A child of less than thirty days is wrapped in three swaddling cloths.

Recitation During the Dressing

A special recitation is made during the *halbashah* (the dressing of the body).°

Order of Dressing a Deceased Female

1. The hair is held together in its loose form—neatly, and

See below, p. 213.

without knots. Combing is permitted *only* to achieve these purposes, and should be kept to a minimum.

2. The veil is placed on the forehead and tied at the back. A cap is placed on top of this, covering the entire head.

3. The trousers are put on. They are to reach the waist. When pull-through bands are provided, they are to be tied around the waist and the ends wound around four times with two bows pointing towards the head.

4. The shirt (*k'tonet*) is put on, the sleeves placed on the hands, and the garment slipped over the head.

5. The *kittel* is placed over the shirt onto the body.

6. The *avnet* is tied over the *kittel* as a belt. The ends are wound around four times and tied in three bows in the shape of the Hebrew letter *shin*, the bows pointing toward the head.

7. The *sovev* is spread in the casket in a diamondlike slanting position.

Order of Dressing a Deceased Male

1. The *mitznefet* is placed on the head and drawn down to cover the head, neck, and the nape of the neck.

2. The trousers are put on. The ends of the band at the waist are wound around four times. The band is tied with two bows pointing towards the head. When pull-through bands are provided at the feet, the right ankle is tied before the left.

3. The shirt (*k'tonet*) is put on, the sleeves placed over the hands, and the garment slipped over the head and drawn down over the body. The band near the neck is tied in the same way as the waist-band of the trousers.

4. The *kittel* is put on in the same way as the *k'tonet*. The *chevra kadisha* should make sure that the sleeves extend to the wrists.

5. The *avnet* is tied around the waist as a belt, over the *kittel*. The ends are wound around four times and tied with three bows in the shape of the Hebrew letter *shin*. These bows should point to the head.

6. The *sovev* is spread diagonally over the inside of the casket, overlapping the sides.
7. The *tallit* is put in the casket over the *sovev*. The removed fringe is tucked into a corner of the *tallit*.

Dressing a Deceased Infant

1. A child who has lived for less than a year is wrapped in four swaddling cloths. The body is wrapped with the first, from the armpits to over the feet. The second cloth is folded into a triangle, and wrapped around the head and neck. The third is also folded into a triangle and placed under the nape of the neck, like a scarf. The two ends are pulled to the front, and the shoulders and arms are covered with them. The fourth cloth serves as a bed sheet.
2. A child who has not lived for thirty days is covered with three swaddling cloths, and is buried in a casket.

Beautifying and Preserving the Remains is Forbidden

The artificial preservation or beautification of the deceased is forbidden. Neither embalming nor cosmetic treatment of a Jewish body for esthetic purposes is permitted.

Placing the Body in the Casket

1. The casket is to be prepared before the *taharah*. When the body has been dressed, some straw and a handful of earth are placed in the pillow upon which the head of the deceased will rest in the casket.
2. Only then is the *sovev* (and in the case of a deceased male, his *tallit*) placed in position in the casket.
3. When the body is placed in the casket, a liturgical selection is recited.°
4. The body is gently lifted and carefully placed in the casket.

° See below pp. 213–214.

5. The entire body is wrapped around with the *sovev*.
6. Before the body is covered, some earth from the Holy Land is sprinkled over the eyes, heart and private parts of the deceased. Broken pieces of earthenware are placed over the eyes and mouth.
7. The *chevra kadisha* asks the deceased for forgiveness for any indignity he or she may have suffered at their hands, notwithstanding the loving care and concern which they exercised during the *taharah* procedures.
8. The casket is closed. Under *most* circumstances it is not to be opened up again before burial. There is one exception to this rule. If the deceased was not previously identified by a relative (as required), the identification can take place after the body has been placed in the casket.

CHAPTER EIGHT

Funeral and Interment

EXPRESSING GRIEF BY RENDING GARMENTS

Psychologists agree that repression of grief is unhealthy. Repressed anguish is bound to surface eventually—frequently in disturbing, neurotic phobias, fantasies and conduct. The healthy response to grief is *expression* rather than *repression*.

To be sure, grief can be expressed in many ways. It can be handled intellectually, by speaking about one's loss and philosophizing about the situation. It can also be vented emotionally, by giving unabashed expression to one's feelings in tears, protest, and hurt.

As a physical sign of grief, primitive man mutilated his body, as if to say: "In the face of my great loss, I do not care about my own life." But self-mutilation is dangerous and counterproductive. It is dangerous because it can become life-threatening. It is also counterproductive, because instead of helping us to handle our grief in a life-affirming manner, it responds to death by suggesting that the survivors should also mortally wound themselves—or ever after live with guilt for merely having survived unscarred. Besides, how much self-mutilation is enough? Can we ever really adequately express our grief in this way? For all these reasons, Scripture prohibited this pagan practice (Deuteronomy 14:1).

However, what we cannot express physically, we *can* express symbolically. Symbols articulate our deepest feelings far more effectively than words do. They stir the profoundest depths of our souls. They help us to act out those feelings of which we are aware, and to focus the feelings of which we are not conscious. They stimulate and express our grief, and grant us psychological relief without doing us bodily harm.

Our biblical ancestors gave inspired symbolic expression to their grief by rending their garments. On one level this is a harmless, meaningful, and effective sublimation of self-mutilation. On another, the rending of garments is a positive, healthy, and formalized expression of rage—channeled in a traditionally hallowed way. It is comforting to know that even our anger at our great loss is natural and acceptable.

On a more cognitive level, rending of garments is the symbolic expression of the impermanent, ephemeral nature of material things.

On the noblest spiritual level, it symbolizes the relation of the body to the soul. Our mystics stated it precisely: "The body is nothing more than the outer garment of the eternal soul." Just as tearing our clothes does not affect our bodies, so the death of our body does not affect our deathless soul.

So effective is the tearing of our garments as the visible sign of our broken hearts that our sages ruled out any compromise on this expression of our mourning. In other aspects of the mourning process, we are permitted to follow the more lenient of conflicting practices. With regard to *keri'ah*, the rending of garments, the stricter view is always followed.

Unfortunately, many people have demeaned this marvelous, many-faceted, deeply meaningful symbol of grief. They pin a black button or a piece of black ribbon on the outerwear of grieving mourners, depriving them of the catharsis of tearing their garments, and of the rich and ancient traditional Jewish expression of grief. They substitute the inauthentic for the Jewishly authentic. They introduce alien symbols which, while attractive to uninformed Jews, result in the loss of much more than the saving of the price of a used garment. *A black ribbon is not a valid alternative for the rending of garments. Wearing such a ribbon—even if it is cut— does not release the wearer from his/her obligation of having to rend garments later on.* In short, the use of ribbons is inappropriate.

KERI'AH: HALAKHIC CHECKLIST

For Whom Do We Rend?

1. According to ancient custom, if one was present at the side of any worthy Jew at the time of his/her passing, one would rend one's garments. However, since this practice might discourage the presence of people at the deathbed, it was substantially modified—as follows:
2. One tears one's clothing at the passing of one of one's seven closest relatives—father, mother, brother (or half brother), sister (or half sister), son, daughter, spouse.
3. One does not tear garments for a spouse from whom one was divorced according to Jewish law (by obtaining a *get*).
4. One tears garments after the passing of one's principal teacher of Torah.

When Do We Rend?

1. The most desirable period for rending extends from the moment of the death of our beloved to his/her interment.
2. The precise time for the rending varies with custom. Some perform *keri'ah* if they are present at the time of death—especially in the case of a parent. Some perform *keri'ah* before leaving their homes for the funeral/burial. Some perform *keri'ah* at the funeral home before the service. Some perform *keri'ah* after the eulogy at the funeral home. Some perform *keri'ah* at the graveside before the casket is covered. It is preferable to perform *keri'ah* at the funeral after the eulogy—for several compelling reasons. The eulogy stirs pent-up emotions, preparing the bereaved psychologically for the rending. All the mourners are usually present, allowing for greater empathy and sympathy. The rabbi or other learned, experienced persons are present to help direct the *keri'ah*.

3. If one knew about the death and began to sit *shiv'ah* but had forgotten to perform *keri'ah,* one does so during the *shiv'ah* period, but without reciting the accompanying blessing.

4. If, in these circumstances, one has not performed *keri'ah* during the *shiv'ah* period, one does not perform *keri'ah* subsequently.

5. However, one may simply not have heard of the passing within seven days of the interment. Under these conditions, one can perform *keri'ah* for one's six close kin up to the end of *sheloshim* (thirty days). In the case of a parent, the obligation to perform *keri'ah* has no time limit.

6. If the body is unavailable, as, for example, when a person is lost at sea, *keri'ah* should be performed as soon as the *Beth Din* (Rabbinical Court) has declared the person dead.

7. A bride or groom may postpone *keri'ah* until after the seven days of rejoicing which follow their marriage. During this period of rejoicing, they should not go to the cemetery.

8. *Keri'ah* is forbidden on the Sabbath and holy days, although the blessing *Dayyan ha-Emet* is recited.

9. If the interment takes place on *Chol ha-Mo'ed,* according to Ashkenazic custom, *keri'ah* is performed immediately only for a parent. If it is postponed for more than three days, an abbreviated version of the blessing (without reference to the divine Name or sovereignty) is recited. For the other six closest relatives, *keri'ah* is postponed until after *Yom Tov.* According to Sefardic custom, *keri'ah* is performed for all seven of one's closest kin on *Chol ha-Mo'ed.*

10. If one is notified of a death (which has occurred previously) during *Chol ha-Mo'ed:*
    a. *In the case of a parent* one rends immediately—provided that the notification is within thirty days of the interment. If notification is delayed longer, one postpones the rending until after the festival.
    b. According to Sefardic custom, one rends immediate-

ly for the six other closest kin *also*, provided that thirty days have not elapsed since interment.

c. According to Ashkenazic custom, one rends for the six closest kin (other than parents) at once, if thirty days after burial will have elapsed by the end of the festival. If not, one postpones the *keri'ah* until after the festival.

Which Garments Should Be Torn?

1. One may rend only garments which one owns.
2. One need not rend one's best, most expensive garments.
3. One rends only those items of outerwear which are worn at home in normal room temperatures, such as a jacket, vest, sweater, shirt, or blouse. One does not rend underwear, a *tallit-katan*, or such special weather outerwear as overcoats or rain coats.

How is Keri'ah Performed?

General Rules

1. One stands when one's garments are torn.
2. The garment should be cut vertically, at a point high in the lapel area.
3. The tear should *not* be made on a seam, where it might be thought to be accidental rather than deliberate.
4. The rending can be started by another adult with a blade, knife, scissors, or other instrument.
5. The rending is always done on a minor by an adult.
6. The tear should not be more than a *tefach*—three and a half inches.
7. No blessing is said on the actual rending, since an act of destruction is not celebrated with a blessing.
8. *Following* the rending, the blessing accepting and acknowledging God's inexorable judgment is recited: "Blessed are Thou, O Lord, King of the Universe, the true Judge." °

Keri'ah for a Parent

1. All outer garments normally worn at home at normal

° See below, p. 215.

room temperature should be torn. Thus, a shirt, as well as a jacket, should be cut.

2. The tear begins with an initial cut in the left side of the garment. It commences in the lapel area of a jacket, vest, or sweater, or the upper front button area of a shirt or blouse, over the heart.
3. The mourner himself/herself should then tear it vertically downwards by hand for three and a half inches.
4. If, another person performs the entire tear for one, it need not be repeated.
5. The tearing should be performed in public, and should be visible throughout the *shiv'ah* period.
6. If the tear were erroneously made on the right side, it need not be repeated.
7. For reasons of modesty, a woman may pin up or cover the tear, or even sew it up crudely.
8. *Every change of torn outerwear during* shiv'ah *necessitates a new* keri'ah.

Keri'ah for Other Relatives

1. Only one outer garment need be torn.
2. The cut is made on the *right* side of the garment, in the lapel or upper front button area.
3. It is commenced by another adult and continued by the mourner for three and a half inches.
4. An instrument may be used to make the whole tear.
5. If it is erroneously torn on the left side, it need not be repeated.
6. For reasons of modesty, a woman may pin up or cover the tear, or even sew it up crudely.
7. The tear need be neither performed in public nor visible.
8. A change of clothing during the *shiv'ah* does *not* necessitate a new *keri'ah*. However, one should avoid changing outerwear during *shiv'ah*.

Keri'ah for Several Relatives Simultaneously

1. In general, the rule is that a single tear and blessing may suffice for several relatives, although the passing of a

parent always demands a special full-fledged *keri'ah*.

2. If one were informed simultaneously of the deaths of more than one close relative, other than a parent, a single tear and blessing suffices.

3. If one were informed simultaneously of the deaths of a parent and another close relative, one should first perform *keri'ah* for one's parent, and then having left space of an inch, tear for the other relative.

4. The same procedure should be followed if one performed *keri'ah* for a parent and was then informed of the passing of another close relative.

5. If one were informed of the passing of a close relative during *shiv'ah* observances for another relative, another tear of three and one-half inches should be made. If one were informed after *shiv'ah*, a slight additional tear suffices.

6. However, if after the completion of *shiv'ah* for another close relative, one were informed of the passing of a parent, an inch should be left and an additional entirely new *keri'ah* performed for one's parent.

How Long Should Torn Garments Be Worn?

Torn clothes may be changed after *shiv'ah*.

Can the Tear Be Mended?

1. In the case of garments torn to express one's grief at the passing of one's parent, the tear may never be mended invisibly. However, the garment may be more crudely mended after the *sheloshim* or before a festival which occurs during the *sheloshim*.

2. In the case of the six other closest kin, the tear may be crudely mended after *shiv'ah*, and permanently, invisibly mended after *sheloshim*. The invisible mending may be done shortly before a festival which occurs, respectively, during *shiv'ah* or *sheloshim*.

THE FUNERAL

When Should the Funeral Be Held?

Prompt burial is a Jewish ideal. "Thou shalt bury him on the same day," declares Scripture. "His body shall not remain all night" (Deuteronomy 21:23). This injunction benefits both the living and the departed. The living are not kept in a state of limbo. The anguish created by extensive delays is avoided, and the bereaved are enabled to deal with their loss more rapidly through the reality of the funeral service and the inexorability of the interment. Death has completed the sojourn of the departed on earth. Delay of burial belies this fact. Moreover, the fact that the departed has to be unnecessarily "preserved" through refrigeration is regarded as a profound indignity. Indeed, our sages believed that the final divine judgment of the soul depends, in large measure, upon the disintegration of the body after burial. Any unnecessary delay postpones the ultimate atonement of the eternal soul of the deceased.

Notwithstanding the ideal of an undelayed burial, funerals do not take place on the Sabbath, Yom Kippur, and the first and seventh days of the pilgrim festivals. To prevent unnecessary desecration of festivals—which would dishonor the departed—funerals are also not held on the second and eighth days of festivals.

TIMING OF THE FUNERAL: HALAKHIC CHECKLIST

1. Burial should take place on the day of death or as soon as possible thereafter.
2. It is legitimately delayed by government regulations, which may require unavoidable postmortem examinations, completion of documentation, and so on.
3. Reasonable delay, which reflects special honor on the deceased, is also sanctioned. Such delay may be occasioned by allowing close relatives to arrive from faraway places. It may also be occasioned by allowing for the arrival of a large crowd of participants in the funeral of a great personality.
4. A funeral may be delayed if a suitable casket or shrouds are not available earlier.

5. In all circumstances, any delay should be kept to an absolute minimum.

Where Should The Funeral Be Held?

Various customs determine the location of the funeral. Funeral services may take place in the home of the deceased. In some communities they take place in the synagogue. Even where the custom is to hold funeral services elsewhere, the remains of extraordinarily outstanding members of the community are brought to the synagogue, where either a full funeral service is held or additional psalms recited and eulogies made. Most often, funerals take place in a funeral home. Many communities—especially smaller communities—have facilities for funeral services (an *ohel*) in the community cemetery. This is, in many respects, a good arrangement, since the participants in the funeral services will also participate in the burial service. The more people who do so, the greater is the respect shown for the deceased. In some communities the funeral services take place at the graveside. This is the most inexpensive arrangement, and is fully sanctioned by ancient Jewish custom. In Jerusalem no delays are allowed and burial may take place at night.

Flowers

The floral decoration of the funeral chapel is a widespread gentile practice. It has no place in a contemporary Jewish funeral home. A well-known funeral director recently told this writer that his establishment destroys thousands of dollars worth of flowers each week. This waste is unconscionable. Sympathizers should be encouraged to send donations to a worthy charity rather than flowers to a chapel. Such donations are meaningful memorials. They benefit the living. They enshrine the wonderful ideal that, at the very end, the deceased leaves this world a little better than he/she found it.

If people insist on sending flowers, they should be urged to instruct the funeral director to display them unostentatiously, and to send them to hospitals and nursing homes after the service. If they insist on having their flowers placed on the grave, this should be done after the interment.

The Funeral Service

The Jewish funeral service is a model of brief, simple dignity. It consists of four elements: a recitation from the Book of Psalms (usually the Twenty-third Psalm), a collage of various psalms, the memorial prayer, and the eulogy.°

The Twenty-third Psalm is the quintessential expression of faith: "Yea, though I walk through the valley of the shadow of death, I shall fear no evil, for Thou art with me. Thy rod and staff, they comfort me." It brings consolation, comfort, and serene reassurance to the broken-hearted bereaved. The collage has been aptly titled: "What is Man?" Its purpose is to remind the mourners of the essential brevity of life, so that they may resolve to fill their days with meaningful activity—inspired by the memory of the ideals and attainments of the deceased.

The purpose of the memorial prayer is our plea to divine Providence to embrace the soul of the departed, and to grant the departed his/her full spiritual reward. Interestingly, the plea is conditional. The mourners pledge charity on this occasion—both to assure the Almighty that they are as willing to help others as He is willing to help them, and also to demonstrate that the deceased has left survivors as dedicated to a life of good works as he/she was.

The Eulogy

The function of the eulogy (*hesped*) is twofold. In the first place, it is meant to focus upon the worthy characteristics and attainments of the deceased. In cases where the rabbi is not personally acquainted with the deceased, the bereaved should make sure that every relevant fact is shared with him, so that he can emphasize the special virtues of the departed in his presentation. There is nobody about whom something good cannot be said, since each of us is unique and special.

The second function of the eulogy is to arouse the emotions of the listeners. For this reason, a eulogy is inappropriate on those intrinsically joyful occasions when the public display of sadness is forbidden.

° See below, p. 216.

HESPED: HALAKHIC CHECKLIST

1. Every Jew is worthy of a eulogy.
2. It may be delivered at any time in the twelve-month period following his/her demise.
3. Eulogies should be factual and free of untruths, focusing on the special qualities of the deceased.
4. Eulogies are not delivered during the major festivals or on the day immediately following.
5. They are not delivered on Chanukah, Purim, or Rosh Chodesh (the first day of the Hebrew month), since these are regarded as minor holidays.
6. They are not delivered on the afternoons preceding major festivals or the minor holidays listed above. Nor are they delivered on Friday afternoons, since the mood of joy is anticipated a few hours prior to the actual commencement of the joyful occasion.
7. These prohibitions may, in exceptional circumstances and with the approval of a reliable rabbinic authority, be partially relaxed, by making *brief* references to those attributes of the deceased which can serve as models for survivors.
8. The clearly articulated request of the deceased that a eulogy be omitted from his funeral service should be respected. In the absence of such a clearly enunciated request, the bereaved survivors may not demand omission of a *hesped*.

Special Rituals: Fraternal Rites

There is no objection to the recitation of the funeral liturgies of fraternal orders, provided that a competent rabbi has determined that the recitation in no way whatsoever conflicts with Jewish theological principles. There is also no objection to fraternal ritual processionals and recessionals. However, under no circumstances may any item of fraternal paraphernalia be placed in the casket. The casket, it will be recalled, is to remain closed after the completion of the *taharah* (ritual purification). *The practice of including a fraternal apron with the shrouds is absolutely prohibited.*

TRANSPORTATION OF THE REMAINS

Long-Distance Transportation: — The Problem of Embalming

State and national governments are legitimately concerned about the decomposition of bodies which are transported over great distances. Wooden caskets may leak. The cargo areas of airplanes and airports may come to smell of decaying human tissue. Understandably, governmental authorities have ruled that these unpleasant aspects of long-distance transportation of bodies must be avoided.

The most common procedure for avoiding these problems is embalming. An incision is made in a major artery and in a major vein. Formaldehyde is pumped into the artery, and the blood pours from the vein down the drain.

Embalming is abhorrent to Jews. The blood is considered to be the seat of human vitality and cannot be discarded like dirty water. It is a halakhically inseparable part of the human body, and must be buried with it. The prohibition against the substitution of formaldehyde for blood is absolute.

Fortunately, embalming can be legally avoided. Sensitive funeral directors can be persuaded that their licenses will not be placed in jeopardy if they transport the ritually purified, unembalmed remains in a sealed *Ziegler Case* or in a similar metal-lined container, which is leakproof and which does not permit the escape of odor. Almost all states and countries sanction this alternative to embalming. Government officials should be approached in a sensitive, sincere, and persuasive manner on grounds of inviolable religious principle. Indeed, the State of Israel has sanctioned the use of a lightweight wooden casket lined with aluminum.

One should be careful to ensure that a Jew is always traveling with the remains—either in the hearse or on the airplane.

TRANSFER FOR BURIAL: HALAKHIC CHECKLIST

1. Upon leaving the chapel, participants in the funeral service should wash their hands with a special vessel.
2. The remains of the deceased should be accompanied to the airport or to the cemetery (as the case may be) by at least one Jew.

3. It is a great *mitzvah* for all participants to accompany the remains for at least six and a half feet on their final journey.
4. The larger the procession (*levayah*), the greater is the honor paid to the departed.

INTERMENT

The Jewish Cemetery

Consecrated Ground

A Jewish cemetery is consecrated ground. It is usually consecrated at a special service.° It must be separated from unconsecrated ground by a surrounding wall, solid hedge, or fence. It must have its own entrances and exits.

Gentile Family Members

A Jewish cemetery is consecrated for the interment of members of the Jewish faith. Only a person born to a Jewish mother or converted to Judaism in accordance with the strict requirements of the Halakhah may be buried in a Jewish cemetery. Painful though it may be, a non-Jew may not be interred next to his or her Jewish spouse, and the unconverted children of a non-Jewish mother may not be buried with their Jewish father. At best, they may be buried in an unconsecrated adjacent area, fenced off from the Jewish cemetery. This is the bitter price of mixed marriage and the neglect of Jewish commitments during life—and one of the consequences of rupturing connections with the Jewish people by choosing to "marry out."

Acquiring Burial Plots

Many of us are reluctant to purchase burial plots. We simply do not wish to contemplate our own passing. Some of us even harbor

° See below, p. 258.

the irrational fear that merely planning our burial will somehow bring it about prematurely. Obviously, such fears are absurd. On the contrary, it is wise to purchase a family burial plot while we are physically and mentally competent. Only in this way can we be certain that our final resting place will be where we desire, and that we shall permanently lie near our most dearly beloved relatives.

It should be noted that purchasing a burial plot does not prevent the owner from disposing of it at any time prior to its intended use. The location of our plot certificates and all our other important documents should be made known to our family members. It is prudent to have burial plot information on file in your synagogue.

Family Plots

It is a good idea for husband and wife to purchase a family plot. In some cases, additional plots are purchased for the use of the extended family. In this context, the wife is customarily considered to be part of her husband's family.

Family Plots and Remarriage

In the event of remarriage following the death of one's spouse, ownership of a family plot presents special perplexing problems. With which mate should the deceased be buried? There are no firm rules, but some guidelines are useful.

BURIAL GUIDELINES FOR THE REMARRIED

1. Under all circumstances, the preference of the deceased should be respected.
2. If no preference was expressed, the deceased should be buried with the other natural parent of his/her children.
3. If both spouses had children with the deceased, preference is usually given the first wife/husband.

Burial Means Interment

Burial in the Ground

Because God fashioned the first man from the dust of the ground (*afar min ha-adamah*), He called him Adam. After Adam's expulsion from Eden, God informed him that he would die and be buried in the earth: "By the sweat of thy brow shalt thou eat bread, till thou return unto the ground; for out of it wast thou taken; for dust thou wast and unto dust thou shalt return" (Genesis 3:19). It was made clear elsewhere in the Bible that this was to be the fate not only of Adam, but of all his descendants after him: "The dust shall return to the earth as it was, and the spirit shall return to God who gave it" (Ecclesiastes 12:7). Thus, burial in the ground is a scriptural imperative rather than merely a widespread custom. To emphasize its mandatory nature, the Bible repeats the verb *kavor*, "to bury": "And bury, shalt thou bury him" (Deuteronomy 21:23). Jews are not granted "options". *Burial means interment*—being placed in the ground. Nothing else is acceptable. To do anything else is tantamount to leaving the body unburied. From a Judaic perspective, there are few things more shameful.

Concrete Vaults

Because the ultimate atonement of the earthly transgressions of the deceased is associated with the disintegration of his/her remains, conditions which will postpone the process of disintegration are avoided. It is for this reason, among others, that embalming is forbidden. It is for this reason, also, that an easily biodegradable, plain wooden casket is used. Indeed, in Israel, caskets are not generally used. The dead are usually placed directly into their graves, so that the process of physical disintegration is not delayed.

Clearly, therefore, lining a grave with concrete is not ideal, The purpose of such vaults is obviously the preservation of the landscaping. But the effect is the postponement of the disintegration of the remains. It unquestionably frustrates the primary purpose of burial in the ground—the speedy return of dust to dust. In unusual circumstances, however, the construction of in-the-ground vaults may be mandated by local governmental health authorities or by cemetery owners. Unstable ground and abnormal moisture content, for example, may be factors which influence this kind of burial legislation. Under such circumstances, Jews may comply with the requirement of the local legislators. This is because underground vaults are *technically* considered to be joined to and part of the ground. In some places substantial holes at the bottom of the vaults are part of their design, permitting "dust to return to dust." On these grounds, therefore, an individual who is buried in an under-ground vault is considered to be buried in the ground.

Mausoleums

In ancient times, buildings of brick and stone or other materials were constructed on the graves of especially prominent individuals. A structure of this kind was meant to draw attention to the extra-ordinary status of the person who lay beneath its foundation. It was, in fact, nothing more than an elaborate memorial, and was called a *nefesh*. Nowadays, also, *nefesh* structures can be seen in some Jewish cemeteries. However, a contemporary mausoleum does not simply mark a grave. It replaces it. It effectively substitutes above-the-ground *storage* of human remains for the Jewish imperative of burial in the ground. It frustrates the atoning goal of the return of dust to dust. Clearly, therefore, the placing of Jewish bodies in mausoleums is an intolerable aberration from Jewish tradition. Such warehousing of the dead is prohibited.

Cremation

The widespread practice of cremating Jewish bodies is a tragic commentary on the erosion of Jewish norms and values. Cremation is a gentile practice. It harks back to the pagan funeral pyre. It nul-lifies the atoning process of the body's underground disintegration. Cremation is unreservedly forbidden. There is no room for compro-mise on this issue. No technical, *ex post facto*, justification can be found. *The expressed will of a Jew to be cremated should be ig-nored.* No funeral rites are offered for cremated Jews. Their sur-vivors do not mourn their passing by observing *shiv'ah, sheloshim,* or the year of mourning. They do not even recite *Kaddish* in their honor.

Cremated ashes may *not* be buried in a Jewish cemetery, unless the deceased was incinerated in an accident, by murderers, or in war. Obviously, in such tragic cases the horrifying mode of death secures atonement.

Burial in Unusual Circumstances

Suicide

We have already emphasized the life-affirming nature of Judaism. We are charged with preserving, dignifying, and sanctifying our lives—but are not granted absolute title over our lives and bodies. Life is a gift from God. We are responsible to Him for its preservation. Judaism does not acknowledge the "right to die." Life and death are in the hands of God. "*I* kill, and I make alive" (Deuteronomy 32:39), declares God. "Behold, all souls are mine" (Ezekiel 18:14). This notion is eloquently and movingly expressed in the Confession of the Dying: "I acknowledge before Thee, that my life is in Thy hand and my death is in Thy hand . . . and if my appointed time to die has arrived, Thou art righteous [in decreeing] all that befalls me."

In these terms, suicide is no less culpable than murder. It may, in a sense, be even worse, since it is a denial of divine Providence and of personal immortality. According to our sages, death itself achieves atonement. When death, however, is a defiant rejection of God's will, it loses its atoning qualities and adds, unspeakably, to the burden of sin of the person who has commited suicide.

Owing to the gravity of his transgression, the committer of suicide was to be denied the honor and dignity usually accorded to the deceased—even to the extent of assigning him a burial plot separated from Jewish graves by at least thirteen feet. Traditionally, also, the only bereavement practices to be observed were those whose omission would cause hurt, shame, and embarrassment to the bereaved family.

In practice, however, a person who commits suicide is rarely treated differently from any other Jewish deceased person. Most rabbinic authorities are of the opinion that nobody in his right mind would kill himself. How could he imagine that death would provide an escape from suffering and responsibility? Surely, if he had been aware that life goes on beyond the grave, and that he would have to give account to God for this terrible transgression, he would never have killed himself! If he were really fully rational, he would never have exposed those who love him to the pain of his demise and to the shame of his suicide.

Accordingly, one who commits suicide is regarded as being at least temporarily insane and no more culpable than any other insane person. For these reasons he is usually accorded the same respectful, loving treatment as every other Jew.

Apostates

Although even the most unrepentant of sinners is prepared for burial in strict accordance with the Halakhah, and is interred—albeit not necessarily in a place of honor—in a consecrated cemetery, a person who has renounced his or her Jewish faith and has accepted another religion is in another category altogether. *Technically*, the apostate remains Jewish, for even though a Jew sins, he is considered to be Jewish. But having shunned his or her faith completely, the apostate cannot expect to be granted its comforts. *Keri'ah is* performed—but at the time of the act of apostasy. Mourning *is* observed—but on the day that Judaism is formally renounced. When an unrepentant apostate dies, no *aninut* is observed, no *taharah* is performed, and the Jewish community is not obliged to busy itself with his or her burial. The seven closest relatives are not required to observe the laws of mourning.

However, if it is believed that the apostasy was the result of brainwashing, psycho-social problems, or other obviously extenuating circumstances, the apostate is treated no differently than are other Jewish transgressors.

Burial of the Stillborn

A stillborn child requires interment. If the child is a male, ritual circumcision (without its attendant blessing) should be performed prior to burial. A name is given to the stillborn infant before its interment. Obviously, there are no funeral or burial rites in such cases. Nor is it necessary for the parents to be present at the interment. The *chevra kadisha* should reserve an area in the communal cemetery for the burial of the stillborn. Many Jewish funeral establishments have set a number of plots aside for this purpose.

Burial of Limbs

The obligation to bury Jewish remains is absolute. It includes not only a complete body, but body parts also. Unhappily, this situation arises when a patient undergoes amputation. The family should make sure that the amputated limb is not incinerated by the hospital authorities. The *chevra kadisha* should arrange to have a Jewish funeral home collect the limb, cleanse it, and bury it as close as possible to where the person himself/herself will ultimately be interred. No burial rites are required for the burial of limbs.

BURIAL RITES

The Presence of Family and Friends

The separation of the funeral service from the burial is an unfortunate consequence of metropolitan living. The location of cemeteries at great distances from the city center, and the convenient location of funeral chapels within easy reach of one's home or place of business, have had the effect of ensuring our attendance at the service in the chapel, while accounting for our absence from the burial service—which is the ultimate farewell to our beloved departed.

It is tragic that there is often difficulty in securing a *minyan* for the final rites at the graveside—after an impressive and well-attended funeral service at the chapel. The loyalty of family and friends should not be determined by urban geography. The ultimate act of loving kindness is to accompany the deceased to his/her final resting place.

The Burial Service

The Jewish burial service reflects our concern both for the deceased and for the bereaved. At the same time it helps us to come to terms with God, who, in His infinite, often ineffable wisdom has decreed our separation from our loved ones.

Our concern for the *deceased* is reflected in the quiet dignity of the interment, in the loving care with which he or she is laid to rest in the prescribed manner, and in the beautiful texts which are recited. These readings affirm our faith that our beloved is at peace—secure in the protection of God.

Our concern for the *bereaved* is expressed in several ways. At times of joyful communal celebration (when *Tachanun* is not recited,° both the processional and the interment rites are abbreviated. This helps avoid conflict and confusion on the part of the bereaved, for it would be unreasonable to expect the bereaved to oscillate between joy and sorrow.

The requirement that the casket be fully covered with soil in the presence of and with the participation of the bereaved has a crucial psychological function. It makes us come to terms with the reality of our loved one's death. It does not permit us the neurotic, reality-avoiding response of denial. It compels us to accept the inevitable, and obliges us to deal with that reality in a healthy manner.

The death of a loved one often leads us to question the goodness of God. How, we sometimes wonder, can a loving God hurt us so badly? How can a good God do seemingly bad things? To be sure, these are ultimate questions, and cannot always be answered adequately. The Jewish tradition does not deny the validity of such questions, but understands that they are more readily dealt with from the standpoint of faith than from soul-destroying doubt. This is the message of the Bible, particularly of the Book of Job. It is also the theme of the burial service.

The burial service is called *Tzidduk ha-Din*—our justification of the divine decree. This moving recitation consists of our stoic acceptance of God's ineffable decree of death, our thanks to Him for His having granted us the gift of the precious life which brought us such joy, and our prayer for the survivors.

The burial *Kaddish* also seeks to shore up our faith and to ease the pain of our loss. It is an affirmation of man's immortality, of our expectation of the messianic period of universal peace and the reinstitution of uncontested Jewish statehood and Temple worship—in short, of God's providential concern for all His creatures.

° See below, p. 222.

THE BURIAL SERVICE: HALAKHIC CHECKLIST

Conduct at the Cemetery

1. A special blessing is recited by those who have not visited a Jewish cemetery within thirty days.° This blessing should be recited at a distance of about seven and a half feet from the graves.
2. At this distance from a grave, one may not exchange greetings, eat, drink, smoke, worship, study, or even carry a sacred book. One's *tzitzit* should be concealed.

Pallbearers

1. The customs relating to pallbearers apply whether the deceased is carried on their shoulders or in another manner, or is wheeled on a special vehicle.
2. Only Jewish males may serve as pallbearers since in ancient times the sons of Jacob carried their Jewish father to his final resting place, notwithstanding the fact that great Egyptian dignitaries were present.
3. For this reason, also, it is appropriate that those who are related to the deceased serve as his/her pallbearers.
4. The sons and brothers of the deceased should perform this function, if the strain of doing so is not intolerable.
5. Other relations and friends may act as pallbearers.
6. Pallbearers may serve in relays, a new set taking over at each stop during the processional.
7. Some misinformed individuals attempt to frustrate the objective of the full participation of the mourners in the last rites by keeping them at a distance from the grave while the casket is anonymously transferred from the hearse to the grave—often by gentiles. This practice is totally unacceptable and should be avoided. It is explained away on the basis of liability insurance. The excuse is lame. The funeral director and cemetery owners carry adequate insurance. They will allow volunteer Jewish pallbearers to perform their labor of love without hindrance.

° See below, p. 222.

The Processional

1. The ritual processional commences at a distance of at least seventeen yards from the grave.
2. This processional is punctuated by stops which are made by the pallbearers. These stops are known as *ma'amadot*.
3. In some places, three stops are made. However, the usual custom is to make seven stops.
4. At each stop a different set of bearers may be invited to carry the casket.
5. At each stop, Psalm 91 is recited—up to the verse "For He shall give His angels charge over thee, to help thee in all thy ways." This verse consists of seven words. At each subsequent stop one more word of this verse is added to the preceding words and verses of Psalm 91, so that the entire verse is recited at the last stop. *
6. On those days when *Tachanun* is not recited, no stops are made, and Psalm 91 is not recited.

The Interment

1. The grave should be at least forty inches deep (some Kabbalists excavate as much as sixty-eight inches) and long enough and wide enough to easily accommodate the casket.
2. As the casket is lowered into the grave, the officiant takes leave of the deceased with the prescribed recitation. *
3. The casket is positioned in the grave with the deceased facing upwards, and with his or her feet pointing to the gates of the cemetery.
4. The grave is filled with earth by the participants. At the very least they should continue to shovel earth onto the casket until it is fully covered, assuming "the form of a grave." Ideally, the shoveling by the participants should go on until the entire grave is filled with earth.

° See below, p. 225.
° See below, p. 226.

5. The shovel should not be passed from hand to hand, but replaced in the pile of earth before being taken up by the next participant (in order to express our prayer that death should not be contagious).

6. Usually, however, the *Tzidduk ha-Din* is recited after the grave has been filled with earth, or, in exceptional circumstances, after the casket has been fully covered by earth.°

7. After the recitation of *Tzidduk ha-Din*, the enlarged Burial *Kaddish* is recited.†

8. The *Tzidduk ha-Din* and the Burial *Kaddish* may be said only in the presence of a *minyan*.

9. On those days when *Tachanun* is not said, both *Tzidduk ha-Din* and the Burial *Kaddish* are omitted—on Friday and festival eve afternoons, on the afternoon of Purim eve, on Purim and on Shushan Purim, Purim Katan; on Rosh Chodesh; during the entire month of Nisan; on Lag b'Omer; during the first fourteen days of Sivan; on the ninth and fifteenth of Av; on New Year's eve; from Yom Kippur eve until two days after Simchat Torah; on Chanukah; on the fifteenth of Shevat.

10. The usual Mourner's *Kaddish* may be recited in the presence of a *minyan*, even when one does not recite the Burial *Kaddish*.

11. The memorial prayer *El-Malei Rachamim* is not recited when the *Tzidduk Ha-din* must be omitted. Another, also very beautiful, prayer may be substituted.††

LEAVING THE CEMETERY

During the interment, the major focus of our attention is obviously the deceased. Immediately afterwards the focus shifts to the bereaved. The participants form two parallel rows through which the mourners pass. As they pass, the assembled people recite the traditional formula of consolation: "May the Lord comfort you among all the other mourners of Zion and Jerusalem."

° According to some customs, *Tzidduk ha-Din* precedes interment.
† See below, p. 226
†† See below, pp. 232–233.

Before leaving the cemetery, those who attended the funeral place a small stone upon the grave and ask the deceased to forgive them for any hurt, however unintentional, they have caused him or her. The placing of stones is the "calling card" of the visitor. It also recalls the ancient practice of *stimat ha-golel*—actually sealing the opening of a grave with a large stone. It is our final concrete act of taking leave of a departed relative or friend. The plea for forgiveness is a profoundly Jewish ethical custom.

Nothing more strikingly reminds us of our mortality and of the brevity of our existence than does our participation in an interment. We symbolize this renewed awareness of human transience by plucking grass from the ground and throwing it behind us. Truly, we can say with the Psalmist: "Man's days are like the grass" (Psalm 103:15).

When we leave the cemetery we wash our hands with water from a vessel. Like the shovel which was used for covering the casket, and for the same reasons, this vessel is not passed directly from hand to hand.

LEAVING THE CEMETERY: HALAKHIC CHECKLIST

1. At a distance of about seven and a half feet from the grave, two parallel lines of at least five people in each— or one line consisting of ten people—are formed.
2. It is customary for male mourners to pass barefooted between the double line or before the single line.
3. At this time the prayer of consolation is offered by the bystanders.
4. The formation of the line (*shurah*) takes place even on those days when *Tzidduk ha-Din* is omitted.
5. When one leaves the cemetery, water is poured onto the hands from a vessel. The vessel is not passed from person to person. While pouring the water onto one's hands, it is customary to say the verse: "He hath swallowed up death forever, and the Lord hath wiped tears from off all faces" (Isaiah 25:8).
6. The hands should be allowed to drip dry.
7. One should not enter one's home or place of work without having washed one's hands, as above.

DISINTERMENT AND REINTERMENT

When we uncover the decomposed remains of an individual—or even his skeleton—we detract significantly from the dignity which he once enjoyed. For this reason, among many others, our sages *forbade the opening of a grave* after burial. Even if something of great monetary value was accidentally left in the grave with the deceased, our sages were reluctant to permit the rescue of that valuable item at the expense of the dignity of the deceased. Only the most compelling of motives could overcome this reluctance—the circumcision of an infant who had been buried uncircumcised, for example, and even then only within a day or two of burial, before the onset of decomposition. The opening of a grave would also be permitted in order to place a forgotten part of the shrouds *near* the body.

If the mere *opening* of a grave after burial is permitted only under exceptional circumstances, how much more compelling must our reasons be for *removing* human remains from one grave to another. Our sages hold that after the dead has been laid to rest, his/her rest should be undisturbed. And since disinterment and reinterment, as we shall see, reinstates some of the practices of mourning, stirs up old hurts, and opens old wounds, removal of the remains is permitted only for certain specified reasons.

VALID REASONS FOR REBURIAL: A HALAKHIC CHECKLIST

From an Unsuitable Grave

1. If the original grave was open to constant vandalism, flooding, or any other unusual natural or social abuse.
2. If the original grave was located among gentile graves.
3. If it subsequently becomes known that the deceased had wished to be buried elsewhere.
4. If the deceased was *accidentally* buried next to a woman/man not related to him/her.
5. If the original grave was in "no-man's land" (*hefker*).
6. If the deceased was accidentally placed in a grave purchased by somebody else who is unwilling to exchange graves or sell that grave.

7. Relatives of an apostate may have his or her remains removed *from* a family plot if they so desire.

Redevelopment of Cemetery Land for Other Purposes

1. By the government, for the rerouting of a highway, for example—over the strenuous objections of the Jewish community.
2. According to Jewish law, although the grave, once used, is consecrated ground and cannot be used for other purposes, local Jewish leaders may decree an existing grave to be hazardous to the general public, and order reburial of the remains elsewhere.

Removal to a More Desirable Location

1. To a family plot elsewhere, provided that the spouse or other family members are buried there or at least in that cemetery.
2. If the initial burial was conditional upon subsequent reburial—and if the deceased so willed it.
3. Transfer of remains to Israel is not only permitted, it is also desirable, since such reburial effects atonement for the deceased.

It should be noted that even when reburial is permitted, a period of twelve months should elapse before exhumation is undertaken. By this time, the process of decomposition should be over. The sages regarded the transfer of *bones* as more anonymous and less of an assault on the dignity of the deceased than the transfer of a decomposing but recognizable body. Nevertheless, even after the twelve-month period, the casket should not be opened during the transfer. If the casket has rotted or where burial is customary without a casket, the earth around the remains (to a depth of about three inches) should also be transferred for reburial with the remains.

The grave from which the remains have been removed for reburial elsewhere may be assigned to another deceased person, provided that it is dug about a foot deeper than when it was originally used for burial.

DISINTERMENT AND REINTERMENT: HALAKHIC CHECKLIST

1. Disinterment and reinterment should not be undertaken on joyous occasions, such as the intermediate period of a festival, nor within twelve months of the first interment.
2. A son should not be personally active in the process. If the son is a *kohen,* he may *not* defile himself for this purpose.
3. A person who has remarried should not be personally active in the removal for reburial of a former spouse.
4. The same respect is required in transporting the remains as when the deceased was *originally* prepared for burial. The remains should be transported in a container not too dissimilar to the original—and certainly not in a sack.
5. Care should be taken not to mix the remains of different people.
6. The remains should not be left unattended.
7. The *shomer* who is entrusted to be with the remains is exempted from the performance of *mitzvot.*
8. Although no formal eulogy is said, one may speak publicly in praise of the deceased.
9. Although one should accompany the remains for a short distance, one does so as an expression of respect and not as the performance of a *mitzvah.*
10. Although close family members enter into a short period of mourning, we do not have to form parallel lines through which they pass, as is usually done at the commencement of mourning. Nor is the formula of condolence recited.
11. Some rites of mourning are imposed—
    a. if the bones are collected from the first grave and then reburied elsewhere in a casket; or
    b. if the bones are moved in the original casket and then laid to rest elsewhere directly in the ground.

12. At the moment of *likut atzamot* (gathering of the bones), the close relative tears his/her garment, as he/she did before, and asks the deceased for forgiveness for any indignity the transfer may involve.

13. A period of mourning commences at the moment of *likut atzamot* but extends only until nightfall of that day, even if the reinterment has not yet been accomplished. The brief mourning rites are those which normally are observed during *shiv'ah.*°

14. However, under these circumstances, the mourner puts on *tefillin* on the day of *likut atzamot*. He/she may eat meat and drink wine.

° See below pp. 117-119.

CHAPTER NINE

The *Shiv'ah* Period

THE VALUE AND PURPOSE OF THE *SHIV'AH* PERIOD

The period of seven days of intense mourning for our closest relatives is mentioned in the Bible (Genesis 50:10). During this period we should not pursue our regular daily business routines undisturbed and unperturbed by our enormous loss.

Traditional Judaism had the wisdom to devise intelligent measures for that healthy working-out of grief which contemporary psychologists counsel. The creation of an unashamed atmosphere of sorrow is a sound confrontation with the reality of death. The *shiv'ah* period enables us to ponder the ultimate issues of life and death. It allows us the bittersweet recollection of precious moments shared with our beloved departed, and gradually prepares us for a healthy reaccommodation to life's routines.

It also enables us to reaffirm our personal relationship with Him who is the source of life and death, by transforming our home into a house of worship, by magnifying His great Name in our regular recitation of the *Kaddish*, and by regular study of our sacred literature.

This time of reassessment, readjustment, and introspection is given a special dimension by the presence of understanding and sympathetic friends and relatives, who cater to our needs, share our grief, support us in our sorrow, console us on our great loss, and strengthen us to meet life's challenges anew.

The fact that *shiv'ah* is usually observed in the house where the departed lived, prayed, loved, and counseled those who mourn is especially poignant. It is most fitting that he or she is memorialized thrice daily with special prayers in an environment which is crowded with living memories.

Shiv'ah reminds us of the centrality of the Jewish home—from cradle to grave.

PREPARING THE HOUSE FOR *SHIV'AH* OBSERVANCES

When we described the burial rites in the last chapter, we pointed out that the recessional after the interment marks a major shift of concern from the deceased to the bereaved. This concern should not terminate with the interment. It should continue throughout the *shiv'ah* period—and beyond.

We can effectively demonstrate our concern by helping to prepare the house in which the bereaved will be "sitting *shiv'ah*." During this period they will not be able to leave the house to do shopping. Many of their friends will visit. In addition to paying "*shiv'ah* calls" (visiting), some will join the mourners in daily worship.

Specifically, we can help by covering all the mirrors in the "*shiv'ah* house." We can either drape a cloth or sheet over them or simply apply a window wax to them. The covering of the mirrors accomplishes at least two purposes. Mirrors are the most egocentric of all our furniture. They reflect *our* images. During *shiv'ah* the thoughts of the bereaved are not with themselves but with those they have lost. In addition, during the prayer services which we hold in a *shiv'ah* house, it is forbidden to worship before a human image. Wall pictures are thus problematic for several reasons— distraction, reflection (by the glass), and human imagery.

A lighted candle is a powerful symbol of the soul's connection with the body. As the flickering, vulnerable flame is attached to and nourished by the candle, so the soul is a flame attached to the body, giving it light and realizing its potential. It is for this reason that a candle is kept burning from the time of death. It should be kindled where the deceased died, lived, or where the bereaved are "sitting *shiv'ah*." It should be kept burning for a full seven days after the commencement of the *shiv'ah* period—even when, as we shall see, the *shiv'ah* period is terminated before seven days have elapsed. In general, funeral homes provide candles for this purpose. But friends, too, can help in this regard. They should bring *yahrzeit* candles to the house of mourning as soon after the passing as possible, because the supply from the funeral home will arrive only after the interment. Sometimes, also, the candles supplied by the funeral home will be insufficient for a given situation. For example, if the interment takes place on an intermediate day of a festival, a flame would have to be kept burning from the time of death (a rabbi should be consulted on the permissibility and method of kindling), throughout the festival period, and for seven days beyond the seventh day of the festival.

Friends can also help by preparing the first meal after the interment (*seudat ha-havra'ah*) and continuing to bring in an adequate supply of food for the entire *shiv'ah* period. The bereaved and their spouses should not have to be confronted with such concerns at this time. In many communities, different families are each allocated the responsibility of providing the bereaved with one meal during the *shiv'ah* period. If this allocation is made fairly, and if the responsibilities are equitably distributed around the congregation, individual members need not be called upon to perform this kindness too frequently in any given period of time.

Neighbors of the bereaved can be of assistance by bringing coatracks and chairs to the house so as to accommodate the many visitors whose arrival is anticipated.

We often fail to think of assuming responsibility for the important routines in which the bereaved are regularly involved. How will their children get to school? With whom do they carpool? Do the children have afterschool activities, dentist appointments, and so on? Real friends will find out and take over.

Synagogue administrators can help the bereaved in a special way. They will have comfortable, low chairs available for mourners—no more than twelve inches above the ground. Often, simple chairs with back support are adapted to this purpose by sawing their legs to a height of twelve inches. These "*shiv'ah* chairs" should be brought to the "*shiv'ah* house." If the Torah can be used at least three times, the synagogue officials will bring a Torah scroll in a specially made, portable ark, and position it in a place of honor. They will also bring adequate supplies of prayer books, and, if necessary, extra sets of *tallit* and *tefillin* and *kippot* for those who will worship with the mourners.

WHO OBSERVES *SHIV'AH?* FOR WHOM?

THE *SHIV'AH* OBLIGATION: A HALAKHIC CHECKLIST

For Whom Is *Shiv'ah* Observed?

1. *Shiv'ah* is observed for our seven closest Jewish relatives—father, mother, brother (or half brother, maternal or paternal), sister (or half sister, maternal or paternal, whether or not she was ever married), son, daughter, and husband or wife (as long as the marriage was *not* terminated by a religious divorce—*get*).
2. It is observed by and for children conceived through artificial insemination.
3. A sympathetic gesture of caring may be offered by the husband or wife of a bereaved spouse. As a demonstration of love and affection, some *shiv'ah* observances may be practiced until the first Shabbat of the *shiv'ah* period. It should be noted that the custom of mourning in "sympathy" is not widespread nowadays.
4. Although they are not *mandated* to do so, adopted children may *choose* to observe *shiv'ah* for their adoptive parents.
5. *Shiv'ah* is observed even if the deceased had instructed the survivors not to do so.

For Whom Is *Shiv'ah* Not Observed?

1. *Shiv'ah* is not observed for an infant who had not lived for a full thirty days. Thus, if one twin passed away within thirty days of birth, and the other on the thirty-first day, *shiv'ah* is observed only for the latter.
2. There are no *shiv'ah* observances for an apostate or for a person who was cremated.
3. A *kohen* does not observe *shiv'ah* for a wife whom he was halakhically forbidden to marry, such as a divorcee.

Who Must Observe *Shiv'ah?*

The obligation to observe *shiv'ah* commences when one becomes *bar* or *bat mitzvah*—thirteen and a day in the case of boys, and twelve and a day in the case of girls.

Who Is Exempted from Observing *Shiv'ah?*

1. A boy or girl who became a *bar* or *bat mitzvah* in the midst of the *shiv'ah* period is exempted not only from all *shiv'ah* observances but from those of *sheloshim* also. The twelve-month period of mourning restrictions for a deceased parent, however, does remain in effect for them.
2. If one was ill (or a woman after childbirth) during the *shiv'ah* period, and could not, as a result, observe *shiv'ah*, one is completely exempted from the obligation, and need not make up for the missed opportunity.

Making Up for Missed *Shiv'ah* Observances

1. In cases other than illness, if one did not observe *shiv'ah* at all, one should attempt to do so during the *sheloshim* period.
2. However, if *shiv'ah* was observed, but the observances were unavoidably *interrupted*—during a period of military duty, for example—the lost time need not later be made up for.

THE DURATION OF THE *SHIV'AH* PERIOD

Shiv'ah Does Not Always Mean "Seven"

The Hebrew word *shiv'ah* means "seven." In this context, the word signifies the seven most intense days of grief and mourning following the interment. However, the word *shiv'ah* should not always be taken literally. Sometimes *shiv'ah* is more than seven. In some circumstances, as we shall see from our halakhic summaries,°

° See below, p. 98.

the period of intense mourning does not begin immediately after the interment. In these cases, the *shiv'ah* period extends beyond the seven days following the burial. In other circumstances, we shall see, individual members of the same family, mourning for the same loved one, begin their *shiv'ah* observances at different times, some observing intensive mourning practices for less than the seven days, some commencing before the interment, and some concluding their intense mourning significantly later than others. Sometimes, too, the *shiv'ah* period may be halakhically abbreviated—lasting less than an hour. Indeed, the last day of the *shiv'ah* period is never a full day, but only a small fraction of that day.

Because, therefore, *shiv'ah* need not actually mean "seven," the computation of the *shiv'ah* period can be rather confusing. To remove this confusion, we have prepared careful summaries of the Halakhah for different circumstances. By referring to the different subheadings, the reader can work out when *shiv'ah* observances commence and terminate under any given set of conditions.

COMMENCEMENT OF *SHIV'AH*: HALAKHIC CHECKLIST

If the Interment Is in One's Own City

1. *Shiv'ah* commences immediately after the interment.
2. If part of the burial took place after sunset, provided that it was over within twenty minutes after sunset and that the mourners had performed any *shiv'ah* observance by that time (such as removing leather footwear or sitting on the ground), it is considered as if they had completed a full day of *shiv'ah* observance. Indeed, some hold that it is so considered even in the absence of any overt act of *shiv'ah* observance.
3. On a late Friday afternoon at dusk, or late on the eve of a festival at dusk, merely facing the synagogue after the interment is regarded as an act of *shiv'ah* observance for the purposes of including that day as part of the *shiv'ah* week. If the interment took place on *Yom Tov* or during *Chol ha-Mo'ed*, *shiv'ah* observances begin after the ter-

mination of the seventh day of the festival. However, the candle should burn (as above), and marital relations, Torah study, shaving, and so on, should cease at once.

If the Interment Is in Another City

1. A mourner, far away from the city where the burial will take place, may begin to observe *shiv'ah* as soon as the news of the passing is received, provided that he or she has no intention of attending the funeral and burial, or of becoming involved with the arrangements. However, some authorities delay the commencement of *shiv'ah* until actually after the burial.
2. If the deceased is to be transferred to another city (or country) for burial, the mourner begins to observe *shiv'ah* from the time when he or she ceases to accompany the casket and takes leave of those who will be doing so.
3. If one must travel a great distance to observe *shiv'ah* with other members of the family, one should commence the *shiv'ah* observances where one is located at the time of being reliably informed of the death. One may travel to join the *shiv'ah* observances of the rest of the family on the second day of the *shiv'ah* period.

If There is No Corpse

1. If the deceased was burned to death, the mourners begin *shiv'ah* as soon as they learn of his or her demise. They do not wait for the interment of the ashes. (Obviously we are not talking of formal cremation. In *such* a case, we have seen, there are *no shiv'ah* observances.)
2. If a husband or wife is missing and has been declared dead by a *Beth Din* (rabbinical court) within thirty days of the abandonment of the search, *shiv'ah* commences immediately after the rabbinic declaration of death.
3. In the case of all other close relatives who are missing— for example, lost at sea—*shiv'ah* commences after the abandonment of the search.

If News of Death Is Delayed

1. One is obliged to observe *shiv'ah*, even if the news of death is delayed, provided that one hears within thirty days of the passing—according to the local time of the person who receives the news.
2. If delayed tidings reach one on the Sabbath, that Sabbath is the first day of *shiv'ah*, even though no public acts of mourning take place on the Sabbath.
3. If one hears the delayed news on a festival or during its intermediate days, the *shiv'ah* commences after that festival.
4. If the delayed tidings reach one within twenty minutes after sunset on a given day, and one immediately performs an act of *shiv'ah* observance (such as the removal of leather shoes), that day is regarded as the first completed day of *shiv'ah*.
5. However, under the above circumstances, if one had already recited the evening prayers (*Ma'ariv*), the recitation signals the commencement of the following day. That following day is then considered to be the first day of *shiv'ah*.
6. If delayed tidings reach one on the thirtieth day before sunset, one must commence the observance of *shiv'ah*, whether or not one has recited one's evening prayers.
7. If delayed tidings reach one on the thirtieth day, and it happens to be a Sabbath, a festival or its intermediate days, only such *shiv'ah* observances as are usually permitted on such days are performed. In this case, the *shiv'ah* ends on the next morning after *Shacharit*.

Bride and Groom

1. Bride and groom fall into a special, separate category. Their private festivities (seven days following a first marriage) are like the public festivals of the Jewish people. Accordingly, their observance of mourning at such times is inappropriate.

2. The commencement of the *shiv'ah* period for the couple will depend upon whether the death occurs before the wedding, after the wedding but prior to the physical consummation of the marriage, or well into the period of festivities.

a. *When a death occurs before the wedding.* Under most circumstances, the wedding is postponed until the conclusion of the *shiv'ah* period unless the wedding feast has been prepared and a huge financial loss will be incurred, or if the death has effectively removed the only person able to organize the wedding at a later date. Under these circumstances the remains are removed, the marriage celebrated and consummated, and the burial then performed. Since the festivities commenced prior to the interment, they are not interrrupted and *shiv'ah* begins only after their conclusion.

b. *When a death occurs after the wedding but before consummation of the marriage.* According to the leading Ashkenazic authorities (and some Sefardic authorities), the wedding ceremony alone does not suffice to postpone the commencement of *shiv'ah* observances. It is the consummation of the marriage which signals the onset of the personal period of rejoicing for the couple, and which postpones their formal mourning. Nevertheless, if the wedding had taken place but the marriage was not consummated because the bride was not able to immerse herself in a *mikveh*, if a day or two elapsed between the wedding and the occurrence of death, and several festive meals had been enjoyed, the *shiv'ah* period commences at the conclusion of the seven- or three-day period (for a second marriage) of wedding festivities.

c. *When a death occurs well into the festive period.* Since the festive period of the couple has truly begun, mourning is most inappropriate. Consequently, there is no *aninut*, no rending of the garments, only a short walk in the funeral procession (if so desired), and no prayer of consolation. The death is formally recognized in two ways: The blessing *Dayyan ha-Emet* is recited,° since it cannot be

See below, p. 15.

said after a significant delay, and physical intimacy is forbidden after the consummation of the marriage.
3. The period of marriage festivities is fully chronological. A portion of the final day does *not* count as a full day.
4. If delayed tidings reach a bride or groom within the period of their marriage festivities, and also within the thirty-day period when *shiv'ah* observances may commence, *shiv'ah* commences after the conclusion of the period of marriage festivities.
5. Under these circumstances, it may so work out that the *shiv'ah* period may be postponed until after the elapse of thirty days from the time of burial. Should this happen, the mourner observes only "one hour" of *shiv'ah* after the conclusion of the marriage-festivity period.

Dementia as a Result of Grief

A person so demented with grief that he or she was oblivious to the burial of a close relative must observe a full seven days of *shiv'ah* from the moment of recovery—provided it is within thirty days of the interment.

Premature Commencement of *Shiv'ah*

If one was wrongly informed of the death of a close relative and thus began to observe *shiv'ah* a day or two prematurely, one simply completes the *shiv'ah* period which one has begun. No additional days need be added.

Termination of Shiv'ah

Jewish breavement practices are both intensely personal but also socially determined. We experience our pain, sorrow, and grief personally. Pain and suffering are our own-most thing. Nobody else can fully comprehend or even accurately imagine our feelings. But we do not grieve alone. Other members of the family share our loss. With whom else can we reminisce as meaningfully about the deceased? Who else is haunted by well-remembered accents and never-to-be-forgotten little incidents? Who else is party to privileged information? Bereavement is a shared family experience no less than it is a private reaction to painful separation.

The Halakhah recognizes that mourning is an expression of family solidarity. As we have seen, different individuals—members of the same family, grieving for the same loved one—may commence the *shiv'ah* observances at different times. They do so precisely because they *are* different individuals, whose situations are different, and who experience their grief differently.

However, under some circumstances, the notion of family solidarity transcends individual differences, and the family members unite as one group, becoming a single bereaved entity, and concluding the *shiv'ah* period together—regardless of the fact that they may have commenced their *shiv'ah* period individually, at different times. We have seen, for example, that a bride and groom postpone their *shiv'ah* until after their seven days of festivities. We shall see in our halakhic summaries that they may, nevertheless, terminate their *shiv'ah* observances with the rest of the family, even if this drastically abbreviates their *shiv'ah* period—even to the briefest part of a single day.

For our purposes, family solidarity is determined by the leader of the family, the *gadol ha-bayit*, around whose axis the family revolves. The *gadol ha-bayit* is the mourner who will be mainly responsible for disposing of the assets of the deceased and/or for making funeral arrangements. The chief family member may be either young (as young as thirteen years old) or old, male or female (although a husband may assume the role of *gadol ha-bayit* on behalf of his wife), or not even an individual person. If all the mourners have equal responsibility, the majority of them, gathered together at one time, constitute a collective *gadol ha-bayit*.

If the *gadol ha-bayit* is "sitting *shiv'ah*" with the family, the family coalesces around him or her. Even though some members begin to "sit *shiv'ah*" later, after the *shiv'ah* period has commenced, the mourners often all terminate their *shiv'ah* together, incorporating the latecomers in a striking demonstration of family solidarity.

The notion of solidarity has a further dimension. Just as the mourner may not isolate himself from his family, so may he not isolate himself from his people. If the rest of the Jewish people is commanded to joyfully celebrate a festival, the mourner must also respond to that imperative. He must make the truly heroic gesture of prematurely terminating his *shiv'ah* observances, and of shifting his mood full circle from sorrow to celebration.

TERMINATION OF *SHIV'AH*: HALAKHIC CHECKLIST

General Rules

1. For the purpose of computing the *shiv'ah* period, a part of
   a day may be considered as a full day. Thus, any part of
   the day before nightfall of the day of interment (or when
   the bereaved stopped accompanying the casket to another
   city) counts as the first day of *shiv'ah*. Similarly, any part
   of the seventh day during daylight hours counts as the
   whole of the last day of *shiv'ah*.
2. *Shiv'ah* usually ends after *Shacharit* (morning) services on
   the seventh day. If no male mourners are present, female
   mourners terminate their *shiv'ah* observances as soon as
   they awaken on the seventh day.

Incorporating Latecomers into Unified Family Mourning: Role of the *Gadol ha-Bayit*

There are four instances in which the members of the
family are considered as a single unit with latecomers for
shiv'ah observances.

a. When members of the family begin the *shiv'ah* in one
location and another member subsequently joins them.

b. When they are all together initially and some members
subsequently accompany the deceased to his/her burial.

c. When they are together initially, and then the *gadol
ha-bayit* leaves, and another family member arrives to
join the rest of the family.

d. When a bride/groom concludes his/her seven days of
marriage festivities during the course of *shiv'ah* for a close
member of the family.

The First Case: A latecomer joins the rest of the family.

He may complete his *shiv'ah* with them only if five conditions are met:

a. He had not commenced his mourning prior to his joining the rest of the family.

b. The *gadol ha-bayit* was there with the rest of the family.

c. They are "sitting *shiv'ah*" in either the city of the demise of the deceased or of his/her burial.

d. He arrived before the rest of the family had completed their mourning on the seventh day.

e. He arrived from a place no further than a day's journey away—even by plane.

All five conditions must be satisfied for the latecomer to complete his/her *shiv'ah* with the rest of the family. Thus, if the *gadol ha-bayit* was himself the latecomer (condition b above not having been satisified), he must count for himself, and will conclude his *shiv'ah* after the rest of the family.

The Second Case: Some members accompany the body and subsequently return.

a. Since all of them (including the *gadol ha-bayit*) were together initially, they are considered to be part of the family which remained behind, regardless of whether or not the *gadol ha-bayit* subsequently stays or leaves.

b. Those who remain behind begin their *shiv'ah* early, as soon as the party accompanying the deceased leaves town. Nevertheless, those who rejoin them end *shiv'ah* with them, although *their shiv'ah* observances began only after the burial.

c. Those who rejoin the family count together with them only if they return before those who have remained behind complete *their shiv'ah*. Thus, if they returned on the morning of the seventh day, they must count *shiv'ah* for themselves from the day of burial.

d. Those who rejoin the rest of the family before the latter have completed their *shiv'ah* count with them even if they had come from a place more than a day's journey distant.

e. Those who rejoin the rest of the family before the latter have completed their *shiv'ah* count with them even if they have commenced mourning practices in the distant location.

Variation on Second Case: The *gadol ha-bayit* delays termination of the *shiv'ah* of those who remained.

a. In this case, the *gadol ha-bayit* was with the rest of the family in the city of demise, and then left to accompany the deceased.

b. Only if he planned to rejoin the members of the family who remained behind, do the latter begin to count when the deceased leaves the city. Since the *gadol ha-bayit* counts from the time of burial, his *shiv'ah* will be abbreviated when he rejoins those who remained before the latter have concluded their *shiv'ah*.

c. But if the *gadol ha-bayit* had no intention of rejoining those who remained behind because his residence was elsewhere, those who remained in the city of demise must wait for the *gadol ha-bayit* to begin counting (after the burial) *before* they can count, even though they did not accompany the deceased (and would otherwise have begun to count when the deceased was removed from the city).

d. However, even if the *gadol ha-bayit* were to go elsewhere—to his own residence, for example, to complete the *shiv'ah*, *if the burial took place on the fourth day after demise (or later)*, those who remain behind in the city of demise begin to count from the time that the deceased is removed from the city.

First and Second Cases Combined: The *gadol ha-bayit* leaves to accompany the deceased and another member arrives from another city to join the remaining family members.

a. If the *gadol ha-bayit* rejoins the remaining members before the latter have completed their *shiv'ah*, it is as if the *gadol ha-bayit* had been with them all along.

b. The latecomer is thus considered to have been together with the *gadol ha-bayit* as soon as the latecomer joined the family "sitting *shiv'ah*." Therefore he/she counts with the rest of the family.

c. If the *gadol ha-bayit* returns after those who remained behind have concluded their *shiv'ah,* the *gadol ha-bayit* must count alone. Therefore the latecomer must also count alone.

First and Second Cases Combined: The whole family accompanies the deceased and the latecomer arrives at the city of demise to await their return.

a. The whole family (apart from the latecomer) begins *shiv'ah* at the time of and in the city near which the burial took place.

b. If they returned during the first three days of *shiv'ah,* the latecomer counts with them, always providing that the *gadol ha-bayit* returns before the end of the *shiv'ah* of the other returning members.

c. This will shorten the *shiv'ah* of the latecomer only if the latter arrived at the city of demise *after* the burial, since the rest of the family begins to count *shiv'ah* only at that time.

d. Should the latecomer have reached the city of demise before the burial of the deceased elsewhere, he must begin *shiv'ah* at once, since he will not be present at the interment. Thus he begins to count *ahead* of the rest of the family. Should he be required to end his *shiv'ah* together with the returning members, his *shiv'ah* will actually be extended through family solidarity. One authority (*Pachad Yitzchak*) does not require solidarity in this case and rules that the latecomer counts *shiv'ah* alone, thus completing his *shiv'ah* ahead of the returning members.

The Third Case: During the absence of the *gadol ha-bayit*, another member of the family arrives.

a. If the family were together in the city of demise, and the *gadol ha-bayit* had to leave, the latecomer counts with the rest of the family only if the *gadol ha-bayit* returns before the end of *shiv'ah*, provided that all five conditions (above in "The First Case" and "First and Second Cases Combined," items a and b) are satisified.

b. If the *gadol ha-bayit* did not return to rejoin the rest of the family on account of his preoccupation with the deceased (for example, to procure a monument), he is regarded as though he *had* actually returned, and the latecomer can still count with the rest of the family, provided that he had joined them during the first three days of *shiv'ah*.

c. If the *gadol ha-bayit* did not return to rejoin the rest of the family for reasons unconnected with the needs of the deceased (for example, to complete his *shiv'ah* observances in the comfort of his own home), the latecomer must count his own *shiv'ah* alone, regardless of the fact that he joined the rest of the family during the first three days of their *shiv'ah*.

The Fourth Case: Bride or groom join the rest of the family during the *shiv'ah*.

If the seven days of rejoicing come to a close during the *shiv'ah* period as computed by the *gadol ha-bayit*, the bride/groom concludes her/his *shiv'ah* with the *gadol ha-bayit* and the rest of the family, provided that the bride/groom has observed at least one *shiv'ah* practice before the family *shiv'ah* period concludes.

Abbreviation on Account of the Intervention of *Yom Tov*

The intervention of a *Yom Tov* (Rosh ha-Shanah, Yom Kippur, Sukkot, Shemini Atzeret, Pesach, Shavu'ot) terminates the *shiv'ah* period, provided that the bereaved observed at least one aspect of the *shiv'ah* prior to the arrival of that *Yom Tov*. The candle, however, should go on burning for the full seven days.

Interment in Israel: Computing the *Shiv'ah*

Because transporting the remains for burial in Israel has become so widespread, it is useful to summarize the *shiv'ah* obligations, both of those who remain behind and of those who accompany the casket.

1. *Those who remain behind* commence their *shiv'ah* observances the moment they take leave of the deceased and stop accompanying the casket, provided that the *gadol ha-bayit* remains behind with them, *or* he will rejoin them before the end of their *shiv'ah* period, *or* if his not returning was occasioned by his preoccupation with the needs of the deceased, *or* if he did not return for personal reasons but the burial took place on the fourth day (or later) after the demise.

2. *Those who accompany the deceased* to Israel may "sit *shiv'ah*" there, reckoning their *shiv'ah* period from the end of the interment.

3. They may choose to return home to "sit *shiv'ah*" with the family members who have remained behind. This is case one and case two, above.

SE'UDAT HA-HAVRA'AH: THE MEAL OF CONDOLENCE

Bread is the very staff of life. Breaking bread, therefore, is an affirmation of life. Confronted by death and the dreadful pain of separation, there is often a tendency to despise life, and to reject its most fundamental routines. "Why," the bereaved may think, "should I be entitled to satisfy my physical needs while my beloved will forever be deprived of such elementary pleasures?" To avoid such feelings of guilt, and to affirm the legitimacy of life's regular patterns, a special meal was ordained for mourners following their return from the cemetery.

This meal of condolence, the *se'udat ha-havra'ah*, has an additional purpose. It confirms, for the bereaved, the caring and commitment of their community and friends, who become their providers and sustainers. They are reminded that they are not alone. Therefore our sages decreed that the bereaved should not eat after the interment until nightfall *unless* his/her neighbors provide the food.

The menu of the *se'udat ha-havra'ah* symbolizes this occasion. Its centerpiece is bread, life's major nutrient. The peeled, hard-boiled eggs or cooked lentils evoke, through their roundness, the cycle of life. Their self-enclosedness conjures up the numb, dumb paralysis of grief, when our mouths are, as it were, closed to rational discourse. Eggs are, in addition, the universal symbol of mourning. They represent unfinished life, its potential not fully realized. This universal symbol reminds us that death is our common destiny. Tea or coffee or another beverage completes and normalizes this meal.

SE'UDAT HA-HAVRA'AH: HALAKHIC CHECKLIST

1. Mourners may neither eat nor drink anything between the interment and the *se'udat ha-havra'ah*.
2. The *se'udat ha-havra'ah* is mandatory only on the day of the interment of those relatives for whom one is obliged to mourn.
3. When the day of interment is a public fast-day, the obligation to have a *se'udat ha-havra'ah* falls away, since the *se'udat ha-havra'ah* obligation terminates after nightfall of the day of interment.
4. If the interment takes place at night, the *se'udat ha-havra'ah* may be eaten at any time till nightfall of the following day.
5. The *se'udat ha-havra'ah* is mandatory on the day that late tidings of the demise are received, if that day is after the interment but within thirty days of burial.
6. A *se'udat ha-havra'ah* is served on Rosh Chodesh, Chanukah, Purim, and *Chol ha-Mo'ed*.
7. On Fridays or on the eve of festivals it is not served beyond three quarters of the daylight period (or beyond midday for those who normally refrain from eating after noon so as to enhance the later enjoyment of the festive meal). Under these circumstances it need not be eaten after the termination of the Sabbath or festival.
8. The *se'udat ha-havra'ah* consists of bread, peeled hard-boiled eggs or lentils, and a beverage.

9. At least the bread for that meal should not have been acquired by the mourner, or by his or her spouse. It must be provided by a friend. It may, however, be provided by a child who has become independent of the bereaved parent.

10. If several close relatives have been buried on the same day, a single *se'udat ha-havra'ah* fulfills the complete obligation of the mourners in this respect.

11. If another close relative is buried within the same *shiv'ah* period, another *se'udat ha-havra'ah* is served.

12. A male mourner should avoid eating the *se'udat ha-havra'ah* in the company of more than one other male mourner, to avoid saying the grace after meals with a *zimmun* (quorum of three adult males). The *zimmun* should not be avoided during the remaining meals of the *shiv'ah* period.

13. The special additions to the grace after meals should be recited after this (and every other) meal during *shiv'ah.*°

14. Nonmourners should not partake of the *se'udat ha-havra'ah.* The meal of condolence is anything but a social occasion.

WORSHIP AND STUDY IN A HOUSE OF MOURNING

Ideally, mourners should not have to leave the house of mourning. Ideally, too, they should recite their daily prayers in the company of a congregation consisting of at least ten male Jews beyond *bar-mitzvah* age—a *minyan.* To make both of these ideals attainable, regular worship services are held in the house of mourning.

By worshipping in a *minyan,* the mourner is able to recite the *Kaddish,* and thus lovingly sanctify the divine Name and accept the divine Judgment. Regular worship and the *Kaddish*—praise of God—reaffirm our faith when it is most sorely challenged, and condition our reentry into the community. Three times a day, as an integral part of that community, the mourner is able to transcend his feelings of isolation from the living.

° See below, pp. 272–275.

The worship service in a house of mourning is only a slightly modified form of the usual liturgy—as we shall see in the halakhic summary which follows.° However, in addition to the statutory morning and evening worship, Psalm 49 (or its substitute on days when the *Tachanun* supplication is omitted) is† recited, which helps us to ponder the meaning of life and death. The recitation of the *Kaddish* following the Psalm is reserved for those who are "sitting *shiv'ah*." A very touching memorial prayer for the departed and a moving prayer for the healing of the pain of the bereaved conclude the morning and evening worship.

The custom of publicly studying a *mishnah* twice daily both honors and elevates the soul of the departed. The Mishnah is the oldest component of the Talmud. It is made up of six orders. Each order consists of a number of different tractates (or volumes). Each tractate is divided into chapters, and every chapter is made up of numbered paragraphs. Each of these paragraphs is called a *mishnah*. Its subject-matter is usually of a legal nature.

The tradition of studying a *mishnah* derives from the fact that the word *mishnah* is an anagram for the word *neshamah*, "soul." They have the same Hebrew consonants.

But the significance of public study is far more profound: Personal immortality is of two kinds—life beyond the grave, which we discussed at the beginning of this volume, and life *through* those who are left behind. To the extent that our loved ones keep alive the values to which we subscribe, our life has not been lived in vain. The study of sacred classics is considered to be a great religious act. Therefore, the study of a *mishnah* demonstrates the commitment of the survivors to the value system of the deceased, and justifies his/her life retroactively—although, as we shall see in the halakhic summary, joyful, regular Torah study during the *shiv'ah* period is otherwise forbidden.

There are, to be sure, two additional purposes for the twice-daily public study. It elevates the tone of the assembly in the *shiv'ah* house from the merely social to the Jewishly significant. It also gives the teacher of the *mishnah* an opportunity of using the text as a springboard for extolling the virtues of the deceased, for discuss-

° See below, p. 113.
† See below, p. 230.

ing the purpose of the *shiv'ah* period, and for analyzing the Jewish concepts of life and death.°

WORSHIP IN THE HOUSE OF MOURNING: HALAKHIC SUMMARY

1. A male mourner should put on *tefillin* on the morning of the day following the burial, but not on the morning when he receives tidings of his loss (within thirty days of the passing).
2. A *minyan*, of which the male mourner is a part, must be present at all daily services following the interment.
3. If he cannot assemble a *minyan*, he should go to the closest synagogue, attempting, if at all possible, to be driven there by someone else (if the synagogue is not in easy walking distance).
4. Although the mourner may lead the worship from the very first day of *shiv'ah*, some hold that he does so from the third day only.
5. If the mourner leads the prayers, he omits *Titkabbel* from the *Kaddish*. *Others* who lead the prayers in the house of mourning include *Titkabbel*.
6. The mourner recites the blessing: "Who has attended to all my needs."
7. If a male mourner is present, the following are omitted, no matter who leads the service: (a) the *Yehi Ratzon* at the end of the *Birkot ha-Shachar*; (b) the priestly blessing in the repetition of the *Amidah*; (c) *Tachanun, El Erekh Apayim, La-menatze'ach,* and *Va'ani Zot Beriti*.
8. Psalm 49 is added to the regular morning and evening services. When *Tachanun* is not said, Psalm 16 is substituted for Psalm 49.
9. The mourner should not study Torah during the *shiv'ah* period—apart from the tragic books of the Bible and the laws of mourning. Thus it is customary that one of the

° See below, pp. 280–389 for a selection of Mishnah passages and their interpretation and application to the *shiv'ah* situation.

visitors learns a *mishnah* in honor of the soul of the departed. This session of Torah study is followed by the memorial prayers and the *Kaddish d'Rabbanan* (rabbinic *Kaddish*).

10. A *Sefer Torah*, conveyed in an ark, and placed in a place of prominence, may be brought to a *shiv'ah* house. Every effort should be made to read the Torah three times. The mourner, however, should not read the Torah or accept an *aliyah*. (He may, however, be called to the Torah on the afternoon of the seventh day, should that be a public fast-day.)

11. On public fast-days and during the Ten Days of Penitence, *Avinu Malkeinu* is recited.

12. On Rosh Chodesh, *Hallel* is omitted or recited after the mourners have been asked to leave the room. However, if Rosh Chodesh coincides with the seventh day of *shiv'ah*, the mourner should recite it alone, following the departure of fellow worshippers from his home after *Shacharit*. Should the seventh day coincide with the Sabbath, however, the mourner may recite the *Hallel* with the congregation in synagogue.

13. On Chanukah, the mourner should leave the room when *Hallel* is recited, and say it alone.

14. When *Selichot* are recited, they may be led by the mourner, and terminated after the *Shema Koleinu* supplication.

15. If a mourner fails to have a *minyan* at home he may lead the service in the synagogue. However, to ensure that no subsequent passages are omitted from the public worship, he should be replaced by another reader at the end of the silent *Amidah*. If nobody else is present who can conduct public worship, the mourner completes the service without alteration, but omits his personal *Tachanun*.

CONDUCT OF VISITORS IN A HOUSE OF MOURNING

A *shiv'ah* is not a wake, and a *shiv'ah* call is not a social outing or a mere formality. It is a sacred obligation. Its purpose is to share the sorrow of one's friends and relatives, to condole with the mourners, and to support them with one's comforting presence. For this reason, it is inappropriate to eat, drink, and socialize during condolence calls.

THE *SHIV'AH* CALL:
HALAKHIC GUIDELINES FOR CONDUCT

1. A visitor should not initiate conversation with a mourner. The mourner, however, may choose to initiate a conversation.
2. Visitors should not extend greetings and indulge in inappropriate jokes and small talk.
3. Although a visitor should not extend greetings to the mourner, if he/she has done so, the mourner should not respond during the first two days of *shiv'ah*. For this reason, some follow the custom of refraining from making *shiv'ah* calls before the third day.
4. However, a visitor may wish the mourner well, and even congratulate him or her upon a happy event which has taken place.
5. The mourner is not to acknowledge the arrival of any visitor, no matter how important, by rising.
6. When leaving, the visitor should address the condolence formula to all the assembled mourners collectively.°
7. The condolence formula is not addressed to mourners on the Sabbath after the recitation of the Sabbath Psalm (Psalm 92) at the conclusion of *Kabbalat Shabbat*.

CONDUCT OF MOURNERS DURING
THE *SHIV'AH* PERIOD

Indulgence in personal pleasures, conduct of business or preoccupation with our livelihood, participation in joyful celebration, and unnecessary moving about are obviously inconsistent with the mood of the *shiv'ah* observances. A mourner is, at this time, restricted in various ways, each of which will be summarized for convenient reference.

° See below, p. 235.

RESTRICTION OF MOVEMENT:
HALAKHIC CHECKLIST

1. One should observe the *shiv'ah* where one's near one passed away, or at least where he or she lived. However, if that is not possible, one can "sit *shiv'ah*" wherever it is most convenient. But it is not desirable to split the *shiv'ah* period up so as to spend various parts of that period in the homes of different mourners.

2. If one cannot assemble a "private" *minyan*, one can say the *Kaddish* in the nearest synagogue.

3. If necessary, a mourner may return to his/her home late at night, returning to the *shiv'ah* house early each morning.

4. A mourner may not go into the street unless he/she has a good reason, (to get *tefillin*, for example). However, he/she may sit alone on the porch, balcony, or in the backyard. Casual social contact should be avoided.

5. During one's *shiv'ah* one may go to the hospital for elective surgery if a long delay will result from rescheduling the operation—with potentially harmful consequences.

6. One may celebrate the wedding of one's son or daughter, provided that one does not say the *Sheva Berakhot*, and that one eats each course of the meal at a different table. One may dance "*mitzvah*" dances to gladden the hearts of the bridal couple.

7. One may attend even a delayed *brit millah* or the *pidyon ha-ben* of one's own son, wearing different clothes and leather footwear, but one should try to avoid accepting an *aliyah*. One may remain for the meal. The *mohel* and/or *sandek* can attend a *brit* during his *shiv'ah*, but should not remain for the festive meal. One may *not* attend a *kiddush* nor a *shalom zakhar*.

8. One may attend the funeral of a close relative.

9. On Friday afternoon, one calculates the time needed to prepare for Shabbat, and gets up from *shiv'ah* at that time. The norm is an hour and a quarter before sunset. If pressed for time, one may rise two and a half hours before sunset. One may travel home from the *shiv'ah*

house, even if the journey requires one to leave the *shiv'ah* house early on Friday morning. These rules also obtain on the eve of a festival.

10. One attends Sabbath services in the synagogue.

RESTRICTION OF PERSONAL PLEASURE: HALAKHIC CHECKLIST

1. Unless required to do so for medical reasons, one should not luxuriate in a bath or a shower. Bathing should be strictly for hygienic reasons, if one feels dirty or has perspired a great deal.
2. One should not indulge in marital relations or other intimate demonstrations of affection.
3. One should not shave, take a haircut, cut one's fingernails, or use cosmetics. One who regularly combs one's hair may do so during *shiv'ah*, if neglect of this practice is uncomfortable.
4. One should not change one's outer clothing, although underwear, socks, and stockings may be changed. One should not have one's clothes washed or laundered unless they are visibly soiled or full of perspiration and one has no change of clothing. The clothes of children in mourning can be washed.
5. One should not wear leather footwear, unless medically required to do so.
6. A woman may not wear any jewelry apart from her wedding ring.
7. One must not study Torah or recite Psalms. Only the books of Job, Lamentations, and the laws of mourning may be studied—and then, only superficially. This rule applies to Shabbat and *Yom Tov* also.
8. One may not listen to music.
9. One should not have little children on one's lap, since this is a great source of pleasure.
10. When sitting, one should use a very low stool or chair. Ideally one should sit no higher than a foot above the floor. One may sit on the floor, of course.
11. One may sleep in a bed.

RESTRICTION OF OCCUPATIONAL ACTIVITIES: HALAKHIC CHECKLIST

1. One may not pursue one's business, trade, occupation, or profession during *shiv'ah*. One may not even appoint agents to do so on one's behalf. Household chores like sweeping the floor are permissible.

2. If at all possible, one's business should be closed for *at least* the first three days of *shiv'ah*. If this will involve one in significant, irreparable, financial loss, one's business should have been sold during the *aninut* period, as we have seen. Should it not be possible to sell one's business, and should one also be liable to pay the salaries of employees, one may keep it open *and* retain the profits. If one's business is such that it *cannot* be sold, one can conduct it even oneself (even during the first three days) so as to avoid an irreparable and significant loss.

3. If one has contracted to perform some work, and a delay may cause great financial loss, the work may be subcontracted to others.

4. If a contractor arranged to do work for a mourner before his/her near one passed away, the contracted job may be completed. This rules applies if the work is not being done in the *shiv'ah* house, and if it is not apparent to casual observers that the work is being done for the mourner.

5. If a mourner is a partner in a business, that business should be closed for at least the first three days. If the partners operate in different locations, only the mourner need close his store/office. In the event of severe loss, the mourner may, during *aninut*, sell his share to his partner(s) who is/are entitled to return his share of the profits after *shiv'ah* as an unconditional gift.

6. If the mourner's partner also passes away during the mourner's *shiv'ah*, the business should be closed, since the partnership lapses. However, a sale may be arranged during *aninut* in the case of great financial loss.

7. If others will suffer irreplacable loss through the

mourner's cessation of work, that work may be done by
him (if he is the only ritual slaughterer or scribe for *gittin*
[Jewish divorces] in town, for example) though appoint-
ment of a substitute is preferable.

8. A physician or surgeon should engage a substitute for
the *shiv'ah* period. In an emergency, however, or if the
patient insists upon having his or her own doctor in
attendance, the physician or surgeon should do what is
necessary for the good of the patient.

9. A rabbi in mourning may answer halakhic questions if he
is the most qualified to do so. On these grounds, he may
also perform a private wedding ceremony in his home—
without instrumental music.

10. An employee, too, must not work during *shiv'ah*,
although he may engage a substitute.

CONDUCT BY MOURNERS ON MINOR FESTIVALS: HALAKHIC CHECKLIST

1. We have noted that Rosh ha-Shanah, Yom Kippur, and
the Pilgrim Festivals cancel the *shiv'ah*.

2. On Chanukah, one should kindle the lights at home,
with all the accompanying blessings. However, a mourner should not kindle the first Chanukah light in the
synagogue.

3. Although Purim does not cancel the *shiv'ah*, no public
mourning is permitted. Hence, one can sit on a regular
chair, use leather footwear, send *mishlo'ach manot* to
one person, and eat the Purim meal with one's own family. However, one's friends should refrain from sending
one *mishlo'ach manot*, although one may accept such
gifts in order to spare friends embarrassment. One may
go to synagogue to hear the reading of the *megillah*. One
should not read the *megillah* for others, unless one is the
most qualified (or is alone able) to do so.

4. There is no public mourning on Shushan Purim.

5. One may attend all synagogue services on Tisha b'Av
and accept an *aliyah*, since all worshippers are regarded
as mourners on that day.

6. A mourner who is firstborn may *not* leave home to attend a *siyyum* on the eve of Passover. However, the *siyyum* may be held in the *shiv'ah* house.

CONDUCT ON THE SABBATH OF THE *SHIV'AH* WEEK: HALAKHIC CHECKLIST

1. Although the Sabbath does not cancel *shiv'ah*, no public mourning is permitted. *Private* mourning continues, and precludes marital intercourse.
2. Since no public demonstration of grief is permitted, one may, as we have seen, return home from the *shiv'ah* house on Friday in time to prepare for the Sabbath. If one is "sitting *shiv'ah*" at home, one rises an hour and a quarter before sunset. If one is pressed for time, one can rise two and a half hours before sunset. The Sabbath preparations do *not* include taking a shave, bath or shower.
3. One should change one's outer garments, although one should not wear one's usual Sabbath best. One may wear leather shoes. One may use one's special Sabbath *tallit*.
4. One may be in synagogue for the late Friday *Minchah* service, but should remain outside during *Kabbalat Shabbat*. One is ushered into the synagogue immediately prior to the recitation of the Sabbath Psalm and greeted with the condolence formula. One omits the study of *bameh madlikin*.
5. In synagogue, one should sit in a different seat, at least six and a half feet from one's regular place of worship.
6. One should not lead the community in prayer or read the Torah unless one is alone qualified to do so. Nor may one accept an *aliyah* or recite the Hymn of Glory (*Anim Zemirot*).
7. One may exchange the *Shabbat Shalom* greeting. However, the formula of consolation is not addressed to mourners after the recitation of the Sabbath Psalm on Sabbath eve.

8. At home, one may sit on a regular chair, and sing all *zemirot* except for *Shalom Aleikhem*—which is simply omitted.
9. If a *minyan* assembles in the *shiv'ah* house for the Sabbath afternoon prayers, *Va-ani Tefillati* is omitted but *Tzidkatekha Tzedek* is recited.
10. If one does so regularly, one may study the *sedra* with Rashi's commentary or a translation (*Shenayim Mikra ve-echad Targum*).
11. All other personal restrictions remain in force.
12. At the conclusion of the Sabbath, the mourner follows the usual liturgy (including *Vi-hi No'am*), but he makes the sanctification of the new moon privately—without the *Shalom Aleikhem* greeting.
13. He commences *Havdallah* with the blessing over the wine.

CHAPTER TEN

The *Sheloshim* and *Yud Bet Chodesh* Periods

REMOVAL OF SOME *SHIV'AH* RESTRICTIONS

After the close of the *shiv'ah* period, some of the restrictions are discontinued. They fall into three categories.

The first relates to the restriction of movement, which prevents us from resuming our usual occupations. After *shiv'ah* we are no longer confined to our homes, made to sit on low chairs, forbidden to wear leather footwear and to pursue our businesses, trades, or professions.

The second category relates to the study of Torah. Although Torah study is regarded as a source of great personal pleasure, it occupies a very high place in the hierarchy of the *mitzvot*. For this reason, notwithstanding the great joy it gives us, its suspension is justified only in the most extraordinary of circumstances—and then only for the shortest possible time. Accordingly, suspension of Torah study is not required beyond the *shiv'ah* period.

The third and final category relates to the most intimate of our personal relationships. The marital communion of husband and wife is a necessarily shared experience, with each partner fulfilling the needs of the other. Unreasonable postponement of this aspect of the marital relationship in reaction to the grief of the one partner is unfair to the other. Furthermore, the marital act transcends the merely pleasurable. It is the sacred seal of a precious relationship, an affirmation of life and love even in the wake of death. As such, it should not be delayed beyond *shiv'ah* by the requirements of mourning.

REMOVAL OF *SHIV'AH* RESTRICTIONS: HALAKHIC CHECKLIST

The following restrictions are removed:

1. Marital abstinence.
2. Prohibition against the wearing of leather footwear.
3. Prohibition against the study of Torah.
4. Sitting on a low chair.
5. Remaining indoors.
6. Prohibition against pursuing one's business or other occupation—except that one should not participate in trade fairs and in business and professional conventions, where social festivities are as much a part of the nature of the gathering as is the business at hand. However, if non-participation will cause significant financial loss, one may attend such gatherings.

MOURNING PARENTS: MOURNING OTHER RELATIVES

The Halakhah distinguishes between formal mourning for deceased parents and for other deceased close relatives. When we mourn the loss of a parent, a full twelve-month period is allowed for the halakhic expression of our grief. In Hebrew, this period is known as *yud bet chodesh*. When we mourn for those other close relatives for whom we are obliged to observe *shiv'ah* restrictions, a period of thirty days is allowed for the halakhic expression of our grief. This period is known as *sheloshim*. We shall see that the *yud bet chodesh* restrictions are, with a few exceptions, identical to those of the *sheloshim* period.

There are several compelling reasons for the extension of restrictions following the loss of a parent. Honor and respect for our parents is biblically ordained. The Ten Commandments single out honor due to parents. Extended mourning practices reflect this special relationship with our parents. They also reflect another special obligation to them. We believe that the heavenly judgment of the departed takes up to twelve months. We also believe that the halakhic behavior of sorrowing children influences the positive outcome of the process of the judgment. Thus our compliance with the Halakhah through daily worship, more intense Torah study, and good deeds is regarded as a measure of the success of our parents in bringing us up. They are seen to have passed on the ancient traditions of our people—and they are judged accordingly.

The distinction between the *yud bet chodesh* period of mourning for parents and the much briefer *sheloshim* period of mourning for other close relatives is often challenged by logic and experience. It is argued that the passing of parents in the lifetime of their children is natural and expected. Therefore the sadness, however great, is tempered by the anticipated inevitability of the event. On the other hand, the passing of a child is out of the natural sequence, and is an unanticipated trauma of unspeakable dimensions. Surely, it is argued, the mourning observances in this tragic case should be more extensive than those for parents.

To be sure, the *experience* of grief is not the same in the two cases. But it is precisely *because* of the different nature of our grief experience that we relate to the periods of mourning differently.

On the one hand, because the death of parents is perceived as inevitable after a full life, and is often preceded by a long illness, the natural tendency may be to grieve their passing less. If the Halakhah were to reflect our *actual* feelings of grief, it would not give clear expression to the special obligations we have towards our parents. Furthermore, we might also feel guilt at our comparative lack of feeling, since we are aware that we owe our parents so very much. The fixed twelve-month period of mourning addresses all these problems.

On the other hand, the danger exists that, left to our own devices, we might find it impossible to *terminate* our mourning for deceased children, or for the loss of a beloved life's companion of many, many years, because such wounds are never fully healed. The termination of formal mourning after thirty days addresses this problem, emphasizing that there *are* acceptable limits to the expression of sadness.

In the final analysis, therefore, the twelve-month period prevents us from mourning our parents too little, while the thirty-day period prevents us from mourning the unbearable loss of our closest relatives too long.

SHELOSHIM AND *YUD BET CHODESH* AS PERIODS OF TRANSITION

Sheloshim and *yud bet chodesh* are periods of transition. During *shiv'ah*, we move from the paralyzing grief of the first three days through the comparatively less intense grief of the remaining days. This period is characterized, as we have seen, by significant restrictions upon our personal movement and everday pursuits. With the completion of *shiv'ah*, we are encouraged to resume most of our normal routines. We are no longer confined to our homes, and can again devote ourselves more fully to family, business, occupational, and professional commitments. By retaining some restrictions of the *shiv'ah* period while releasing us from others, the remaining portion (post-*shiv'ah*) of the thirty-day and twelve-month period of mourning—as the case may be—allows us a gradual transition into and preparation for our full resumption of a way of life unrestricted by formal expressions of grief.

SHELOSHIM IS NOT ALWAYS "THIRTY"

Sheloshim may translate into English as "thirty," but the *sheloshim* period does not necessarily last for thirty days. As was the case when we counted *shiv'ah*, the final day is *always* abbreviated—on the principle that the smallest "part of the day counts as a complete day." Sometimes the period is further abbreviated by the intervention of a major holy day, and sometimes the spirit of joy of a major holy day actually *cancels* the *sheloshim* observances. For these reasons, the duration of the *sheloshim* period is subject to a number of variables, and needs to be spelled out in detail.

DURATION OF *SHELOSHIM*: HALAKHIC CHECKLIST

Commencement

1. The *sheloshim* period begins as soon as interment has taken place.
2. However, since *shiv'ah* begins simultaneously (under most circumstances), and since *shiv'ah* restrictions are more severe than *sheloshim* restrictions, *shiv'ah* overshadows *sheloshim*. The characteristic restrictions of

sheloshim manifest themselves only when the *shiv'ah* ends.

3. When *shiv'ah* observances are postponed, as, for example, when burial takes place on *Yom Tov* or *Chol ha-Moed*, *sheloshim* restrictions begin immediately after interment, are then overshadowed by the *shiv'ah* restrictions which begin after *Yom Tov*, and after the termination of *shiv'ah*.

Termination

1. *The Usual Case.* Under normal circumstances, the *sheloshim* period terminates on the thirtieth day *after burial.* On the principle that a small "part of the day counts as a complete day," the *sheloshim* period ends after the *Shacharit* prayer on the thirtieth day.

2. *Cancellation of Sheloshim.* The spirit of joy which pervades major holy days (including Yom Kippur) overwhelms the mood of sorrow which follows the burial of a loved one. It actually cancels out the *sheloshim* period, provided that the *shiv'ah* period has been terminated either by the completion of the *shiv'ah* period on the seventh day, or by the termination of the *shiv'ah* observances *after they have been at least minimally performed* by the intervention of a major holy day. Specifically—

a. If one completed *shiv'ah* before Rosh ha-Shanah, Rosh ha-Shanah will cancel *sheloshim*.

b. If Rosh ha-Shanah intervened after one had begun (but not yet completed the observances of *shiv'ah* period, Rosh ha-Shanah will cancel *shiv'ah*, and Yom Kippur will cancel *sheloshim*.

c. If one completed *shiv'ah* before Yom Kippur, Yom Kippur will cancel *sheloshim*.

d. If Yom Kippur intervened after one had begun (but not completed) the observances of *shiv'ah*, Yom Kippur will cancel *shiv'ah*, and Sukkot will cancel *sheloshim*.

Note: Sukkot, Shemini Atzeret, and Simchat Torah are regarded as a *single unit* (rather than two distinct festivals) for the cancellation of *sheloshim*.

Abbreviation of *Sheloshim*

1. The same holy day *cannot* cancel *both shiv'ah* and *sheloshim*. We have just seen that *one* holy day cancels *shiv'ah*, and the *next holy day*, if it occurs within the thirty-day period, cancels *sheloshim*.
2. However, even if the next holy day does not occur within the thirty-day period (and thus *does not* cancel *sheloshim*), the holy day which cancelled *shiv'ah* also shortens *sheloshim*.
3. If the following holy days intervene after one has begun (but not completed) one's *shiv'ah* obligations, they are counted as either seven or eight days of the thirty-day *sheloshim* period:
   a. Pesach = 8 days (7 in Israel).
   b. Shavu'ot = 8 days (7 in Israel).
   c. Sukkot = 7 days (everywhere).
   d. Shemini Atzeret and Simchat Torah = 8 days (7 in Israel).

Note: Sukkot and Shemini Atzeret/Simchat Torah are regarded as two separate units for shortening *sheloshim*.

4. Thus, if one had completed *part* of one's *shiv'ah* obligations before the intervention of—
   a. Pesach, the completed part (even one hour) of *shiv'ah* = 7 days, and Pesach = 8 days, making 15 days completed, and leaving 15 additional days of *sheloshim* observances.
   b. Shavu'ot, the completed part (even one hour) of *shiv'ah* = 7 days, and Shavu'ot = 8 days, making 15 days completed, and leaving 15 additional days of *sheloshim* observances.
   c. Sukkot, the completed part (even one hour) of *shiv'ah* = 7 days, Sukkot = 7 days, and Shemini Atzeret/Simchat Torah = 8 days, making 22 days completed, and leaving 8 additional days of *sheloshim* observances.

Effect of Sukkot and Shemini Atzeret/Simchat Torah on
***Sheloshim* computation.**

1. For cancellation of *sheloshim* they are a *single unit.*
2. For abbreviation of *sheloshim* they are *two units.*
3. But if burial took place at any time during Sukkot (so that *sheloshim* observances *precede shiv'ah* observances), Shemini Atzeret and Simchat Torah *each* count as only one day of the *sheloshim* period.

LIMITING PLEASURE

The restriction of pleasure is the most obvious expression of our grief. The periods of *sheloshim* and *yud bet chodesh*, therefore, are characterized by the restriction of various types of pleasure.

The Joy of Friendship

The Halakhah recognizes the universal nature of certain categories of pleasure. Foremost among these is the special joy of fellowship. The pleasure of fellowship is termed *simchat mere'im* or *mere'ut.* Specifically, the classical sources of Judaism distinguish between four varieties of *simchat mere'im:*

1. *Bet ha-Simchah.* This is a joyous assembly in which instrumental music (*mazmutei chatan ve-kallah*) is of the very essence of the celebration. A wedding ceremony and feast in a catering establishment is a prime example of this variety of *simchat mere'im.*
2. *Bet ha-Mishteh.* When, for example, the wedding ceremony is held in a synagogue, and the festive meal with its instrumental music and dancing is held afterwards in a catering establishment, that meal is designated as being in a *bet ha-mishteh.* The fellowship of celebration itself constitutes the pleasure, even if one does not partake of the meal.
3. *Se'udat Mere'im.* This is a meal enjoyed in the company of friends and relatives beyond the immediate family circle. It may have merely social purposes or may be in celebration of the ful-

fillment of a *mitzvah (se'udat mitzvah)*. In this case, the meal itself defines the *simchat mere'im*, even in the absence of instrumental music and dancing. One's mere transient presence (if one does not eat) is not regarded as pleasurable. In *some* circumstances mourners are not restricted from this category of *simchat mere'im*, as we shall see.

4. *Chedvat Mere'im.* This variety of *simchat mere'im* is based upon the classical model of *shayarah*, a group excursion. Originally denoting a group traveling together to do business, it was extended to excursions for other purposes also, since irrespective of the ultimate goal of the excursion, the fellowship enjoyed by the participants is a great source of pleasure.

In each variety of *simchat mere'im*, the *group as a whole* celebrates an event or occasion. The participant is not part of an unconnected crowd of individuals, but rather an integral part of a group especially constituted to celebrate a specific event. A wedding party is an excellent example of a group of this kind. A spectator in a crowded football stadium, on the other hand, is one of a host of individuals. He purchases his ticket as an individual. As such, a football game is not a *simchat mere'im*, unless he attends as a member of an organized group making an excursion to the game. In this case the group activity comes under the heading of *chedvat mere'im*.

Joyful Fellowship: Sacred and Profane: Exemptions for a *Se'udat Mitzvah*

We have, thus far, distinguished between four categories of joyful fellowship. The Halakhah makes a further distinction. A social event may be celebrated with a meal whose purposes are sacred. Such a meal is known as a *se'udat mitzvah*. It may, on the other hand, have no religious motivation. In this case, it is called a *se'udat reshut*. Under some circumstances mourners are permitted to participate in a *se'udat mitzvah*. In one instance they are even permitted to participate in a *se'udat reshut*. We shall analyze these situations in some detail as a case study in the halakhic methodology which is reflected in the checklists which punctuate this volume.

The distinction is first made by the Talmud. One source precludes a mourner from participating in joyful fellowship for twelve months following the loss of a parent, and for thirty days following the loss of any of the six other closest kin, unless the gathering is "for the sake of heaven"—*le-shem shamayim* (*Semachot* 9). The Jerusalem Talmud suspends the prohibition in the case of a "gathering for sacred purposes" (*chavurat mitzvah*) or for the sanctification of the new moon (*Mo'ed Katan* 3:8). The same source permits a mourner for close relatives to issue a reciprocal invitation to friends within the *sheloshim*, while forbidding such reciprocation during the twelve-month period of mourning for a parent.

How are we to understand the notions of a gathering "for the sake of heaven" and "for sacred purposes"? What is the concept of reciprocated hospitality?

It would appear that a reciprocation of hospitality is permitted in most cases because it is routine rather than especially celebratory and joyful. This is the only case of a permitted *se'udat reshut*. Most commentators maintain that it applies when a group of families extend hospitality to one another on a regular rotating basis, and the turn has come for the mourner to open his/her home for fellowship. However, during the twelve-month period of mourning for a parent not even such reciprocation is permitted.

The definition of gathering "for the sake of heaven" and for "sacred purposes" is the subject of an ongoing debate among halakhic authorities.

The simplest definition is offered by Rabbi Moses of Coucy in his *Sefer Mitzvot Gadol* in the name of prominent Tosafists. It includes any meal which celebrates the performance of a *mitzvah* (*se'udat mitzvah*), including a wedding meal. This view is *not* codified by Rabbi Joseph Karo in the authoritative Code of Jewish Law, *Shulchan Arukh*, nor by Rabbi Moses Isserles in his glosses on that work.

The two definitions which do appear in the codes are those of the schools of thought represented by Rabbi Abraham ben David of Posquières (*Rabad*), on the one hand, and by Rabbi Joseph ibn Habiba, the author of *Nimukkei Yosef*, on the other.

The view of Rabad is the most restrictive. It holds that almost every *se'udat mitzvah* is a joyful fellowship, and is thus forbidden. There are only two exceptions to this rule. The wedding festivities of orphans and the poor for whose arrangement the mourner has taken responsibility. Such festivities may be held in his/her presence. (It has been suggested that if the absence of the mourner will deeply upset the unfortunate celebrants, his/her presence at the festivities also comes within this definition.) A *se'udat mitzvah* celebrating the personal fulfillment of a *mitzvah* by the mourner himself is the second exception—such as being part of the company which ate the paschal lamb in biblical times, and, it has been suggested, the celebration of his own completion of the study of a tractate of Talmud (*siyyum*) in contemporary times. According to Rabbi Sabetai Cohen (*Shakh*), these exemptions apply only to mourners for their parents *after* the completion of the *sheloshim*. They do not apply to other mourners during the *sheloshim*. Rabbi Yechiel Mikhel Epstein in his *Arukh ha-Shulchan* cites the differing opinion of Rabbi Joel Sirkes (*Bach*) and other authorities as being authoritative. These authorities claim that the two exceptions apply to mourners for their parents after the completion of their *sheloshim*, and to other mourners during their *sheloshim*. This is the view which we have elected to follow.

Rabad's restrictive view is softened by more recent and contemporary authorities, by extending the notion that the mourner may attend a *se'udat mitzvah* when his/her absence would cause great pain to the celebrants. It is further softened by Rabbi Moshe Feinstein, who applied the notion that public mourning is forbidden on the Sabbath. Thus he rules that a mourner may attend the *bar mitzvah* celebration of a friend who insists on his/her presence, and any *bar mitzvah* celebration in the synagogue which he customarily attends, lest his/her absence be regarded as public mourning. Both extenuating circumstances are invoked in permitting a mourner to attend a *shalom zakhar*. Notwithstanding the softening of Rabad's position, Rabbi Feinstein follows the view of the Shakh that the exceptions apply only after the conclusion of the *sheloshim*.

Rabbi Joseph ibn Habiba maintains that *only* the *se'udat mitzvah* following a wedding is intrinsically joyful. For this reason, we add the formula "Blessed is He in whose dwelling is joyful celebration" to the introduction to the grace after meals. Accordingly, in the absence of the "for the sake of heaven" motivation which we have described, a mourner cannot attend a wedding feast. The *se'udat mitzvah* following a ritual circumcision is *not* intrinsically joyful. The special formula is omitted from the grace on account of the pain suffered by the infant (*tza'ara d'yenuka*), which mitigates the joy expressed in the verse "I rejoice at thy word as one that findeth great spoil" (Psalms 119:62). Since a ritual circumcision is thus not intrinsically joyful, it may be attended by mourners. Rabbi Yechiel Mikhel Epstein suggests that the granting of permission to mourners to attend the *se'udat mitzvah* following a circumcision is archetypal. It simply *illustrates* the more general principle that all *se'udot mitzvah* which lack the formula "in whose dwelling is joyful celebration" cannot be judged to be intrinsically joyful assemblies. They are, therefore, gatherings "for the sake of heaven" and "for sacred purposes." They may thus be attended by mourners—after thirty days following the burial of a parent and during the *sheloshim* period following the loss of other close relatives.

Rabbi Moses Isserles cites the views of the representatives of both the lenient and the restrictive tendencies, and determines that the custom is according to the restrictive view of Rabad—except that one can participate in a *se'udat mitzvah* (apart from a wedding feast) in one's own home. In the case of his own *mitzvah*, for instance a *sandek*, a *mohel*, or a father at the circumcision of his son, the mourner may attend the *se'udat mitzvah* which is held elsewhere also.

Rabbi Epstein's conclusion on this subject is noteworthy: "It seems, in my humble opinion, that, in case of need, one can rely upon the lenient views, since the Halakhah follows the lenient view in the [laws of] mourning."

Since this work is intended to encourage the widest possible audience of readers to observe the laws of mourning, our Halakhic Checklist will take note of the more lenient as well as the more restrictive of the tendencies.

Universal Personal Pleasures: Music During Mourning

We have noted that *mazmutei chatan ve-kallah*, the musical entertainments which are an inseparable part of a wedding celebration, are intrinsic to the *bet ha-simchah* and *bet ha-mishteh* categories of the pleasures of fellowship. The early sources of the Halakhah confine their restrictions on the enjoyment of music to these contexts alone. Later halakhic authorities, however, extend the restriction to the personal sphere also. They hold that listening to music is a universal source of *personal* pleasure, and restrict the enjoyment of both live and recorded music. This restriction is not total. Listening to incidental music, such as that in commercials, background, and at intermission at sports events, is permitted.

Universal Personal Pleasures: Grooming and Hygiene

There are two more categories of universal personal pleasure which are restricted during mourning. The first relates to the pleasure we have in pampering ourselves. We enjoy luxuriating and taking pride in looking good in public. This luxuriating is restricted during the *sheloshim period.*

Universal Personal Pleasures: Enjoyment of the New and the Fresh

The second category relates to our delight in new possessions and improvements to our property which our friends and neighbors will admire. These include buying new homes, redecorating our homes, acquiring new furniture, and wearing new clothes—unless, of course, these purchases and improvements are unavoidable.

Subjective Personal Pleasures

While we have discussed what the rabbis consider to be universal sources of pleasure, we are aware of the essentially subjective, personal nature of pleasure. What one person enjoys, another may detest. What gives joy to one person may leave another unaffected. What provides cheer to one person may be wearisome to another. And since some forms of pleasures are socially conditioned, the pleasurable experiences of one society may be incomprehensible to another, and pleasures which are common in one period of time may be quite unpleasurable in another.

Grief, too, is a personal, subjective experience, which cannot be reduced to a robotlike behaviorism. Consequently, if a person feels that a particular activity which is a source of great personal pleasure is not consonant with the experience of grief, that activity can be restricted during the mourning period. The rabbis merely establish rules which apply to the overwhelming majority of people. As such, their restrictions reflect the feelings of most of us, and our level of consciousness to our situation of loss. They also express our respect for those we mourn, and assure us that we are doing no less than can be legitimately required of us. If we wish to do more, we may restrict ourselves further—but in full awareness that our tradition does not require us to do so.

SHELOSHIM RESTRICTIONS: HALAKHIC CHECKLIST

To Whom Do *Sheloshim* Restrictions Apply?

1. *Sheloshim* restrictions apply to one who has lost one's father, mother, brother (or half brother), sister (or half sister), son, daughter, husband, or wife (to whom one was married in compliance with the Halakhah, and from whom one was not divorced with a *get*).
2. These restrictions apply even if the deceased has clearly requested that no formal mourning be observed for him/her. Such instructions are to be ignored.

Personal Grooming and Hygiene

Bathing and Showering

1. Since the sages distinguished between washing oneself for the sake of personal cleanliness—which they generally permitted—and bathing as a pleasurable luxury, only the latter category was forbidden during *sheloshim*.
2. Thus, if one has become dirty, the dirt may be removed with soap and water.
3. Although there is no intrinsic prohibition against bathing the entire body after the completion of *shiv'ah*, the authorities regarded this practice as inappropriately luxurious, and counseled alternative methods of preserving personal cleanliness, such as the thorough washing of different parts of the body separately—with the following notable exceptions:

   a. Bathing or showering in cold water is not considered a luxury and is always permitted during *sheloshim*.

b. A person who bathes or showers daily, and would feel most uncomfortable were he/she to cease doing so for an extended period, may continue to do so during *sheloshim*—making the shower as brief as possible.

c. Hot baths and showers ordered by a physician should be taken.

d. A woman should bathe as usual prior to going to the *mikvah*, but should alter her normal routine to remain mindful of her mourning.

Trimming of Nails

1. Clippers or scissors should not be used for this purpose during *sheloshim*.
2. Clippers or scissors may be used by a woman in preparation for going to the *mikveh*. If possible, her nails should be trimmed by another woman.

Haircuts and Shaving

1. Haircuts and shaving are prohibited until the end of *sheloshim*.
2. If one's unshaven appearance after *shiv'ah* and *prior* to the conclusion of *sheloshim* will *significantly* obstruct one's livelihood, a learned rabbi should be consulted.
3. A groom may shave on his wedding day.
4. A married woman may go to the hairdresser during *sheloshim*, but may not have her hair dyed a different color. She may remove such body hair as bothers her.
5. If *Yom Tov* cancels *sheloshim*, one may shave and take a haircut on the day before *Yom Tov*—particularly in the case of Pesach, since one may not shave or take a haircut in the subsequent *sefirah* period or during *Chol ha-Moed*. The latter consideration will permit one to shave and take a haircut before Sukkot which cancels *sheloshim*.
6. If the *sheloshim* end on a Shabbat, one may *not* shave and take a haircut on the preceding day.
7. If the *sheloshim* ended during the *sefirah* period, or in the period between the seventeenth of Tammuz and Rosh Chodesh Av, one may trim and cut one's hair if it is too long and heavy for comfort.

Cosmetics, Colognes, Etc.

1. Perfumes, deodorants, hairsprays, etc., are permitted.
2. Unmarried women should not use makeup during the *sheloshim*. However, married women are not included in this restriction, since it is mandatory for them to be attractive to their husbands. The same exception applies to women who are engaged or attempting to meet their life's companion.

New Purchases

1. One should neither purchase for oneself nor wear *expensive* clothing. Everyday, inexpensive clothes may be purchased and worn by somebody else before being put on by the mourner. This provision does not apply to socks, stockings, underwear, and everyday footwear, which may be put on directly by the mourner. Old clothing should not be dry-cleaned or dyed. Freshly dry-cleaned or dyed clothing should be worn by someone else before being put on by the mourner.
2. One should neither buy nor rent an apartment or house, unless great loss will be incurred by the delay.
3. One should not buy major items of new furniture.
4. One may not *paint* one's home.

Entertainment and Social Gatherings

1. One may not greet a mourner, although a mourner may extend and respond to greetings.
2. If one had not greeted a mourner with the formula of condolence during his/her *shiv'ah*, one may do so during the *sheloshim* period.
3. A mourner should not listen to live or recorded music unless the music is incidental—as background in commercials, and during intermission.
4. A mourner should not accept invitations to social gatherings which are celebrated with a festive meal (*se'udot reshut*) such as wedding anniversaries. Since the celebration of the acquisition of a new home (*chanukat ha-bayit*)

is not universally celebrated, it is to be considered a *se'udat reshut* for these purposes.

5. However, a mourner for close relatives other than parents may extend reciprocal hospitality during the period of mourning, if reciprocation is routine and customary, since *this* instance of *se'udat reshut* is not considered to be very pleasurable.

6. Participation in the following *se'udot mitzvah* is permitted to those who mourn close relatives *other than* parents:

Brit Millah (Circumcision)

a. All authorities permit mourners to be present at the circumcision itself, and to have some food before leaving. They should not, in this view, enjoy a full, formal meal.
b. All authorities permit the mourner to enjoy the entire formal meal if the event takes place in his/her home.
c. All authorities permit the father and/or grandfather of the child, the *sandek*, and the *mohel* to enjoy the entire formal meal.
d. If the meal is held on Shabbat, some authorities permit all mourners to participate fully.
e. The lenient school of thought does not regard this as a joyful *se'udat mitzvah* and permits mourners to participate fully.

Pidyon ha-Ben (Redemption of the Firstborn Son)

a. Most authorities permit the parents to attend and to participate fully in the formal meal.
b. They permit the presiding *kohen*, when in mourning, to do the same, even if other *kohanim* are present.
c. In the lenient view, this *se'udat mitzvah* is not an intrinsically joyful occasion. Mourners may therefore participate fully.

Bar/Bat Mitzvah

a. Most authorities permit parents and grandparents of the celebrant to participate fully in the formal meal, without sitting at the top table, under two conditions: If the event was planned prior to the bereavement, or if its cancellation would be very costly.

b. Some authorities allow other mourners to attend if the celebrant urges him to do so, or if the *se'udah* takes place on the actual date when the celebrant becomes a *bar/bat mitzvah*, or if the *se'udah* is characterized as a *se'udat mitzvah* by *divrei Torah* (expositions of Torah themes).

Siyyum Masekhet (The Completion of Study of Talmudic Tractate)

a. All authorities permit one completing his own study of a tractate of the Talmud to participate fully in the formal celebratory *se'udat mitzvah*.

b. The lenient view permits mourners to attend such a *se'udat mitzvah* without qualification.

Chanukah Celebration

a. Some authorities disqualify such an event as a *se'udat mitzvah* within the framework of the laws of mourning.

b. Others regard it as such, provided that it is characterized as such by *divrei Torah*, permitting full participation of the mourners.

Chanukat ha-Bayit (Housewarming Celebrations)

The views in item (a) of *Siyyum Masekhet*, above, apply here too.

7. Mourners (other than for parents) may attend any of the following events, although they are not *se'udot mitzvah*:

a. A *kiddush* in one's regular place of worship on Shabbat to prevent appearances of public mourning on the Sabbath.

b. A *shalom zakhar* of a close friend, at his insistence, and also to prevent appearances of public mourning on the Sabbath.

c. A "*le-chayim*" with a few friends, since it is not a formal meal.

d. A meal in a hotel, restaurant, or convention is permitted, since it is regarded as if it were in one's own home, provided that the dimension of *shayarah* (see above p. 131) is not present.

Engagements, Marriages, and Wedding Celebrations

Engagements

1. A mourner may attend an engagement celebration where there is neither music nor a formal meal. A mourner may both give and receive an engagement ring.
2. A mourner may not attend a *tena'im* ceremony unless it is celebrated with a *devar Torah*, making it a *se'udat mitzvah*.

Getting Married During *Sheloshim*

1. A mourner should not marry during the *sheloshim* period. However, if the groom had no children of his own, or if the wedding was planned prior to the demise of the close relative, and its cancellation or postponement will be *very* costly, a bride and/or groom who is a mourner/are mourners may marry during the *sheloshim* period. *In that event:*
   a. The groom, if he is in mourning, wears a *kittel* under the *chupah*.
   b. The music and dancing should not be cancelled.
   c. Their seven festive days count as part of the *sheloshim*.
   d. No mourning takes place during the seven festive days.

2. If he *has* small children and cannot adequately care for them on his own, a mourner may marry during his *sheloshim* period, but may not have marital relations until after the *sheloshim* period.
3. If one's close relative dies during one's seven festive days, one's mourning commences *after* the seven festive days.
4. A widower cannot remarry until all three pilgrim festivals have passed in any sequence. Shemini Atzeret is a separate pilgrim festival for this purpose. A *childless* widower

may remarry after *shiv'ah*. A widow must wait for three months to pass prior to her remarriage.

Attending a Wedding Celebration

1. Mourners who are not very close to the bridal couple and whose absence from the wedding will cause them no great pain, should not accept an invitation to attend even the *chupah*.

2. Parents and grandparents of the bride and/or groom may attend the wedding although they are in mourning. They may shave (but not take haircuts), and attend the wedding meal. They may even sit at the top table, but should eat each course of the feast at a different table. They may even participate in "*mitzvah* dancing," if their not doing so would upset the bridal couple.

3. The brother, sister, stepfather, stepmother, and aunts and uncles who are particularly close to the bridal couple may attend the reception prior to the *chupah*, participate in the procession to the *chupah*, stand under the *chupah* itself, and even recite a blessing under the *chupah* if invited to do so. Since they are in mourning, however, they may not attend the wedding feast after the *chupah*. Permission is granted to them to attend the reception and *chupah*, since their absence will pain the bridal couple greatly, and since the main festivity and rejoicing takes place at the festive meal after the *chupah*.

4. On this basis, it would seem that permission to attend at least the *chupah* should be granted to close friends in mourning, whose absence would be painful and detract from the joy, especially if the *chupah* is held in a synagogue.

Attending *Sheva Berakhot*

1. Mourners who may attend the *chupah* may also be present at meals where *sheva berakhot* are recited on Shabbat and *Yom Tov*.

2. Mourners may attend the festive meal where *sheva berakhot* are recited, if there will be no *minyan* without them.

When *Sheloshim* Restrictions Restrict One's Usual Income

1. The restrictions which limit mourners from listening to music and attending large social functions during *sheloshim* aim at restricting *pleasure*. They are not meant to curtail a mourner's regular source of income.
2. Thus professional musicians may play and sing during their *sheloshim* period, photographers may attend social functions where music is played, caterers may attend parties which they cater, cantors may eat at receptions where their duty calls them, and so on.
3. Some nonprofessionals utilize this "loophole" to allow them to attend social functions at which music is played, by serving as photographers, etc., during their *sheloshim* period. While some rabbis permit them to do so, others regard such permissiveness as contraverting the spirit of the *sheloshim* restrictions and their essential purpose. This "loophole" may be used only by close relatives of the bridal couple.
4. A rabbi may certainly conduct a wedding ceremony during his *sheloshim* period. He and the cantor may even attend the subsequent festive meal, without eating, if by not doing so they will jeopardize their positions.

Synagogue Practice During *Sheloshim*

1. A mourner should not wear his/her *usual* Sabbath clothes, but should dress tastefully for synagogue.
2. A mourner should change his/her usual synagogue seat to one no more prominent, and at least six and a half feet away. This rule applies to Shabbat and *Yom Tov* also. It applies to Yeshiva students, who should change their seats in the *bet midrash*. The rabbi of a congregation need move only to the next seat.
3. A mourner may not lead the congregation in worship on Shabbat, *Yom Tov*, and *Chol ha-Mo'ed*, unless he is the only one qualified to do so.
4. On other occasions when *Hallel* is recited, a mourner may lead the congregation in prayer only at *Minchah* and *Ma'ariv* services, even if he is observing *yahrzeit*.

5. On a holy day, when *kohanim* "duchen" (recite the priestly blessing in unison before the Holy Ark), a mourner who is a *kohen* should leave the synagogue before the priestly blessing, unless he is the only *kohen* who is present. Some authorities permit the *kohen* to "duchen" on the grounds this is a divine imperative of love rather than an opportunity for personal pleasure.

6. During Sukkot, a mourner should not perform *hakafot* with *lulav* and *etrog*. However, one leading authority permits these *hakafot* on *Yom Tov* and Hoshanah Rabbah.

7. If a mourner accepts a *hakafah* on Simchat Torah, he should not participate in the singing and dancing.

8. On Purim, a mourner may send *mishloach manot* to one person only. He/she should eat the festive meal with the close family only. A teacher may remain at a Purim party with his students.

9. A teacher may receive gifts on Chanukah, and may remain at the party given by his students.

If One Is Notified of a Death More Than Thirty Days After The Burial

1. If the delayed tidings refer to the death of a *parent*, one should briefly remove one's shoes or sit on a low stool. Other rules of *shiv'ah* and *sheloshim* do not apply. However, the twelve-month period of restriction still applies.

2. If delayed tidings refer to one of the other close relatives for whom one must mourn, one need only remove one's shoes briefly or sit on a low stool.

3. If the delayed tidings reached one on Shabbat, *Yom Tov*, or *Chol ha-Mo'ed*, the brief demonstration of formal mourning takes place after they have ended.

4. If the delayed tidings arrived during worship, the brief demonstration of formal mourning takes place after the completion of the worship.

5. If one did not mourn briefly on the day of notification, one should do so on the next day.

YUD BET CHODESH RESTRICTIONS

As we pointed out earlier, most of the restrictions which apply during the *sheloshim* period of mourning for other close relatives also apply for the *yud bet chodesh* period of mourning for our parents.

In some instances the restrictions upon us when we mourn for our parents are greater throughout the *entire* twelve months than they are during the thirty days of mourning for other close relatives. In other instances, however, after the *sheloshim*, the restrictions are relaxed. For the sake of clarity we shall summarize the instances where the *yud bet chodesh* restrictions are greater than *sheloshim* restrictions, and where they are less severe. Where the restrictions are unchanged we shall not reiterate them, since they can be found in the halakhic summary of the *sheloshim* restrictions.

YUD BET CHODESH RESTRICTIONS: HALAKHIC CHECKLIST

Computing the *Yud Bet Chodesh*

1. The mourning period for a deceased parent is twelve *full* Jewish calendar months.
2. In computing the termination of the *yud bet chodesh*, we do not regard part of the day as equivalent to a complete day. On the contrary, the mourning continues to the *end* of the day which completes the twelve-month period.

Where *Yud Bet Chodesh* Is Less Severe Than *Sheloshim*

Personal Hygiene and Grooming.

1. One can take a haircut after the end of *sheloshim* when one's unkempt appearance becomes socially unacceptable or interferes with one's business (*she-yiga'aru bo*—when colleagues protest one's appearance).
2. The usual standard for collegial protest is *either* three months from the time of the last haircut—including the full *sheloshim* period—or the advent of a major festival following the conclusion of *sheloshim*.

3. If a delayed haircut will really jeopardize one's business, one may take a haircut earlier.
4. A community spokesman may take a haircut even during *sheloshim* (or even *shiv'ah*) to enhance his efforts on behalf of the community.
5. An unkempt mustache may be trimmed earlier to facilitate eating.
6. In the case of *shaving*, the standard for collegial protest is more lenient than for taking a haircut. Thus one can shave immediately after *sheloshim*.
7. All other restrictions on personal hygiene and grooming fall away, such as those on bathing, trimming nails, and applying cosmetics.

New Purchases

1. The *sheloshim* restrictions on new purchases remain in force.
2. However, if one runs out of wearable clothing, new outerwear may be purchased and worn, provided that—
3. The new clothes are worn for a day or two by somebody else before the mourner puts them on.
4. Clothing may be dry-cleaned after the *sheloshim*.

Entertainment and Social Gatherings

1. One may address the formula of condolence to a mourner for his/her parent at any point before the end of the twelve-month period.
2. A *mohel, sandek,* father, or grandfather who is mourning the loss of a parent may fully partake of the meal following a *brit millah* after the termination of *sheloshim*.
3. The stricter school of halakhic authority allows a mourner for a parent to celebrate a *se'udat mitzvah* only at the conclusion of *his own* study of a tractate of Talmud after *sheloshim*. The more lenient school permits him to attend a celebration of somebody else's study also.
4. The stricter school allows mourners for parents after *sheloshim* to attend other *se'udot mitzvah* (such as *bar/bat*

mitzvahs) only in the presence of other extenuating circumstances, such as the pain of their absence to the celebrant and the prohibition of public mourning on the Sabbath. The lenient school requires no such extenuating circumstances after the conclusion of *sheloshim*.

5. Group excursions for business purposes are always permitted after *sheloshim*, if colleagues insist and the main purpose is business rather than pleasure.

6. A mourner for a parent may attend a fund-raising dinner in aid of a worthy charity, and may even be its guest of honor, after the termination of *sheloshim*.

7. A woman in mourning for a parent may accompany her husband to a social gathering after the termination of her *sheloshim*, if her absence will cause him real embarrassment.

8. Some authorities permit a mourner for a parent to receive *mishlo'ach manot* on *Purim* after the termination of *sheloshim*.

Marriages and Wedding Celebrations

1. *Getting married.* A bride or groom who mourn a parent may marry after *sheloshim*, even in the absence of those extenuating circumstances which enable them to marry during the *sheloshim*.

2. *Attending a wedding.* A mourner for a parent may attend a wedding ceremony in a synagogue after the termination of *sheloshim*.

3. *Attending sheva berakhot.* After *sheloshim*, a mourner for a parent may take full part in a *sheva berakhot* celebration on a Shabbat or *Yom Tov*, whether or not they would be permitted to attend the wedding itself during *sheloshim*.

Where the *Yud Bet Chodesh* Is More Severe Than *Sheloshim*

1. A minor who becomes *bar/bat mitzvah* during *shiv'ah* or *sheloshim* is not bound by their restrictions. Nevertheless, a minor who becomes *bar/bat mitzvah* during the twelve-

month period following the death of a parent is bound
(after attaining religious maturity) by the *yud bet chodesh*
restrictions.

2. A mourner for the passing of a close relative (other than a
parent) may reciprocate a dinner-party invitation during
sheloshim. A mourner for a parent may not do so for the
full twelve-month period.

THE *KADDISH*

The recitation of the *Kaddish* by mourners at public worship
services—morning, afternoon, and evening—is one of the most
striking characteristics of the Jewish response to the death of a loved
one.

It is significant that the Mourner's *Kaddish* makes no reference to
death or dying. The Mourner's *Kaddish* is simply an ancient hymn
of praise to the Almighty. In fact, it is but one of five versions of this
moving paean of praise.

A shorter version, the half *Kaddish,* indicates the conclusion of a
minor section of the public prayer service. The full *Kaddish* is
sometimes referred to as the *Kaddish Titkabbel,* on account of the
inclusion of a stanza which pleads with God to accept our prayers.
For this reason, it is recited at the end of each segment of our public
worship. *Kaddish D'Rabbanan* includes a stanza which is directed
to the well-being of those who study and teach Torah. This version
of the *Kaddish* is recited at the end of a lesson in rabbinic literature.
The only version of the *Kaddish* which makes reference to death is
the *Kaddish D'Itchadeta'a,* which is recited at the conclusion of one
or more tractates of the Talmud, and after burial. And even in this
case the reference to death is oblique. It is made in a general prayer
for the ultimate establishment of God's Kingdom on earth, the messianic era, which is characterized by the restoration of Jerusalem in
its pristine spiritual glory, the rebuilding of the Temple and the
reinstitution of the Temple services, the disappearance of all forms
of idolatry and false religion, and ultimately, the resurrection of the
dead.

The origin of the *Kaddish* is shrouded in mystery. It has been
suggested that it was composed following the destruction of the

First Temple and the exile of the Jewish people to Babylon. Its authors sought to console the population with their faith that, although God's ways are inscrutable and His creatures suffer inexplicable setbacks, His plan for His world will eventually be realized in the messianic restoration. By expressing this profound faith, our sages publicly sanctified His great Name.

So moved was the general populace by the magnificent cadences of this great hymn of praise and awesome declaration of faith that it was recited in the language of the common man in ancient Israel—Aramaic. So popular and beloved did it become in its original form that all efforts to translate it into languages which replaced Aramaic as the common language of the Jewish people were vigorously resisted.

It is probable that the earliest version of this prayer was the form which was recited after studying a portion of rabbinic literature, praising the Giver of Torah and praying for its devotees. On the principle that one should honor those who teach the Torah in the same way as one honors the Torah itself, the epilogue to the Torah text eventually became the epilogue to its teachers. Tractate *Soferim*, in fact, records that the rabbinic *Kaddish* came to be recited at the conclusion of the *shiv'ah* observances following the passing of a great sage.

Not surprisingly, in consequence of our belief in the unique and infinite value of *every* human being, the distinction between sages and simple people was eradicated. The *Kaddish,* in a form appropriate to all Jews, became the epilogue of every Jewish life. Also, not surprisingly, the *Kaddish D'Itchadeta'a,* which was recited at the conclusion of the study of a talmudic tractate or tractates, came to be recited at the interment of every Jew. The Jew is, in many respects, likened to the Torah. The elements of his soul correspond to the number of its books, and the destruction of the Torah, like the passing of a Jew, is marked by the rending of the garments of the mourners. It was eminently reasonable, then, that the epilogue of the Torah should serve as the epilogue of members of that people which treasures it above all else.

The association of the *Kaddish* with bereavement is not exhausted by its historical origins. The infinite worth of the human being derives from his having been created in the image of God. With the passing of every human being there is, as it were, a diminution of the divine image. This is compensated for by our declaring: "Magnified and sanctified be Thy great Name in the world which Thou didst create in accordance with Thy will."

It has been well said elsewhere that there is an additional dimension to the *Kaddish*. It reflects the defiant, triumphant faith of Job, who declared, in response to his terrible, undeserved suffering, "Yea, though He slay me, I shall nevertheless trust in Him" (Job 13:15). God's ways are inscrutable to us, and often appear to challenge us to disbelief. The sufferings of the righteous, the sudden termination of a life which is full of promise, with dreams unrealized and hopes unfulfilled, the passing of a loved one without whose presence life appears barren and bereft of meaning—all these can shake our faith in the beneficent Creator. Instead, our response is the sanctification of His Name, perhaps reluctantly—even defiantly—at first, but, by dint of daily repetition, in loving reconciliation in the end. Subliminally, at least, we begin to respond to the lesson of the *Kaddish*. The world is His. He created it, and directs it according to His will, with infinite, surpassing wisdom. Although the workings of His wisdom are beyond us, although it is not clear why individuals and even nations suffer and perish, we become convinced that, ultimately, His kingdom will be established on earth, and that suffering will have been recompensed. In the light of the glory of the end, the means to its attainment, unreasonable in the short term, will eventually be perceived as having been eminently reasonable. To this extent, the *Kaddish* is not only a hymn of praise (*tushbechata*), but also a song of consolation (*nechemata*).

Our consolation is heightened by the requirement that the *Kaddish* be recited publicly, in a *minyan*. We soon see that we are not alone. Others share our pain. Other people are also tormented by grief, and join us in our recitation of the *Kaddish*. Our anguish is not isolated. We are part of a community of the bereaved, which is united in its experience of the most inescapable aspect of life—its inexorable termination.

The *Kaddish* has an additional purpose which is, perhaps, of overriding significance in the context of our grieving for a loved one. Apart from our personal spiritual immortality, to which reference was made in an earlier chapter, we receive an additional measure of immortality through our children. If our children personify the ideals for which we stand, our values live in them. A child who sanctifies the Name of God reflects the values of his parents. In a real sense, then, we are judged by the conduct of our children. This judgment extends into the realm of the metaphysical. The ultimate divine judgment to which our parents are subject beyond the grave depends upon the manner in which we sanctify his Name.

It is for this reason that a bereft child recites the *Kaddish* for eleven months only. An ancient tradition has it that divine judgment never extends beyond a year. Our filial piety is reflected in our confidence that our parents are judged worthy of His reward before the termination of the judgment period.

There are at least three clear implications in this treatment of the *Kaddish:*

1. If parents are judged through the deeds of their children, there can be no proxy sanctification of God's name by a "hired *Kaddish.*" If one is physically able to do so, one should regularly recite the *Kaddish* oneself. It is absurd to believe that a proxy can be paid to pray for one.
2. If the purpose of the regular recitation of the *Kaddish* is to reflect the value system of the departed and to affect their ultimate Judgment, mourners should not confine themselves to the *Kaddish* as the exclusive means of sanctifying God's name. They should avail themselves of *every* opportunity of sanctifying His great Name in public. This object is attained by living righteously, by giving charity generously, and by fixing times for spiritual growth through the regular study of the Torah. In the final analysis, these means of sanctifying the Name of God are by no means inferior to the regular recitation of the *Kaddish* and the leadership of public worship. On the contrary, without them, the *Kaddish* alone is an inadequate mode of sanctification.
3. Since the *Kaddish* also serves to compensate for the diminution of His image with the passing of a human being, it should be regularly recited even in the absence of a surviving child. It is only under such circumstances that a substitute should be found—and even recompensed—to serve this purpose.

MOURNER'S *KADDISH*: HALAKHIC CHECKLIST

1. The *Kaddish* should be recited regularly. One should ignore the clear instruction of the deceased that *Kaddish* need not be said.

2. A son, even under *bar mitzvah, must* say *Kaddish* for the first eleven months of his twelve-month period of mourning. A daughter is not obliged to do so. However, she may, should she so wish, recite the *Kaddish* while male mourners are doing so.

3. A son who has received late tidings of his parent's passing must say *Kaddish* until the end of the eleventh month. If he hears of his/her passing during the twelfth month, he should say *Kaddish* throughout that month. If he hears after the end of the twelfth month, he is not obligated to say *Kaddish.*

4. If the deceased left no son, his/her other close relatives are obligated to say the *Kaddish.* Any one of them may choose to continue to say the *Kaddish* thrice daily after *sheloshim,* and until *one week* before the end of the twelve-month period.

5. A stepson or adopted son may say *Kaddish.*

6. A person whose parents are alive may say *Kaddish* for someone else only with the expressed permission of his parents.

7. A person other than the son of the deceased, who is saying *Kaddish,* should do so for eleven months and three weeks.

8. Ideally, one should hire a person to say *Kaddish* for the deceased only if one knows that he is, simultaneously, saying *Kaddish* for nobody else.

LEADING PUBLIC WORSHIP

We have seen that the regular, thrice-daily recitation of *Kaddish* by a mourner is not the only way in which he can publicly sanctify God's Name. He can—if he is able to do so with fluency and understanding of what he is saying—also lead public worship services on non-holy days. (We have already designated the occasions when a mourner may not lead the services.)

Since it is likely that several qualified mourners may be available to lead the services at the same time, an order of precedence has been established in order to avoid conflict.

PRECEDENCE IN LEADING PUBLIC WORSHIP: HALAKHIC CHECKLIST

1. There is special merit in a mourner's leading public worship.
2. A mourner for his parents takes precedence over one who mourns for other relatives.
3. A mourner for both parents does not take precedence over a mourner for one parent.
4. A mourner during *sheloshim* takes precedence over a mourner whose *sheloshim* period has passed.
5. A mourner whose *sheloshim* period was terminated by a *Yom Tov* has the same right to lead public worship as a mourner during *sheloshim*. The right extends for thirty days after interment.
6. A son on the *yahrzeit* of his parent has precedence in leading public worship over a mourner during his *sheloshim*..
7. If there is another synagogue in reasonably close proximity, a member of the congregation has precedence over a nonmember in leading public worship.

CHAPTER ELEVEN

From Grief to Remembrance

BRIDGING THE GAP

The Role of the Community

We have repeatedly emphasized the therapeutic effects of the Jewish rites of mourning. We achieve these effects through the *expression* of grief rather than its *repression*. Through its unreserved expression, we experience a gradual coming to grips with the reality of the separation. The Jewish process of mourning represents a step-by-step conditioning of the mourner to the full resumption of life's normal demands, activities, and responsibilites.

The participation of relatives and friends in the normalization process is a central feature of Jewish practice. The mourner is scarcely left alone during the periods of the most intense trauma and grief. He/she is made to feel fully part of a caring community.

During the paralyzing period of *aninut,* the *chevra kadisha* relieves the bereaved of much of the heavy burden of involvement in funeral arrangements. It organizes the transportation of the remains, and lovingly attends to the final cleansing, dressing, and laying out of the deceased in an appropriate casket.

Friends and family inform other friends and relatives of the time of the funeral, and are at the beck and call of the bereaved. The synagogue sends cards with *shiv'ah* arrangements to all its members.

The community prepares the meal of condolence for the mourners when they return from the interment, and helps prepare the home for the *shiv'ah* observances by covering the mirrors, arranging a room for prayers, and providing adequate supplies of food for the bereaved.

The *shiv'ah* period is the special responsibility of all sectors of the community. The *chevra kadisha* provides prayer books, head coverings, prayer shawls (*tallitot*), a portable ark, a Torah scroll, a charity box, and low chairs for the mourners. It ensures the presence of at least a *minyan* of worshippers at services in the morning, late afternoon, and evening. It arranges for a person who can lead the study of an appropriate *mishnah*, and—if necessary—for an experienced prayer-leader to conduct the worship.

Members of the community (not only the close friends of the mourners) visit the bereaved as often as possible. They do not engage in frivolous small talk, but do what they can to direct the conversation of the bereaved to the virtues of the deceased, facilitating the mourner's expression of his/her deepest feelings about his/her great loss. The discussions are of inestimable therapeutic value.

Community solidarity does not end with the termination of *shiv'ah*. People should continue to drop in, and members of the congregation should be assigned to call up several times a week for the first several months. The rabbi should indicate a sincere willingness to discuss the loss with the bereaved, and should follow up on his offer.

Attendance at daily services will reinforce the mourner's sense of communal solidarity. The fact that others are also reciting the *Kaddish* makes him or her part of an extended family of the bereaved, providing the comforting assurance that he or she is not alone, and that others empathize with his or her pain and grief. The fact that other worshippers have completed their mourning rites, and still continue to attend daily services is an encouraging reminder both that faith can be kindled in the face of death and that the days of mourning will be ended and regular   routines resumed.

Bereavement Therapy

The companionship of a caring community and the healing effects of the rites of mourning are usually adequate for coming to terms with our loss, and for helping us take the first steps toward the resumption of normal living.

In some instances, however, these factors alone are not effective in bridging the gap from debilitating grief to healthy remembrance. In these cases, the mourners cannot accept the reality of their loss. For months after the passing of the person near and dear to them, they may fantasize about his/her presence—especially after a long, fulfilling, and mutually dependent relationship. They may "see" his face in a crowd, "hear" her key in the lock, answer his "voice," remember to bring her favorite food to "her" in the apartment, rush home to turn up the heat for her disabled "husband," and so on. Sleep patterns may be destroyed, and eating will be neglected and sporadic. The mourners may suffer loss of weight, and may become listless and depressed. Simple, routine chores, such as cleaning the apartment, may take inordinate amounts of time to accomplish. The bereaved may remain obsessed with thoughts of the departed. They may demonstrate the conflicting emotions of denial and anger, sadness and gladness—sadness at the loss, and gladness that *they* have survived—and guilt because of these confusing feelings. They may panic at their abandonment and at their imagined inability to cope alone in accomplishing unaccustomed tasks. They may perceive their future as impossibly bleak.

Children, too, may show complex, disturbed emotions—fear for their *own* survival, terror that those who take care of them may also die, guilt and anger. They may express these feelings in games, in drawings, and in sudden changes of behavior.

If these emotions and complex feelings do not gradually dissipate, bereavement therapy is called for—and should be sought out.

Some agencies in larger cities, the New York Board of Rabbis, for example, train rabbis, ministers, priests, and nurses in pastoral bereavement-counseling techniques. At no cost to the bereaved, they provide a caring, empathetic, therapeutic setting to allow the mourner to express and soon come to terms with his/her feelings. They "reflect" the feelings of the mourner, helping him/her to identify them. They react to such "theological" questions as "Why has God done this to me?" nonjudgmentally, by gently responding, "I understand how you are feeling. You are very angry." They reflect accounts of fantasies of keys turning in the lock by responding, "You are feeling so, so alone. I feel with you"—and so on. Without preaching, without offering privileged sources of "secret knowledge," without attempting to justify God, they gradually facilitate the easy expression of repressed feelings, which allows the mourner to take the first steps to normal routine. They reinforce feelings of progress, and, later in the process, offer the solace of the wisdom of their common religious tradition.

These therapeutic sessions should never take more than eight visits, each not exceeding one hour. In the overwhelming majority of cases, four sessions will suffice to help the mourner through persistent grief, and the symptoms described above will begin to disappear.

Brief bereavement therapy (which can, incidentally, be taught to sensitive, empathetic, caring, emotionally mature members of most communities) may be the final bridge between grief and remembrance. But if the symptoms do not disappear, and if the pastoral bereavement counselor does not see significant progress by the eighth session, the grief is probably pathological, and should be referred to a clinical psychologist or psychiatrist for further treatment.

LASTING REMEMBRANCES

Kever Avot: Graveside Visits of Prayer and Remembrance

There are four compelling reasons for periodic visits to the graves of people we love. The first is to express our ongoing respect and esteem, to indicate that though they are no longer with us in the flesh, our beloved departed are neither out of mind nor totally out of sight. The second is to reinforce memory with contact. The third, during the twelve-month period following their passing, is to pray for the elevation of their souls. The fourth is to pray to Almighty God in their presence, as it were, invoking their merit, and transforming our prayer into a prayer which joins the generations, and transcends the divisions wrought by death.

In this connection it is most important to bear in mind that we never pray to the dead. That is utterly forbidden. We pray directly to God in their presence and in their merit. We reject the notion of prayer through mediators as being totally un-Jewish in character.

Our periodic visits to the graves of our near and dear ones are made more meaningful by our recitation of special meditations.°

° See below, p. 249.

Our contact with our beloved departed is symbolized by our touching the monument or grave (if, of course, we are not *kohanim*). The grass or sod we leave on the grave before we end our visits reminds us again of the transient, ephemeral, impermanent nature of life, and of our own vulnerability. The stone which is often placed on the monument or grave is our symbolic "calling card."

KEVER AVOT: HALAKHIC CHECKLIST

Whose Graves Are Visited?

1. One visits the graves of departed parents, primarily, but also those of departed relatives for whom one is obligated to observe *shiv'ah*.
2. A woman who has remarried following the death of her first husband may visit his grave only if such a visit will cause no hurt or offence to her second husband. A man may visit the grave of his first wife only if such a visit will neither hurt nor offend his second wife.
3. The students of a great Torah sage should visit his grave.

When to Schedule Visits

1. Visits are often made at the conclusion of the *shiv'ah* period.
   a. If *shiv'ah* ends on the Sabbath, *kever avot* is scheduled on the next day (Sunday).
   b. If *shiv'ah* ends on a festival or is cancelled by a festival, *kever avot* is scheduled on the first day after the festival (*isru chag*). Some people postpone the *kever avot* to the conclusion of the *sheloshim* if the *shiv'ah* ends or is cancelled by the first days of Pesach or Sukkot.

2. *Kever avot* visits are scheduled at the end of the *sheloshim* period.
   a. If that period ends on a Sabbath, the visit can be scheduled either the following day (Sunday) or the previous day (Friday).

b. If the *sheloshim* period ends on a *Yom Tov* other than Pesach or Sukkot, the visit is scheduled on the day after the *Yom Tov* (*isru chag*).

c. If the *sheloshim* period ends on the first day of Pesach or Sukkot, the visit is scheduled on the day *before* the festival.

3. *Kever avot* visits are scheduled on the *yahrzeit* of the departed.

a. If the *yahrzeit* occurs on the Sabbath, the visit is scheduled the preceding Friday or the following Sunday.

b. If the *yahrzeit* occurs on the first days of Pesach or Sukkot, the visit is scheduled on the first day before the festival.

c. If the *yahrzeit* occurs on another festival, the visit is scheduled on *isru chag*.

4. *Kever avot* visits are often scheduled on the Ninth of Av and on the eve of Rosh ha-Shanah and Yom Kippur. Sefardic Jews schedule visits on the eve of the months of Elul and Nissan.

5. *Kever avot* visits may be scheduled even on those days when the *El-Malei Rachamim* prayer is not said.° A beautiful prayer is substituted.†

6. *Kever avot* visits are *not* scheduled on ha-Moed.

The Blessing on Visiting a Jewish Cemetery

1. One washes one's hands before entering the cemetery, and again as soon as one leaves.

2. If one has not visited a Jewish cemetery for a period of at least thirty days, one recites a special blessing and prayer when one crosses within six and a half feet of a grave.°

3. If one sees a Jewish cemetery at a distance or through a

° See below, p. 167.
† See below, pp. 232 ff.
° See below, p. 222.

window, one does not recite the blessing. However, since one *did*, in fact, see the cemetery, one does not recite the blessing if one again comes into a Jewish cemetery within thirty days.
4. If one carried the casket or was part of a funeral procession, one does not say the blessing, because one who is busy with a *mitzvah* is exempted from performing another *mitzvah* simultaneously. However, since one did, in fact, see a Jewish cemetery, one does not recite the blessing if one again comes into a Jewish cemetery within thirty days.
5. This blessing is made upon seeing a Jewish cemetery, and not upon seeing only a single Jewish grave.

Procedures at the Graveside

1. A moving meditation is recited. Spontaneous prayers may be added.†
2. One places one's left hand on the grave (or memorial monument) and recites: "And the Lord shall guide you continually and satisfy your soul in drought, and make strong your bones; and you shall be like a watered garden and like a spring of water whose waters fail not" (Isaiah 58:11). "Rest in peace until He cometh who comforts and announces peace."
3. One places some grass and sod on the grave, or a small stone on the memorial monument.
4. One should behave with reverence and respect. Jokes and small talk are inappropriate and in bad taste.
5. One should not visit a cemetery twice in the same day.

Yizkor: The Holy Day Remembrance

Mourning is both the most personal and the most universal of our experiences. It is the most personal of experiences because of our unique relationship with those we mourn. It is the most universal of experiences because there is nobody who is not confronted by the painful disruption of a precious relationship by death's intrusion. Our *kever avot* and *yahrzeit* observances reflect the personal nature

°†See below, p. 250.

of our remembrance. The *yizkor* (memorial) service reflects our remembrance as part of a community of the bereaved.

The practice of collective remembrance of our departed ancestors is very old. It is mentioned in the Second Book of Maccabees (12:44) and in several early rabbinic sources. In all likelihood, the *yizkor* service was originally held on Yom Kippur only. As late as the year 1208 C.E., the *Machzor Vitry*, a primary source of our liturgy, mentions the *yizkor* exclusively on the Day of Atonement.

Characteristically, its original purpose was not merely sentimental remembrance. Its central feature was the commitment of the living to offer charity in memory of the departed, reflecting the view that the meritorious behavior of surviving descendants assists in the spiritual elevation of the souls of departed ancestors. On the Day of Atonement, therefore, remembrance by children of their parents through acts of loving-kindness achieves atonement for them.

The association of charity with *yizkor* accounts for its later (eighteenth century) introduction into the pilgrim festival services—on the last day of Pesach and Shavuot and on Shemini Atzeret (the Eighth day of Solemn Assembly). On those days the scriptural reading ends with a call for donations (*matnat yad*).

> Three times a year shall all your males appear before the Lord your God in the place which He shall choose: on the feast of unleavened bread, and on the feast of weeks, and on the feast of Tabernacles; and they shall not appear before the Lord empty-handed. Every man shall give as he is able, according to the blessing of the Lord your God which He has given you. (Deuteronomy 16:16–17)

It would appear that the names of community martyrs were originally read during the memorial serivces. In time, these death rolls (called *kuntresim* or *memorbucher* or *yizkerbucher*) came to include the names of the other members of the community, and eventually, comparatively recently, evolved to the point of becoming memorial prayers for individuals.

Our custom reflects all three stages of the development of the memorial service. The *yizkor* paragraphs recited by individuals make specific mention of individual departed members of our families. The *El-Malei Rachamim* prayer, recited by the cantor or prayer leader, makes collective mention of departed members of the community, of victims of the Nazi Holocaust, and of the fallen defenders of the State of Israel. The *Av ha-Rachamim* prayer, with which the *yizkor* service concludes, was probably composed as a eulogy for the Jewish communities which were wiped out during the first Crusade in 1096. It has now become a memorial prayer for the martyrs of every period of Jewish history. Always the concluding segment of *yizkor*, this prayer was originally also recited on the Sabbaths preceding Shavuot and Tisha B'Av. This remains the custom of Jews originating in Southwestern Germany. Most other Ashkenazic Jewish communities recite this prayer on all Sabbaths—except as indicated in our halakhic summary of *yahrzeit* observances.°

YIZKOR REMEMBRANCE: HALAKHIC CHECKLIST

1. One is obligated to recite *yizkor* for deceased parents, but may also do so for other relatives (even minors) and for friends.
2. The *yizkor* service is held after the Torah reading on Yom Kippur, the last day of Pesach, the second day of Shavuot, and on Shemini Atzeret.
3. An Israeli, temporarily in the diaspora, should follow the diaspora dates of *yizkor*, i.e., the eighth day of Pesach and the second day of Shavuot, as well as the shared dates of Yom Kippur and Shemini Atzeret.
4. A memorial light should burn in one's home or in one's synagogue on Yom Kippur in memory of the departed.
5. On the pilgrim festivals it may be kindled from a pre-existing flame even during the day. For Yom Kippur, it must be kindled before the fast begins.
6. In the absence of a candle, an electric memorial light, switched on prior to the holy day, may be used.
7. The essence of the *yizkor* memorial is the commitment to give charity in memory of the departed.

8. The names of several individuals can be included in a single memorial prayer. The Ashkenazic custom is to refer to the deceased by his/her given name and that of his/her father. The Sefardic custom is to refer to the deceased by his/her given name and that of his/her mother.

9. *Yizkor* is recited even during the year of mourning for one's parents, even though it may stimulate grief and anguish not in keeping with the festive mood.

10. A child below *bar/bat mitzvah* should recite *yizkor* if he/she understands its purpose.

11. *Yizkor* may be recited for a first husband/wife even after one's remarriage.

12. In the overwhelming majority of communities, children with parents still living leave the synagogue during *yizkor*—for two reasons:
    a. Not to constitute a separate group within the community of the bereaved.
    b. Not to identify themselves prematurely as mourners, lest their doing so become a self-fulfilling prophecy (*ayin ha-ra*).
    In some few communities they remain in synagogue—also for two reasons:
    a. To pray for the good health of their parents.
    b. To include themselves among the mourners for our martyrs throughout the ages.

13. Although memorial prayers are part of communal worship, there is no technical requirement of a *minyan*, and the *yizkor* recitations can be made privately.

14. There is no "statute of limitations" on the *yizkor* observance for parents. Their children continue to observe *yizkor* throughout the course of their lives.

15. *Yizkor* is recited even for unworthy, sinful parents—for whom it is especially efficacious.

Yahrzeit: An Annual Remembrance

Anniversaries are natural occasions for remembrance. The anniversary of the passing of someone near and dear, the *yahrzeit*, is no exception. It evokes bittersweet emotions. Echoes of voices long silenced are still heard. Images of experiences once shared crowd in upon us. Smiling faces, never fully erased from our memory, capture our attention. Special gestures, special customs, special scenes are especially vivid on *yahrzeit* days. We relive pleasant occasions, and, sadly, relive times of sadness too. When it is possible to do so, we visit the graves of our loved ones at such times, allowing our stream of consciousness to join us to them through the miracle of memory.

But the *yahrzeit* of a person near and dear to us is more than just an occasion for sentiment and sadness. It reestablishes links which transcend the passing of time, links which are forged by the ongoing acceptance of responsibility for those we love—even beyond the grave.

We have already discussed the Jewish view of the immortality of the soul, our unshakeable conviction that conscious life continues beyond the death of the body. Disembodied life occurs in a realm which we call *heaven*. Heaven is not a place. It is a state of being, unrestricted by our bodies, unimpeded by pain and illness. But heaven is not a monolithic, undifferentiated state. It has more and less desirable gradations, which are defined in terms of their nearness to God—the Ground of all Being. Closeness to God bestows existence in its fullest sense. Distance from Him represents diminution of existence. "Hell," therefore, in the Jewish view, is nothing more and nothing less than being absolutely cut off from His presence. It is the total absence of existence.

In our analysis of the *Kaddish*, and elsewhere, we pointed out that those who are near and dear to us are judged by our actions. If our lives reflect fine values, *their* lives are justified by the good qualities which they transmitted to us.

Our mystic tradition maintains that the initial judgment of our loved ones takes place within twelve months of their passing. However, it also holds that the elevation of their souls at that time is not final. Through *our* continued commitment to our faith and our unceasing pursuit of good deeds, we help assure their continued progress through the heavenly spheres, enhancing their existence as they draw ever nearer to God—the Source of all existence. The same mystic tradition has it that the spiritual progression of our beloved departed takes place in annual stages, and that their progress is determined on each *yahrzeit*.

It is for this reason that our *yahrzeit* observances are marked by attitudes of penitence, study of Torah, acts of loving-kindness, the public sanctification of the Divine Name through the recitation of *Kaddish* and the leading of public worship, and by the renewal of faith-commitments.

YAHRZEIT OBSERVANCES: HALAKHIC CHECKLIST

For Whom Is *Yahrzeit* Observed?

1. One is obligated to observe *yahrzeit* only for one's parents, but may elect to do so for others, especially if nobody else does so.
2. One is not obligated to observe the *yahrzeit* of a minor.
3. The *yahrzeit* of a spouse from a previous marriage should not be observed openly by lighting a candle if this will cause hurt and resentment to one's new spouse.

Computing the *Yahrzeit* Date

1. If burial took place within three days of death, the first *yahrzeit* is observed on the Jewish calendar anniversary of the *passing*.
2. If the burial took place more than three days after the passing, the first *yahrzeit* is observed according to the Jewish calendar on the anniversary of the *burial*.
3. *All* subsequent *yahrzeits* are observed on the anniversary of the passing.
4. The *yahrzeit* is computed according to the time zone in which the death occured.
5. If the death occurred during the evening twilight, the *yahrzeit* date is computed as of the following day.
6. If only the date of burial is known, but not the date of

death, the *yahrzeit* will be the Jewish calendar anniversary of the date of burial.

7. If neither the date of death nor the date of burial is
known, a Hebrew date, other than the *yahrzeit* of the
other parent, should be chosen as the *yahrzeit* date, and
kept consistently each year. In this event, the mourner
may not take precedence over one who is observing an
actual yahrzeit in respect to leading the service, being
called to the Torah, etc.

8. *Yahrzeit* computations *can* be complicated by peculiari-
ties of the Jewish calendar—notably by the insertion of a
second Adar month in Jewish leap years (seven times in
every cycle of nineteen years)—and by the fact that the
number of days in some months is not always consistent,
as follows:

When Death Occurred in the Month of Adar

Of a Leap Year

1. The first *yahrzeit* is observed on the day and month of
passing—or burial (see "Computing the *Yahrzeit* date,"
item 1 or 2)—even though thirteen months may have
passed since the demise. (In this case the laws of mourning have not applied during the thirteenth month.)

2. The *yahrzeit* date will subsequently be the day and
month of passing—in a leap year on the appropriate
Adar, and in the only Adar of a regular year.

3. But if death occurred on the thirtieth day of the first
Adar, and the following year was *not* a leap year, since
Adar has only twenty-nine days in a regular year, *yahr-
zeit* is observed on Rosh Chodesh Nisan.

Of a Regular Year

1. In subsequent *regular* years the *yahrzeit* is established in
accordance with "Computing the *Yahrzeit* Date," items
1 and 2.

2. In subsequent *leap* years, the custom varies. Some establish the *yahrzeit* date in the first Adar, and others in both

Adars. One should be consistent in one's custom.

3. If the death occurred on the first day of Rosh Chodesh Adar, since that day is really the thirtieth of Shevat, in a leap year, *yahrzeit* will be observed on the first day of Rosh Chodesh on the *first* Adar only.

When Death Occurred on Rosh Chodesh Kislev or Rosh Chodesh Tevet

1. If the death occurred in a year with only one day of Rosh Chodesh, in a subsequent year with two days of Rosh Chodesh, *yahrzeit* is observed on the second day (since the first day probably belongs to the previous month).
2. If the death occurred on the *first day* of Rosh Chodesh, and the anniversary year has only one day of Rosh Chodesh, *yahrzeit* is nonetheless observed on Rosh Chodesh.

Yahrzeit Observances

1. A candle should burn in every residence where children observe the *yahrzeit* of their parents. It should be kindled before sunset, burn for the entire day until it goes out on its own.
2. On the first *yahrzeit*, the restrictions of the *yud bet chodesh* period of mourning continue.
3. In subsequent years, one does not attend a wedding or become married on a parent's *yahrzeit*.
4. Many people fast on the *yahrzeit*, unless it occurs on a day when *Tachanun* is omitted,° during the seven festive days following one's marriage, or if one is the father, *mohel*, or *sandek* of a male child entering the covenant of circumcision. The father and the *kohen* presiding at a *pidyon ha-ben* (redemption of the firstborn son) are exempted from fasting. One who celebrates his own completion of a rabbinic text (*siyyum*) is also exempted. The fast is initiated by its formal acceptance in the afternoon prayer preceding the *yahrzeit*. However one fasts

See below, p. 167.

even in the absence of the formal acceptance if fasting is an annual custom.

5. It is customary to receive an *aliyah* to the Torah on the day of or closest to the *yahrzeit* of a parent.

6. It is customary to have the memorial prayer recited after the Torah reading closest to the *yahrzeit*. This *El-Malei Rachamim* prayer is omitted at the following times:

a. Rosh Chodesh
b. Chanukah
c. The fifteenth of Shevat
d. The two days of Purim
e. The fourteenth and fifteenth of Adar Rishon
f. The entire month of Nisan
g. The fourteenth of Iyyar
h. Lag Ba-Omer
i. From the first to the thirteenth of Sivan
j. On the fifteenth of Av
k. On the eve of Rosh ha-Shanah
l. On the eve of Yom Kippur
m. From Yom Kippur to Sukkot
n. From Sukkot to Rosh Chodesh Cheshvan
o. When there is a *brit millah* in the synagogue and the father, *mohel,* or *sandek* worship there on that day
p. When a groom is in synagogue on the day of his wedding or during the seven days following
q. On Shabbat when the new month is blessed
r. On the four special *Shabbatot—Zakhor, Parah, Shekalim,* and *ha-Chodesh* (on the latter two the new month is blessed anyway).
s. During festivals and *Chol ha-Mo'ed*—except when *yizkor* is recited.

7. Although several names may be included in the same memorial prayer, it is customary to recite separate memorial prayers for each person near and dear to one.

8. It is customary to visit the graves of parents on their *yahrzeit* unless the expense of doing so is too great. If the *yahrzeit* occurs when the memorial prayer is *not* said, the visit can be made before or after the actual *yahrzeit*, but

as close as possible to it. Special recitations are made at the graveside.° Only the recitation of the *Kaddish* requires a *minyan*.

9. In the absence of another mourner in the synagogue, a son leads the worship on Saturday evening prior to his parent's *yahrzeit*.

10. A son has precedence over other worshippers in leading worship on the *yahrzeit* of his parents.

11. If one accidentally forgot to observe *yahrzeit*, one may do so on another day, as soon as the omission becomes known.

12. It is customary to study Mishnah texts on the *Yahrzeit* date. A selection is appended.†

The Memorial Monument: A Lasting Remembrance

The consecration of a lasting monument at the grave of a person near and dear is a custom which has been sanctified by time, and which originates in the biblical period: "And Rachel died, and was on the way to Ephrat, which is Bethlehem. And Jacob set a monument by her grave; that is the monument of Rachel's grave unto this very day" (Genesis 35:19–10).

The classical sources of Judaism have three names for graveside monuments, each reflecting a different purpose for their erection. The first word used by the Torah (as in the reference to Rachel's grave, above) is *matze'vah*—that which is lasting or firmly established. In this sense the memorial is to be a lasting remembrance, marking a burial place for visitation and for prayer.

Prophetic literature refers to a graveside monument as a *tziyyun*—a marker. In this sense its purpose is to indicate to *kohanim* that they must stay away from the site in order to avoid ritual defilement. If the perimeter of the grave was clearly marked, these markings (a so-called brass bed, plant-lined edges, or a slab covering the entire grave) would serve this particular function of the monument.

The designation for a graveside monument in rabbinic literature is *nefesh*—a soul. This refers to a monument, sometimes even a

° See below, pp. 248 ff.
† See below, p. 281.

most elaborate structure, erected over the grave as a token of respect for the soul of the departed, which was believed to frequent the area. In time, probably in response to the injunction of Rabban Gamliel that rich and poor should not be differentiated by death, the tendency developed to simplify the nature of graveside monuments. Although the injunction of Rabban Gamliel originally aimed at providing all Jews with uniform and inexpensive shrouds, the extension of the principle to the type of monuments erected in Jewish cemeteries is a welcome development. The creation of "forests" of expensive granite and marble is a shameful waste of money which can be usefully directed to charitable purposes.

A simple stone, modest in size, easily visible, and meaningfully inscribed, fulfills all three purposes of the graveside monument. It clearly marks the grave; it is a token of respect for the departed; and it is a lasting remembrance.

Interestingly, the inscriptions on centuries-old monuments have provided historians with otherwise unobtainable information about many master builders of Jewish history.

THE GRAVESIDE MONUMENT: HALAKHIC CHECKLIST

1. The graves of all Jews, even minors, should be clearly marked.
2. Although it is not common practice to demarcate the individual burial sites of buried body parts, of infants who have survived for less than thirty days, and of stillborn and aborted fetuses, the section of the cemetery where these remains are buried should be clearly marked off, so that *kohanim* will avoid ritual defilement.
3. If the estate of the deceased does not suffice for the erection of a suitable monument, the children should defray expenses from their personal resources, since the commandment of honoring parents extends beyond the grave.
4. If both parents die and the children can afford only one stone, it is consecrated to the parent who died first.
5. One should ignore any prior request of a deceased parent

not to erect a stone in his or her memory. The erection of a small, simple monument is the best compromise in such a situation.

6. The monument should be erected as soon as possible after the end of *shiv'ah* period. Many authorities object to the widespread custom of delaying the erection for twelve months. That custom is rationalized by its supporters on the grounds that the memory of the departed is still vivid within the twelve-month period, owing to the regular observance of various mourning practices. Only thereafter, when the normal rhythms and routines of life are resumed, is the need felt by many people for a lasting material remembrance.

7. The inscriptions on Jewish tombstones are almost as varied as the people they memorialize, and as those who compose them. What they have in common is:

a. The monuments are simple slabs, not statuettes, etc.

b. They contain the *Hebrew* name of the deceased and his/her father's Hebrew name in the Ashkenazic tradition or his/her mother's name in the Sefardic tradition.

c. Any "added" names which were given the deceased during serious illness should be included as part of the Hebrew name only if the individual recovered from that illness.

d. The date of death on the *Jewish* calendar.

e. The first line of the inscription usually consists of the two Hebrew letters *peh* and *nun*, abbreviating the sentence *poh nitman*, "here is buried."

f. The end of the inscription usually consists of the Hebrew letters *tav, nun, tzadik, bet* and *heh*, abbreviating the words *tehei nafsho(ah) tzerurah bitzror hachayyim*, "may his/her soul be bound up in the band of life."

g. Additional inscriptions, should they be desired, should be appropriate descriptions of the deceased for whom they will serve as a lasting memorial. These descriptions may be in Hebrew and in the vernacular.

8. The names of relatives who have disappeared and are

presumed dead, as in the case of Holocaust victims may be added to the monument of, say, a parent.

9. One may erect a monument to honor a person whose actual burial place is unknown, as in the case of a victim of the Holocaust.

10. It is permissible to erect a double monument, if only one grave is presently used. When the second grave is used, the second inscription may be added, without obliterating the words on the first, even if smaller letters must be used in the space left over after the first inscription.

11. A moving series of prayers, psalms, readings, and a short eulogy are recited at the service of consecration of a tombstone.°

12. A person who has remarried may attend the service of the consecration of the monument of the deceased spouse, if it will not cause real hurt or deep resentment to the new spouse.

13. The service of consecration should not be scheduled on a day when *Tachanun* is not said,° nor thirty days before a festival.

14. One should not lean or sit upon or derive any benefit from a monument belonging to or designated for another, although it may be donated for the grave of a poor person.

15. A monument erected in error at the wrong gravesite may be relocated to its appropriate location.

° See below, p. 241.
° See above, p. 84.

Glossary

Adar. Hebrew month. In a Jewish leap year there are two months of Adar. Purim falls on the fourteenth of Adar of a regular year. In a leap year, that date is called Purim Katan, and Purim itself is celebrated a month later, on the fourteenth of Adar II. Shushan Purim occurs on the day after Purim.

Aliyah. Ascent to the platform to read from the Torah; ascent (immigration) to Israel.

Amidah. Lit. "Standing [prayer]." The nineteen-blessing prayer par excellence of each daily worship service.

Anim Zemirot. Hymn of glory. Ecstatic mystical adoration of God.

Aninut. The period between death and burial. First stage of the mourning process.

Ashkenazi(c). Of European extraction. One of the two major segments of the Jewish people, each having its own customs (*minhagim*).

Av Hebrew month. The ninth is a solemn fast-day. The fifteenth is the anniversary of happier events.

Av ha-Rachamim. Prayer in tribute to Jewish martyrs, originating at the time of the Crusades.

Avinu Malkeinu. "Our Father, our King." A series of supplications recited on public fast-days and during the Ten Days of Penitence, between the New Year and the Day of Atonement.

Avnet. Belt, part of shrouds.

Ayin ha-Ra. Lit. "The evil eye."

Ba'al kore. Torah reader.

Ba'al tefillah. Prayer leader.

Ba'al teshuvah. Lit. "A penitent." Applied to a Jew who either returns to a life of commitment and observance or assumes such a commitment for the first time.

Bameh Madlikin. "Wherewith does one kindle [the Sabbath lights]?" A portion of the *mishnah* (chap. 2) studied during Friday evening services.

Bar Mitzvah. Attainment by a Jewish boy of religious majority, at age thirteen years and a day.

Bat Mitzvah. Attainment by a Jewish girl of religious majority, at age twelve years and a day.

173

Berakhah (pl. *berakhot*). Blessing.

Beth Din. Rabbinical court.

Bet ha-Mishteh. Lit. "House of banqueting." Place where events are celebrated by eating, drinking, and dancing to instrumental music.

Bet ha-Simchah. Lit. "House for festive occasions." Place where festive events are celebrated.

Birkat (pl. *Birkot*) *ha-Shachar.* Blessing recited at the very beginning of the morning service.

Brit [*Millah*]. Ritual circumcision. The method of entering into the covenant of Abraham.

Chametz. Leaven; forbidden on Passover.

Chanukah. The festival of lights.

Chanukat ha-Bayit. Consecration of a new home. A religiously oriented housewarming celebration.

Chatan Bereishit. Person called to begin the reading of the Torah on the festival of the Rejoicing of the Law.

Chatan Torah. Person called to complete the reading of the Torah on the festival of the Rejoicing of the Law.

Chedvat Mere'im. A group excursion; business and professional convention, whose emphasis is primarily upon good fellowship.

Chevra Kadisha. Lit. "Holy Brotherhood." The men and women who occupy themselves with preparing the dead for burial and with services to the bereaved.

Chol ha-Mo'ed. Intermediate days of the festivals of Passover and Tabernacles.

Chullin. Unconsecrated foodstuffs; in contradistinction to food which, in ancient times, was sanctified for sacrificial purposes.

Dayyan ha-Emet. Lit. "The true Judge." A blessing recited after bereavement, justifying the divine decree.

El Erekh Apayim. "God who is long-suffering." A short supplication.

El-Malei Rachamim. "God, the merciful King." The memorial prayer par excellence.

Erev. The eve of, e.g., Sabbath or festival.

Etrog. Citron; used on the festival of Tabernacles.

Gadol ha-Bayit. Head of the family.

Get. Bill of divorcement.

Goses. A dying person; one whose death is imminent, expected to occur within seventy-two hours, and who has lost his swallowing reflex.

Halakhah. Jewish law, based upon Scriptures and the Talmud, and codified in the great codes, such as Maimonides' *Mishneh Torah* and Joseph Karo's *Shulchan Arukh*. It also comprises the responses of great authorities to questions of law.

Halakhic. The adjectival form of the noun *halakhah*.

Hakafot. Processions around the synagogue.

Halbashah. Dressing the deceased.

Hallel. A collection of psalms (Psalms 113–117) recited on festivals both major and minor.

Hashkavah. Laying out the dead.

Havdallah. Blessing at the end of the Sabbath and festivals distinguishing them from work-days.

Hefker. No-man's-land. Ownerless property.

Hesped. Eulogy.

Isru chag. The day after a festival.

Kabbalat Shabbat. The introductory portion of the Friday evening service. Psalms 95–99, 29, 92, and 93. The hymn "Come, my beloved" precedes the last-mentioned two psalms.

Kaddish. Prayer of praise recited, *inter alia*, by mourners.

Kaddish d'Itchadeta'a. The *Kaddish* recited at the graveside and upon completion of a tractate of the Talmud; contains prayer for messianic age and the resurrection of the dead.

Kaddish Titkabbel. The whole *Kaddish*, signifying the end of a portion of the statutory worship service.

Karet. The divine punishment of excision, of being cut off from God's presence in the realm beyond the grave. This is absolute extinction. Some define *karet* as the divine sentence of dying childless.

Kav (pl. Kabin). A liquid measure. Nine *kabin* of water are used in the purification rites.

Keri'ah. Ritual rending of garments as an expression of grief.

Kever Avot. Lit. "Ancestral graves." The religious act of paying a graveside visit to the departed at his/her burial place.

Kiddush. Declaration of the holiness of Sabbaths and festivals; a blessing normally recited over wine. A gathering in which the foregoing ceremony is observed.

Kippah (pl. *Kippot*). Head covering, always worn by the observant and by most others during worship and Torah-study.

Kittel. White outergarment worn, *inter alia*, by the bridegroom. It is also worn at the Passover *seder* meal and on Yom Kippur. Part of the shrouds.

Kohen (pl. *kohanim*). A priest, a descendant of Aaron, brother of Moses. *Inter alia*, *kohanim* are enjoined from contact with the dead.

K'tonet. Shirt, Part of the shrouds.

Kuntres. Memorial roll of martyrs.

Lag B'Omer. The *omer* is the period of mourning between Passover and Pentecost. On the thirty-third day (*lag*), a historic tragedy ceased and it became a time of rejoicing.

La-menatze'ach. A psalm (Psalm 20) recited at the end of the morning worship.

Le-Chayyim. Lit. "To life"; a toast; a gathering of a few friends for drinks.

Likkut Atzamot. Collection of bones for reburial.

Lulav. Palm branch used in the Tabernacles worship services.

Ma'amadot. Stops in the burial procession.

Ma'avar Yabok. The classical work on death and mourning, written by Rabbi Aharon Berakhyah ben Moshe of Modena; contains mystic elements, customs, and halakhic practices.

Maimonides. The great medieval philosopher, physician, and codifier of Jewish law (1035–1104).

Mamzer. Offspring of an adulterous or incestuous union.

Massekhet. Tractate of Talmud.

Matnat yad. Offering.

Matzevah. Memorial; headstone on grave.

Megillah. Book of Esther. Read on Purim.

Memorbuch. Martyrs' memorial roll.

Mikhnasayim. Trousers. Part of shrouds.

Minchah. Afternoon service.

Minyan. A quorum of at least ten Jewish males aged thirteen and over. The term is also used as a synonym for a group of worshippers.

Mishlo'ach Manot. Sending of two portions of edibles to at least one friend. A Purim practice.

Mishnah. The foundation of the Talmud. A collection of legal rulings of the sages, originally preserved in oral form over the many centuries of its evolution, and edited by Rabbi Judah the Prince, ca. 200 C.E.

Mitzvah (**pl.** *mitzvot*). Pious deed, mandated either by Scripture or by rabbinic authorities.

Mitznefet. Headdress. Part of shrouds.

Mohel. Ritual circumciser.

Nefesh. Soul. Also designates a memorial constructed over ancient Jewish graves.

Nisan. Hebrew month. The festival of Passover is celebrated from the fifteenth to the twenty-third of Nisan.

Ohel. Lit. "Tent." In practive anything which is over a dead body or grave.

Onen (**Fem.** *onenet;* **pl.** *onenim*). The title given to a mourner in the period between the death and burial of one of his/her seven closest family members.

Perutah. Name of the smallest coin.

Pesach. Passover.

Pidyon ha-Ben. Redemption of the firstborn son on the thirty-first day of his life.

Piku'ach Nefesh. The imperative to save or preserve life, overriding Sabbath prohibitions.

Pilgrim Festivals. Passover (Pesach), Pentecost (Shavuot), and Tabernacles (Sukkot). When the Temple existed in Jerusalem, pilgrimages were made on these occasions.

Po nitman Lit. "Here is buried."

Purim. Festival of lots.

Purim Katan. See *Adar.*

Rashi. Rabbi Shlomo ben Yitzchak. The Bible and Talmud commentator par excellence, he set up a school of higher Jewish learning which established a centuries-long European tradition of text analysis, following the decimation of Torah scholars during the First Crusade (1096).

Rosh Chodesh. New moon; a semi-holiday.

Rosh ha-Shanah. The Jewish New Year.

Sandek. One who holds the baby during his ritual circumcision.

Seder. The evening meal eaten on the first two nights of Passover. The story of the Exodus is read before the meal. The meal is characterized by a great many customs and symbolic practices.

Sefardi(c). Of Eastern/Spanish/North African extraction. One of the two major segments of the Jewish people. Has its own customs (*minhagim*).

Sefer Torah. Scroll.

Sefirah. The counting period. In our context, "The counting of the *omer.*" The period of semi-mourning between Passover (Pesach) and Pentecost (Shavuot).

Selichot. Penitential prayers.

Se'udah. Meal.

Se'udat ha-havra'ah. The meal eaten by mourners returning home from the interment.

Se'udat mere'im/mere'ut. A meal celebrated in fellowship with companions.

Se'udat mitzvah. A meal at which the fulfillment of a religious precept is celebrated.

Se'udat reshut. A meal or an event which is not regarded as a religious imperative.

Shabbat. The Jewish Sabbath, commencing at sunset on Friday afternoon, and extending into dark on Saturday night.

Shabbat shalom. Lit. "Sabbath peace." A greeting exchanged by Jews on the Sabbath.

Shacharit. The morning service.

Shalom aleikhem. Lit. "Peace be unto you." A greeting exchanged by Jews.

Shalom zakhar. Welcome celebration for a newborn male child. Occurs on the first Friday night of the infant's life.

Shavuot. Pentecost. Fifty days after Passover. Celebrates the giving of the Torah at Mount Sinai.

Shayarah. A group excursion.

She-yigaru bo. Lit. "When they remonstrate with him." The complaint of close friends and family members about the unkempt appearance of the unshaven, unshorn mourner.

Sheloshim. The thirty-day period of mourning for close relatives, commencing after the interment.

Shema Koleinu. Lit. "Hear our voice." A heartrending plea. Part of the *Selichot* service.

Shemirah. The function performed by the *shomer/shomrim*—the person/people who remain(s) with the dead at all times between passing and burial.

Shenayim mikra ve-echad Targum. The ancient practice of reviewing the weekly Torah portion, twice in Hebrew and once in Aramaic translation.

Sheva berakhot. The seven blessings recited after grace after meals at each meal at which a *minyan* is present during the seven festive days following a wedding. By extension, the meals themselves have come to be called *sheva berakhot.*

Shevat. Hebrew month.

Shiv'ah. The seven-day period of intense mourning which commences following interment.

Shomer (pl. *shomrim*). Those who stay with the deceased prior to the funeral and interment.

Shulchan Arukh. Code of Jewish Law, written by Rabbi Joseph Karo.

Shurah. The parallel lines formed by those attending the burial service, through which the bereaved pass for consolation after the interment.

Shushan Purim. The day after Purim; a partial holiday outside of Jerusalem and certain other ancient cities, where it is equivalent to Purim itself.

Siddur. Prayer book.

Simchah. Festive occasion.

Simchat mere'im/mere'ut. Festive fellowship; festive get-together of companions.

Simchat Torah. Festival of the Rejoicing of the Torah.

Sivan. Hebrew month. The festival of Pentecost falls on the sixth and seventh of Sivan.

Siyyum/siyyum massekhet. Completion of a tractate(s) of the Talmud. Celebrated with a festive meal.

Sovev. Linen sheet for wrapping the dead.

Stimat ha-Golel. Lit. "The closing of the sepulcher." In ancient times, a stone was rolled into the entrance of the burial cave.

Sukkah. Booth, constructed for the festival of Tabernacles.

Sukkot. The festival of Tabernacles.

Tachanun. Meditation, highly personal, following the main (*Amidah*) prayer.

Taharah. Ritual cleansing of the dead.

Takhrichin. Shrouds.

Tallit (pl. *tallitot*). Prayer shawl.

Tallit katan. Small, four-cornered undergarment with fringes at each corner.

Talmud. The classical postbiblical sacred text of the Jewish people. The record of rabbinic discussions and analyses of Scripture, Mishnah, and other rabbinic texts. Originally an evolving oral tradition, it was edited in two versions, one in ancient Palestine (the *Yerushalmi*), and one, the more authoritative, in Babylon (the *Bavli*).

Tefach. Handbreadth; a rabbinic measure.

Tefillah. Prayer.

Tefillat ha-derekh. Prayer on going on a journey.

Tefillin. Phylacteries, leather boxes worn on the head and arm during morning prayers, containing scriptural passages, mandated by the Bible (Exodus 13:9, 13:16; Deuteronomy 6:8, 21:18).

Tena'im. Lit. "Conditions." A prenuptial contract between fathers of bride and groom, agreeing, *inter alia*, to the date of the proposed marriage.

Ten Days of Penitence. The solemn period of introspection between the Jewish New Year and the Day of Atonement.

Tiltul min ha-tzad. Halakhically permissible manner of carrying an object which may otherwise not be moved on the Sabbath or festivals.

Tish'a B'Av. The ninth day of the month Av. Solemn fast-day. Day of collective mourning for the destroyed Temple in Jerusalem.

Titkabbel. Stanza in the *Kaddish* beseeching God to accept our prayers.

Torah. Technically, the Five Books of Moses. More broadly, the entire Scriptures. Sometimes, the oral Tradition as well.

Tza'ara d'yenukah. Distress suffered by the infant at his circumcision.

Tzidkatekha tzedek. A paragraph following the *Amidah* prayer on Sabbath afternoons. A justification of the divine decree of human mortality.

Tzidduk ha-Din. Lit. "Justification of God's judgment." Usually said at the interment.

Tzitzit. Four-cornered garment with fringes, mandated by scripture (Numbers 15:37–41).

Tziyyun. Memorial marker; headstone on grave.

Va'ani tefillati. Lit. "As for me, this is my prayer." Introduction to the Sabbath afternoon Torah-reading service.

Va'ani zot beriti. Lit. "As for me, this is my covenant." A verse recited toward the close of the morning service.

Vi-hi no'am. A verse praying for a pleasant upcoming working week.

Yahrzeit. Anniversary of a person's demise.

Yehi ratzon. Lit. "May it be Thy will." A formula of supplication.

Yizkorbuch. Death roll, usually of martyrs, read at memorial services.

Yizkor. The memorial service which takes place on Passover, Pentecost, the Day of Atonement, and the Eighth Day of Solemn Assembly.

Yom Kippur. Day of Atonement.

Yom Tov. Jewish religious festival.

Yud bet chodesh. The twelve-month period of mourning for parents.

Zemirot. Sabbath and festival table hymns.

Zimun. Quorum of three for public recitation of the grace after meals.

Bibliography

Basry, Ezra. *Sefer ha-Tzava'ot.* Jerusalem, n.d.

————. *I Hereby Bequeath: A Comprehensive Guide to Jewish Wills.* Trans. Eliyahu Touger. Jerusalem, n.d.

Bender, A. "Beliefs, Rites and Customs of the Jews Connected with Death, Burial and Mourning." *Jewish Quarterly Review* 7, pp. 101–118, 259–270.

Brayer, Menachem. "The Psychology of Bereavement." *Gesher* 8 (1966): 56–71.

Epstein, Yechiel Mikhel. *Arukh ha-Shulchan: Yoreh Deah* 335–405. Jerusalem and Tel Aviv, n.d.

Fassler, Joan. *My Grandpa Died Today.* New York, 1971.

Felder, Aaron. *Yesodei Smochos.* New York, 1976.

Feldman, Emanuel. "Death as Estrangement: The *Halakhah* of Mourning." *Judaism* 21, no.1 (Winter 1972): 59–67.

Folkman, J. "The Role of the Rabbi in Bereavement." *CCAR Journal* 324 (1959): 52–56.

Freud, Sigmund. *Mourning and Melancholia.* In *The Standard Edition of the Complete Psychological Works of Sigmund Freud,* vol. 14, pp. 237–258. London, 1958.

Goodman, Arnold. *A Plain Pine Box: A Return to Simple Jewish Funerals and Eternal Traditions.* New York, 1981.

Gorer, Geoffrey. *Death, Grief and Mourning.* New York, 1965.

Greenberg, Sidney, ed. *A Treasury of Comfort.* New York, 1954.

Greenwald, Yekutiel Yehudah. *Kol Bo al Avelut.* New York, 1965.

Grollman, Earl A., ed. *Explaining Death to Children.* Boston, 1967.

Grosberg, Chanokh Zundel, ed. *Chazon le-Mo'ed: Hilkhot Semachot.* Jerusalem, 1965.

Hirsch, W. *Rabbinic Psychology.* London, 1947. (Standard text on personal immortality.)

Karo, Yosef. *Shulchan Arukh: Yoreh Deah* 335–405.

————. *Shulchan Arukh: Yoreh Deah.* Trans. Chaim N. Denberg. Montreal, 1954.

Kidorf, Irwin. "The *Shiva:* A Form of Group Psychotherapy." *Journal of Religion and Health* 5 (1966): 43–47.

Kubler-Ross, Elizabeth. *On Death and Dying.* New York, 1969.

Lamm, Maurice. *The Jewish Way in Death and Mourning.* New York, 1981.

Linzer, Norman, ed. *Understanding Bereavement and Grief.* New York, 1976.

Maimonides, Moses. *Mishneh Torah: Hilkhot Evel.* Jerusalem, 1959.

Modena, Aharon Berakhya. *Ma'avar Yabok.* Vilna, 1896.

Parkes, C.M. *Bereavement: Studies of Grief in Adult Life.* New York, 1972.

————. "Bereavement Counselling: Does It Work?" *British Medical Journal* 281 (1980): 3–6.

Rabinowicz, H. *A Guide to Life: Jewish Laws and Customs of Mourning.* London, 1969.

Rozwaski, Chaim. "On Jewish Mourning Psychology." *Judaism* 17, no. 3. (Summer 1968): 335–345.

Rubenstein, Shmuel. *The Jewish Funeral.* New York, 1977.

Schneidman, Edwin, ed. *Death: Current Perspectives.* Pal Alto, Calif., 1976.

Siggins, L. "Mourning: A Critical Survey of the Literature." *International Journal of Psychoanalysis* 47 (1966): 418–38.

Spiro, Jack D. *A Time to Mourn: Judaism and the Psychology of Bereavement.* New York, 1967.

Toper, Shlomo Pesach, ed. *Eternal Life: A Handbook for the Mourner.* Newcastle upon Tyne, 1972.

Tukechinsky, Yechiel Mikhel. *Gesher ha-Chayyim.* 2 vols. Jerusalem, 1960.

Ushpol, Isaac B. *Darkei Chesed: Summary of Laws and Customs Applying to the "Chevra Kadisha."* Excerp. and trans. Abraham Stone. New York, 1974.

Wordan, J. William. *Grief Counselling and Grief Therapy: A Handbook for the Mental Health Practitioner.* New York, 1982.

Zlotnick, Dov. *The Tractate "Mourning."* New Haven, 1966.

Part Two

Family Preparedness Checklist

This form should be completed and duplicated. A copy should be left with next of kin, the synagogue, the rabbi, the *chevra kadisha*, and with other valuable documents.

Name: _____

Address: _____

Birthdate: _____

Physicians: _____ Phone: _____

Who to contact in event of death: _____ Phone: _____

_____ Phone: _____

Insurance agents: _____ Phone: _____

_____ Phone: _____

_____ Phone: _____

Location of policies: _____

Location of Last Will and Testament: _____

Attorney who drew up this document: ____ Phone: _____

_____

Rabbi: _____ Phone: _____

Synagogue: _____ Phone: _____

Chevra Kadisha: _____ Phone: _____

_____

Location of burial plot: Cemetery: _____

Block: _____ #: _____

Cemetery manager: _____ Phone: _____

Prepaid arrangements: _____

Funeral home: _____ Phone: _____

STATEMENT ON AUTOPSY: I, the undersigned, forbid the performance of a non-rabbinically mandated autopsy on me.

ORGAN DONATIONS: I, the undersigned, permit use of such of my organs as my rabbi will sanction.

STATEMENT TO THE FUNERAL HOME: I, the undersigned, insist on a halakhically mandated *shemirah, taharah,* shrouds, casket, as approved by my rabbi.

SIGNATURE: _____

APPROVAL OF RABBI: Autopsy: YES ____   Organ gifts: YES ____

NO ____   NO ____

Funeral Home arrangements: YES ____

NO ____

SIGNATURE OF RABBI: _____

o o o o o o o o o

When Death Occurs:

CHECKLIST FOR *CHEVRA KADISHA*

1. Name of deceased (English): _____
   (Hebrew)

2. Address of deceased: _____
   _____

3. Current location of deceased (Hospital, etc.): _____
   _____

4. Member of Synagogue: YES ____
                           NO ____

5. Physician of deceased: _____   Phone: _____

6. Death certificate signed?   YES ____
                      NO ____   Number: _____

7. Intervention required with officials, Re: Autopsy, etc.?YES ____
                                              NO ____

8. Member of *Chevra Kadisha* assigned for intervention: _____
   _____ Phone: _____

9. Family member responsible for arrangements: _____
   _____ Phone: _____

10. Member of *Chevra* assigned to visit/contact that family member:
    _____ Phone: _____

11. Member of *Chevra* assigned to be with the deceased until arrival at
    funeral home: _____
    Phone: _____   Phone: _____

12. Name(s) of funeral director(s): ——————————————
——————————————— Phone: —————
Phone: ————————————————————

13. Location of burial plot: Cemetery: ————————————
Block: ——— #: ——————

14. (A) Transportation required to another city/country: YES ——
NO ——

(B) Name of organizer of transportation: ——————————
Phone: ——————— Phone: ———————

15. *Chevra* members to do *Shemirah* at funeral home: ————
——————————————— Phone: —————
Phone: ————————————————————

16. Names of *Chevra* members to do *Taharah*:
1. ——————————— Phone: —————
2. ——————————— Phone: —————
3. ——————————— Phone: —————
4. ——————————— Phone: —————

17. Names of *Chevra* members to help with funeral arrangements (transportation of friends, *minyan* at interment, phone calls, etc.):
1. ——————————— Phone: —————
2. ——————————— Phone: —————
3. ——————————— Phone: —————

18. Names of officiating Rabbis:
1. ——————————— Phone: —————
2. ——————————— Phone: —————

19. Time of funeral: ——————— Date of funeral: —————

20. Location of funeral: ——————————————————
——————————————————————

21. List any problems with funeral home (costs, equipment, etc.): —
——————————————————————

22. Names of *Chevra* members to place newspaper notice and "spread the word":

    1. _____ Phone: _____
    2. _____ Phone: _____
    3. _____ Phone: _____

23. Copy of notice:

24. Names of *Chevra* members to provide *Se'udat ha-Havra'ah*, other meals, preparation of *Shiv'ah* house:

    1. _____ Phone: _____
    2. _____ Phone: _____
    3. _____ Phone: _____
    4. _____ Phone: _____
    5. _____ Phone: _____

25. Names of *Chevra* members responsible for:
    (A) *Shiv'ah Minyanim*:

    1. _____ Phone: _____
    2. _____ Phone: _____
    3. _____ Phone: _____

    (B) *Shiv'ah* house equipment: _____

    _____ Phone: _____

    Chairs: YES ____   *Sefer Torah*: YES ____
            NO ____   NO ____
    Siddurim: YES ____   *Kippot* and *tallitot*: YES ____
               NO ____   NO ____

    (C) Who will lead *Mishnah* study?

    1. _____ When? _____ Phone: _____
    2. _____ When? _____ Phone: _____

3. _____ When? _____ Phone: _____

4. _____ When? _____ Phone: _____

5. _____ When? _____ Phone: _____

6. _____ When? _____ Phone: _____

(D) Who will lead services?

1. _____When? _____ Phone: _____

2. _____ When? _____ Phone: _____

3. _____ When? _____ Phone: _____

4. _____ When? _____ Phone: _____

(E) Who will read Torah? _____

_____ Phone: _____

(F) Was card dispatched to members of congregation:YES ____

NO ____

Shiv'ah information on card:

Name of deceased: _____

Address: _____

(relationship with) Member: _____

From: Minchah Ma'ariv Shacharit   Date: ____ Time: ____

To: Shacharit   Date: ____ Time: ____

(Sunday times: Shacharit: ____ Minchah: ____ Ma'ariv: ____

26. Comments: _____

_____

_____

_____

27. Signature of President of Chevra Kadisha/Synagogue officer:

_____

Halakhically Mandated
Bequest Form

BACKGROUND INFORMATION

Halakhic Prioritization of Beneficiaries

Under Jewish law the property of a person is disposed of after death in accordance with halakhic rules of descent and distribution; in other words, unlike American civil law, a person may not freely dispose of his property in a "last will." The decedent's heirs, as determined by the Halakhah, have the right to go before the Jewish court and have any attempted disposition of property made contrary to the Halakhah declared invalid.

The following is a brief overall summary of the manner in which property is distributed after death under the Halakhah.

1. Male children are the basic "heirs" of a decedent's property. Daughters are not entitled to the decedent's property if the decedent had male children. (Unmarried daughters, however, are entitled to a certain form of support from the male heirs.) The father's firstborn son (not the mother's!) is entitled to a double share of his father's property (note: not his mother's). It is interesting to note that if a male child predeceases his parent, then the deceased male child's heirs would take their father's inheritance.
2. In the event that there were no male children, the daughters of the decedent are granted equal shares.
3. The decedent's wife is not considered a legal heir. She is, however, entitled to certain forms of support, either under her marriage contract (*ketubah*) or as general support and maintenance until such time as she remarries (*mezonot*).

193

4. In the event that the decedent had no children (and, therefore, no grandchildren), the father of the decedent is the next
in line. If the father is not living, then the brothers of the
decedent would be granted the inheritance.

5. In the case of a convert (*ger*), all children prior to the conversion are not considered heirs under the Halakhah;
however, children born after conversion are subject to the
Halakhah. We would recommend, however, that a person
should consult a competent rabbi if he is a converted Jew;
likewise, if an otherwise legal heir has converted to another
religion, competent rabbinical authority should be consulted.

Alternative Designees for Disbursement

*For whatever reason, however, a person may wish to make a dis-
position of his property after death to persons other than those
strictly designated by law.* For example, he may wish to provide for
his wife (who is not considered an heir under Jewish law). He may
wish to give a greater share to his children who are in greater need
of money, or he may wish to give property to his daughters (who are
not considered heirs if the decedent is survived by a son). *In such
cases, additional documentation must be created to effectuate the
testator's last wishes.*

Method of Effecting Alternative Designation

Conceptually, the testator creates a written obligation which
exceeds his estimated testamentary estate in favor of persons to
whom he wishes to give property upon his/her death who are not
legal heirs (under the *Halakhah*). This obligation is payable one
hour before death, and is secured by all of the testator's property
owned by him at the time of his death.

*In addition, the testator makes the usual civil will wherein he
expresses his desires for the disposition of his property after death.*
The indebtedness, which vests one hour before death, is subject to
divestment by a condition subsequent; to wit, if all of the decedent's heirs agree to be bound by the terms of the civil will (i.e.,
they all agree not to contest the will in a Jewish court), then the

obligation (which runs in favor of the testator's intended beneficiaries) is discharged.

Conceptually, in order to effectuate their parent's last wishes (as expressed in his will), the heirs freely give away all or part of their inheritance to those persons whom their parent wished to own his property. An heir who contests the will stands to lose his entire inheritance which would be used up in satisfying his parent's substantial obligation, which comes into force one hour prior to his death. Given the alternative of potentially losing their entire inheritance, the heirs will no doubt readily accept their parent's last wishes as expressed in the will.

This formulation finds a counterpart in American jurisprudence, which upholds testamentary gifts conditional upon a legatee not contesting the will—the famous *in terrorem* clause, which revokes all legacies made to a beneficiary who interposes objection to, or contests, the will.

The Sample Form

The sample form below is used in conjunction with the execution of a civil will. Lawyers are encouraged to advise their Jewish clients of the importance of executing such a document in order to ensure that the client's legatees do not unintentionally take property in violation of the *Halakhah* or do not become involved in bitter family disputes involving the disposition of property after death.

HALAKHICALLY VALID BEQUEST DOCUMENT

I, the undersigned, do hereby state that I am indebted to[1]

_____

_____

in the amount of \$_____[2] payable one hour before my death. To secure the aforesaid debt, I hereby pledge all my property—

---

1. List only those intended beneficiaries who are either (a) not considered heirs under the Halakhah or (b) heirs under the Halakhah to whom the testator wishes to give more under the will than would otherwise be their share under the Halakhah.

2. The testator should estimate his testamentary estate and include an amount in this document substantially greater than the anticipated testamentary estate.

both real and personal—by virtue of the Talmudic Act of Acquisition known as "Movable Property Gained Together with Real Property," whereby movable property can be pledged as a consequence of pledging real property. The above-mentioned indebtedness and pledge were made with *kinyan sudar*.

Notwithstanding the foregoing, this obligation shall be rendered null and void if the wishes expressed in my Last Will be carried out and if none of my heirs contest the disposition of my property set forth therein.

In the event that all my heirs contest or make objection to the disposition of my property made in my Last Will, whether before a civil court or before a Jewish court, then the aforesaid obligation to the obligee(s) above named shall be deemed to vest absolutely.

If one or more of my heirs contest the disposition of my property made in my Will ("Contesting Heirs") and some of my heirs are willing to abide by my last wishes ("Non-Contesting heirs"), then

> (a) With respect to my Non-Contesting Heirs, the above-named obligee(s) shall release such Non-Contesting Heirs from honoring his (their) share of this obligation. In the event any of the above named obligee(s) fail or refuse to release a Non-Contesting Heir(s), then this obligation shall be null and void with respect to any such obligee(s);
> (b) With respect to a Contesting Heir(s), any Contesting Heir will be required to honor his (their) share of this obligation to the extent of his (their) share of the inheritance.

The foregoing has been done in a legal manner, in accord with Talmudic Jurisprudence, with effective conditions and stipulations in the manner of the children of Gad and the children of Reuven, and with effective acts of property transfer, and not in the manner of speculation. This instrument is not an impractical document, but a bona fide legal document, and even if it be in my possession at the time of my death, shall not be deemed invalid by reason of either proof of payment or failure of delivery.[3]

Dated: _____ Signed:[4] _____

Halakhically Valid Bequest Document

אני החתום מטה מודה בהודאה גמורה שהתחייבתי עצמי _____ _____

סך _____ $ דולר וזמן הפרעון יהי' שעה אחת קודם מיתתי _____

ושיעבדתי _____ כל נכסי מטלטלין אג"ק. אך תנאי התניתי שבאם יקיימו יורשיי כל

מה שכתוב בצוואה אז החוב בטל ומבוטל לגמרי כי לא התחייבתי עצמי רק בתנאי הנ"ל

ואם מקצת מיורשיי ירצו לקיים מה שכתוב בהוויי"ל ומקצת מיורשיי לא ירצו לקיים מה

שכתוב בהוויי"ל אז התניתי עם הזוכים הנ"ל שיוותרו היורשים הרוצים לקיים מה

שכתוב בצוואה על החוב המגיע לחלקם, ואם לא יוותרו על החוב המגיע לחלקם אז כל

החוב בטל ומבוטל, באופן שרק אלו היורשים שאין רוצים לקיים את הווייי"ל יצטרכו

לשלם את החוב כפי חלקם וכ"ז נעשה באופן המועיל בתנאי גמור בתנאי ב"ג וב"ר

ובקנין גמור דלא כאסמכתא ודלא כטופסי שטרות ושטר זה אעפ"י שיהי' מונח תחת

ידי יהי' לראי' ברורה לכל הנ"ל ולא יועיל שום טענה של פירעון או חזרה וכדומה.

_____

במקום שיש בכור

אני החתום מטה מודה בהודאה גמורה שהתחייבתי עצמי _____ _____

סך _____ והזמן פרעון יהי' שעה אחת קודם מיתתי ושיעבדתי להם כל נכסי

מטלטלין אג"ק אך תנאי התניתי שאם בני בכורי _____ יסלק עצמו

מחלק בכורתו ולא יקח יותר מחלק פשוט ויקיים מה שכתוב בצוואה אז החוב הנ"ל

בטל ומבוטל וכ"ז נעשה בקנין גמור באופן המועיל ודלא כאסמכתא ודלא כטופסי

שטרות ובתנאי גמור כתנאי ב"ג וב"ר. ושטר זה אעפ"י שיהיה מונח תחת ידי יהי'

לראי' ברורה לכל הנ"ל ולא יועיל שום טענה של פירעון או חזרה וכדומה.

_____

3. Although the last clause of the document negates possible claims of invalidity in the event that the document is found in the possession of the decedent at the time of his death, better practice dictates that a trusted third party (e.g., rabbi, lawyer, etc.) be asked to hold the document.

4. The testator should execute this document in the presence of an observant Jew (*shomer mitzvah*) with a proper "act of transfer" (*kinyan sudar*), which requires (a) the obligee or his representative giving a thing of value to the testator, and (b) delivery of the document to the obligee. To accomplish the foregoing, the attorney who draws the will can act on behalf of the obligee by giving a pen to the testator, who can thereupon deliver the document to the lawyer as agent of the obligee.

Recitations Prior to Death

PRAYERS TO BE RECITED BY/FOR A SICK PERSON

Psalm 23. A Psalm of David

The Lord is my shepherd; I shall not want. He maketh me to lie down in green pastures: he leadeth me beside the still waters. He restoreth my soul: he guideth me in the paths of righteousness for his name's sake. Yea, though I walk through the valley of the shadow of death, I will fear no evil; for thou art with me: thy rod and thy staff, they comfort me. Thou preparest a table before me in the presence of mine enemies: thou hast anointed my head with oil; my cup runneth over. Surely happiness and loving-kindness will follow me all the days of my life; and I shall dwell in the house of the Lord for evermore.

תפלה לחולה

תהלים כ"ג

מִזְמוֹר לְדָוִד יְהוָה רֹעִי לֹא אֶחְסָר: בִּנְאוֹת דֶּשֶׁא יַרְבִּיצֵנִי עַל־מֵי מְנֻחוֹת יְנַהֲלֵנִי: נַפְשִׁי יְשׁוֹבֵב יַנְחֵנִי בְמַעְגְּלֵי־צֶדֶק לְמַעַן שְׁמוֹ: גַּם כִּי־אֵלֵךְ בְּגֵיא צַלְמָוֶת לֹא־אִירָא רָע כִּי־אַתָּה עִמָּדִי שִׁבְטְךָ וּמִשְׁעַנְתֶּךָ הֵמָּה יְנַחֲמֻנִי: תַּעֲרֹךְ לְפָנַי שֻׁלְחָן נֶגֶד צֹרְרָי דִּשַּׁנְתָּ בַשֶּׁמֶן רֹאשִׁי כּוֹסִי רְוָיָה: אַךְ טוֹב וָחֶסֶד יִרְדְּפוּנִי כָּל־יְמֵי חַיָּי וְשַׁבְתִּי בְּבֵית־יְהוָה לְאֹרֶךְ יָמִים:

Psalm 103. A Psalm of David

Bless the Lord, O my soul; and all that is within me, bless his holy name. Bless the Lord, O my soul, and forget not all his benefits: who forgiveth all thine iniquity; who healeth all thy diseases; who redeemeth thy life from the pit; who crowneth thee with loving-kindness and tender mercies: who satisfieth thy years with good things; so that thy youth is renewed like the eagle's. The Lord executeth righteous acts, and judgments for all that are oppressed. He made known his ways unto Moses, his doings unto the children of Israel. The Lord is merciful and gracious, slow to anger, and abounding in loving-kindness. He will not always contend; neither will he keep his anger for ever. He hath not dealt with us after our sins, nor requited us after our iniquities. For as the heaven is high above the earth, so mighty is his loving-kindness over them that fear him. As far as the east is from the west, so far hath he removed our transgressions from us. Like a father hath mercy upon his children, so the Lord hath mercy upon them that fear him. For he knoweth our frame; he remembereth that we are dust. As for man, his days are as grass; as the flower of the field, so he flourisheth. For the wind passeth over it, and it is gone; and the place thereof shall know it no more. But the loving-kindness of the Lord is from everlasting to everlasting upon them that fear him, and his righteousness unto children's children, to such as keep his covenant, and to those that remember his precepts to do them. The Lord hath established his throne in the heavens; and his kingdom ruleth over all. Bless the Lord, ye his angels: ye mighty in strength, that fulfill his word, hearkening unto the voice of his word. Bless the Lord, all ye his hosts; ye ministers of his, that do his will. Bless the Lord, all ye his works, in all places of his dominion: bless the Lord, O my soul.

תהלים ק״ג

לְדָוִד בָּרְכִי נַפְשִׁי אֶת־יְהֹוָה וְכָל־קְרָבַי אֶת־שֵׁם קָדְשׁוֹ: בָּרְכִי נַפְשִׁי אֶת־יְהֹוָה וְאַל־
תִּשְׁכְּחִי כָּל־גְּמוּלָיו: הַסֹּלֵחַ לְכָל־עֲוֹנֵכִי הָרֹפֵא לְכָל־תַּחֲלוּאָיְכִי: הַגּוֹאֵל מִשַּׁחַת חַיָּיְכִי
הַמְעַטְּרֵכִי חֶסֶד וְרַחֲמִים: הַמַּשְׂבִּיעַ בַּטּוֹב עֶדְיֵךְ תִּתְחַדֵּשׁ כַּנֶּשֶׁר נְעוּרָיְכִי: עֹשֵׂה צְדָקוֹת
יְהֹוָה וּמִשְׁפָּטִים לְכָל־עֲשׁוּקִים: יוֹדִיעַ דְּרָכָיו לְמֹשֶׁה לִבְנֵי יִשְׂרָאֵל עֲלִילוֹתָיו: רַחוּם וְחַנּוּן
יְהֹוָה אֶרֶךְ אַפַּיִם וְרַב־חָסֶד: לֹא־לָנֶצַח יָרִיב וְלֹא לְעוֹלָם יִטּוֹר: לֹא כַחֲטָאֵינוּ עָשָׂה לָנוּ
וְלֹא כַעֲוֹנֹתֵינוּ גָּמַל עָלֵינוּ: כִּי כִגְבֹהַּ שָׁמַיִם עַל־הָאָרֶץ גָּבַר חַסְדּוֹ עַל־יְרֵאָיו: כִּרְחֹק מִזְרָח
מִמַּעֲרָב הִרְחִיק מִמֶּנּוּ אֶת־פְּשָׁעֵינוּ: כְּרַחֵם אָב עַל־בָּנִים רִחַם יְהֹוָה עַל־יְרֵאָיו: כִּי־הוּא
יָדַע יִצְרֵנוּ זָכוּר כִּי־עָפָר אֲנָחְנוּ: אֱנוֹשׁ כֶּחָצִיר יָמָיו כְּצִיץ הַשָּׂדֶה כֵּן יָצִיץ: כִּי רוּחַ
עָבְרָה־בּוֹ וְאֵינֶנּוּ וְלֹא־יַכִּירֶנּוּ עוֹד מְקוֹמוֹ: וְחֶסֶד יְהֹוָה מֵעוֹלָם וְעַד־עוֹלָם עַל־יְרֵאָיו
וְצִדְקָתוֹ לִבְנֵי בָנִים: לְשֹׁמְרֵי בְרִיתוֹ וּלְזֹכְרֵי פִקֻּדָיו לַעֲשׂוֹתָם: יְהֹוָה בַּשָּׁמַיִם הֵכִין כִּסְאוֹ
וּמַלְכוּתוֹ בַּכֹּל מָשָׁלָה: בָּרְכוּ יְהֹוָה מַלְאָכָיו גִּבֹּרֵי כֹחַ עֹשֵׂי דְבָרוֹ לִשְׁמֹעַ בְּקוֹל דְּבָרוֹ: בָּרְכוּ
יְהֹוָה כָּל־צְבָאָיו מְשָׁרְתָיו עֹשֵׂי רְצוֹנוֹ: בָּרְכוּ יְהֹוָה כָּל־מַעֲשָׂיו בְּכָל־מְקֹמוֹת מֶמְשַׁלְתּוֹ
בָּרְכִי נַפְשִׁי אֶת־יְהֹוָה:

Psalm 139. For the Chief Musician. A Psalm of David

O Lord, thou hast searched me, and knowest me. Thou knowest my downsitting and mine uprising, thou understandest my thoughts afar off. Thou siftest my path and my lying down, and art familiar with all my ways. For while there is not yet a word on my tongue, lo, thou, O Lord, knowest it all. Thou hast beset me behind and before, and laid thine hand upon me. Such knowledge is too wonderful for me; it is too high, I cannot attain unto it. Whither can I go from thy spirit? or whither can I flee from thy presence? If I ascend into heaven, thou art there; or if I make the grave my bed, behold, thou art there. If I take the wings of the morning, and dwell in the uttermost parts of the sea, even there shall thy hand lead me, and thy right hand shall hold me. If I say, Let deep darkness cover me, and the light about me be night; even the darkness darkeneth not from thee, but the night is light as the day—the darkness is as the light. For thou didst form my veins, thou didst weave me together in my mother's womb. I will give thanks unto thee, for that I am fearfully and wonderfully made: wonderful are thy works; and that my soul knoweth right well. My frame was not hidden from thee, when I was made in secret, and curiously wrought in the depths of the earth. Thine eyes did see mine unshapen substance; and in thy book the days, even all of them that were to be formed, were written, and for it also there was one among them. How precious unto me are thy thoughts, O God! How great is the sum of them! If I would count them, they are more in number than the sand: when I awake, I am still with thee. O that thou wouldst slay the wicked, O God: depart from me, ye bloodthirsty men: they who mention thee for treachery, thine adversaries who take thy name in vain. Do not I hate them, O Lord, that hate thee? and do not I strive with those that rise up against thee? I hate them with perfect hatred: they are become mine enemies. Search me, O God, and know my heart: try me, and know my thoughts: and see if there be any way of sorrow in me, and lead me in the way everlasting.

תהלים קל״ט

לַמְנַצֵּחַ לְדָוִד מִזְמוֹר יְהֹוָה חֲקַרְתַּנִי וַתֵּדָע: אַתָּה יָדַעְתָּ שִׁבְתִּי וְקוּמִי בַּנְתָּה לְרֵעִי מֵרָחוֹק: אָרְחִי וְרִבְעִי זֵרִיתָ וְכָל־דְּרָכַי הִסְכַּנְתָּה: כִּי אֵין מִלָּה בִּלְשׁוֹנִי הֵן יְהֹוָה יָדַעְתָּ כֻלָּהּ:

אָחוֹר וָקֶדֶם צַרְתָּנִי וַתָּשֶׁת עָלַי כַּפֶּכָה: פְּלִיאָה דַעַת מִמֶּנִּי נִשְׂגְּבָה לֹא־אוּכַל לָהּ: אָנָה אֵלֵךְ מֵרוּחֶךָ וְאָנָה מִפָּנֶיךָ אֶבְרָח: אִם־אֶסַּק שָׁמַיִם שָׁם אָתָּה וְאַצִּיעָה שְּׁאוֹל הִנֶּךָּ: אֶשָּׂא כַנְפֵי־שָׁחַר אֶשְׁכְּנָה בְּאַחֲרִית יָם: גַּם־שָׁם יָדְךָ תַנְחֵנִי וְתֹאחֲזֵנִי יְמִינֶךָ: וָאֹמַר אַךְ־חֹשֶׁךְ יְשׁוּפֵנִי וְלַיְלָה אוֹר בַּעֲדֵנִי: גַּם־חֹשֶׁךְ לֹא־יַחְשִׁיךְ מִמֶּךָּ וְלַיְלָה כַּיּוֹם יָאִיר כַּחֲשֵׁיכָה כָּאוֹרָה: כִּי־אַתָּה קָנִיתָ כִלְיֹתָי תְּסֻכֵּנִי בְּבֶטֶן אִמִּי: אוֹדְךָ עַל כִּי נוֹרָאוֹת נִפְלֵיתִי נִפְלָאִים מַעֲשֶׂיךָ וְנַפְשִׁי יֹדַעַת מְאֹד: לֹא־נִכְחַד עָצְמִי מִמֶּךָ אֲשֶׁר־עֻשֵּׂיתִי בַסֵּתֶר רֻקַּמְתִּי בְּתַחְתִּיּוֹת אָרֶץ: גָּלְמִי רָאוּ עֵינֶיךָ וְעַל־סִפְרְךָ כֻּלָּם יִכָּתֵבוּ יָמִים יֻצָּרוּ וְלוֹ אֶחָד בָּהֶם: וְלִי מַה־יָּקְרוּ רֵעֶיךָ אֵל מֶה עָצְמוּ רָאשֵׁיהֶם: אֶסְפְּרֵם מֵחוֹל יִרְבּוּן הֱקִיצֹתִי וְעוֹדִי עִמָּךְ: אִם־תִּקְטֹל אֱלוֹהַּ רָשָׁע וְאַנְשֵׁי דָמִים סוּרוּ מֶנִּי: אֲשֶׁר יֹמְרוּךָ לִמְזִמָּה נָשׂוּא לַשָּׁוְא עָרֶיךָ: הֲלוֹא־מְשַׂנְאֶיךָ יְהֹוָה אֶשְׂנָא וּבִתְקוֹמְמֶיךָ אֶתְקוֹטָט: תַּכְלִית שִׂנְאָה שְׂנֵאתִים לְאֹיְבִים הָיוּ לִי: חָקְרֵנִי אֵל וְדַע לְבָבִי בְּחָנֵנִי וְדַע שַׂרְעַפָּי: וּרְאֵה אִם־דֶּרֶךְ־עֹצֶב בִּי וּנְחֵנִי בְּדֶרֶךְ עוֹלָם:

A prayer of the afflicted when he fainteth, and poureth out his complaint before the Lord. Hear my prayer, O Lord, and let my cry come unto thee. Hide not thy face from me in the day of my distress: incline thine ear unto me; in the day when I call answer me speedily. I beseech thee, O Lord, Healer of all flesh, have mercy upon me, and support me in thy grace upon my bed of sickness, for I am weak. Send me and all who are sick among thy children relief and cure. Assuage my pain, and renew my youth as the eagle's. Bestow wisdom upon the physician that he may cure my wound, so that my health may spring forth speedily. Hear my prayer, prolong my life, let me complete my years in happiness, that I may be enabled to serve thee and keep thy statutes with a perfect heart. Give me understanding to know that this bitter trial hath come upon me for my welfare, so that I may not despise thy chastening nor weary of thy reproof.

תְּפִלָּה לְעָנִי כִי־יַעֲטֹף וְלִפְנֵי יְיָ יִשְׁפֹּךְ שִׂיחוֹ יְיָ שִׁמְעָה תְפִלָּתִי וְשַׁוְעָתִי אֵלֶיךָ תָבוֹא: אַל־תַּסְתֵּר פָּנֶיךָ מִמֶּנִּי בְּיוֹם צַר־לִי הַטֵּה־אֵלַי אָזְנֶךָ בְּיוֹם אֶקְרָא מַהֵר עֲנֵנִי: אָנָּא יְיָ רוֹפֵא כָל בָּשָׂר. רַחֵם עָלַי וּסְעָדֵנִי בְּחַסְדְּךָ הַגָּדוֹל עַל עֶרֶשׂ דְּוָי. כִּי אֻמְלָל אָנִי: שְׁלַח לִי תְּרוּפָה וּתְעָלָה בְּתוֹךְ שְׁאָר חוֹלֵי בָנֶיךָ: רְפָא אֶת־מַכְאֹבִי וְחַדֵּשׁ כַּנֶּשֶׁר נְעוּרָי: תֵּן בִּינָה לָרוֹפֵא וְיִגְהֶה מִמֶּנִּי מְזוֹרִי. וַאֲרוּכָתִי מְהֵרָה תִצְמָח: שְׁמַע תְּפִלָּתִי וְהוֹסֵף יָמִים עַל יָמַי וַאֲכַלֶּה שְׁנוֹתַי בַּנְּעִימִים. לְמַעַן אוּכַל לַעֲבוֹד עֲבוֹדָתֶךָ וְלִשְׁמוֹר פִּקּוּדֶיךָ בְּלֵב שָׁלֵם: הֲבִינֵנִי וְאֵדְעָה כִּי לִשְׁלוֹמִי מַר־לִי מָר. וְאַל־אֶמְאַס אֶת מוּסָרְךָ וּבְתוֹכַחְתְּךָ אַל־אָקוּץ:

O God of forgiveness, who art gracious and merciful, slow to anger and abounding in lovingkindness, I confess unto thee with a broken and contrite heart that I have sinned, and have done that which is evil in thy sight. Behold, I repent me of my evil way, and return unto thee with perfect repentance. Help me, O God of my salvation, that I may not again turn unto folly, but walk before thee in truth and uprightness. Rejoice the soul of thy servant, for unto thee, O Lord, do I lift up my soul. Heal me, O Lord, and I shall be healed, save me, and I shall be saved, for thou art my praise. Amen, and Amen!

אֱלוֹהַּ סְלִיחוֹת חַנּוּן וְרַחוּם אֶרֶךְ אַפַּיִם וְרַב־חָסֶד. מוֹדֶה אֲנִי לְפָנֶיךָ בְּלֵב נִשְׁבָּר וְנִדְכֶּה כִּי חָטָאתִי וְהָרַע בְּעֵינֶיךָ עָשִׂיתִי: הִנֵּה נִחַמְתִּי עַל רָעָתִי. וְאָשׁוּב בִּתְשׁוּבָה שְׁלֵמָה לְפָנֶיךָ: עָזְרֵנִי אֱלֹהֵי יִשְׁעִי. וְלֹא אָשׁוּב לְכִסְלָה וְאֶתְהַלֵּךְ לְפָנֶיךָ בֶּאֱמֶת וּבְתָמִים: שַׂמֵּחַ נֶפֶשׁ עַבְדֶּךָ. כִּי אֵלֶיךָ יְיָ נַפְשִׁי אֶשָּׂא: רְפָאֵנִי יְיָ וְאֵרָפֵא הוֹשִׁיעֵנִי וְאִוָּשֵׁעָה. כִּי תְהִלָּתִי אָתָּה. אָמֵן וְאָמֵן:

CONFESSION ON A DEATHBED

I acknowledge unto thee, O Lord my God and God of my fathers, that both my cure and my death are in thy hands. May it be thy will to send me a perfect healing. Yet if my death be fully determined by thee, I will in love accept it at thy hand. O may my death be an atonement for all the sins, iniquities and transgressions of which I have been guilty against thee. Bestow upon me the abounding happiness that is treasured up for the righteous. Make known to me the path of life: in thy presence is fulness of joy; at thy right hand, bliss for evermore.

Thou who art the father of the fatherless and judge of the widow, protect my beloved kindred with whose soul my own is knit. Into thy hand I commend my spirit; thou hast redeemed me, O Lord God of truth. Amen, and Amen!

When the end is approaching:—

The Lord reigneth; the Lord hath reigned; the Lord shall reign for ever and ever. (*To be said three times.*)

Blessed be his name, whose glorious kingdom is for ever and ever. (*To be said three times.*)

The Lord he is God. (*To be said seven times.*)

Hear, O Israel: the Lord our God, the Lord is one.

וידוי שכיב מרע

מוֹדֶה אֲנִי לְפָנֶיךָ יְיָ אֱלֹהַי וֵאלֹהֵי אֲבוֹתַי שֶׁרְפוּאָתִי וּמִיתָתִי בְּיָדֶךָ: יְהִי רָצוֹן מִלְּפָנֶיךָ שֶׁתִּרְפָּאֵנִי רְפוּאָה שְׁלֵמָה. וְאִם הַמָּוֶת כָּלָה וְנֶחֱרַץ מֵעִמְּךָ אֲקַחֶנּוּ מִיָּדְךָ בְּאַהֲבָה. וּתְהִי מִיתָתִי כַּפָּרָה עַל כָּל חֲטָאִים וַעֲוֹנוֹת וּפְשָׁעִים שֶׁחָטָאתִי וְשֶׁעָוִיתִי וְשֶׁפָּשַׁעְתִּי לְפָנֶיךָ. וְתַשְׁפִּיעַ לִי מֵרַב טוּב הַצָּפוּן לַצַּדִּיקִים. וְתוֹדִיעֵנִי אֹרַח חַיִּים שְׂבַע שְׂמָחוֹת אֶת פָּנֶיךָ נְעִימוֹת בִּימִינְךָ נֶצַח:

אֲבִי יְתוֹמִים וְדַיַּן אַלְמָנוֹת. הָגֵן בְּעַד קְרוֹבַי הַיְקָרִים אֲשֶׁר נַפְשִׁי קְשׁוּרָה בְנַפְשָׁם: בְּיָדְךָ אַפְקִיד רוּחִי פָּדִיתָה אוֹתִי יְיָ אֵל אֱמֶת. אָמֵן וְאָמֵן:

בשעת יציאת הנשמה:

יְיָ מֶלֶךְ. יְיָ מָלָךְ. יְיָ | יִמְלוֹךְ לְעוֹלָם וָעֶד:
(*to be said three times.*)

בָּרוּךְ שֵׁם כְּבוֹד מַלְכוּתוֹ לְעוֹלָם וָעֶד:
(*to be said three times.*)

יְיָ הוּא הָאֱלֹהִים:
(*to be said seven times.*)

שְׁמַע יִשְׂרָאֵל יְיָ אֱלֹהֵינוּ יְיָ אֶחָד:

BLESSING TO BE RECITED WHEN ONE IS PRESENT AT THE PASSING OF ONE OF ONE'S SEVEN CLOSEST RELATIVES OR ONE'S PRINCIPAL TEACHER

Blessed art thou, O Lord our God, King of the universe, the true Judge.

בָּרוּךְ אַתָּה יְיָ אֱלֹהֵינוּ מֶלֶךְ הָעוֹלָם. דַּיַּן הָאֱמֶת:

BLESSING TO BE RECITED WHEN ONE IS PRESENT AT THE PASSING OF ANY PERSON OTHER THAN THE ABOVE

Blessed is the true Judge.　　　　　　　　בָּרוּךְ דַּיַּן הָאֱמֶת:

Deed of Sale of Business by Onen

I, the undersigned[1] _____ hereby sign to the effect that I have today sold absolutely and permanently to Mr. _____, an individual residing at _____ _____, the _____ business/factory, located at _____ _____, for the price established between us, a sum of $_____.[2]

I have to date, received the sum of $_____[3] from him, having granted him the remainder as a loan which he must repay me within _____ years[4] from this date.

The above-mentioned business/factory belongs to Mr. _____ _____, the above-mentioned purchaser and/or his representatives as of this date, without leaving any residual rights of ownership over to us/me or my/our representative(s).

By the method of selling movables along with real property, I have also sold him the goods and articles which are located there, viz. _____.[5] I have now sold the above-mentioned items to Mr. _____, the above-mentioned purchaser, for the price established between us, the sum of $_____.[2] I have, to date, received the sum of $_____[3] from him, having granted him the remainder as a loan which he must also repay me within _____ years[4] from this date.

---

1. If the seller has a partner, the following language should be added here: "and in the name of my partner _____;" If it is a limited company, the name of that company should be added.
2. This should be a realistic price for the business.
3. A modest sum, e.g., $50.
4. The period of time makes no difference. One might suggest ten years.
5. This depends on the nature of the business, whether there is machinery, etc.
° Relying upon the *Arukh ha-Shulchan, Choshen Mishpat* 22, we have omitted the inclusion of the designation of *arev kablan*—an unconditionally responsible guarantor.

I have reached agreement with him that I and/or one of my representatives will stay on as manager of the business/factory for a period of _____ years[4] from now, to faithfully administer all the affairs of the business, without any interference from the above-mentioned purchaser. The purchaser is obligated to pay me or my representative an unencumbered salary of $_____.[2] The above-mentioned purchaser has neither the right nor the power to remove me or my representative from this my position until he has paid me in full what he owes me, both for the business and for the goods therein, etc.

Furthermore, all workers and laborers, Jews and gentiles, presently employed in the business will remain in place in the business in terms of the existing conditions of service.

Furthermore, should there arise the need to have other workers and laborers, or to fire any of them, I, the undersigned, or my representative shall have the right to do whatever we deem to be in the best interests of the business.

I, or my representative, have the further right to withdraw funds from the business to pay all the expenses of administering the business—in addition to my salary and the salaries of the workers and laborers.

All these transactions will be recorded and accounts kept. At the termination of _____ years[4] from now I am obligated to render account to the above-mentioned purchaser, subtracting from the above-mentioned sum which he still owes me for the purchase all the profits accruing to me after defraying my expenses. He is obligated to pay me what he owes me.

With regard to that reckoning in the event of a dispute arising between us, I and/or my representative will be believed, rather than the purchaser and/or his representative.

It has been explicitly agreed with the aforementioned purchaser that if there be in this sale anything which will not give effect to the sale and transfer of ownership according to the law of the Torah, the sale of other items included, this deed will not thereby be invalidated. Similarly, if any of the acts of ownership of transfer shall be deemed to be ineffectual, it will not thereby invalidate whatever act(s) of transfer of ownership is (are) effective in making this a valid sale.

All this has been effected by the act of symbolic transfer of ownership known as *kinyan agav sudar,* by a handshake, and by transfer of ownership of movable property along with fiscal property (*kinyan agav karka*) to further strengthen this transaction. It employs all those methods of transfer of ownership which are effective under the law of the holy Torah and the legislation of our Sages of blessed memory without any invalidating reservations or limitations of any kind.

In proof hereof I _____[1] do hereby sign on this _____ day of the week, the _____ day of the month of _____ in the year _____, here at _____

SIGNATURE OF SELLER _____

o o o o o o o o o o

STATEMENT BY WITNESS

In the presence of us the undersigned, the seller, Mr. _____ signed to all the contents of the above instrument. We sign to this effect on this _____ day of _____ in the year _____, here _____

SIGNATURE OF WITNESS _____
SIGNATURE OF WITNESS _____

שטר מכירה

אני הח"מ _____ הנני בא בזה על החתום[1] איך שמכרתי כהיום במכירה גמורה וחלוטה לצמיתות עלמין למר _____ _____ מ_____ _____ [הכתובת] את בית המשחיר והחרושת של _____ [סוג המסחר ובית החרושת] הנמצא ב_____ _____ [הכתובת] במחיר שהשוחינו בינינו, סך _____$[2] דולר וקבלתי כעת ממנו סך _____$[3] דולר, ואת המותר זקפתי עליו כמלווה לשלם עד _____ שנים[4] מהיום*, ומעתה בית המסחר והחרושת הנ"ל ולבאי כוחו מבלי כל שיור כל שהוא לעצמנו או באי כוחנו וע"ג קרקע הנ"ל מכרתי לו גם כן את כל הסחורה הנמצאת שם, היינו כל _____ כל[5]. הנ"ל מכרתי כעת לקונה _____ הנ"ל במחיר שהשוחינו בינינו, היינו סך _____$[2] דולר

וקבלתי כעת מהקונה סך _____\$[3] דולר. את המותר זקפתי עליו במלווה לשלם לי
גם כן עד _____ שנים[4] מהיום. והתניתי עמו שאני (ו) או אחד מבאי כוחי נשאר בתור
מנהל של בית המסחר/החרושת מעתה ועד _____ שנים[4] לנהל באמונה את כל ענייני
העסק באופן בלתי מוגבל מצד הקונה הנ״ל, ועל הקונה לשלם לי או לב״כ משכורת
חפשית בסך _____\$[2] דולר. ואין לקונה, הנ״ל רשות וכוח לסלק אותי או ב״כ
ממשרתי בטרם ישלם כל הסכום המגיע ממנו, הן בעד העסק והן בעד הסחורה וכו'
במלואם. וכן כל העובדים והפועלים כעת בעסק, בין יהודים בין שאינם יהודים,
כולם ישארו במקומותיהם בעסק על פי התנאים והאופנים שהיו קשורים בהם עד
עכשיו. וכן אם יהיה צורך לשכור עוד פועלים ועובדים, או לפטר את מי מהם —
תהיה לי החח״מ או ב״כ הרשות לעשות בכל זה כפי שאמצא נכון לטובת העסק. וגם
להוציא מקופת העסק נוסף למשכורתי ומשכורת הפועלים והעובדים, את כל ההוצאות
הדרושות לניהול העסק, והכל יירשם ויובא בחשבון. ואחר כלות _____ שנים[4]
מהיום, עלי לעשות חשבון עם הקונה הנ״ל ולנכות מהחוב שהוא חייב נשאר חייב לי בעד
קניית העסק, כאמור לעיל, את כל הרווח שיגיע לי אחר ניכוי ההוצאות, ועליו יהיה
לשלם לי את הכסף המגיע לי עוד ממנו לפי החשבון. ויהיה לי או לב״כ כל דין תורת
נאמנות נגד הקונה וב״כ בכל הנוגע לחשבונות אלו ובפירוש הותנה עם הקונה הנ״ל
שאם יהיה במכירה הזאת איזה דבר מהדברים שלא יועילו בהם המכירה והקנין ע״פ
ד״ת שלא תבטל עי״ז מכירת שאר הדברים האמורים בשטר זה, וכן שלא יהיה קנין
אחד שאינו מועיל יכול לבטל את הקנין המועיל במכירה הזאת. [והרשות ביד הקונה
הנ״ל לתרגם את כל הנ״ל לשפת המדינה ולעשות כל דברי תוקף הקניין והמכירה ע״פ
חוקי המדינה והממשלה. ועליו יהיה לשלם מכיסו את כל הוצאות התרגום והמיסים
כפי חוקי המדינה.] כל זה נעשה בקגא״ס ובאנד שלאג ובקניין אגב קרקע ליתר
שאת על הקניינים הנ״ל ובכל אופן המועיל ע״פ דין תוה״ק ותקחז״ל דלא כאסמכתא
ודלא כטופסי דשטרי.
ולראיה באתי על החתום[1]
ביום _____ בשבת, _____ בחודש _____ שנת _____ פה _____
_____ נאום
בפנינו החח״מ חתם ר' _____ (המוכר) על כל הנ״ל
ובזה באנו על החתום יום ושנה הנ״ל פה _____
_____ נאום
_____ נאום

ACKNOWLEDGMENT BY PURCHASER

I, the undersigned _____ declare that all that is written above has been explained to me, and that I agree to and accept fully the contents of and all the conditions set out in the above document.

SIGNED ON THIS DAY _____ AT _____

_____

SIGNATURE OF PURCHASER _____

Recitations at Taharah

PRAYER PRECEDING *TAHARAH*
OF A JEWISH FEMALE

Lord of the Universe, have mercy upon _____ the daughter of _____,° who has passed on, and who is the daughter of Abraham, Isaac, and Jacob, Thy servants. Grant that her soul be given repose among the righteous, for it is Thou who revivest the dead and causest the living to die. Blessed art Thou, who pardons and forgives the sins and the iniquities of those who are dead among Thy people, Israel, with great compassion.

May it also be Thy will, O God, and God of our fathers, that angels of mercy will encompass Thy departed servant _____ daughter of Thy servant _____.° O our God, and God of our fathers, enlighten Thy poor servant. Keep her secure from all troubles and evil, and from the judgment of Gehennom.

Blessed art Thou, whose mercy is great, and who art compassionate.

Blessed art Thou, who makes peace in His lofty heavens for His servants and for those who revere His name.

Blessed is He who mercifully redeems His people, Israel, from all manner of tribulation.

Blessed art Thou, who mercifully establishes His covenant of mercy.

In mercy, conceal and cause the iniquities of Thy departed servant _____° to vanish, that she be not consumed. She is, indeed, in need of Thy great mercies, for Thou, O Lord our God, art good, and pardon those who call upon Thee.

Blessed art Thou, who art great in counsel and find ways to be merciful. Thou art with Thy righteous ones in paradise. O, guard Thou Thy pious ones.

Blessed art Thou, who bestows great mercy and kindness to the departed of Israel, Thy people.

°Supply name of deceased: _____ bat _____ (mother's name).

רִבּוֹנוֹ שֶׁל עוֹלָם חֲמוֹל עַל* פְּלוֹנִית בַּת פְּלוֹנִי הַמֵּתָה הַלָּזוֹ שֶׁהִיא בַּת)¹אַבְרָהָם יִצְחָק
וְיַעֲקֹב עֲבָדֶיךָ וְתָנוּחַ נַפְשָׁהּ וְנִשְׁמָתָהּ עִם הַצַּדִּיקִים כִּי אַתָּה מְחַיֶּה הַמֵּתִים וּמֵמִית חַיִּים.
בָּרוּךְ אַתָּה מוֹחֵל וְסוֹלֵחַ לַחַטָּאִים וְלָעֲוֹנוֹת מִמֵּתֵי יִשְׂרָאֵל בְּתַחֲנוּנִים: וּבְכֵן יְהִי
רָצוֹן מִלְּפָנֶיךָ יְיָ אֱלֹהֵינוּ וֵאלֹהֵי אֲבוֹתֵינוּ שֶׁתְּסַבֵּב מַלְאֲכֵי רַחֲמִים לִפְנֵי הַמֵּתָה שֶׁהִיא
אֲמָתְךָ בַּת אֲמָתֶךָ: וְאַתָּה יְיָ אֱלֹהֵינוּ וֵאלֹהֵי אֲבוֹתֵינוּ מַשְׂכִּיל אֶל דָּל מַלְּטֶהָ מִכָּל צָרָה
וּמִיּוֹם רָעָה וּמִדִּינָהּ שֶׁל גֵּיהִנֹּם: בָּרוּךְ אַתָּה גָּדוֹל אַתָּה הַחֶסֶד וּבַעַל הָרַחֲמִים: בָּרוּךְ אַתָּה
הָעֹשֶׂה שָׁלוֹם בִּמְרוֹמָיו לַעֲבָדָיו וּלִירֵאָי שְׁמוֹ: בָּרוּךְ פּוֹדֶה עַמּוֹ יִשְׂרָאֵל מִמִּינֵי פּוּרְעָנִיּוֹת
בְּרַחֲמִים: בְּרַחֲמִים הַסְתֵּר וְהַעֲלֵם פִּשְׁעֵי הַמֵּתָה הַזֹּאת אַמָּתֶךָ מִשְׂרֶפֶת אֵשׁ תַּחְלִיצֶהָ
שֶׁהִיא צְרִיכָה לְרַחֲמֶיךָ הָרַבִּים: וְאַתָּה יְיָ אֱלֹהֵינוּ טוֹב וְסַלָּח לְכָל קוֹרְאֶיךָ. בָּרוּךְ אַתָּה
גָּדוֹל הָעֵצָה וְרַב הָעֲלִילִיָּה בְּרַחֲמִים עִם רַגְלֵי צַדִּיקִים בְּגַן עֵדֶן תִּדְרֹךְ כִּי מְקוֹם יְשָׁרִים
הוּא רַגְלֵי חֲסִידָיו יִשְׁמֹר: בָּרוּךְ אַתָּה הַנּוֹתֵן רַחֲמִים גְּדוֹלִים וְרֹב תַּחֲנוּנִים לְמֵתֵי עַמּוֹ
יִשְׂרָאֵל אָמֵן כֵּן יְהִי רָצוֹן:

PRAYER PRECEDING *TAHARAH* OF A JEWISH MALE

Note: The English translation of the prayer for a Jewish female can be used appropriately, and in the masculine form. It should be adapted.

רִבּוֹנוֹ שֶׁל עוֹלָם חֲמוֹל עַל פְּלוֹנִי בֶּן פְּלוֹנִי הַמֵּת הַלָּז שֶׁהוּא בֶּן אַבְרָהָם יִצְחָק וְיַעֲקֹב
עֲבָדֶיךָ וְתָנוּחַ נַפְשׁוֹ וְנִשְׁמָתוֹ עִם הַצַּדִּיקִים כִּי אַתָּה מְחַיֶּה הַמֵּתִים וּמֵמִית חַיִּים. בָּרוּךְ
אַתָּה מוֹחֵל וְסוֹלֵחַ לַחַטָּאִים וְלָעֲוֹנוֹת מִמֵּתֵי יִשְׂרָאֵל בְּתַחֲנוּנִים: וּבְכֵן יְהִי רָצוֹן
מִלְּפָנֶיךָ יְיָ אֱלֹהֵינוּ וֵאלֹהֵי אֲבוֹתֵינוּ שֶׁתְּסַבֵּב מַלְאֲכֵי רַחֲמִים לִפְנֵי הַמֵּת שֶׁהוּא עַבְדְּךָ בֶּן
אֲמָתֶךָ: וְאַתָּה יְיָ אֱלֹהֵינוּ וֵאלֹהֵי אֲבוֹתֵינוּ מַשְׂכִּיל אֶל דָּל מַלְּטֵהוּ מִכָּל צָרָה וּמִיּוֹם רָעָה
וּמִדִּינָהּ שֶׁל גֵּיהִנֹּם: בָּרוּךְ אַתָּה גָּדוֹל הַחֶסֶד וּבַעַל הָרַחֲמִים: בָּרוּךְ אַתָּה הָעֹשֶׂה שָׁלוֹם
בִּמְרוֹמָיו לַעֲבָדָיו וּלִירֵאָי שְׁמוֹ: בָּרוּךְ פּוֹדֶה עַמּוֹ יִשְׂרָאֵל מִמִּינֵי פּוּרְעָנִיּוֹת בְּרַחֲמִים:
וּבְכֵן יְהִי רָצוֹן מִלְּפָנֶיךָ יְיָ אֱלֹהֵינוּ וֵאלֹהֵי אֲבוֹתֵינוּ שֶׁתִּזְכּוֹר זְכוּת בְּרִית קֹדֶשׁ שֶׁבִּבְשָׂרוֹ
וְיִהְיֶה פִּדְיוֹן לוֹ מִשְׂרֶפֶת גֵּיהִנֹּם וְתַחֲלִיצֵהוּ. בָּרוּךְ אַתָּה כּוֹרֵת הַבְּרִית בְּרַחֲמִים בְּרַחֲמִים:
בְּרַחֲמִים הַסְתֵּר וְהַעֲלֵם פִּשְׁעֵי הַמֵּת הַזֶּה עַבְדְּךָ מִשְׂרֶפֶת אֵשׁ תַּחֲלִיצֵהוּ. שֶׁהוּא צָרִיךְ
לְרַחֲמֶיךָ הָרַבִּים: וְאַתָּה יְיָ אֱלֹהֵינוּ טוֹב וְסַלָּח לְכָל קוֹרְאֶיךָ. בָּרוּךְ אַתָּה גָּדוֹל הָעֵצָה וְרַב
הָעֲלִילִיָּה בְּרַחֲמִים עִם רַגְלֵי צַדִּיקִים בְּגַן עֵדֶן יִדְרֹךְ כִּי מְקוֹם יְשָׁרִים הוּא רַגְלֵי חֲסִידָיו
יִשְׁמֹר: בָּרוּךְ אַתָּה הַנּוֹתֵן רַחֲמִים גְּדוֹלִים וְרֹב תַּחֲנוּנִים לְמֵתֵי עַמּוֹ יִשְׂרָאֵל אָמֵן כֵּן יְהִי
רָצוֹן:

PRAYER PRIOR TO WASHING

Rabbi Akiva said: "Happy are you. O Israel. Before whom do you purify yourselves, and who is He who purifies you? It is your Father in heaven—as it says: And I shall sprinkle pure water upon you and you will be purified of all your iniquities. Of all your uncleanliness shall I cleanse you. And Scripture declares: "The Lord is the *Mikveh* of Israel."

Thou art a fountain of gardens, a well of living waters, and flowing streams from Lebanon.

Surely the Lord hath washed away the dirt of the daughters of Zion, and shall cast away the blood of Jerusalem from the midst thereof with a spirit of justice and cleansing.

And I shall sprinkle pure water upon you, and you will be purified of all your impurities. of all your uncleanliness shall I cleanse you.

אָמַר רַבִּי עֲקִיבָא אַשְׁרֵיכֶם יִשְׂרָאֵל לִפְנֵי מִי אַתֶּם מִטַּהֲרִין וּמִי מְטַהֵר אֶתְכֶם אֲבִיכֶם
שֶׁבַּשָּׁמַיִם שֶׁנֶּאֱמַר וְזָרַקְתִּי עֲלֵיכֶם מַיִם טְהוֹרִים וּטְהַרְתֶּם מִכֹּל טֻמְאוֹתֵיכֶם וּמִכָּל
גִּלּוּלֵיכֶם אֲטַהֵר אֶתְכֶם: וְאוֹמֵר מִקְוֵה יִשְׂרָאֵל יְיָ מַה הַמִּקְוֶה מְטַהֵר אֶת הַטְּמֵאִים אַף
הַקָּדוֹשׁ בָּרוּךְ הוּא מְטַהֵר אֶת יִשְׂרָאֵל:

מַעְיַן גַּנִּים בְּאֵר מַיִם חַיִּים וְנוֹזְלִים מִן לְבָנוֹן: אִם רָחַץ יְיָ אֵת צוֹאַת בְּנוֹת צִיּוֹן וְאֶת
דְּמֵי יְרוּשָׁלַיִם יָדִיחַ מִקִּרְבָּהּ בְּרוּחַ מִשְׁפָּט וּבְרוּחַ בָּעֵר: וְזָרַקְתִּי עֲלֵיכֶם מַיִם טְהוֹרִים
וּטְהַרְתֶּם מִכֹּל טֻמְאוֹתֵיכֶם וּמִכָּל גִּלּוּלֵיכֶם אֲטַהֵר אֶתְכֶם:

RECITATION DURING WASHING

His head is like the most fine gold; his heaps of curls are black as a raven.

His eyes are like doves beside the water-brooks, bathing in milk and fitly set.

His cheeks are like a bed of spices, towers of sweet herbs.

His lips are roses dripping flowing myrrh.

His arms are golden cylinders set with beryl,

His body is as polished ivory overlaid with sapphires.

His legs are pillars of marble set upon foundations of fine gold,

His appearance is like Lebanon, as select as the cedars.

His mouth is most sweet and he is altogether precious.
This is my beloved and this is my friend, daughters of Jerusalem.

רֹאשׁוֹ כֶּתֶם פָּז קְוֻצּוֹתָיו תַּלְתַּלִּים שְׁחֹרוֹת כָּעוֹרֵב: עֵינָיו כְּיוֹנִים עַל אֲפִיקֵי מָיִם
רֹחֲצוֹת בֶּחָלָב יֹשְׁבוֹת עַל מִלֵּאת: לְחָיָו כַּעֲרוּגַת הַבֹּשֶׂם מִגְדְּלוֹת מֶרְקָחִים שִׂפְתוֹתָיו
שׁוֹשַׁנִּים נֹטְפוֹת מוֹר עֹבֵר: יָדָיו גְּלִילֵי זָהָב מְמֻלָּאִים בַּתַּרְשִׁישׁ מֵעָיו עֶשֶׁת שֵׁן מְעֻלֶּפֶת
סַפִּירִים: שׁוֹקָיו עַמּוּדֵי שֵׁשׁ מְיֻסָּדִים עַל אַדְנֵי פָז מַרְאֵהוּ כַּלְּבָנוֹן בָּחוּר כָּאֲרָזִים: חִכּוֹ
מַמְתַּקִּים וְכֻלּוֹ מַחֲמַדִּים זֶה דוֹדִי וְזֶה רֵעִי בְּנוֹת יְרוּשָׁלָיִם:

RECITATION DURING DRESSING

I shall surely rejoice in the Lord. My soul will delight in my God.
For he hath clothed me in garments of salvation. He hath drawn
the cloak of righteousness upon me. And I said:

> Let them place a pure headdress on his head. And they placed the pure
> headdress on his head and dressed him with clothes. And the angel of
> the Lord was standing by. For as the earth will bring forth its growth,
> and as a garden will make its seed to grow, thus will the Lord God cause
> righteousness and praise to flourish in the presence of all the nations.
> And the Lord will guide you continually. He will satisfy your soul in
> drought. And He will make fat your bones. And you will be like a
> watered garden, and like a spring of water, whose waters do not fail.

שׂוֹשׂ אָשִׂישׂ בַּיָי תָּגֵל נַפְשִׁי בֵּאלֹהַי כִּי הִלְבִּישַׁנִי בִּגְדֵי יֶשַׁע מְעִיל צְדָקָה יְעָטָנִי כֶּחָתָן
יְכַהֵן פְּאֵר וְכַכַּלָּה תַּעְדֶּה כֵלֶיהָ: וְאֹמַר יָשִׂימוּ צָנִיף טָהוֹר עַל רֹאשׁוֹ וַיָּשִׂימוּ הַצָּנִיף
הַטָּהוֹר עַל רֹאשׁוֹ וַיַּלְבִּישֻׁהוּ בְּגָדִים וּמַלְאַךְ יְיָ עֹמֵד: כִּי כָאָרֶץ תּוֹצִיא צִמְחָהּ וּכְגַנָּה
זֵרוּעֶיהָ תַצְמִיחַ כֵּן יְיָ אֱלֹהִים יַצְמִיחַ צְדָקָה וּתְהִלָּה נֶגֶד כָּל הַגּוֹיִם: וְנָחֲךָ יְיָ תָּמִיד
וְהִשְׂבִּיעַ בְּצַחְצָחוֹת נַפְשֶׁךָ וְעַצְמֹתֶיךָ יַחֲלִיץ וְהָיִיתָ כְּגַן רָוֶה וּכְמוֹצָא מַיִם אֲשֶׁר לֹא יְכַזְּבוּ
מֵימָיו:

RECITATION WHEN THE BODY
IS PLACED IN THE CASKET

But they shall not go to see when the holy things are covered, lest
they die. Behold his couch, which is Solomon's. Threescore valiant

men are about it, of the valiant of Israel. They all hold swords, being expert in war; every man hath his sword upon his thigh because of fear of the night.

May the Lord bless you and protect you. May the Lord cause His face to shine upon you and be gracious unto you.

His scent is as the Lebanon.

I have seen, and behold, a candlestick all of gold, with a bowl upon the top of it, and its seven lamps thereon; there are seven pipes, yea seven, to the lamps, which are upon the top thereof. And two olive trees by it, one upon the right side of the bowl, and the other upon the left side thereof.

Who art thou, O great mountain, before Zerubbabel thou shalt become a plain. And he shall bring forth the top stone with shoutings of: "Grace, grace, unto it." But as I live, the glory of the Lord shall fill the whole of the world.

וְלֹא יָבוֹאוּ לִרְאוֹת כְּבַלַּע אֶת הַקֹּדֶשׁ וָמֵתוּ:

הִנֵּה מִטָּתוֹ שֶׁלִּשְׁלֹמֹה שִׁשִּׁים גִּבּוֹרִים סָבִיב לָהּ מִגִּבּוֹרֵי יִשְׂרָאֵל: כֻּלָּם אֲחֻזֵי חֶרֶב מְלֻמְּדֵי מִלְחָמָה אִישׁ חַרְבּוֹ עַל יְרֵכוֹ מִפַּחַד בַּלֵּילוֹת: יְבָרֶכְךָ יְיָ וְיִשְׁמְרֶךָ: יָאֵר יְיָ פָּנָיו אֵלֶיךָ וִיחֻנֶּךָּ: יִשָּׂא יְיָ פָּנָיו אֵלֶיךָ וְיָשֵׂם לְךָ שָׁלוֹם: יֵלְכוּ יוֹנְקוֹתָיו וִיהִי כַזַּיִת הוֹדוֹ וְרֵיחַ לוֹ כַּלְּבָנוֹן: רָאִיתִי וְהִנֵּה מְנוֹרַת זָהָב כֻּלָּהּ וְגֻלָּהּ עַל רֹאשָׁהּ וְשִׁבְעָה נֵרֹתֶיהָ עָלֶיהָ שִׁבְעָה וְשִׁבְעָה מוּצָקוֹת לַנֵּרוֹת אֲשֶׁר עַל רֹאשָׁהּ: וּשְׁנַיִם זֵיתִים עָלֶיהָ אֶחָד מִימִין הַגֻּלָּה וְאֶחָד עַל שְׂמֹאלָהּ:

מִי אַתָּה הַר הַגָּדוֹל לִפְנֵי זְרֻבָּבֶל לְמִישׁוֹר וְהוֹצִיא אֶת הָאֶבֶן הָרֹאשָׁה תְּשֻׁאוֹת חֵן חֵן לָהּ: וְעַתָּה יִגְדַּל נָא כֹּחַ אֲדֹנָי כַּאֲשֶׁר דִּבַּרְתָּ לֵאמֹר: וְאוּלָם חַי אָנִי וְיִמָּלֵא כְבוֹד יְיָ אֶת כָּל הָאָרֶץ:

Blessing Following Rending
of Garments

Blessed art Thou, O Lord our God, King of the universe, the true
Judge.　　　　　　　　בָּרוּךְ אַתָּה יְיָ אֱלֹהֵינוּ מֶלֶךְ הָעוֹלָם. דַּיַּן הָאֱמֶת:

ABBREVIATED FORM OF THE ABOVE

Blessed is the true Judge.　　　　　　　　בָּרוּךְ דַּיַּן הָאֱמֶת:

215

The Funeral Service

Read either Psalm 23 or Psalm 130.

Psalm 23

The Lord is my shepherd; I shall not want. He maketh me to lie down in green pastures: He leadeth me beside the still waters. He restoreth my soul: He guideth me in the paths of righteousness for His name's sake. Yea, though I walk through the valley of the shadow of death, I will fear no evil; for Thou art with me: Thy rod and Thy staff, they comfort me. Thou preparest a table before me in the presence of mine enemies: Thou hast anointed my head with oil; my cup runneth over. Surely happiness and loving-kindness will follow me all the days of my life; and I shall dwell in the house of the Lord for evermore.

תהלים כ"ג

מִזְמוֹר לְדָוִד יְהוָה רֹעִי לֹא אֶחְסָר: בִּנְאוֹת דֶּשֶׁא יַרְבִּיצֵנִי עַל־מֵי מְנֻחוֹת יְנַהֲלֵנִי:
נַפְשִׁי יְשׁוֹבֵב יַנְחֵנִי בְמַעְגְּלֵי־צֶדֶק לְמַעַן שְׁמוֹ: גַּם כִּי־אֵלֵךְ בְּגֵיא צַלְמָוֶת לֹא־אִירָא רָע
כִּי־אַתָּה עִמָּדִי שִׁבְטְךָ וּמִשְׁעַנְתֶּךָ הֵמָּה יְנַחֲמֻנִי: תַּעֲרֹךְ לְפָנַי שֻׁלְחָן נֶגֶד צֹרְרָי דִּשַּׁנְתָּ בַשֶּׁמֶן
רֹאשִׁי כּוֹסִי רְוָיָה: אַךְ טוֹב וָחֶסֶד יִרְדְּפוּנִי כָּל־יְמֵי חַיָּי וְשַׁבְתִּי בְּבֵית־יְהוָה לְאֹרֶךְ יָמִים:
שִׁיר הַמַּעֲלוֹת מִמַּעֲמַקִּים קְרָאתִיךָ יְהוָה: אֲדֹנָי שִׁמְעָה בְקוֹלִי תִּהְיֶינָה אָזְנֶיךָ קַשֻּׁבוֹת
לְקוֹל תַּחֲנוּנָי: אִם־עֲוֹנוֹת תִּשְׁמָר־יָהּ אֲדֹנָי מִי יַעֲמֹד: כִּי־עִמְּךָ הַסְּלִיחָה לְמַעַן תִּוָּרֵא:
קִוִּיתִי יְהוָה קִוְּתָה נַפְשִׁי וְלִדְבָרוֹ הוֹחָלְתִּי: נַפְשִׁי לַאדֹנָי מִשֹּׁמְרִים לַבֹּקֶר שֹׁמְרִים לַבֹּקֶר:
יַחֵל יִשְׂרָאֵל אֶל־יְהוָה כִּי־עִם־יְהוָה הַחֶסֶד וְהַרְבֵּה עִמּוֹ פְדוּת: וְהוּא יִפְדֶּה אֶת־יִשְׂרָאֵל
מִכֹּל עֲוֹנוֹתָיו:

Psalm 130

Out of the depths have I cried unto Thee, O Lord. Lord, hear my voice: let Thine ears be attentive to the voice of my supplications. If

Thou, Lord, shouldst mark iniquities, O Lord, who could stand?
But there is forgiveness with Thee, that Thou mayest be feared. I
wait for the Lord, my soul doth wait, and in His word do I hope.
My soul waiteth for the Lord, more than watchmen wait for the
morning; yea, more than watchmen for the morning. O let Israel
hope in the Lord; for with the Lord there is loving-kindness, and
with Him is plenteous deliverance. And He shall deliver Israel from
all his iniquities.

Or read the following scriptural selection:

O Lord, Thou hast been a dwelling-place unto us in all generations. Before the mountains were brought forth, or ever Thou
gavest birth to the earth and the world, even from everlasting to
everlasting Thou art God. Thou turnest man back to dust, and
sayest, Return, ye children of men. For a thousand years in Thy
sight are but as yesterday when it is past, and as a watch in the
night. The days of our years are threescore years and ten, or even by
reason of strength fourscore years; yet is their pride but travail and
nothingness; for it is soon gone by, and we fly away. So teach us to
number our days, that we may get us a heart of wisdom.

Seek ye the Lord while He may be found, call ye upon Him while
He is near; let the wicked forsake his way, and the unrighteous man
his thoughts; and let him return unto the Lord, and He will have
mercy upon him; and to our God, for He will abundantly pardon.
For My thoughts are not your thoughts, neither are your ways My
ways, saith the Lord. For as the heavens are higher than the earth,
so are My ways higher than your ways, and My thoughts than your
thoughts.

אֲדֹנָי מָעוֹן אַתָּה הָיִיתָ לָּנוּ בְּדֹר וָדֹר: בְּטֶרֶם הָרִים יֻלָּדוּ וַתְּחוֹלֵל אֶרֶץ וְתֵבֵל וּמֵעוֹלָם
עַד־עוֹלָם אַתָּה אֵל: תָּשֵׁב אֱנוֹשׁ עַד־דַּכָּא וַתֹּאמֶר שׁוּבוּ בְנֵי־אָדָם: כִּי אֶלֶף שָׁנִים בְּעֵינֶיךָ
כְּיוֹם אֶתְמוֹל כִּי יַעֲבֹר וְאַשְׁמוּרָה בַלָּיְלָה: יְמֵי שְׁנוֹתֵינוּ בָהֶם שִׁבְעִים שָׁנָה וְרָהְבָּם עָמָל
וָאָוֶן כִּי גָז חִישׁ וַנָּעֻפָה: לִמְנוֹת יָמֵינוּ כֵּן הוֹדַע וְנָבִיא לְבַב חָכְמָה:
דִּרְשׁוּ יְיָ בְּהִמָּצְאוֹ קְרָאֻהוּ בִּהְיוֹתוֹ קָרוֹב: יַעֲזֹב רָשָׁע דַּרְכּוֹ וְאִישׁ אָוֶן מַחְשְׁבֹתָיו
וְיָשֹׁב אֶל־יְיָ וִירַחֲמֵהוּ וְאֶל־אֱלֹהֵינוּ כִּי־יַרְבֶּה לִסְלוֹחַ: כִּי לֹא מַחְשְׁבוֹתַי מַחְשְׁבוֹתֵיכֶם וְלֹא
דַרְכֵיכֶם דְּרָכָי נְאֻם יְיָ: כִּי גָבְהוּ שָׁמַיִם מֵאָרֶץ כֵּן גָּבְהוּ דְרָכַי מִדַּרְכֵיכֶם וּמַחְשְׁבֹתַי
מִמַּחְשְׁבֹתֵיכֶם:

Continue with the following reading:

As for man, his days are as grass; as the flower of the field, so he flourisheth. For the wind passeth over it, and it is gone; and the place thereof shall know it no more. But the loving-kindness of the Lord is from everlasting to everlasting upon them that fear Him, and His righteousness unto children's children. In the way of righteousness is life; and in the pathway thereof there is no death. And the dust returneth to the earth as it was, but the spirit returneth unto God, who gave it. Whom have I in heaven but Thee? And there is none upon earth that I desire beside Thee. My flesh and my heart faileth: but God is the strength of my heart and my portion for ever. How precious is Thy loving-kindness, O God! And the children of men take refuge under the shadow of Thy wings. For with Thee is the fountain of life; in Thy light do we see light.

אֱנוֹשׁ כֶּחָצִיר יָמָיו כְּצִיץ הַשָּׂדֶה כֵּן יָצִיץ: כִּי רוּחַ עָבְרָה־בּוֹ וְאֵינֶנּוּ וְלֹא־יַכִּירֶנּוּ עוֹד מְקוֹמוֹ: וְחֶסֶד יְיָ מֵעוֹלָם וְעַד־עוֹלָם עַל־יְרֵאָיו וְצִדְקָתוֹ לִבְנֵי בָנִים: בְּאֹרַח צְדָקָה חַיִּים וְדֶרֶךְ נְתִיבָה אַל־מָוֶת: וְיָשֹׁב הֶעָפָר עַל הָאָרֶץ כְּשֶׁהָיָה וְהָרוּחַ תָּשׁוּב אֶל הָאֱלֹהִים אֲשֶׁר נְתָנָהּ: מִי לִי בַשָּׁמָיִם וְעִמְּךָ לֹא־חָפַצְתִּי בָאָרֶץ: כָּלָה שְׁאֵרִי וּלְבָבִי צוּר־לְבָבִי וְחֶלְקִי אֱלֹהִים לְעוֹלָם: מַה־יָּקָר חַסְדְּךָ אֱלֹהִים וּבְנֵי אָדָם בְּצֵל כְּנָפֶיךָ יֶחֱסָיוּן: כִּי עִמְּךָ מְקוֹר חַיִּים בְּאוֹרְךָ נִרְאֶה־אוֹר:

Read one of the following.

For a Man

Who may ascend the mountain of the Lord? And who may stand in His holy place? He that hath clean hands and a pure heart; who hath not set his desire upon vanity, and hath not sworn deceitfully. He shall receive a blessing from the Lord, and righteousness from the God of his salvation.

Let us hear the conclusion of the whole matter: Fear God, and keep His commandments: for this is the whole duty of man.

The day is short, and the work is great, and the laborers are sluggish, and the reward is much, and the Master of the house is urgent.

It is not thy duty to complete the work, but neither art thou free to desist from it. Faithful is thy Employer to pay thee the reward of thy labor; and know that the grant of reward unto the righteous will be in the time to come.

מִי־יַעֲלֶה בְהַר יְיָ וּמִי־יָקוּם בִּמְקוֹם קָדְשׁוֹ: נְקִי כַפַּיִם וּבַר לֵבָב אֲשֶׁר לֹא נָשָׂא לַשָּׁוְא נַפְשִׁי וְלֹא נִשְׁבַּע לְמִרְמָה: יִשָּׂא בְרָכָה מֵאֵת יְיָ וּצְדָקָה מֵאֱלֹהֵי יִשְׁעוֹ: סוֹף דָּבָר הַכֹּל נִשְׁמָע אֶת הָאֱלֹהִים יְרָא וְאֶת מִצְוֹתָיו שְׁמוֹר כִּי זֶה כָּל הָאָדָם: הַיּוֹם קָצֵר וְהַמְּלָאכָה מְרֻבָּה וְהַפּוֹעֲלִים עֲצֵלִים וְהַשָּׂכָר הַרְבֵּה וּבַעַל הַבַּיִת דּוֹחֵק: לֹא עָלֶיךָ הַמְּלָאכָה לִגְמוֹר וְלֹא־אַתָּה בֶן־חוֹרִין לְהִבָּטֵל מִמֶּנָּה: נֶאֱמָן הוּא בַּעַל מְלַאכְתְּךָ שֶׁיְשַׁלֶּם לְךָ שְׂכַר פְּעֻלָּתֶךָ. וְדַע שֶׁמַּתַּן שְׂכָרָם שֶׁל־צַדִּיקִים לֶעָתִיד לָבוֹא:

For a Woman

The portions in brackets to be omitted according to circumstances.

A woman of worth who can find? For her price is far above rubies. [The heart of her husband trusteth in her; and he shall have no lack of gain. She doeth him good and not evil all the days of her life.] She stretcheth out her hand to the poor; yea, she putteth forth her hands to the needy. Strength and majesty are her clothing; and she laugheth at the time to come. She openeth her mouth with wisdom; and the law of loving-kindness is on her tongue. [She looketh well to the ways of her household, and eateth not the bread of idleness. Her children rise up and call her happy; her husband also, and he praiseth her, saying: Many daughters have done worthily, but thou excellest them all.] Give her of the fruit of her hands; and let her works praise her in the gates.

The Lord recompense thy works, and a full reward be given thee of the Lord God of Israel, under whose wings thou art come to trust.

אֵשֶׁת חַיִל מִי יִמְצָא וְרָחוֹק מִפְּנִינִים מִכְרָהּ: [בָּטַח בָּהּ לֵב בַּעְלָהּ וְשָׁלָל לֹא יֶחְסָר: גְּמָלַתְהוּ טוֹב וְלֹא רָע כֹּל יְמֵי חַיֶּיהָ:] דָּרְשָׁה צֶמֶר וּפִשְׁתִּים וַתַּעַשׂ בְּחֵפֶץ כַּפֶּיהָ: הָיְתָה כָּאֳנִיּוֹת סוֹחֵר מִמֶּרְחָק תָּבִיא לַחְמָהּ: וַתָּקָם בְּעוֹד לַיְלָה וַתִּתֵּן טֶרֶף לְבֵיתָהּ וְחֹק לְנַעֲרֹתֶיהָ: זָמְמָה שָׂדֶה וַתִּקָּחֵהוּ מִפְּרִי כַפֶּיהָ נָטְעָה כָּרֶם: חָגְרָה בְעוֹז מָתְנֶיהָ וַתְּאַמֵּץ זְרוֹעֹתֶיהָ:

טַעֲמָה כִּי טוֹב סַחְרָהּ לֹא יִכְבֶּה בַלַּיְלָה נֵרָהּ: יָדֶיהָ שִׁלְּחָה בַכִּישׁוֹר וְכַפֶּיהָ תָּמְכוּ פָלֶךְ: כַּפָּהּ פָּרְשָׂה לֶעָנִי וְיָדֶיהָ שִׁלְּחָה לָאֶבְיוֹן: לֹא תִירָא לְבֵיתָהּ מִשָּׁלֶג כִּי כָל בֵּיתָהּ לָבֻשׁ שָׁנִים: מַרְבַדִּים עָשְׂתָה לָּהּ שֵׁשׁ וְאַרְגָּמָן לְבוּשָׁהּ: נוֹדָע בַּשְּׁעָרִים בַּעְלָהּ בְּשִׁבְתּוֹ עִם זִקְנֵי אָרֶץ: סָדִין עָשְׂתָה וַתִּמְכֹּר וַחֲגוֹר נָתְנָה לַכְּנַעֲנִי: עוֹז וְהָדָר לְבוּשָׁהּ וַתִּשְׂחַק לְיוֹם אַחֲרוֹן: פִּיהָ פָּתְחָה בְחָכְמָה וְתוֹרַת חֶסֶד עַל לְשׁוֹנָהּ: [צוֹפִיָּה הֲלִיכוֹת בֵּיתָהּ וְלֶחֶם עַצְלוּת לֹא תֹאכֵל: קָמוּ בָנֶיהָ וַיְאַשְּׁרוּהָ בַּעְלָהּ וַיְהַלְלָהּ: רַבּוֹת בָּנוֹת עָשׂוּ חָיִל וְאַתְּ עָלִית עַל כֻּלָּנָה:] שֶׁקֶר הַחֵן וְהֶבֶל הַיֹּפִי אִשָּׁה יִרְאַת יְהֹוָה הִיא תִתְהַלָּל: תְּנוּ לָהּ מִפְּרִי יָדֶיהָ וִיהַלְלוּהָ בַשְּׁעָרִים מַעֲשֶׂיהָ:

יְשַׁלֵּם יְיָ פָּעֳלֵךְ וּתְהִי מַשְׂכֻּרְתֵּךְ שְׁלֵמָה מֵעִם יְיָ אֱלֹהֵי יִשְׂרָאֵל אֲשֶׁר בָּאת לַחֲסוֹת תַּחַת כְּנָפָיו:

Continue with "O Lord, who art full of compassion."

O Lord who art full of compassion, who dwellest on high-God of forgiveness, who art merciful, slow to anger, and abounding in loving-kindness, grant pardon of transgressions, nearness of salvation, and perfect rest beneath the shadow of Thy divine presence, in the exalted places among the holy and pure, who shine as the brightness of the firmament, to _____ who hath gone to his [her] eternal home. We beseech thee, O Lord of compassion, remember unto him [her] for good all the meritorious and pious deeds which he [she] wrought while on earth. Open unto him [her] the gates of righteousness and light, the gates of pity and grace. O shelter him [her] for evermore under the cover of Thy wings; and let his [her] soul be bound up in the bond of eternal life. The Lord is his [her] inheritance; may he [she] rest in peace. And let us say, Amen.

אֵל מָלֵא רַחֲמִים שׁוֹכֵן בַּמְּרוֹמִים אֵלֹהַּ סְלִיחוֹת חַנּוּן וְרַחוּם אֶרֶךְ אַפַּיִם וְרַב חֶסֶד. הַמְצֵא כַּפָּרַת פֶּשַׁע וְהַקְרָבַת יֶשַׁע וּמְנוּחָה נְכוֹנָה תַּחַת כַּנְפֵי הַשְּׁכִינָה בְּמַעֲלוֹת קְדוֹשִׁים וּטְהוֹרִים כְּזֹהַר הָרָקִיעַ מַזְהִירִים. אֶת נִשְׁמַת פב״פ שֶׁהָלַךְ (שֶׁהָלְכָה) לְעוֹלָמוֹ (לְעוֹלָמָהּ): אָנָּא בַּעַל הָרַחֲמִים זָכְרָה לוֹ (לָהּ) לְטוֹבָה כָּל זְכֻיּוֹתָיו (זְכֻיּוֹתֶיהָ) וְצִדְקוֹתָיו (וְצִדְקוֹתֶיהָ) בְּאַרְצוֹת הַחַיִּים. וּפְתַח לוֹ (לָהּ) שַׁעֲרֵי צֶדֶק וְאוֹרָה שַׁעֲרֵי חֶמְלָה וַחֲנִינָה. בְּסֵתֶר כְּנָפֶיךָ תַּסְתִּירֵהוּ (תַּסְתִּירֶהָ) לְעוֹלָמִים. וּצְרוֹר בִּצְרוֹר הַחַיִּים אֶת נִשְׁמָתוֹ (נִשְׁמָתָהּ). יְיָ הוּא נַחֲלָתוֹ (נַחֲלָתָהּ). וְיָנוּחַ (וְתָנוּחַ) בְּשָׁלוֹם עַל מִשְׁכָּבוֹ (מִשְׁכָּבָהּ) וְנֹאמַר אָמֵן:

In case of a child, read the following:

O God, who art full of compassion, who dwellest on high, grant perfect rest beneath the shadow of thy divine presence, in the exalted places among the holy and pure, who shine as the brightness of the firmament, to the child _____ who hath gone to his [her] eternal rest. We beseech thee, O Lord of compassion, shelter his [her] soul for evermore under the cover of Thy wings. The Lord is his [her] portion. May he [she] rest in peace. And let us say, Amen!

אֵל מָלֵא רַחֲמִים שׁוֹכֵן בַּמְּרוֹמִים. הַמְצֵא מְנוּחָה נְכוֹנָה תַּחַת כַּנְפֵי הַשְּׁכִינָה. בְּמַעֲלוֹת קְדוֹשִׁים וּטְהוֹרִים. כְּזֹהַר הָרָקִיעַ מַזְהִירִים. אֶת־נִשְׁמַת הַיֶּלֶד (הַיַּלְדָּה) פב״פ שֶׁהָלַךְ (שֶׁהָלְכָה) לְעוֹלָמוֹ (לְעוֹלָמָהּ) אָנָּא בַּעַל הָרַחֲמִים הַסְתִּירֵהוּ (הַסְתִּירֶהָ) בְּסֵתֶר כְּנָפֶיךָ לְעוֹלָמִים. וּצְרוֹר בִּצְרוֹר הַחַיִּים אֶת נִשְׁמָתוֹ (נִשְׁמָתָהּ). יְיָ הוּא נַחֲלָתוֹ (נַחֲלָתָהּ) וְיָנוּחַ (וְתָנוּחַ) בְּשָׁלוֹם עַל מִשְׁכָּבוֹ (מִשְׁכָּבָהּ) וְנֹאמַר אָמֵן:

Eulogy

The Mishnah lessons found below on pp. 280–389 can form the basis of the eulogy.

The Burial Service

1. *Those who have not been in a cemetery for thirty days say the following blessing:*

Blessed be the Lord our God, King of the universe, who formed you in judgment, who nourished and sustained you in judgment, who brought death on you in judgment, who knoweth the number of you all in judgment, and will hereafter restore you to life in judgment. Blessed art Thou, O Lord, who quickenest the dead.

Thou, O Lord, art mighty for ever, Thou revivest the dead, Thou art mighty to save.

Thou sustainest the living with loving-kindness, revivest the dead with great mercy, supportest the falling, healest the sick, loosest the bound, and keepest thy faith to them that sleep in the dust. Who is like unto Thee, Lord of mighty acts, and who resembleth Thee, O King, who causest death and revivest, and causest salvation to spring forth? Yea, faithful art Thou to revive the dead.

בָּרוּךְ אַתָּה יְהֹוָה אֱלֹהֵֽינוּ מֶֽלֶךְ הָעוֹלָם אֲשֶׁר יָצַר אֶתְכֶם בַּדִּין וְזָן אֶתְכֶם בַּדִּין וְכִלְכֵּל אֶתְכֶם בַּדִּין וְהֵמִית אֶתְכֶם בַּדִּין וְיוֹדֵעַ מִסְפַּר כֻּלְּכֶם וְעָתִיד לְהַחֲיוֹתְכֶם בַּדִּין. בָּרוּךְ אַתָּה יְהֹוָה מְחַיֵּה הַמֵּתִים.

אַתָּה גִבּוֹר לְעוֹלָם אֲדֹנָי מְחַיֵּה מֵתִים אַתָּה רַב לְהוֹשִׁיעַ.

מְכַלְכֵּל חַיִּים בְּחֶֽסֶד מְחַיֵּה מֵתִים בְּרַחֲמִים רַבִּים סוֹמֵךְ נוֹפְלִים וְרוֹפֵא חוֹלִים וּמַתִּיר אֲסוּרִים וּמְקַיֵּם אֱמוּנָתוֹ לִישֵׁנֵי עָפָר. מִי כָמֽוֹךָ בַּֽעַל גְּבוּרוֹת וּמִי דֽוֹמֶה לָּךְ מֶֽלֶךְ מֵמִית וּמְחַיֶּה וּמַצְמִֽיחַ יְשׁוּעָה. וְנֶאֱמָן אַתָּה לְהַחֲיוֹת מֵתִים.

2. *When* Tachanun *is not said, the following is recited:*

Guard me, O God, for in Thee do I take refuge. I say unto the Lord, Thou art my lord: I have no good beyond Thee. As for the saints that are in the earth, they are the noble ones in whom is all

222

my delight. Their sorrows will be multiplied that have gotten unto themselves another god: their drink offerings of blood will I not pour out, nor take their names upon my lips. The Lord is the portion of mine inheritance and of my cup: Thou maintainest my lot. The lines are fallen unto me in pleasant places; yea, I have a delightsome heritage. I will bless the Lord, who hath given me counsel: yea, my reins admonish me in the night seasons.

I have set the Lord always before me: because He is at my right hand, I shall not be moved. Therefore my heart rejoiceth and my glory is glad: my flesh also will dwell in safety. For Thou wilt not abandon my soul to the grave: neither wilt Thou suffer thy loving one to see the pit. Thou wilt make known to me the path of life: in Thy presence is fullness of joy; at Thy right hand, bliss for evermore.

מִכְתָּם לְדָוִד שָׁמְרֵנִי אֵל, כִּי חָסִיתִי בָךְ: אָמַרְתְּ לַיהֹוָה אֲדֹנָי אָתָּה, טוֹבָתִי בַּל עָלֶיךָ: לִקְדוֹשִׁים אֲשֶׁר בָּאָרֶץ הֵמָּה, וְאַדִּירֵי כָּל חֶפְצִי בָם: יִרְבּוּ עַצְּבוֹתָם אַחֵר מָהָרוּ, בַּל אַסִּיךְ נִסְכֵּיהֶם מִדָּם, וּבַל אֶשָּׂא אֶת שְׁמוֹתָם עַל שְׂפָתָי: יְהֹוָה מְנָת חֶלְקִי וְכוֹסִי, אַתָּה תּוֹמִיךְ גּוֹרָלִי: חֲבָלִים נָפְלוּ לִי בַּנְּעִימִים אַף נַחֲלָת שָׁפְרָה עָלָי: אֲבָרֵךְ אֶת יְהֹוָה אֲשֶׁר יְעָצָנִי, אַף לֵילוֹת יִסְּרוּנִי כִלְיוֹתָי: שִׁוִּיתִי יְהֹוָה לְנֶגְדִּי תָמִיד, כִּי מִימִינִי בַּל אֶמּוֹט: לָכֵן שָׂמַח לִבִּי וַיָּגֶל כְּבוֹדִי, אַף בְּשָׂרִי יִשְׁכֹּן לָבֶטַח: כִּי לֹא תַעֲזֹב נַפְשִׁי לִשְׁאוֹל, לֹא תִתֵּן חֲסִידְךָ לִרְאוֹת שָׁחַת: תּוֹדִיעֵנִי אֹרַח חַיִּים, שׂוֹבַע שְׂמָחוֹת אֶת פָּנֶיךָ, נְעִימוֹת בִּימִינְךָ נֶצַח:

3. *On all other occasions, the service commences as follows:*

The Rock, His work is perfect, for all His ways are judgment: a God of faithfulness and without iniquity, just and right is He.

The Rock, perfect in every work, who can say unto Him, What workest Thou? He ruleth below and above; He causeth death and reviveth: He bringeth down to the grave, and bringeth up again.

The Rock, perfect in every deed, who can say unto Him, What doest Thou? O Thou who speakest and doest, of Thy grace deal kindly with us, and for the sake of him who was bound like a lamb, O hearken and do.

Just in all thy ways art thou, O perfect Rock, slow to anger and full of compassion. Spare and have pity upon parents and children, for Thine, Lord, is forgiveness and compassion.

Just art Thou, O Lord, in causing death and in reviving, whose hand is the charge of all spirits: far be it from Thee to blot out our remembrance: O let Thine eyes mercifully regard us, for Thine, Lord, is compassion and forgiveness.

If a man live a year or a thousand years, what profiteth it him? He shall be as though he had not been. Blessed be the true Judge, who causeth death and reviveth.

Blessed be He, for his judgment is true, and His eye discerneth all things, and He awardeth unto man his reckoning and his sentence, and all must render acknowledgment unto Him.

We know, O Lord, that Thy judgment is righteous: Thou art justified when Thou speakest, and pure when Thou judgest, and it is not for us to murmur at Thy method of judging; just art Thou, O Lord, and righteous are Thy judgments.

O true and righteous Judge! Blessed be the true Judge, all whose judgments are righteous and true.

The soul of every living thing is in Thy hand; Thy right hand is full of righteousness. Have mercy upon the remnant of the flock of Thy hand, and say unto the angel, Stay thy hand.

Thou art great in counsel and mighty in deed; Thine eyes are open upon all the ways of the children of men, to give unto every one according to his ways, and according to the fruit of his doings. To declare that the Lord is upright; He is my Rock, and there is no unrighteousness in Him.

The Lord gave, and the Lord hath taken away; blessed be the name of the Lord. And He, being merciful, forgiveth iniquity and destroyeth not: yea, many a time He turneth his anger away, and doth not stir up all His wrath.

הַצוּר תָּמִים פָּעֳלוֹ כִּי כָל־דְּרָכָיו מִשְׁפָּט אֵל אֱמוּנָה וְאֵין עָוֶל צַדִּיק וְיָשָׁר הוּא:

הַצּוּר תָּמִים בְּכָל פֹּעַל. מִי יֹאמַר לוֹ מַה תִּפְעָל. הַשַּׁלִּיט בְּמַטָּה וּבְמַעַל. מֵמִית וּמְחַיֶּה מוֹרִיד שְׁאוֹל וַיָּעַל:

הַצּוּר תָּמִים בְּכָל מַעֲשֶׂה. מִי יֹאמַר לוֹ מַה תַּעֲשֶׂה. הָאוֹמֵר וְעֹשֶׂה. חֶסֶד חִנָּם לָנוּ תַעֲשֶׂה. וּבִזְכוּת הַנֶּעֱקַד כְּשֶׂה. הַקְשִׁיבָה וַעֲשֵׂה: צַדִּיק בְּכָל־דְּרָכָיו הַצּוּר תָּמִים. אֶרֶךְ אַפַּיִם וּמָלֵא רַחֲמִים. חֲמוֹל נָא וְחוּס נָא עַל אָבוֹת וּבָנִים. כִּי לְךָ אָדוֹן הַסְּלִיחוֹת וְהָרַחֲמִים:

צַדִּיק אַתָּה יְהֹוָה לְהָמִית וּלְהַחֲיוֹת. אֲשֶׁר בְּיָדְךָ פִּקְדוֹן כָּל־רוּחוֹת. חָלִילָה לְךָ זִכְרוֹנֵנוּ לִמְחוֹת. וְיִהְיוּ נָא עֵינֶיךָ בְּרַחֲמִים עָלֵינוּ פְקוּחוֹת. כִּי לְךָ אָדוֹן הָרַחֲמִים וְהַסְּלִיחוֹת:

אָדָם בֶּן שָׁנָה יִהְיֶה. אוֹ אֶלֶף שָׁנִים יִחְיֶה. מַה יִּתְרוֹן לוֹ. כְּלֹא הָיָה יִהְיֶה. בָּרוּךְ דַּיַּן הָאֱמֶת מֵמִית וּמְחַיֶּה:

בָּרוּךְ הוּא כִּי אֱמֶת דִּינוֹ. וּמְשׁוֹטֵט הַכֹּל בְּעֵינוֹ. וּמְשַׁלֵּם לְאָדָם חֶשְׁבּוֹנוֹ וְדִינוֹ. וְהַכֹּל לִשְׁמוֹ הוֹדָיָה יִתֵּנוּ:

יָדַעְנוּ יְהֹוָה כִּי צֶדֶק מִשְׁפָּטֶיךָ. תִּצְדַּק בְּדָבְרֶךָ. וְתִזְכֶּה בְּשָׁפְטֶךָ. וְאֵין לְהַרְהֵר אַחַר מִדַּת שָׁפְטֶךָ. צַדִּיק אַתָּה יְהֹוָה וְיָשָׁר מִשְׁפָּטֶיךָ:

דַּיַּן אֱמֶת. שׁוֹפֵט צֶדֶק וֶאֱמֶת. בָּרוּךְ דַּיַּן הָאֱמֶת. שֶׁכָּל־מִשְׁפָּטָיו צֶדֶק וֶאֱמֶת:

נֶפֶשׁ כָּל חַי בְּיָדֶךָ. צֶדֶק מָלְאָה יְמִינְךָ וְיָדֶךָ. רַחֵם עַל פְּלֵיטַת צֹאן יָדֶךָ. וְתֹאמַר לְמַלְאָךְ הֶרֶף יָדֶךָ:

גְּדֹל הָעֵצָה וְרַב הָעֲלִילִיָּה. אֲשֶׁר עֵינֶיךָ פְקֻחוֹת עַל־כָּל־דַּרְכֵי בְּנֵי אָדָם. לָתֵת לְאִישׁ כִּדְרָכָיו וְכִפְרִי מַעֲלָלָיו: לְהַגִּיד כִּי יָשָׁר יְהֹוָה צוּרִי וְלֹא עַוְלָתָה בּוֹ:

יְהֹוָה נָתַן וַיהֹוָה לָקָח. יְהִי שֵׁם יְהֹוָה מְבֹרָךְ: וְהוּא רַחוּם יְכַפֵּר עָוֹן וְלֹא יַשְׁחִית. וְהִרְבָּה לְהָשִׁיב אַפּוֹ. וְלֹא יָעִיר כָּל חֲמָתוֹ:

4. *The processional is punctuated by seven stops. At each, the following portion of Psalm 91 is recited:*

Psalm 91

He that dwelleth in the shelter of the Most High abideth under the shadow of the Almighty. I say of the Lord, He is my refuge and my fortress: my God, in whom I trust. For He shall deliver thee from the snare of the fowler, and from the noisome pestilence. He shall cover thee with His pinions, and under His wings shalt thou take refuge: His truth shall be a shield and a buckler. Thou shalt not be afraid of the terror by night, nor of the arrow that flieth by day; of the pestilence that walketh in darkness, nor of the plague that ravageth at noon day. A thousand may fall at thy side, and ten thousand at thy right hand; it shall not come nigh unto thee. Only with thine eyes shalt thou look on, and see the retribution of the wicked. For Thou, O Lord, art my refuge. Thou hast made the Most High Thy dwelling place; there shall no evil befall thee, neither shall any scourge come nigh thy tent.

צ"א

יֹשֵׁב בְּסֵתֶר עֶלְיוֹן, בְּצֵל שַׁדַּי יִתְלוֹנָן. אֹמַר לַיהֹוָה מַחְסִי וּמְצוּדָתִי, אֱלֹהַי אֶבְטַח בּוֹ. כִּי הוּא יַצִּילְךָ מִפַּח יָקוּשׁ, מִדֶּבֶר הַוּוֹת. בְּאֶבְרָתוֹ יָסֶךְ לָךְ וְתַחַת כְּנָפָיו תֶּחְסֶה, צִנָּה וְסֹחֵרָה אֲמִתּוֹ. לֹא תִירָא מִפַּחַד לָיְלָה, מֵחֵץ יָעוּף יוֹמָם. מִדֶּבֶר בָּאֹפֶל יַהֲלֹךְ, מִקֶּטֶב יָשׁוּד צָהֳרָיִם. יִפֹּל מִצִּדְּךָ אֶלֶף וּרְבָבָה מִימִינֶךָ, אֵלֶיךָ לֹא יִגָּשׁ. רַק בְּעֵינֶיךָ תַבִּיט וְשִׁלֻּמַת רְשָׁעִים תִּרְאֶה. כִּי אַתָּה יְהֹוָה מַחְסִי, עֶלְיוֹן שַׂמְתָּ מְעוֹנֶךָ. לֹא תְאֻנֶּה אֵלֶיךָ רָעָה וְנֶגַע לֹא יִקְרַב בְּאָהֳלֶךָ.

The next verse consists of seven words. At each stop an additional word is added to the preceding portion of Psalm 91, so that Psalm 91 to the end of the following verse is read at the last stop.

For He shall give his angels charge over thee, to keep thee in all thy ways.

כִּי מַלְאָכָיו יְצַוֶּה־לָּךְ לִשְׁמָרְךָ בְּכָל־דְּרָכֶיךָ:

5. *When the casket is lowered into the grave, the following is said:*

May he come to his place in peace.

עַל מְקוֹמוֹ יָבֹא בְשָׁלוֹם:

May she come to her place in peace.

עַל מְקוֹמָהּ תָּבֹא בְשָׁלוֹם:

6. *The burial* Kaddish *is recited.*

Mourners. May His great name be magnified and sanctified in the world that is to be created anew, where He will revive the dead, and raise them up unto life eternal; will rebuild the city of Jerusalem, and establish His temple in the midst thereof; and will uproot all alien worship from the earth and restore the worship of the true God. O may the Holy One, blessed be He, reign in His sovereignty and glory during your life and during your days, and during the life of all the house of Israel, even speedily and at a near time, and say ye, Amen.

Cong. and Mourners. Let His great name be blessed for ever and to all eternity.

Mourners. Blessed, praised and glorified, exalted, extolled and honored, magnified and lauded be the name of the Holy One, blessed be He; though He be high above all blessings and hymns, praises and consolations, which are uttered in the world; and say ye, Amen.

Mourners. May there be abundant peace from heaven, and life for us and for all Israel; and say ye, amen.

Mourners. He who maketh peace in his high places, may He make peace for us and for all Israel; and say ye, Amen.

יִתְגַּדַּל וְיִתְקַדַּשׁ שְׁמֵהּ רַבָּא, בְּעָלְמָא דְהוּא עָתִיד לְאִתְחַדָּתָא, וּלְאַחֲיָא מֵתַיָּא, וּלְאַסָּקָא לְחַיֵּי עָלְמָא, וּלְמִבְנֵי קַרְתָּא דִירוּשְׁלֵם, וּלְשַׁכְלֵל הֵיכָלֵהּ בְּגַוַּהּ, וּלְמֶעֱקַר פּוּלְחָנָא נוּכְרָאָה מֵאַרְעָא, וּלְאָתָבָא פּוּלְחָנָא דִשְׁמַיָּא לְאַתְרֵהּ, וְיַמְלִיךְ קוּדְשָׁא בְּרִיךְ הוּא בְּמַלְכוּתֵהּ וִיקָרֵהּ, בְּחַיֵּיכוֹן וּבְיוֹמֵיכוֹן, וּבְחַיֵּי דְכָל בֵּית יִשְׂרָאֵל, בַּעֲגָלָא וּבִזְמַן קָרִיב, וְאִמְרוּ אָמֵן.

יְהֵא שְׁמֵהּ רַבָּא מְבָרַךְ, לְעָלַם וּלְעָלְמֵי עָלְמַיָּא.

יִתְבָּרַךְ וְיִשְׁתַּבַּח, וְיִתְפָּאַר וְיִתְרוֹמַם וְיִתְנַשֵּׂא, וְיִתְהַדָּר וְיִתְעַלֶּה וְיִתְהַלָּל, שְׁמֵהּ דְקוּדְשָׁא, בְּרִיךְ הוּא. לְעֵילָא מִן כָּל בִּרְכָתָא וְשִׁירָתָא, תֻּשְׁבְּחָתָא וְנֶחֱמָתָא, דַּאֲמִירָן בְּעָלְמָא, וְאִמְרוּ אָמֵן.

יְהֵא שְׁלָמָא רַבָּא מִן שְׁמַיָּא, וְחַיִּים טוֹבִים עָלֵינוּ, וְעַל כָּל יִשְׂרָאֵל, וְאִמְרוּ אָמֵן.

עֹשֶׂה שָׁלוֹם בִּמְרוֹמָיו, הוּא בְּרַחֲמָיו יַעֲשֶׂה שָׁלוֹם עָלֵינוּ, וְעַל כָּל יִשְׂרָאֵל, וְאִמְרוּ אָמֵן.

7. The Memorial Prayer is recited.

For an Adult

O Lord, who art full of compassion, who dwellest on high—God of forgiveness, who art merciful, slow to anger and abounding in loving-kindness, grant pardon of transgressions, speedy salvation and perfect rest beneath the shadow of Thy divine presence, in the exalted places among the holy and pure, who shine as the brightness of the firmament, to _____ who hath gone to his [her]

eternal home. We beseech thee O Lord of compassion, remember
unto him [her] for good all the meritorious and pious deeds which
he [she] wrought while on earth. Open unto him [her] the gates of
righteousness and light, the gates of pity and grace. O shelter him
[her] for evermore under the cover of Thy wings; and let his [her]
soul be bound up in the bond of the eternal life. The Lord be his
[her] inheritance; may he [she] rest in peace. And let us say, Amen.

אֵל מָלֵא רַחֲמִים שׁוֹכֵן בַּמְּרוֹמִים אֱלוֹהַּ סְלִיחוֹת חַנּוּן וְרַחוּם אֶרֶךְ אַפַּיִם וְרַב חֶסֶד.
הַמְצֵא כַּפָּרַת פֶּשַׁע וּמְנוּחָה נְכוֹנָה תַּחַת כַּנְפֵי הַשְּׁכִינָה בְּמַעֲלוֹת קְדוֹשִׁים וּטְהוֹרִים כְּזֹהַר
הָרָקִיעַ מַזְהִירִים. לְנִשְׁמַת פב״פ שֶׁהָלַךְ (שֶׁהָלְכָה) לְעוֹלָמוֹ (לְעוֹלָמָהּ). אָנָּא בַּעַל הָרַחֲמִים
זָכְרָה־לּוֹ (לָהּ) לְטוֹבָה כָּל זְכִיּוֹתָיו (זְכִיּוֹתֶיהָ) וְצִדְקוֹתָיו (וְצִדְקוֹתֶיהָ) בְּאַרְצוֹת הַחַיִּים. וּפְתַח
לוֹ (לָהּ) שַׁעֲרֵי צֶדֶק וְאוֹרָה שַׁעֲרֵי חֶמְלָה וַחֲנִינָה. בְּסֵתֶר כְּנָפֶיךָ תַּסְתִּירֵהוּ (תַּסְתִּירֶהָ)
לְעוֹלָמִים. וּצְרוֹר בִּצְרוֹר הַחַיִּים אֶת נִשְׁמָתוֹ (נִשְׁמָתָהּ). יְיָ הוּא נַחֲלָתוֹ (נַחֲלָתָהּ). וְיָנוּחַ
(וְתָנוּחַ) בְּשָׁלוֹם עַל מִשְׁכָּבוֹ (מִשְׁכָּבָהּ) וְנֹאמַר אָמֵן:

For a Child

O God, who art full of compassion, who dwellest on high, grant
perfect rest beneath the shadow of thy divine presence, in the
exalted places among the holy and pure, who shine as the brightness of the firmament, to the child _____ who hath gone to
his [her] eternal rest. We beseech thee, O Lord of compassion,
shelter him [her] for evermore under the cover of Thy wings; and
let his [her] soul be bound up in the bond of eternal life. The Lord
be his [her] inheritance; may he [she] rest in peace. And let us say,
Amen.

אֵל מָלֵא רַחֲמִים שׁוֹכֵן בַּמְּרוֹמִים. הַמְצֵא מְנוּחָה נְכוֹנָה תַּחַת כַּנְפֵי הַשְּׁכִינָה.
בְּמַעֲלוֹת קְדוֹשִׁים וּטְהוֹרִים. כְּזֹהַר הָרָקִיעַ מַזְהִירִים. אֶת־נִשְׁמַת הַיֶּלֶד (הַיַּלְדָּה) פ״ב״פ
שֶׁהָלַךְ (שֶׁהָלְכָה) לְעוֹלָמוֹ (לְעוֹלָמָהּ). אָנָּא בַּעַל הָרַחֲמִים הַסְתִּירֵהוּ (הַסְתִּירֶהָ) בְּסֵתֶר
כְּנָפֶיךָ לְעוֹלָמִים. וּצְרוֹר בִּצְרוֹר הַחַיִּים אֶת נִשְׁמָתוֹ (נִשְׁמָתָהּ) יְיָ הוּא נַחֲלָתוֹ (נַחֲלָתָהּ) וְיָנוּחַ
(וְתָנוּחַ) בְּשָׁלוֹם עַל מִשְׁכָּבוֹ (מִשְׁכָּבָהּ) וְנֹאמַר אָמֵן:

8. *Two lines are formed through which the mourners pass. They are consoled with the following formula:*

May the Almighty comfort you among the other mourners for Zion and Jerusalem.

הַמָּקוֹם יְנַחֵם אֶתְכֶם בְּתוֹךְ שְׁאָר אֲבֵלֵי צִיּוֹן וִירוּשָׁלָֽיִם:

9. *When leaving the cemetery, one plucks some grass and says:*

And they of the city shall flourish like the grass of the earth. He remembereth that we are dust.

וְיָצִֽיצוּ מֵעִיר כְּעֵֽשֶׂב הָאָֽרֶץ:

זָכוּר כִּי־עָפָר אֲנָֽחְנוּ:

10. *One washes one's hands and declares:*

He maketh death to vanish in life eternal; and the Lord God wipeth away tears from off all faces; and the reproach of His people shall He take away from off all the earth: for the Lord hath spoken it.

בִּלַּע הַמָּֽוֶת לָנֶֽצַח וּמָחָה אֲדֹנָי יֱהֹוִה דִּמְעָה מֵעַל כָּל־פָּנִים וְחֶרְפַּת עַמּוֹ יָסִיר מֵעַל כָּל־הָאָֽרֶץ כִּי יְהֹוָה דִּבֵּר:

Special Readings
Following Regular Worship
in the *Shiv'ah* House

Psalm 49

Hear this, all ye peoples; give ear, all ye inhabitants of the world:
both low and high, rich and poor, together. My mouth shall speak
wisdom; and the meditation of my heart shall be of understanding.
I will incline my ear to a parable: I will open my riddle to the lyre.
Wherefore should I fear in the days of evil, when the iniquity of
them that would supplant me compasseth me about, even of them
that trust in their wealth, and boast themselves in the multitude of
their riches? None of them can by any means redeem his brother,
nor give to God a ransom for him: (for the redemption of their soul
is costly, and must be let alone for ever:) that he should still live
always, that he should not see the pit. For he will see that wise men
die, the fool and the brutish together perish, and leave their wealth
to others. Their inward thought is, that their houses shall continue
for ever, and their dwelling places to all generations; they call their
lands after their own names. But man that is in glory abideth not:
he is like the beasts that perish. This is the way of them that are
foolish, and of those who after them take pleasure in their speech.
(Selah.) Like sheep they are laid in the grave; death shall be their
shepherd: but the upright shall have dominion over them in the
morning; and their form shall be for the grave to consume, that
there be no habitation for it. But God will redeem my soul from the
grasp of the grave; for He will receive me. (Selah.) Be thou not
afraid when a man becometh rich, when the glory of his house is
increased: for at his death he shall carry nothing away; his glory
shall not descend after him. Though while he lived he blessed his
soul, and though men praise thee that thou doest well unto thyself,

he shall go to the generation of his fathers, who shall never see the light. Man that is in glory, but without understanding, is like the beasts that perish.

תהלים מ״ט

לַמְנַצֵּחַ לִבְנֵי־קֹרַח מִזְמוֹר: שִׁמְעוּ־זֹאת כָּל־הָעַמִּים הַאֲזִינוּ כָּל־יֹשְׁבֵי חָלֶד: גַּם־בְּנֵי אָדָם גַּם־בְּנֵי־אִישׁ יַחַד עָשִׁיר וְאֶבְיוֹן: פִּי יְדַבֵּר חָכְמוֹת וְהָגוּת לִבִּי תְבוּנוֹת: אַטֶּה לְמָשָׁל אָזְנִי אֶפְתַּח בְּכִנּוֹר חִידָתִי: לָמָּה אִירָא בִּימֵי רָע עֲוֹן עֲקֵבַי יְסוּבֵּנִי: הַבֹּטְחִים עַל־חֵילָם וּבְרֹב עָשְׁרָם יִתְהַלָּלוּ: אָח לֹא־פָדֹה יִפְדֶּה אִישׁ לֹא־יִתֵּן לֵאלֹהִים כָּפְרוֹ: וְיֵקַר פִּדְיוֹן נַפְשָׁם וְחָדַל לְעוֹלָם: וִיחִי־עוֹד לָנֶצַח לֹא יִרְאֶה הַשָּׁחַת: כִּי יִרְאֶה חֲכָמִים יָמוּתוּ יַחַד כְּסִיל וָבַעַר יֹאבֵדוּ וְעָזְבוּ לַאֲחֵרִים חֵילָם: קִרְבָּם בָּתֵּימוֹ לְעוֹלָם מִשְׁכְּנֹתָם לְדֹר וָדֹר קָרְאוּ בִשְׁמוֹתָם עֲלֵי אֲדָמוֹת: וְאָדָם בִּיקָר בַּל־יָלִין נִמְשַׁל כַּבְּהֵמוֹת נִדְמוּ: זֶה דַרְכָּם כֵּסֶל לָמוֹ וְאַחֲרֵיהֶם בְּפִיהֶם יִרְצוּ סֶלָה: כַּצֹּאן לִשְׁאוֹל שַׁתּוּ מָוֶת יִרְעֵם וַיִּרְדּוּ בָם יְשָׁרִים לַבֹּקֶר וְצוּרָם לְבַלּוֹת שְׁאוֹל מִזְּבֻל לוֹ: אַךְ־אֱלֹהִים יִפְדֶּה נַפְשִׁי מִיַּד שְׁאוֹל כִּי יִקָּחֵנִי סֶלָה: אַל־תִּירָא כִּי־יַעֲשִׁר אִישׁ כִּי־יִרְבֶּה כְּבוֹד בֵּיתוֹ: כִּי לֹא בְמוֹתוֹ יִקַּח הַכֹּל לֹא־יֵרֵד אַחֲרָיו כְּבוֹדוֹ: כִּי־נַפְשׁוֹ בְּחַיָּיו יְבָרֵךְ וְיוֹדֻךָ כִּי־תֵיטִיב לָךְ: תָּבוֹא עַד־דּוֹר אֲבוֹתָיו עַד־נֵצַח לֹא יִרְאוּ־אוֹר: אָדָם בִּיקָר וְלֹא־יָבִין נִמְשַׁל כַּבְּהֵמוֹת נִדְמוּ:

Psalm 16

This is substituted for Psalm 49 on days when Tachanun is not recited.

Guard me, O God, for in Thee do I take refuge. I say unto the Lord, Thou art my lord: I have no good beyond Thee. As for the saints that are in the earth, they are the noble ones in whom is all my delight. Their sorrows will be multiplied that have gotten unto themselves another god: their drink offerings of blood will I not pour out, nor take their names upon my lips. The Lord is the portion of mine inheritance and of my cup: Thou maintainest my lot. The lines are fallen unto me in pleasant places; yea, I have a delightsome heritage. I will bless the Lord, who hath given me counsel: yea, my reins admonish me in the night seasons.

I have set the Lord always before me: because He is at my right hand, I shall not be moved. Therefore my heart rejoiceth and my glory is glad: my flesh also will dwell in safety. For Thou wilt not abandon my soul to the grave: neither wilt Thou suffer thy loving one to see the pit. Thou wilt make known to me the path of life: in Thy presence is fullness of joy; at Thy right hand, bliss for ever-more.

מִכְתָּם לְדָוִד שָׁמְרֵנִי אֵל, כִּי חָסִיתִי בָךְ: אָמַרְתְּ לַיהוָה אֲדֹנָי אַתָּה, טוֹבָתִי בַּל עָלֶיךָ: לִקְדוֹשִׁים אֲשֶׁר בָּאָרֶץ הֵמָּה, וְאַדִּירֵי כָּל חֶפְצִי בָם: יִרְבּוּ עַצְּבוֹתָם אַחֵר מָהָרוּ, בַּל אַסִּיךְ נִסְכֵּיהֶם מִדָּם, וּבַל אֶשָּׂא אֶת שְׁמוֹתָם עַל שְׂפָתָי: יְהוָה מְנָת חֶלְקִי וְכוֹסִי, אַתָּה תּוֹמִיךְ גּוֹרָלִי: חֲבָלִים נָפְלוּ לִי בַּנְּעִימִים אַף נַחֲלַת שָׁפְרָה עָלָי: אֲבָרֵךְ אֶת יְהוָה אֲשֶׁר יְעָצָנִי, אַף לֵילוֹת יִסְּרוּנִי כִלְיוֹתָי: שִׁוִּיתִי יְהוָה לְנֶגְדִּי תָמִיד, כִּי מִימִינִי בַּל אֶמּוֹט: לָכֵן שָׂמַח לִבִּי וַיָּגֶל כְּבוֹדִי, אַף בְּשָׂרִי יִשְׁכֹּן לָבֶטַח: כִּי לֹא תַעֲזֹב נַפְשִׁי לִשְׁאוֹל, לֹא תִתֵּן חֲסִידְךָ לִרְאוֹת שָׁחַת: תּוֹדִיעֵנִי אֹרַח חַיִּים, שֹׂבַע שְׂמָחוֹת אֶת פָּנֶיךָ, נְעִימוֹת בִּימִינְךָ נֶצַח:

Memorial Prayer

O Lord and King, who art full of compassion, God of the spirits of all flesh, in whose hand are the souls of the living and the dead, receive, we beseech Thee, in thy great loving-kindness the soul of

_____

אָנָּא יְהוָה מֶלֶךְ מָלֵא רַחֲמִים. אֱלֹהֵי הָרוּחוֹת לְכָל־בָּשָׂר. אֲשֶׁר בְּיָדְךָ נַפְשׁוֹת הַחַיִּים וְהַמֵּתִים. אָנָּא קַבֵּל בְּחַסְדְּךָ הַגָּדוֹל אֶת־נִשְׁמַת _____

For a man say:

who hath been gathered unto his people.   אֲשֶׁר נֶאֱסַף אֶל עַמּוֹ:

°Have mercy upon him; pardon all his transgressions, for there is none righteous upon the earth, who doeth only good, and sinneth not. Remember unto him the righteousness which he wrought, and let his reward be with him, and his recompense before him.°

Oh shelter his soul in the shadow of Thy wings. Make known to him the path of life: in Thy presence is fullness of joy; at Thy right hand, bliss for evermore. Bestow upon him the abounding happiness that is treasured up for the righteous,

חוּס וַחֲמוֹל עָלָיו. סְלַח וּמְחַל לְכָל־פְּשָׁעָיו. כִּי אָדָם אֵין צַדִּיק בָּאָרֶץ אֲשֶׁר יַעֲשֶׂה־
טוֹב וְלֹא יֶחֱטָא: זְכוֹר לוֹ צִדְקָתוֹ אֲשֶׁר עָשָׂה וִיהִי שְׂכָרוֹ אִתּוֹ וּפְעֻלָּתוֹ לְפָנָיו.
אָנָּא הַסְתֵּר אֶת־נִשְׁמָתוֹ בְּצֵל כְּנָפֶיךָ. הוֹדִיעֵהוּ אֹרַח חַיִּים שֹׂבַע שְׂמָחוֹת אֶת־פָּנֶיךָ
נְעִימוֹת בִּימִינְךָ נֶצַח. וְתַשְׁפִּיעַ לוֹ מֵרַב טוּב הַצָּפוּן לַצַּדִּיקִים.

For a woman say:

who hath been gathered unto her people.

אֲשֶׁר נֶאֶסְפָה אֶל עַמָּהּ: חוּס וַחֲמוֹל עָלֶיהָ.

°Have mercy upon her; pardon all her transgressions, for there is
none righteous upon earth, who doeth only good, and sinneth not.
Remember unto her the righteousness which she wrought, and let
her reward be with her, and her recompense before her.°

Oh shelter her soul in the shadow of Thy wings. Make known to
her the path of life: in Thy presence is fullness of joy; at Thy right
hand, bliss for evermore. Bestow upon her the abounding happiness
that is treasured up for the righteous,

סְלַח וּמְחַל לְכָל־פְּשָׁעֶיהָ. כִּי אָדָם אֵין צַדִּיק בָּאָרֶץ אֲשֶׁר יַעֲשֶׂה־טוֹב וְלֹא יֶחֱטָא:
זְכוֹר לָהּ צִדְקָתָהּ אֲשֶׁר עָשְׂתָה וִיהִי שְׂכָרָהּ אִתָּהּ וּפְעֻלָּתָהּ לְפָנֶיהָ:
אָנָּא הַסְתֵּר אֶת־נִשְׁמָתָהּ בְּצֵל כְּנָפֶיךָ. הוֹדִיעֶהָ אֹרַח חַיִּים שֹׂבַע שְׂמָחוֹת אֶת־פָּנֶיךָ
נְעִימוֹת בִּימִינְךָ נֶצַח. וְתַשְׁפִּיעַ לָהּ מֵרַב טוּב הַצָּפוּן לַצַּדִּיקִים.

as it is written, Oh how great is Thy goodness, which Thou hast
laid up for them that fear Thee, which Thou hast wrought for them
that trust in Thee before the children of men!

O Lord, who healest the broken-hearted and bindest up their
wounds, grant Thy consolation unto the mourners.

כְּמוֹ שֶׁכָּתוּב. מָה רַב טוּבְךָ אֲשֶׁר־צָפַנְתָּ לִירֵאֶיךָ פָּעַלְתָּ לַחוֹסִים בָּךְ נֶגֶד בְּנֵי אָדָם:
אָנָּא יְיָ הָרוֹפֵא לִשְׁבוּרֵי לֵב וּמְחַבֵּשׁ לְעַצְּבוֹתָם. שַׁלֵּם נִחוּמִים לָאֲבֵלִים.

[In the case of a male child, include the following:

May the death of this child mark the end of all anguish and tribulation unto his parents.]

וּתְהִי פְּטִירַת הַיֶּלֶד הַזֶּה קֵץ לְכָל־צָרָה וְצוּקָה לְאָבִיו וּלְאִמּוֹ:

[In the case of a female child, include the following:

וּתְהִי פְּטִירַת הַיַּלְדָּה הַזֹּאת קֵץ לְכָל־צָרָה וְצוּקָה לְאָבִיהָ וּלְאִמָּהּ:

May the death of this child mark the end of all anguish and tribulation unto her parents.]

Oh strengthen and support them in the day of their grief and sorrow; and remember them (and their children) for a long and good life. Put into their hearts the fear and love of Thee, that they may serve Thee with a perfect heart; and let their latter end be peace. Amen.

Like one whom his mother comforteth, so will I comfort you, (saith the Lord), and in Jerusalem shall ye be comforted. Thy sun shall no more go down, neither shall thy moon withdraw itself; for the Lord shall be thine everlasting light, and the days of thy mourning shall be ended. He maketh death to vanish in life eternal: and the Lord God wipeth away tears from off all faces; and the reproach of His people shall he take away from off all the earth: for the Lord hath spoken it.

חַזְּקֵם וְאַמְּצֵם בְּיוֹם אֶבְלָם וִיגוֹנָם וְזָכְרֵם [וּבְנֵי בֵיתָם] לְחַיִּים טוֹבִים וַאֲרֻכִּים: תֵּן בְּלִבָּם יִרְאָתְךָ וְאַהֲבָתְךָ לְעָבְדְךָ בְּלֵבָב שָׁלֵם: וּתְהִי אַחֲרִיתָם שָׁלוֹם. אָמֵן: כְּאִישׁ אֲשֶׁר אִמּוֹ תְּנַחֲמֶנּוּ כֵּן אָנֹכִי אֲנַחֶמְכֶם וּבִירוּשָׁלַ͏ִם תְּנֻחָמוּ: לֹא־יָבֹא עוֹד שִׁמְשֵׁךְ וִירֵחֵךְ לֹא יֵאָסֵף. כִּי יְיָ יִהְיֶה־לָּךְ לְאוֹר עוֹלָם. וְשָׁלְמוּ יְמֵי אֶבְלֵךְ. בִּלַּע הַמָּוֶת לָנֶצַח. וּמָחָה יְיָ אֱלֹהִים דִּמְעָה מֵעַל כָּל־פָּנִים. וְחֶרְפַּת עַמּוֹ יָסִיר מֵעַל כָּל־הָאָרֶץ. כִּי יְיָ דִּבֵּר:

Mourner's Kaddish

See p. 246.

Formula of Condolence

This is said by visitors upon leaving the *shiv'ah* house.

May the Almighty comfort you among the other mourners for Zion and Jerusalem.

הַמָּקוֹם יְנַחֵם אֶתְכֶם בְּתוֹךְ שְׁאָר אֲבֵלֵי צִיּוֹן וִירוּשָׁלָיִם:

Yizkor Recitations

On the eighth day of Pesach, the second day of Shavu'ot, and on Shemini Chag Atzeret, the congregation rises for Yizkor, the Memorial service.

Lord, what is man that Thou art mindful of him,
The son of mortal man that Thou takest thought of him?
    Man is like a breath,
    His days are as a passing shadow.
In the morning he flourishes and springs up afresh,
By evening he is cut down and he withers.
    Teach us so to number our days
    That we may attain a heart of wisdom.
Mark, O man, the innocent and look upon the upright,
For there is a future for the man of peace.
    Yea, God will redeem my soul from the power of the grave
    When He receives me. Selah.
My flesh and my heart may fail,
But the rock of my heart and my portion is God forever.
    When the dust returns to the earth that it was,
    The spirit shall return to God who gave it.
And I in righteousness would look upon Thy face;
When I awake I shall be serene with beholding Thy likeness.

יְיָ מָה־אָדָם וַתֵּדָעֵהוּ   בֶּן־אֱנוֹשׁ וַתְּחַשְּׁבֵהוּ:

אָדָם לַהֶבֶל דָּמָה   יָמָיו כְּצֵל עוֹבֵר:

בַּבֹּקֶר יָצִיץ וְחָלָף   לָעֶרֶב יְמוֹלֵל וְיָבֵשׁ:

לִמְנוֹת יָמֵינוּ כֵּן הוֹדַע   וְנָבִא לְבַב חָכְמָה:

שְׁמָר־תָּם וּרְאֵה יָשָׁר   כִּי־אַחֲרִית לְאִישׁ שָׁלוֹם:

אַךְ־אֱלֹהִים יִפְדֶּה־נַפְשִׁי מִיַּד שְׁאוֹל   כִּי יִקָּחֵנִי סֶלָה:

כָּלָה שְׁאֵרִי וּלְבָבִי   צוּר לְבָבִי וְחֶלְקִי אֱלֹהִים לְעוֹלָם:

וְיָשֹׁב הֶעָפָר עַל־הָאָרֶץ כְּשֶׁהָיָה   וְהָרוּחַ תָּשׁוּב אֶל־הָאֱלֹהִים אֲשֶׁר נְתָנָהּ:

אֲנִי בְּצֶדֶק אֶחֱזֶה פָנֶיךָ   אֶשְׂבְּעָה בְהָקִיץ תְּמוּנָתֶךָ:

236

MEMORIAL SUPPLICATIONS

Prayer in Memory of a Departed Father

God, be mindful of the soul of my beloved father who has been called to his eternal home. In his memory I offer charity. May his soul be bound up in the bond of life with the souls of Abraham, Isaac, Jacob, Sarah, Rebecca, Rachel, Leah, and all the other righteous ones in eternal bliss. Amen.

יִזְכֹּר אֱלֹהִים נִשְׁמַת אָבִי מוֹרִי שֶׁהָלַךְ לְעוֹלָמוֹ. בַּעֲבוּר שֶׁאֲנִי נוֹדֵר צְדָקָה בְּעַד הַזְכָּרַת נִשְׁמָתוֹ: בִּשְׂכַר זֶה, תְּהֵא נַפְשׁוֹ צְרוּרָה בִּצְרוֹר הַחַיִּים. עִם נִשְׁמוֹת אַבְרָהָם יִצְחָק וְיַעֲקֹב. שָׂרָה רִבְקָה רָחֵל וְלֵאָה. וְעִם שְׁאָר צַדִּיקִים וְצִדְקָנִיּוֹת שֶׁבְּגַן עֵדֶן. וְנֹאמַר אָמֵן:

Prayer in Memory of a Departed Mother

God, be mindful of the soul of my beloved mother who has been called to her eternal home. In her memory I offer charity. May her soul be bound up in the bond of life with the souls of Abraham, Isaac, Jacob, Sarah, Rebecca, Rachel, Leah, and all the other righteous ones in eternal bliss. Amen.

יִזְכֹּר אֱלֹהִים נִשְׁמַת אִמִּי מוֹרָתִי שֶׁהָלְכָה לְעוֹלָמָהּ. בַּעֲבוּר שֶׁאֲנִי נוֹדֵר צְדָקָה בְּעַד הַזְכָּרַת נִשְׁמָתָהּ: בִּשְׂכַר זֶה, תְּהֵא נַפְשָׁהּ צְרוּרָה בִּצְרוֹר הַחַיִּים. עִם נִשְׁמוֹת אַבְרָהָם יִצְחָק וְיַעֲקֹב. שָׂרָה רִבְקָה רָחֵל וְלֵאָה. וְעִם שְׁאָר צַדִּיקִים וְצִדְקָנִיּוֹת שֶׁבְּגַן עֵדֶן. וְנֹאמַר אָמֵן:

Prayer in Memory of a Departed Husband

God, be mindful of the soul of my beloved husband who has been called to his eternal home. In his memory I offer charity. May his soul be bound up in the bond of life with the souls of Abraham, Isaac, Jacob, Sarah, Rebecca, Rachel, Leah, and all the other righteous ones in eternal bliss. Amen.

יִזְכֹּר אֱלֹהִים נִשְׁמַת בַּעֲלִי . . . שֶׁהָלַךְ לְעוֹלָמוֹ. בַּעֲבוּר שֶׁאֲנִי נוֹדֵר צְדָקָה בְּעַד הַזְכָּרַת נִשְׁמָתוֹ: בִּשְׂכַר זֶה, תְּהֵא נַפְשׁוֹ צְרוּרָה בִּצְרוֹר הַחַיִּים. עִם נִשְׁמוֹת אַבְרָהָם יִצְחָק וְיַעֲקֹב. שָׂרָה רִבְקָה רָחֵל וְלֵאָה. וְעִם שְׁאָר צַדִּיקִים וְצִדְקָנִיּוֹת שֶׁבְּגַן עֵדֶן. וְנֹאמַר אָמֵן:

Prayer in Memory of a Departed Wife

God, be mindful of the soul of my beloved wife who has been called to her eternal home. In her memory I offer charity. May her soul be bound up in the bond of life with the souls of Abraham, Issac, Jacob, Sarah, Rebecca, Rachel, Leah, and all the other righteous ones in eternal bliss. Amen.

יִזְכֹּר אֱלֹהִים נִשְׁמַת אִשְׁתִּי . . . שֶׁהָלְכָה לְעוֹלָמָהּ. בַּעֲבוּר שֶׁאֲנִי נוֹדֵר צְדָקָה בְּעַד הַזְכָּרַת נִשְׁמָתָהּ: בִּשְׂכַר זֶה, תְּהֵא נַפְשָׁהּ צְרוּרָה בִּצְרוֹר הַחַיִּים. עִם נִשְׁמוֹת אַבְרָהָם יִצְחָק וְיַעֲקֹב. שָׂרָה רִבְקָה רָחֵל וְלֵאָה. וְעִם שְׁאָר צַדִּיקִים וְצִדְקָנִיּוֹת שֶׁבְּגַן עֵדֶן. וְנֹאמַר אָמֵן:

Prayer in Memory of a Departed Son

God, be mindful of the soul of my beloved son _____ who has been called to his eternal home. In his memory I offer charity. May his soul be bound up in the bond of life with the souls of Abraham, Isaac, Jacob, Sarah, Rebecca, Rachel, Leah, and all the other righteous ones in eternal bliss. Amen.

יִזְכֹּר אֱלֹהִים נִשְׁמַת בְּנִי הַנֶּחְמָד . . . שֶׁהָלַךְ לְעוֹלָמוֹ. בַּעֲבוּר שֶׁאֲנִי נוֹדֵר צְדָקָה בְּעַד הַזְכָּרַת נִשְׁמָתוֹ: בִּשְׂכַר זֶה, תְּהֵא נַפְשׁוֹ צְרוּרָה בִּצְרוֹר הַחַיִּים. עִם נִשְׁמוֹת אַבְרָהָם יִצְחָק וְיַעֲקֹב. שָׂרָה רִבְקָה רָחֵל וְלֵאָה. וְעִם שְׁאָר צַדִּיקִים וְצִדְקָנִיּוֹת שֶׁבְּגַן עֵדֶן. וְנֹאמַר אָמֵן:

Prayer in Memory of a Departed Daughter

God, be mindful of the soul of my beloved daughter _____ who has been called to her eternal home. In her memory I offer charity. May her soul be bound up in the bond of life with the souls of Abraham, Isaac, Jacob, Sarah, Rebecca, Rachel, Leah, and all the other righteous ones in eternal bliss. Amen.

יִזְכֹּר אֱלֹהִים נִשְׁמַת בִּתִּי הַנֶּחְמָדָה. בַּעֲבוּר שֶׁאֲנִי נוֹדֵר צְדָקָה בְּעַד הַזְכָּרַת נִשְׁמָתָהּ: בִּשְׂכַר זֶה, תְּהֵא נַפְשָׁהּ צְרוּרָה בִּצְרוֹר הַחַיִּים. עִם נִשְׁמוֹת אַבְרָהָם יִצְחָק וְיַעֲקֹב. שָׂרָה רִבְקָה רָחֵל וְלֵאָה. וְעִם שְׁאָר צַדִּיקִים וְצִדְקָנִיּוֹת שֶׁבְּגַן עֵדֶן. וְנֹאמַר אָמֵן:

Prayer in Memory of Other Departed Relatives and Friends

God, be mindful of the soul of _____ and of all those near
and dear to me who have been called to their eternal home. In their
memory I offer charity. May their souls be bound up in the bond of
life with the souls of Abraham, Isaac, Jacob, Sarah, Rebecca,
Rachel, Leah, and all the other righteous ones in eternal bliss.
Amen.

יִזְכֹּר אֱלֹהִים נִשְׁמַת . . . וְנִשְׁמוֹת קְרוֹבַי וִידִידַי שֶׁהָלְכוּ לְעוֹלָמָם. בַּעֲבוּר שֶׁאֲנִי
נוֹדֵר צְדָקָה בְּעַד הַזְכָּרַת נִשְׁמָתָם: בִּשְׂכַר זֶה תִּהְיֶינָה נַפְשׁוֹתֵיהֶם צְרוּרוֹת בִּצְרוֹר הַחַיִּים
עִם נִשְׁמוֹת אַבְרָהָם יִצְחָק וְיַעֲקֹב. שָׂרָה רִבְקָה רָחֵל וְלֵאָה. וְעִם שְׁאָר צַדִּיקִים וְצִדְקָנִיּוֹת
שֶׁבְּגַן עֵדֶן. וְנֹאמַר אָמֵן:

Prayer in Memory of Jewish Martyrs

God, be mindful of the souls of all the martyred children of Israel
who gave their lives for the sanctification of Thy name. In their
memory I offer charity. May their souls be bound up in the bond of
life, with the souls of Abraham, Isaac, Jacob, Sarah, Rebecca,
Rachel, Leah, and all the other righteous ones in eternal bliss.
Amen.

יִזְכֹּר אֱלֹהִים נִשְׁמוֹת כָּל אַחֵינוּ בְּנֵי יִשְׂרָאֵל שֶׁמָּסְרוּ נַפְשָׁם עַל קִדּוּשׁ הַשֵּׁם. בַּעֲבוּר
שֶׁאֲנִי נוֹדֵר צְדָקָה בְּעַד הַזְכָּרַת נִשְׁמָתָם: בִּשְׂכַר זֶה תִּהְיֶינָה נַפְשׁוֹתֵיהֶם צְרוּרוֹת בִּצְרוֹר
הַחַיִּים עִם נִשְׁמוֹת אַבְרָהָם יִצְחָק וְיַעֲקֹב. שָׂרָה רִבְקָה רָחֵל וְלֵאָה. וְעִם שְׁאָר צַדִּיקִים
וְצִדְקָנִיּוֹת שֶׁבְּגַן עֵדֶן. וְנֹאמַר אָמֵן:

Prayer to Be Recited by Those Who Are
Still Blessed With Parents

Almighty God, while those who have lost their parents and their
dear ones call to mind those who have gone to their eternal rest, we
at this solemn moment raise our eyes unto Thee, the Giver of Life,
and from a grateful heart thank Thee for Thy mercies in having
preserved the life of our beloved father and mother.

 May it be Thy will, O Lord our God, and the God of our fathers to bless them with health and strength, so that they may be with us for many years to come. Bless them even as they have blessed us, and guard them even as they have guarded us.

In return for all their affection and the sacrifices which they have made for us, may we bring them joy and lighten their cares. May it be our privilege to help them in every way that lies within our power; may we learn to understand and recognize the duty we owe unto them, that we may never have cause to reproach ourselves when it is too late.

Shield our home from all sorrow. May peace and harmony and Thy spirit ever reign within its walls. Keep us true to Thee and to one another, that we may all form one band to do Thy will with a perfect heart, our Father in Heaven.

Special Hazkarah for our Martyrs Throughout the Ages and for the Six Million

Responsively

O our God and God of our fathers, our Creator and Rock of our salvation, look down from Thy heights and see our affliction.

We come before Thee with a broken heart, we knock at Thy doors with a crushed spirit, O hearken to the voice of our supplication.

Our brothers were sold to human wolves, our sisters were delivered to ferocious beasts, our infants and babes became a prey to the dregs of mankind.

Death, bereavement and widowhood penetrated our windows, parents with their tender children were burned before our eyes, and with the Shema on their lips they perished in the gas chambers.

The lamps of Israel were extinguished in our dwellings, the cedars of Labanon were uprooted from our midst.

Our tongues cleave to our palate, our eyes are a fount of tears, and our soul has drunk in full the cup of sorrow.

Why didst Thou forsake us, O our God? Why didst Thou stand afar at the time of our distress? Why didst Thou keep silent when the tyrants spilt our blood like water?

Where can we find a remedy for our wounds? When shall comfort come for our mourning? How can we forget our beloved ones?

Service at the Consecration
of a Tombstone

Happy is the man that walketh not in the counsel of the wicked, nor standeth in the way of sinners, nor sitteth in the seat of the scornful. But his delight is in the law of the Lord; and in His law doth he meditate day and night. And he shall be like a tree planted by the streams of water, that bringeth forth its fruit in its season, whose leaf also doth not wither; and whatsoever he doeth shall prosper. The wicked are not so; but are like the chaff which the wind driveth away. Therefore the wicked shall not stand in judgment nor sinners in the congregation of the righteous. For the Lord knoweth the way of the righteous, but the way of the wicked shall perish.

אַשְׁרֵי הָאִישׁ אֲשֶׁר לֹא הָלַךְ בַּעֲצַת רְשָׁעִים וּבְדֶרֶךְ חַטָּאִים לֹא עָמָד וּבְמוֹשַׁב לֵצִים
לֹא יָשָׁב: כִּי אִם־בְּתוֹרַת יְהֹוָה חֶפְצוֹ וּבְתוֹרָתוֹ יֶהְגֶּה יוֹמָם וָלָיְלָה: וְהָיָה כְּעֵץ שָׁתוּל עַל־
פַּלְגֵי מָיִם אֲשֶׁר פִּרְיוֹ יִתֵּן בְּעִתּוֹ וְעָלֵהוּ לֹא־יִבּוֹל וְכֹל אֲשֶׁר־יַעֲשֶׂה יַצְלִיחַ: לֹא־כֵן
הָרְשָׁעִים כִּי אִם־כַּמֹּץ אֲשֶׁר־תִּדְּפֶנּוּ רוּחַ: עַל־כֵּן לֹא־יָקֻמוּ רְשָׁעִים בַּמִּשְׁפָּט וְחַטָּאִים
בַּעֲדַת צַדִּיקִים: כִּי־יוֹדֵעַ יְהֹוָה דֶּרֶךְ צַדִּיקִים וְדֶרֶךְ רְשָׁעִים תֹּאבֵד:

For a Man

Who may ascend the mountain of the Lord? And who may stand in His holy place? He that hath clean hands and a pure heart; who hath not set his desire upon vanity, and hath not sworn deceitfully. He shall receive a blessing from the Lord, and righteousness from the God of his salvation.

Let us hear the conclusion of the whole matter: Fear God, and keep His commandments: for this is the whole duty of man.

The day is short, and the work is great, and the laborers are sluggish, and the reward is much, and the Master of the house is urgent.

241

It is not thy duty to complete the work, but neither art thou free to desist from it. Faithful is thy Employer to pay thee the reward of thy labor; and know that the grant of reward unto the righteous will be in the time to come.

מִי־יַעֲלֶה בְהַר יְיָ וּמִי־יָקוּם בִּמְקוֹם קָדְשׁוֹ: נְקִי כַפַּיִם וּבַר לֵבָב אֲשֶׁר לֹא נָשָׂא לַשָּׁוְא נַפְשִׁי וְלֹא נִשְׁבַּע לְמִרְמָה: יִשָּׂא בְרָכָה מֵאֵת יְיָ וּצְדָקָה מֵאֱלֹהֵי יִשְׁעוֹ:

סוֹף דָּבָר הַכֹּל נִשְׁמָע אֶת הָאֱלֹהִים יְרָא וְאֶת מִצְוֹתָיו שְׁמוֹר כִּי זֶה כָּל הָאָדָם:

הַיּוֹם קָצֵר וְהַמְּלָאכָה מְרֻבָּה וְהַפּוֹעֲלִים עֲצֵלִים וְהַשָּׂכָר הַרְבֵּה וּבַעַל הַבַּיִת דּוֹחֵק: לֹא עָלֶיךָ הַמְּלָאכָה לִגְמוֹר וְלֹא־אַתָּה בֶן־חוֹרִין לְהִבָּטֵל מִמֶּנָּה: נֶאֱמָן הוּא בַּעַל מְלַאכְתְּךָ שֶׁיְשַׁלֶּם לְךָ שְׂכַר פְּעֻלָּתֶךָ. וְדַע שֶׁמַּתַּן שְׂכָרָם שֶׁל־צַדִּיקִים לֶעָתִיד לָבוֹא:

For a Woman

A woman of worth who can find? For her price is far above rubies. The heart of her husband trusteth in her; and he shall have no lack of gain. She doeth him good and not evil all the days of her life. She seeketh wool and flax, and worketh willingly with her hands. She is like the merchant-ships; she bringeth her food from afar. She riseth also while it is yet night, and setteth forth provision for her household, and their portion for her maidens. She considereth a field, and buyeth it: with the fruit of her hands she planteth a vine-yard. She girdeth her loins with strength, and maketh strong her arms. She perceiveth that her earnings are good; her lamp goeth not out by night. She putteth her hands to the distaff, and her hands hold the spindle. She stretcheth out her hand to the poor; yea, she putteth forth her hands to the needy. She is not afraid of the snow for her household; for all her household are clothed with scarlet. She maketh for herself coverings of tapestry; her clothing is fine linen and purple. Her husband is known in the gates, when he sitteth among the elders of the land. She maketh linen garments and selleth them; and delivereth girdles unto the merchant. Strength and majesty are her clothing; and she laugheth at the time to come. She openeth her mouth with wisdom; and the law of loving-kindness is on her tongue. She looketh well to the ways of her household, and eateth not the bread of idleness. Her children rise up and call her happy; her husband also, and he praiseth her, saying: Many daughters have done worthily, but thou excellest them all. Favor is false, and beauty is vain; but a woman that feareth the Lord, she shall be praised. Give her of the fruit of her hands; and let her works praise her in the gates.

אֵשֶׁת חַיִל מִי יִמְצָא וְרָחוֹק מִפְּנִינִים מִכְרָהּ: [בָּטַח בָּהּ לֵב בַּעְלָהּ וְשָׁלָל לֹא יֶחְסָר: גְּמָלַתְהוּ טוֹב וְלֹא רָע כֹּל יְמֵי חַיֶּיהָ:] דָּרְשָׁה צֶמֶר וּפִשְׁתִּים וַתַּעַשׂ בְּחֵפֶץ כַּפֶּיהָ: הָיְתָה כָּאֳנִיּוֹת סוֹחֵר מִמֶּרְחָק תָּבִיא לַחְמָהּ: וַתָּקָם בְּעוֹד לַיְלָה וַתִּתֵּן טֶרֶף לְבֵיתָהּ וְחֹק לְנַעֲרֹתֶיהָ: זָמְמָה שָׂדֶה וַתִּקָּחֵהוּ מִפְּרִי כַפֶּיהָ נָטְעָה כָּרֶם: חָגְרָה בְעוֹז מָתְנֶיהָ וַתְּאַמֵּץ זְרוֹעֹתֶיהָ: טָעֲמָה כִּי טוֹב סַחְרָהּ לֹא יִכְבֶּה בַלַּיְלָה נֵרָהּ: יָדֶיהָ שִׁלְּחָה בַכִּישׁוֹר וְכַפֶּיהָ תָּמְכוּ פָלֶךְ: כַּפָּהּ פָּרְשָׂה לֶעָנִי וְיָדֶיהָ שִׁלְּחָה לָאֶבְיוֹן: לֹא תִירָא לְבֵיתָהּ מִשָּׁלֶג כִּי כָל בֵּיתָהּ לָבֻשׁ שָׁנִים: מַרְבַדִּים עָשְׂתָה לָּהּ שֵׁשׁ וְאַרְגָּמָן לְבוּשָׁהּ: נוֹדָע בַּשְּׁעָרִים בַּעְלָהּ בְּשִׁבְתּוֹ עִם זִקְנֵי אָרֶץ: סָדִין עָשְׂתָה וַתִּמְכֹּר וַחֲגוֹר נָתְנָה לַכְּנַעֲנִי: עוֹז וְהָדָר לְבוּשָׁהּ וַתִּשְׂחַק לְיוֹם אַחֲרוֹן: פִּיהָ פָּתְחָה בְחָכְמָה וְתוֹרַת חֶסֶד עַל לְשׁוֹנָהּ: צוֹפִיָּה הֲלִיכוֹת בֵּיתָהּ וְלֶחֶם עַצְלוּת לֹא תֹאכֵל: קָמוּ בָנֶיהָ וַיְאַשְּׁרוּהָ בַּעְלָהּ וַיְהַלְלָהּ: רַבּוֹת בָּנוֹת עָשׂוּ חָיִל וְאַתְּ עָלִית עַל כֻּלָּנָה: שֶׁקֶר הַחֵן וְהֶבֶל הַיֹּפִי אִשָּׁה יִרְאַת יְהוָה הִיא תִתְהַלָּל: תְּנוּ לָהּ מִפְּרִי יָדֶיהָ וִיהַלְלוּהָ בַשְּׁעָרִים מַעֲשֶׂיהָ:

Guard me, O God, for in Thee do I take refuge. I say unto the Lord, Thou art my lord: I have no good beyond Thee. As for the saints that are in the earth, they are the noble ones in whom is all my delight. Their sorrows will be multiplied that have gotten unto themselves another god: their drink offerings of blood will I not pour out, nor take their names upon my lips. The Lord is the portion of mine inheritance and of my cup: Thou maintainest my lot. The lines are fallen unto me in pleasant places; yea, I have a delightsome heritage. I will bless the Lord, who hath given me counsel: yea, my reins admonish me in the night seasons.

I have set the Lord always before me: because He is at my right hand, I shall not be moved. Therefore my heart rejoiceth and my glory is glad: my flesh also will dwell in safety. For Thou wilt not abandon my soul to the grave: neither wilt Thou suffer thy loving one to see the pit. Thou wilt make known to me the path of life: in Thy presence is fullness of joy; at Thy right hand, bliss for evermore.

מִכְתָּם לְדָוִד שָׁמְרֵנִי אֵל כִּי־חָסִיתִי בָךְ: אָמַרְתְּ לַיהֹוָה אֲדֹנָי אָתָּה טוֹבָתִי בַּל־עָלֶיךָ:
לִקְדוֹשִׁים אֲשֶׁר־בָּאָרֶץ הֵמָּה וְאַדִּירֵי כָּל־חֶפְצִי־בָם: יִרְבּוּ עַצְּבוֹתָם אַחֵר מָהָרוּ בַּל־אַסִּיךְ
נִסְכֵּיהֶם מִדָּם וּבַל־אֶשָּׂא אֶת־שְׁמוֹתָם עַל־שְׂפָתָי: יְהֹוָה מְנָת־חֶלְקִי וְכוֹסִי אַתָּה תּוֹמִיךְ
גּוֹרָלִי: חֲבָלִים נָפְלוּ־לִי בַּנְּעִמִים אַף־נַחֲלָת שָׁפְרָה עָלָי: אֲבָרֵךְ אֶת־יְהֹוָה אֲשֶׁר יְעָצָנִי אַף־
לֵילוֹת יִסְּרוּנִי כִלְיוֹתָי: שִׁוִּיתִי יְהֹוָה לְנֶגְדִּי תָמִיד כִּי מִימִינִי בַּל־אֶמּוֹט: לָכֵן ׀ שָׂמַח לִבִּי
וַיָּגֶל כְּבוֹדִי אַף־בְּשָׂרִי יִשְׁכֹּן לָבֶטַח: כִּי ׀ לֹא־תַעֲזֹב נַפְשִׁי לִשְׁאוֹל לֹא־תִתֵּן חֲסִידְךָ לִרְאוֹת
שָׁחַת: תּוֹדִיעֵנִי אֹרַח חַיִּים שֹׂבַע שְׂמָחוֹת אֶת־פָּנֶיךָ נְעִמוֹת בִּימִינְךָ נֶצַח:

The Lord is my shepherd; I shall not want. He maketh me to lie
down in green pasures: He leadeth me beside the still waters. He
restoreth my soul: He guideth me in the paths of righteousness for
His name's sake. Yea, though I walk through the valley of the
shadow of death, I will fear no evil; for Thou art with me: Thy rod
and Thy staff, they comfort me. Thou preparest a table before me
in the presence of mine enemies: Thou hast anointed my head with
oil; my cup runneth over. Surely happiness and loving-kindness
will follow me all the days of my life; and I shall dwell in the house
of the Lord for evermore.

מִזְמוֹר לְדָוִד יְהֹוָה רֹעִי לֹא אֶחְסָר: בִּנְאוֹת דֶּשֶׁא יַרְבִּיצֵנִי עַל־מֵי מְנֻחוֹת יְנַהֲלֵנִי:
נַפְשִׁי יְשׁוֹבֵב יַנְחֵנִי בְמַעְגְּלֵי־צֶדֶק לְמַעַן שְׁמוֹ: גַּם כִּי־אֵלֵךְ בְּגֵיא צַלְמָוֶת לֹא־אִירָא רָע
כִּי־אַתָּה עִמָּדִי שִׁבְטְךָ וּמִשְׁעַנְתֶּךָ הֵמָּה יְנַחֲמֻנִי: תַּעֲרֹךְ לְפָנַי ׀ שֻׁלְחָן נֶגֶד צֹרְרָי דִּשַּׁנְתָּ בַשֶּׁמֶן
רֹאשִׁי כּוֹסִי רְוָיָה: אַךְ ׀ טוֹב וָחֶסֶד יִרְדְּפוּנִי כָּל־יְמֵי חַיָּי וְשַׁבְתִּי בְּבֵית־יְהֹוָה לְאֹרֶךְ יָמִים:

O Lord, thou hast been a dwelling-place unto us in all generations. Before the mountains were brought forth, or ever Thou
gavest birth to the earth and the world, even from everlasting to
everlasting Thou art God. Thou turnest man back to dust, and
sayest, Return, ye children of men. For a thousand years in Thy
sight are but as yesterday when it is past, and as a watch in the
night. The days of our years are threescore years and ten, or even by
reason of strength fourscore years; yet is their pride but travail and
nothingness; for it is soon gone by, and we fly away. So teach us to
number our days, that we may get us a heart of wisdom.

אֲדֹנָי מָעוֹן אַתָּה הָיִיתָ לָּנוּ בְּדֹר וָדֹר: בְּטֶרֶם הָרִים יֻלָּדוּ וַתְּחוֹלֵל אֶרֶץ וְתֵבֵל וּמֵעוֹלָם עַד־עוֹלָם אַתָּה אֵל: תָּשֵׁב אֱנוֹשׁ עַד־דַּכָּא וַתֹּאמֶר שׁוּבוּ בְנֵי־אָדָם: כִּי אֶלֶף שָׁנִים בְּעֵינֶיךָ כְּיוֹם אֶתְמוֹל כִּי יַעֲבֹר וְאַשְׁמוּרָה בַלָּיְלָה: יְמֵי שְׁנוֹתֵינוּ בָהֶם שִׁבְעִים שָׁנָה וְרָהְבָּם עָמָל וָאָוֶן כִּי גָז חִישׁ וַנָּעֻפָה: לִמְנוֹת יָמֵינוּ כֵּן הוֹדַע וְנָבִיא לְבַב חָכְמָה:

Seek ye the Lord while He may be found, call ye upon Him while He is near; let the wicked forsake his way, and the unrighteous man his thoughts; and let him return unto the Lord, and He will have mercy upon him; and to our God, for He will abundantly pardon. For My thoughts are not your thoughts, neither are your ways My ways, saith the Lord. For as the heavens are higher than the earth, so are My ways higher than your ways, and my thoughts than your thoughts.

דִּרְשׁוּ יְיָ בְּהִמָּצְאוֹ קְרָאֻהוּ בִּהְיוֹתוֹ קָרוֹב: יַעֲזֹב רָשָׁע דַּרְכּוֹ וְאִישׁ אָוֶן מַחְשְׁבֹתָיו וְיָשֹׁב אֶל־יְיָ וִירַחֲמֵהוּ וְאֶל־אֱלֹהֵינוּ כִּי־יַרְבֶּה לִסְלוֹחַ: כִּי לֹא מַחְשְׁבוֹתַי מַחְשְׁבוֹתֵיכֶם וְלֹא דַרְכֵיכֶם דְּרָכָי נְאֻם יְיָ: כִּי גָבְהוּ שָׁמַיִם מֵאָרֶץ כֵּן גָּבְהוּ דְרָכַי מִדַּרְכֵיכֶם וּמַחְשְׁבֹתַי מִמַּחְשְׁבֹתֵיכֶם:

As for man, his days are as grass; as the flower of the field, so he flourisheth. For the wind passeth over it, and it is gone; and the place thereof shall know it no more. But the loving-kindness of the Lord is from everlasting to everlasting upon them that fear Him, and His righteousness unto children's children. Mark the innocent man, and behold the upright; for the latter end of that man is peace. In the way of righteousness is life; and in the pathway there-of there is no death. The Lord setteth free the soul of his servants; and none that take refuge in Him shall be condemned. And the dust returneth to the earth as it was, but the spirit returneth unto God, who gave it, Whom have I in heaven but Thee? And there is none upon earth that I desire beside Thee. My flesh and my heart faileth: but God is the strength of my heart and my portion for ever. How precious is Thy loving-kindness, O God! And the children of men take refuge under the shadow of Thy wings. For with Thee is the fountain of life: in Thy light do we see light.

אֱנוֹשׁ כֶּחָצִיר יָמָיו כְּצִיץ הַשָּׂדֶה כֵּן יָצִיץ: כִּי רוּחַ עָבְרָה־בּוֹ וְאֵינֶנּוּ וְלֹא־יַכִּירֶנּוּ עוֹד
מְקוֹמוֹ: וְחֶסֶד יְיָ מֵעוֹלָם וְעַד־עוֹלָם עַל־יְרֵאָיו וְצִדְקָתוֹ לִבְנֵי בָנִים: בְּאֹרַח צְדָקָה חַיִּים
וְדֶרֶךְ נְתִיבָה אַל־מָוֶת: וְיָשֹׁב הֶעָפָר עַל הָאָרֶץ כְּשֶׁהָיָה וְהָרוּחַ תָּשׁוּב אֶל הָאֱלֹהִים אֲשֶׁר
נְתָנָהּ: מִי לִי בַשָּׁמָיִם וְעִמְּךָ לֹא־חָפַצְתִּי בָאָרֶץ: כָּלָה שְׁאֵרִי וּלְבָבִי צוּר־לְבָבִי וְחֶלְקִי
אֱלֹהִים לְעוֹלָם: מַה־יָּקָר חַסְדְּךָ אֱלֹהִים וּבְנֵי אָדָם בְּצֵל כְּנָפֶיךָ יֶחֱסָיוּן: כִּי עִמְּךָ מְקוֹר
חַיִּים בְּאוֹרְךָ נִרְאֶה־אוֹר:

Eulogy

Mourner's *Kaddish**

יִתְגַּדַּל וְיִתְקַדַּשׁ שְׁמֵהּ רַבָּא בְּעָלְמָא דִּי בְרָא כִרְעוּתֵהּ וְיַמְלִיךְ מַלְכוּתֵהּ בְּחַיֵּיכוֹן וּבְיוֹמֵיכוֹן
וּבְחַיֵּי דְכָל בֵּית יִשְׂרָאֵל, בַּעֲגָלָא וּבִזְמַן קָרִיב וְאִמְרוּ אָמֵן: יְהֵא שְׁמֵהּ רַבָּא מְבָרַךְ לְעָלַם
וּלְעָלְמֵי עָלְמַיָּא: יִתְבָּרַךְ וְיִשְׁתַּבַּח וְיִתְפָּאַר וְיִתְרוֹמַם וְיִתְנַשֵּׂא וְיִתְהַדָּר וְיִתְעַלֶּה וְיִתְהַלָּל
שְׁמֵהּ דְּקֻדְשָׁא, בְּרִיךְ הוּא לְעֵלָּא (בעשי"ת וּלְעֵלָּא מִכָּל) מִן כָּל בִּרְכָתָא וְשִׁירָתָא,
תֻּשְׁבְּחָתָא וְנֶחֱמָתָא, דַּאֲמִירָן בְּעָלְמָא, וְאִמְרוּ אָמֵן: יְהֵא שְׁלָמָא רַבָּא מִן שְׁמַיָּא וְחַיִּים
עָלֵינוּ וְעַל כָּל יִשְׂרָאֵל וְאִמְרוּ אָמֵן: עוֹשֶׂה שָׁלוֹם בִּמְרוֹמָיו הוּא יַעֲשֶׂה שָׁלוֹם עָלֵינוּ וְעַל כָּל
יִשְׂרָאֵל וְאִמְרוּ אָמֵן:

Memorial Prayer

אֵל מָלֵא רַחֲמִים שׁוֹכֵן בַּמְּרוֹמִים אֵלֶּה סְלִיחוֹת חַנּוּן וְרַחוּם אֶרֶךְ אַפַּיִם וְרַב חֶסֶד.
הַמְצֵא כַּפָּרַת פֶּשַׁע וְהַקְרָבַת יֶשַׁע וּמְנוּחָה נְכוֹנָה תַּחַת כַּנְפֵי הַשְּׁכִינָה בְּמַעֲלוֹת קְדוֹשִׁים
וּטְהוֹרִים כְּזֹהַר הָרָקִיעַ מַזְהִירִים. אֶת נִשְׁמַת פב"פ שֶׁהָלַךְ (שֶׁהָלְכָה) לְעוֹלָמוֹ (לְעוֹלָמָהּ):
אָנָּא בַּעַל הָרַחֲמִים זָכְרָה לוֹ (לָהּ) לְטוֹבָה כָּל זְכִיּוֹתָיו (זְכִיּוֹתֶיהָ) וְצִדְקוֹתָיו (וְצִדְקוֹתֶיהָ)
בְּאַרְצוֹת הַחַיִּים. וּפָתַח לוֹ (לָהּ) שַׁעֲרֵי צֶדֶק וְאוֹרָה וְשַׁעֲרֵי חֶמְלָה וַחֲנִינָה. בְּסֵתֶר כְּנָפֶיךָ
תַּסְתִּירֵהוּ (תַּסְתִּירֶהָ) לְעוֹלָמִים. וּצְרוֹר בִּצְרוֹר הַחַיִּים אֶת נִשְׁמָתוֹ (נִשְׁמָתָהּ). יְיָ הוּא
נַחֲלָתוֹ (נַחֲלָתָהּ). וְיָנוּחַ (וְתָנוּחַ) בְּשָׁלוֹם עַל מִשְׁכָּבוֹ (מִשְׁכָּבָהּ) וְנֹאמַר אָמֵן:

---

* See p. 256 for English transliteration.

אֵל מָלֵא רַחֲמִים שׁוֹכֵן בַּמְּרוֹמִים. הַמְצֵא מְנוּחָה נְכוֹנָה תַּחַת כַּנְפֵי הַשְּׁכִינָה.
בְּמַעֲלוֹת קְדוֹשִׁים וּטְהוֹרִים. כְּזֹהַר הָרָקִיעַ מַזְהִירִים. אֶת־נִשְׁמַת הַיֶּלֶד (הַיַּלְדָּה) פב״פ
שֶׁהָלַךְ (שֶׁהָלְכָה) לְעוֹלָמוֹ (לְעוֹלָמָהּ) אָנָּא בַּעַל הָרַחֲמִים הַסְתִּירֵהוּ (הַסְתִּירֶהָ) בְּסֵתֶר
כְּנָפֶיךָ לְעוֹלָמִים. וּצְרוֹר בִּצְרוֹר הַחַיִּים אֶת נִשְׁמָתוֹ (נִשְׁמָתָהּ). יְיָ הוּא נַחֲלָתוֹ (נַחֲלָתָהּ)
וְיָנוּחַ (וְתָנוּחַ) בְּשָׁלוֹם עַל מִשְׁכָּבוֹ (מִשְׁכָּבָהּ) וְנֹאמַר אָמֵן:

Recitations When Visiting
A Grave—*Kever Avot*

Blessing to be Recited When One Has Not Visited a Jewish Cemetery for At Least Thirty Days

See p. 222.

Psalms 23 and 130
See p. 216.

MEDITATIONS
For a Father

שָׁלוֹם עָלֶיךָ אֲדוֹנִי אָבִי וּמוֹרִי, הוֹד זִיוִי וַהֲדָרִי, בְּשָׁלוֹם יָנוּחוּ עַצְמוֹתֶיךָ בַּקֶּבֶר בָּעוֹלָם הַזֶּה, וְנִשְׁמָתְךָ הוּבְאָה לְחַיֵּי עַד לְעוֹלָם הַבָּא: וְיָדַעְתִּי כִּי שָׁלוֹם אָהֳלֶךָ, וּמַעְלָה מַעְלָה עָלְתָה נִשְׁמָתֶךָ, יוֹשֶׁבֶת בְּסֵתֶר עֶלְיוֹן, וּבְצֵל שַׁדַּי תִּתְלוֹנָן: אַךְ אֲנִי, אַיֵּה אֶמְצָא מָנוֹחַ וּבַמָּה אֶתְנַחֵם, כָּל־יָמֶיךָ בִּי נִטְפַּלְתָּ וְכָל־מַחְסוֹרִי הָיָה לִי עַל־יָדֶךָ, תָּמִיד הֲטִיבוֹתָ לִי מִטּוּבֶךָ, גַּם בַּתּוֹרָה הֶאֱרַתָּ אֶת־עֵינִי, וְלַמִּצְוֹת הִדְרַכְתָּ פְּעָמַי, וּבַעֲבוֹדַת יְיָ חִזַּקְתָּ אֶת־יָדִי, וּמִדֶּרֶךְ הָרַע מָנַעְתָּ אֶת־רַגְלָי: וְעַתָּה הָלַכְתָּ לְךָ מַנְהִיגִי, וְנִשְׁאַרְתִּי אֲנִי לְבַדִּי, וְאֵין לִי עוֹד מְנַהֵל וְלֹא מוֹרֶה דֵעָה: הֵן צַדִּיק נֶאֱסָף, וּבְנוֹ נֶעֱזָב: עַל־כֵּן הַיּוֹם יָצֵאתִי וְלַמָּקוֹם מְלוֹנְךָ בָּאתִי, וְאֶשְׁתַּטֵּחַ עַל־קִבְרֶךָ וְאֶשָּׂא עֵינַי לֵאלֹהֵי מָרוֹם אֲשֶׁר לוֹ הַיְשׁוּעָה וּמִמֶּנּוּ הַנֶּחָמָה, וְהוּא רַחוּם יוֹשִׁיעֵנִי, וּבְחַסְדּוֹ יִרְפָּאֵנִי: וְגַם אַתָּה אָבִי תִּסְעָדֵנִי, וַעֲמָד־נָא וְהִתְפַּלֵּל בַּעֲדִי, וּבַקֵּשׁ עָלַי רַחֲמִים מֵהָאֵל רֹכֵב שְׁחָקִים, עַד יָבְקַע כַּשַּׁחַר אוֹרִי, וַאֲרוּכָתִי מְהֵרָה תַצְמִיחַ:

אָנָּא יְיָ רִבּוֹן הָעוֹלָמִים רְפָאֵנִי יְיָ וְאֵרָפֵא, הוֹשִׁיעֵנִי וְאִוָּשֵׁעַ, עֲשֵׂה עִמִּי חֶסֶד לְמַעַן

248

שְׁמֶךָ, אָנָּא תְנַחֲמֵנִי וְאַל־תַּעַזְבֵנִי וְתִהְיֶה הַשְׁגָּחָתְךָ עָלַי תָּמִיד לְטוֹבָה, וְתַצְלִיחַ אוֹתִי בְּכָל־עִנְיָנַי, וְתֶן רֶוַח וּבְרָכָה בְּמַעֲשֵׂי יָדַי, וְהָאֵר עֵינַי בְּמִצְוֹתֶיךָ, וְדַבֵּק לִבִּי בְּתוֹרָתֶךָ, וְאַל־תַּשְׁלֶט־בִּי יֵצֶר הָרַע שֶׁלֹּא אָבוֹא לִידֵי חֵטְא, וְתִטַּע בְּלִבִּי עֵצוֹת טוֹבוֹת, וְהָפֵר כָּל־עֲצַת רָעִים מֵעָלַי, וְהַצִּילֵנִי מִדִּין קָשֶׁה וּמִבַּעַל דִּין קָשֶׁה וּמִמְּצָא פָנִים וּמֵאָדָם רַע וּמֵחָבֵר רַע וּמִשָּׁכֵן רַע וּמִמִּקְרֶה רַע וּמִכָּל־שָׁעוֹת רָעוֹת הַמִּתְרַגְּשׁוֹת לָבוֹא לָעוֹלָם, וּתְמַלֵּא מִסְפַּר יָמַי בְּשָׁלוֹם וּבְמִיתָה טוֹבָה, וִיהִי יוֹם מִיתָתִי כְּיוֹם לֵדָתִי, שֶׁלֹּא יִמָּצֵא בִי שׁוּם חֵטְא וְעָוֹן וְאַשְׁמָה וָרֶשַׁע, וְתָנוּחַ נַפְשִׁי בִּצְרוֹר הַחַיִּים וְנַקֵּנִי בְּיוֹם הַדִּין וְצַדְּקֵנִי בַּמִּשְׁפָּט: אָנָּא יְיָ, שְׁמַע קוֹל תְּפִלָּתִי, וַעֲשֵׂה אֶת־שְׁאֵלָתִי וּבַקָּשָׁתִי בְּרַחֲמֶיךָ הָרַבִּים, אָמֵן:

וְגַם אַתָּה אָבִי מוֹרִי, אֲשֶׁר אַתָּה מוֹרָשֵׁי לְבָבִי, יְמַלֵּא יְיָ כָּל־מִשְׁאֲלוֹתֶיךָ, לְהַעֲלוֹת נִשְׁמָתְךָ כְּחֶפְצֶךָ, וְתִשְׁכֹּן בְּצֵל עֵדֶן אֵצֶל הָאָבוֹת הַקְּדוֹשִׁים וְהַתְּמִימִים וְהַטְּהוֹרִים, וְתִזְכֶּה לַעֲמוֹד לִתְחִיָּה, לְגוֹרָלְךָ הַנָּעִים לְקֵץ הַיָּמִים, אָמֵן.

For a Mother

שָׁלוֹם לָךְ אִמִּי מוֹרָתִי. אֲשֶׁר טִפַּחְתְּ וְרִבִּית אוֹתִי. וְנִצְטַעַרְתְּ עָלַי בְּלִי שִׁעוּר כְּפֵאָה וּכְבִכּוּרִים וְכֵרָאֵיוֹן. וְטִפַּלְתְּ בִּי כְּכָל־יָמַיִךְ: וְכָל־מַחְסוֹרִי הָיָה לִי מִיָּדֵךְ: וְעַתָּה מִיּוֹם אֲשֶׁר הָלַכְתְּ בְּדֶרֶךְ כָּל־הָאָרֶץ לֹא נִשְׁאֲרָה לִי אוֹמֶנֶת כָּמוֹךְ. כִּי בְּכָל־עֵת הֲכִנְתְּ אֶת־טוֹבָתִי: וּבִרְאוֹתִי אָרְחִי וְזוֹ צָרָתִי הָלַכְתִּי לִשְׂדֵה בוֹכִים. עַד שֶׁבָּאתִי אֶל־בֵּית אִמִּי וּלְחֶדֶר הוֹרָתִי. וְהִנֵּה הִיא לוּטָה בַשִּׂמְלָה. וְרוּחָהּ עָלְתָה לְמַעְלָה. וְאָמַרְתִּי, שָׁלוֹם לָךְ וְשָׁלוֹם לִמְנוּחָתֵךְ וְשָׁלוֹם לְנִשְׁמָתֵךְ. מְנֻשִׁים בָּאֹהֶל תְּבֹרָךְ, וְתָמִיד יֹאמַר עָלַיִךְ, קוּמִי אוֹרִי כִּי בָא אוֹרֵךְ. וּכְבוֹד יְיָ עָלַיִךְ יִזְרָח: וְלִי אֲנִי עַבְדֵּךְ. יֶהֱמוּ־נָא עָלַי רַחֲמַיִךְ. לְהִתְפַּלֵּל בַּעֲדִי אֶל־יְיָ. שֶׁיִּשְׁמַע קוֹל תַּחֲנוּנִי. בְּאָמְרִי, אָנָּא נוֹרָא וְקָדוֹשׁ הַרְבֵּה מְחִילָתֶךָ, פִּשְׁעֵי לִסְלֹחַ גַּלְגֵּל מְדוֹתֶךָ. יְחַנֵּנִי מִיוֹמַיִם בְּרַחֲמָיו עוֹשֶׂה שָׁלוֹם בִּמְרוֹמָיו. וְיַסְפִּיק לִי מִשְׁמַיִם בַּר וְלֶחֶם וּמָזוֹן בְּרַחֲמָיו. וְאֶל־דִּמְעָתִי אַל־יֶחֱרָשׁ, בְּקָרְאִי מִן־הַמֵּצַר כְּעָנִי וָרָשׁ: יְחָנֵּנִי וְיֹאמַר פְּדָעֵהוּ מֵרֶדֶת שַׁחַת. וְלֹא יֶחְסַר לַחְמוֹ וְלֹא יָמוּת לַשַּׁחַת. וִיזַכֵּנִי לִרְאוֹת בָּנִים וּבְנֵי בָנִים בַּתּוֹרָה וּבְמִצְוֹת עוֹסְקִים. וְיִהְיוּ בַּעֲלֵי מִצְוֹת וְשֵׁם טוֹב וְצַדִּיקִים. וּמִכָּל־עָוֹן וְאַשְׁמָה מְנֻקִּים: וְאַתְּ, נִשְׁמָתֵךְ תִּשְׁכֹּן בְּצֵל עֲצֵי עֵדֶן אֵצֶל הָאִמָּהוֹת הַיְשָׁרוֹת הַקְּדוֹשׁוֹת וְהַטְּהוֹרוֹת. וְתִזְכִּי לַעֲמוֹד לִתְחִיָּה בְּצֵל עֲצֵי עֵדֶן עִם־שְׁאָר נָשִׁים שַׁאֲנַנּוֹת וַחֲסִידוֹת בָּנוֹת עֲלִיָּה. וְתַעַמְדִי לְגוֹרָלֵךְ לְקֵץ הַיָּמִין. כֵּן יַעֲשֶׂה הָאֵל יְיָ, אָמֵן:

For a Child

שָׁלוֹם עָלֶיךָ נִשְׁמָה יְחִידָה, אֲשֶׁר הָיִיתְ מְחַיָּה גּוּף אָדָם אֲשֶׁר נַפְשִׁי לוֹ כָּמַהּ, מוֹצָא
מֵעִי וְיוֹצֵא חֲלָצַי אֲשֶׁר נָתַן לִי אֱלֹהִים בָּזֶה עַל־פְּנֵי תֵבֵל אַרְצוֹ כַּאֲשֶׁר יָשַׁר בְּעֵינָיו.
בִּרְצוֹנוֹ נָתַן וּבִרְצוֹנוֹ נָטַל: חָבִיב הָיָה עָלַי דְּבוּרוֹ. תַּאֲוַת נַפְשִׁי לִשְׁמוֹ וּלְזִכְרוֹ. דּוֹדִי חָמַק
עָבָר, נִגְלָה וְנִכְסָה נִרְאָה וְנִסְתָּר, קְרָאתִיו וְלֹא עָנָנִי בִּקַּשְׁתִּיהוּ וְלֹא מְצָאתִיהוּ: וַאֲנִי לֹא
יָדַעְתִּי כַּבְשֵׁי דְרַחֲמָנָא וְרָזוֹהִי. אִם הָיָה מַתָּנָה עַל־מְנָת לְהַחֲזִירָהּ בִּזְמַנָּהּ. אוֹ אִם־עֲווֹנֵינוּ
עָנוּ בָנוּ לְאִיזוֹ סִבָּה מֵהָעֲווֹנוֹת שֶׁהִתְחַיַּבְתִּי עֲלֵיהֶן לְקַבֵּל הַפֻּרְעָנוּת: בֵּין כַּךְ וּבֵין כַּךְ לֹא
זָכִיתִי לְגַדְּלוֹ יוֹתֵר, וְאַף כִּי אָמַרְתִּי אַחֲרֵי מוֹתִי אֵצֶלֶה בְתָמָר בְּסַנְסַנָּיו, נִפְרְדוּ
נִפְרְצוּ עָלַי בְּגָזְרַת אֲדוֹנָיו, וְאֶלְכָה לִי שָׂדֵה בוֹכִים, אֶל־הַסֶּלַע וְאֶל־הַבּוֹכִים, וְאֶתְפַּלְלָה
אֶל־אֵל עַל־נִשְׁמָתוֹ, יַעֲלֶנָה אֶל־מְכוֹן שִׁבְתּוֹ, וְיַסְתִּירֶנָּה בְּסֵתֶר עֶלְיוֹן יָרוֹם חֶבְיוֹן: וְאַתְּ
נִשְׁמָה עִמְדִי־נָא בִּתְפִלָּה וּבַקָּשָׁה לִפְנֵי אֵל רָם וְנִשָּׂא, שֶׁיְכַפֵּר וְיִסְלַח לַעֲווֹנוֹת וְלַפְּשָׁעִים
וְלַמַּעֲשִׂים הָרָעִים שֶׁחָטָאתִי וְשֶׁעָוִיתִי וְשֶׁפָּשַׁעְתִּי וְשֶׁהֲרֵעוֹתִי, וְיַנְחֲלֵנִי עַל־מֵי מְנוּחוֹת
בְּנַחַת וְשׂוּבָה עַד־זִקְנָה וְשֵׂיבָה, וְיִשְׁמֹר אוֹתִי וּשְׁאָר זַרְעִי מִן־כִּלָּיוֹן נֶחֱרָץ עוֹד כָּל־יְמֵי
הָאָרֶץ, וּמִמִּיתָה שֶׁלֹּא בִזְמַנָּהּ, גַּם מִכָּל־חֳלִי וְכָל־מַכָּה. וְיִשְׁמֹר צֵאתִי וּבוֹאִי לְחַיִּים
וּלְשָׁלוֹם מֵעַתָּה וְעַד עוֹלָם: וְאַתְּ לְכִי לַקֵּץ וּתְנוּחִי וְתַעֲמֹדִי לְגֹרָלֵךְ לְקֵץ הַיָּמִין עִם כָּל־
הַצַּדִּיקִים: וְהוּא רַחוּם יְכַפֵּר עָוֹן, וְלֹא יַשְׁחִית, וְהִרְבָּה לְהָשִׁיב אַפּוֹ, וְלֹא יָעִיר כָּל־חֲמָתוֹ,
וּבְשָׁלְחוֹ אֶת אֵלִיָּה הַנָּבִיא לְפָנֵי בּוֹא הַיּוֹם הַגָּדוֹל וְהַנּוֹרָא, אֲשֶׁר יָבוֹא לְהָשִׁיב לֵב עַל־
בָּנִים עַל־אֲבוֹתָם וְלֵב־אָבוֹת עַל־בָּנִים, אָזַי גַּם לָךְ גַּם יְנַחֵם, אָמֵן:

ADDITIONAL MEDITATIONS

*In addition to the classical Hebrew meditations for parents and
children, we are appending a number of specific shorter meditations for visits to the graves of all departed relatives. These meditations are merely a guide. It is a virtue to offer spontaneous
meditations in the presence of the grave of a loved one.*

Meditation for a Departed Father

Your passing, dear father, has left a void in my life which can
never be filled. How can I ever forget the untiring zeal with which

you labored to provide my every physical and spiritual need? How can I ever forget the sacrifices you so willingly made that I should prosper? You have been a role-model for me in every respect. Whenever I come to a choice point in my life, whenever an important decision demands to be made, I ask myself: What would Father have done? The recollection of your joy in my achievements, your comforting words and gestures which strengthened me at every setback are indelibly inscribed upon my soul. These sacred memories will inspire me to live according to the ideals you treasured. Please keep me in your prayers even as I keep you in mine.

Meditation for a Departed Mother

Dearest mother, whatever I am today I owe to you. What would I be without your tender care, without your love and devotion in my every hour of need? Your gentleness and your concern have been a continual inspiration. I have learned as much from your lovingkindness as from all my formal education. No effort on my behalf was too great for you. You stirred at my every cry; you suffered even my smallest pain with me; your influence enobled my life and molded my personality. May your example ever be my guide. Parted in body our souls remain united. Your love is ever with me. I know that you remember me in your prayers, I remember you in mine.

Meditation for a Departed Husband

My darling, with a heart filled to overflowing, I recall our precious years together. Your tenderness and devoted concern, the strength you were to me in sorrow, the inspiration in all I did, made life together full and meaningful. Your support and trust, and your companionship, brought blessing to my life. Though death has parted us, the bonds we made in the presence of God can never be dissolved. May your sacred memory make me a better person. I shall never forget you. May the Merciful One bless and keep you, until He reunites us. I have you in my prayers. Please remember me in yours.

Meditation for a Departed Wife

My darling, with a heart filled to overflowing I recall our precious years together. Your tenderness and devoted concern, the strength you were to me in sorrow, the inspiration in all I did, made life full and meaningful. Your support and trust, and your companionship, brought blessing to my life. You showed me how to love. You helped me find fulfillment. I miss you so very much. Though death has parted us, the bonds we made in the presence of God can never be dissolved. May your sacred memory make me a better person. May the Merciful One bless you and keep you, until He reunites us. Remember me in your prayers my darling even as I remember you in mine.

Meditation for a Departed Child

My darling, the blessed memories you have left me ever sustain me. I can never forget the joy and happiness it gave me to tend to your every spiritual and physical need. Every minute was sacred, every hour was precious. The soul within me weeps as I recall my dreams for you, as I remember my hopes and plans for your future. In His infinite wisdom, God made other plans for you, and called you back to His loving care. I thank Him for having entrusted your beautiful soul, although too briefly, to my care. I pray that I was faithful to that trust. Your life was a blessing; your memory is an inspiration. May He guard and keep you for me. Remember me in your innocent prayers even as I remember you in mine.

Meditation for a Departed Brother or Sister

Dear _____ , you've been called to your eternal rest, but the passage of time can never erase the precious memories of the countless happy hours of companionship we had together. Thank you for your warmth and friendship, for your patience and understanding, for your loyalty and your support, for your commitment and your caring. I am ever grateful to you for your concern for me. If ever I upset you by word or gesture, please forgive me. The memory of our close bonds of fellowship ever sustains me. May it continue to inspire me in my relationship with others. Remember me in your prayers, I remember you in mine.

Meditation for Other Relatives and Friends

My dear _____ : Time has passed, but you are not forgotten. The precious memory of the time we spent together in close companionship ever sustains me. Your love and loyalty still inspire me. May I be given the strength to do unto others what you unhesitatingly and unstintingly did for me. May the memory of your life guide me in the paths of righteousness and truth. I shall never forget you. I often think of you in my prayers. Please remember me in yours.

MEMORIAL PRAYER

For an Adult

O Lord, who art full of compassion, who dwellest on high—God of forgiveness, who art merciful, slow to anger and abounding in loving-kindness, grant pardon of transgressions, speedy salvation, and perfect rest beneath the shadow of Thy divine presence, in the exalted places among the holy and pure, who shine as the brightness of the firmament, to _____ who hath gone to his [her] eternal home. We beseech Thee O Lord of compassion, remember unto him [her] for good all the meritorious and pious deeds which he [she] wrought while on earth. Open unto him [her] the gates of righteousness and light, the gates of pity and grace. O shelter him [her] for evermore under the cover of Thy wings; and let his [her] soul be bound up in the bond of eternal life. The Lord be his [her] inheritance; may he [she] rest in peace. And let us say, Amen.

For a Child

O God, who art full of compassion, who dwellest on high, grant perfect rest beneath the shadow of thy divine presence, in the exalted places among the holy and pure, who shine as the brightness of the firmament , to the child _____ who hath gone to his [her] eternal rest. We beseech Thee, O Lord of compassion, shelter him [her] for evermore under the cover of Thy wings; and let his [her] soul be bound up in the bond of eternal life. The Lord be his [her] inheritance; may he [she] rest in peace. And let us say, Amen.

Transliterations of the *Kaddish*

THE BURIAL *KADDISH*

Yit-ga-dal ve-yit-ka-dash she-mei raba
B'al-ma dee hoo a-tid le-it-chad'ta
Oo-le-a-cha-ya mei-ta-ya oo-le-a-sa-ka
Yat-hon le-cha-yei al-ma.
Oo-le-miv-neh kar-ta dee--ye-rush-leim
Oo-le-shakh-leil hei-kha-lei be-ga-vah.
Oo-le-me'e-kar pul-cha-na nookh-ra'ah mei-ar'a
Oo-le-a-ta-va pul-cha-na dee--she-ma-ya le-at-rei.
Ve-yim-lakh kood-sha b'rikh hoo be-mal-khu-tei vee-ka-rei
Be-cha-yei-khon oo-ve-yo-mei-khon oo-ve-cha-yei dee--khol
    beit Yis-ra-el
Ba'a-ga-la oo-viz-man ka-riv.
Ve-ee-me-roo: AMEN.

Ye-hei she-mei rab-ba me-va-rakh le-a-lam oo-le-al-mei
    al-ma-ya.

Yit-ba-rakh ve-yish-ta-bach ve-yit-pa'ar ve-yit-ro-mam
Ve-yit-na-sei ve-yit-ha-dar ve-yit-a-leh ve-yit-ha-lal
She-mei dee--kood-sha. B'rikh hoo.
Le-ei-lah min kol bir-kha-ta ve-shee-ra-ta
Toosh-be-cha-ta ve-ne-che-ma-ta
Dee--a-mee-ran b'al-ma.
Ve-ee-me-roo: AMEN.

Ye-hei she-la-ma rab-ba min--she-ma-ya ve-cha-yyim
A-lei-noo ve-al kol Yis-ra-el.
Ve-ee-me-roo: AMEN.

O-seh sha-lom bim-ro-mav hoo ya-a-seh sha-lom
A-lei-noo ve-al kol Yis-ra-el.
Ve-ee-me-roo: AMEN

THE MOURNER'S *KADDISH*

Yit-ga-dal ve-yit-ka-dash she-mei rab-ba
B'al-ma dee--ve-ra khee-re-oo-tei.
Ve-yam-likh mal-khoo-tei be-cha-yei-khon
Oo-ve-yo-mei-khon oo-ve-cha-yei dee--khol beit Yis-ra-el
Ba'a-ga-la oo-viz-man ka-riv.
Ve-ee-me-roo: AMEN.

Ye-hei she-mei rab-ba me-va-rakh le-a-lam oo-le-al-mei
  al-ma-ya.

Yit-ba-rakh ve-yish-ta-bach ve-yit-pa'ar ve-yit-ro-mam
Ve-yit-na-sei ve-yit-ha-dar ve-yit-a-leh ve-yit-ha-lal
She-mei dee--kood-sha. B'rikh hoo.
Le-ei-lah min kol bir-kha-ta ve-shee-ra-ta
Toosh-be-cha-ta ve-ne-che-ma-ta
Dee--a-mee-ran b'al-ma.
Ve-ee-me-roo: AMEN.

Ye-hei she-la-ma rab-ba min--she-ma-ya ve-cha-yyim

A-lei-noo ve-al kol Yis-ra-el.
Ve-ee-me-roo: AMEN.

O-seh sha-lom bim-ro-mav hoo ya-a-seh shalom
A-lei-noo ve-al kol Yis-ra-el.
Ve-ee-me-roo: AMEN.

KADDISH D'RABBANAN

Yit-ga-dal ve-yit-ka-dash she-mei rab-ba
B'al-ma dee--ve-ra khee-re-oo-tei.
Ve-yam-likh mal-khoo-tei be-cha-yei-khon
Oo-ve-yo-mei-khon oo-ve-cha-yei dee--khol beit Yis-ra-el
Ba'a-ga-la oo-viz-man ka-riv.
Ve-ee-me-roo: AMEN.

Ye-hei she-mei rab-ba me-va-rakh le-a-lam oo-le-al-mei
  al-ma-ya

Yit-ba-rakh ve-yish-ta-bach ve-yit-pa'ar ve-yit-ro-mam
Ve-yitna-seh ve-yit-ha-dar ve-yit-a-leh ve-yit-ha-lal
She-mei dee--kood-sha. B'rikh hoo.
Le-ei-lah min kol bir-kha-ta ve-shee-ra-ta
Toosh-be-cha-ta ve-ne-che-ma-ta
Dee--a-mee-ran b'al-ma.
Ve-ee-me-roo: AMEN.

Al Yis-ra-el ve-al rab-ba-nan ve-al tal-mee-dei-hon
Ve-al kol tal-mee-dei tal-mee-dei-hon
Ve-al kol man dee as-kin be-o-raiy-ta
Dee be-at-ra ha-dein ve-dee be-khol a-tar ve-a-tar
Ye-hei le-hon oo-le-khon she-la-ma rab-ba
Chee-na ve-chis-da ve-ra-cha-min ve-cha-yeen a-ree-kheen
Oo-me-zo-na re-vee-cha oo-far-ka-na
Min ko-dam a-voo-hon dee ve-she-ma-ya.
Ve-ee-me-roo: AMEN.

Ye-hei she-la-ma rab-ba min--she-ma-ya ve-cha-yyim to-vim
A-lei-noo ve-al kol Yis-ra-el.
Ve-ee-me-roo: AMEN.

O-seh sha-lom bim-ro-mav hoo be-ra-cha-mav ya-a-seh sha-lom
A-lei-noo ve-al kol Yis-ra-el.
Ve-ee-me-roo: AMEN.

Service for the Consecration of a New Cemetery

Psalm 91

He that dwelleth in the shelter of the Most High abideth under the shadow of the Almighty. I say of the Lord, He is my refuge and my fortress; my God, in whom I trust. For He shall deliver thee from the snare of the fowler, and from the noisome pestilence. He shall cover thee with His pinions, and under His wings shalt thou take refuge: His truth shall be a shield and a buckler. Thou shalt not be afraid of the terror by night, nor of the arrow that flieth by day; of the pestilence that walketh in darkness, nor of the plague that ravageth at noon day. A thousand may fall at thy side, and ten thousand at thy right hand; it shall not come nigh unto thee. Only with thine eyes shalt thou look on, and see the retribution of the wicked. For Thou, O Lord, art my refuge, Thou hast made the Most High thy dwelling place; there shall no evil befall thee, neither shall any scourge come nigh thy tent. For He shall give His angels charge over thee, to keep thee in all thy ways. They shall bear thee upon their hands, lest thou strike thy foot against a stone. Thou shalt tread upon the lion and the adder: upon the young lion and the serpent shalt thou trample. Because he hath set his love upon Me, therefore will I deliver him: I will set him on high, because he knoweth My name. When he calleth upon Me, I will answer him; I will be with him in trouble: I will deliver him and honor him. With length of days will I satisfy him, and will let him see My salvation. *Repeat the last verse.*

יֹשֵׁב בְּסֵתֶר עֶלְיוֹן בְּצֵל שַׁדַּי יִתְלוֹנָן: אֹמַר לַיהֹוָה מַחְסִי וּמְצוּדָתִי אֱלֹהַי אֶבְטַח־בּוֹ: כִּי הוּא יַצִּילְךָ מִפַּח יָקוּשׁ מִדֶּבֶר הַוּוֹת: בְּאֶבְרָתוֹ יָסֶךְ לָךְ וְתַחַת־כְּנָפָיו תֶּחְסֶה צִנָּה וְסֹחֵרָה אֲמִתּוֹ: לֹא־תִירָא מִפַּחַד לָיְלָה מֵחֵץ יָעוּף יוֹמָם: מִדֶּבֶר בָּאֹפֶל יַהֲלֹךְ מִקֶּטֶב יָשׁוּד צָהֳרָיִם: יִפֹּל מִצִּדְּךָ אֶלֶף וּרְבָבָה מִימִינֶךָ אֵלֶיךָ לֹא יִגָּשׁ: רַק בְּעֵינֶיךָ תַבִּיט וְשִׁלֻּמַת רְשָׁעִים תִּרְאֶה:

258

כִּי־אַתָּה יְהֹוָה מַחְסִי עֶלְיוֹן שַׂמְתָּ מְעוֹנֶךָ: לֹא־תְאֻנֶּה אֵלֶיךָ רָעָה וְנֶגַע לֹא־יִקְרַב בְּאָהֳלֶךָ: כִּי מַלְאָכָיו יְצַוֶּה־לָּךְ לִשְׁמָרְךָ בְּכָל־דְּרָכֶיךָ: עַל־כַּפַּיִם יִשָּׂאוּנְךָ פֶּן־תִּגֹּף בָּאֶבֶן רַגְלֶךָ: עַל־ שַׁחַל וָפֶתֶן תִּדְרֹךְ תִּרְמֹס כְּפִיר וְתַנִּין: כִּי בִי חָשַׁק וַאֲפַלְּטֵהוּ אֲשַׂגְּבֵהוּ כִּי־יָדַע שְׁמִי: יִקְרָאֵנִי וְאֶעֱנֵהוּ עִמּוֹ־אָנֹכִי בְצָרָה אֲחַלְּצֵהוּ וַאֲכַבְּדֵהוּ: אֹרֶךְ יָמִים אַשְׂבִּיעֵהוּ וְאַרְאֵהוּ בִּישׁוּעָתִי:

Exodus 30:34–36, 7-8

And the Lord said unto Moses: "Take unto thee sweet spices, stacte, and onycha, and galbanum; sweet spices with pure frankincense; of each shall there be a like weight. And thou shalt make of it incense, a perfume after the art of the perfumer, seasoned with salt, pure and holy. And thou shalt beat some of it very small, and put of it before the testimony in the tent of meeting, where I will meet with thee; it shall be unto you most holy." And it is said again: "And Aaron shall burn thereon incense of sweet spices; every morning, when he dresseth the lamps, he shall burn it. And when Aaron lighteth the lamps at dusk, he shall burn it, a perpetual incense before the Lord throughout your generations."

וַיֹּאמֶר יְהֹוָה אֶל־מֹשֶׁה, קַח־לְךָ סַמִּים נָטָף, וּשְׁחֵלֶת וְחֶלְבְּנָה סַמִּים, וּלְבֹנָה זַכָּה, בַּד בְּבַד יִהְיֶה: וְעָשִׂיתָ אֹתָהּ קְטֹרֶת, רֹקַח מַעֲשֵׂה רוֹקֵחַ, מְמֻלָּח, טָהוֹר, קֹדֶשׁ: וְשָׁחַקְתָּ מִמֶּנָּה הָדֵק, וְנָתַתָּה מִמֶּנָּה לִפְנֵי הָעֵדֻת, בְּאֹהֶל מוֹעֵד אֲשֶׁר אִוָּעֵד לְךָ שָׁמָּה, קֹדֶשׁ קָדָשִׁים תִּהְיֶה לָכֶם: וְנֶאֱמַר, וְהִקְטִיר עָלָיו אַהֲרֹן קְטֹרֶת סַמִּים, בַּבֹּקֶר בַּבֹּקֶר, בְּהֵיטִיבוֹ אֶת־הַנֵּרֹת, יַקְטִירֶנָּה: וּבְהַעֲלֹת אַהֲרֹן אֶת־הַנֵּרֹת בֵּין הָעַרְבַּיִם, יַקְטִירֶנָּה, קְטֹרֶת תָּמִיד לִפְנֵי יְהֹוָה לְדֹרֹתֵיכֶם:

Numbers 17:11–15

And Moses said unto Aaron: "Take thy fire-pan, and put fire therein from off the altar, and lay incense thereon, and carry it quickly unto the congregation, and make atonement for them; for there is wrath gone out from the Lord: the plague is begun." And Aaron took as Moses spoke, and ran into the midst of the assembly; and, behold, the plague was begun among the people; and he put on the incense and made atonement for the people. And he stood between the dead and the living; and the plague was stayed. Now they that died by the plague were fourteen thousand and seven hundred, besides them that died about the matter of Korah. And Aaron returned unto Moses unto the door of the tent of meeting, and the plague was stayed.

וַיֹּאמֶר מֹשֶׁה אֶל אַהֲרֹן, קַח אֶת הַמַּחְתָּה וְתֶן עָלֶיהָ אֵשׁ מֵעַל הַמִּזְבֵּחַ וְשִׂים קְטֹרֶת,
וְהוֹלֵךְ מְהֵרָה אֶל הָעֵדָה וְכַפֵּר עֲלֵיהֶם, כִּי יָצָא הַקֶּצֶף מִלִּפְנֵי יְיָ, הֵחֵל הַנָּגֶף. וַיִּקַּח אַהֲרֹן
כַּאֲשֶׁר דִּבֶּר מֹשֶׁה, וַיָּרָץ אֶל תּוֹךְ הַקָּהָל, וְהִנֵּה הֵחֵל הַנֶּגֶף בָּעָם, וַיִּתֵּן אֶת הַקְּטֹרֶת וַיְכַפֵּר
עַל הָעָם. וַיַּעֲמֹד בֵּין הַמֵּתִים וּבֵין הַחַיִּים, וַתֵּעָצַר הַמַּגֵּפָה. וַיִּהְיוּ הַמֵּתִים בַּמַּגֵּפָה אַרְבָּעָה
עָשָׂר אֶלֶף וּשְׁבַע מֵאוֹת, מִלְּבַד הַמֵּתִים עַל דְּבַר קֹרַח. וַיָּשָׁב אַהֲרֹן אֶל מֹשֶׁה אֶל פֶּתַח
אֹהֶל מוֹעֵד, וְהַמַּגֵּפָה נֶעֱצָרָה.

Psalm 102

A prayer of the afflicted, when he fainteth and poureth out his complaint before the Lord.
O Lord, hear my prayer,
And let my cry come unto Thee.
Hide not Thy face from me in the day of my distress;
Incline Thine ear unto me;
In the day when I call answer me speedily.
For my days are consumed like smoke,
And my bones are burnt as a hearth.
My heart is smitten like grass,
And withered; for I forgot to eat my bread.
By reason of the voice of my sighing
My bones cleave to my flesh
I am like a pelican of the wilderness;
I am become like an owl of the waste places.
I watch, and am become
Like a sparrow that is alone upon the housetop.
Mine enemies taunt me all the day;
They that are mad against me do curse by me.
For I have eaten ashes like bread,
And mingled my drink with weeping.
Because of Thine indignation and Thy wrath;

For Thou hast taken me up, and cast me away.
My days are like a lengthening shadow;
And I am withered like grass.
But Thou, O Lord, sittest enthroned for ever;
And Thy name is unto all generations.
Thou wilt rise and have compassion upon Zion;
For it is time to be gracious unto her,
    for the appointed time is come.
For Thy servants take pleasure in her stones,
And love her dust.
So the nations will fear the name of the Lord,
And the kings of the earth Thy glory;
When the Lord hath built up Zion,
When He hath appeared in His glory;
When He hath regarded the prayer of the destitute,
And hath not despised their prayer.
This shall be written for the generations to come
And a people which shall be created shall praise the Lord.
For He hath looked down from the height of His sanctuary;
From heaven did the Lord behold the earth;
To hear the groaning of the prisoner;
To loose those that are appointed to death;
That men may tell of the name of the Lord in Zion,
And His praise in Jerusalem;
When the peoples are gathered together,
And the kingdoms to serve the Lord.
He weakened my strength in the way;
He shortened my days.
I say: "O my God, take me not away in the midst of my days,
Thou whose years endure throughout all generations."
Of old Thou didst lay the foundations of the earth;
And the heavens are the work of Thy hands.
They shall perish but Thou shalt endure;
Yea, all of them shall wax old like a garment
As a vesture shalt thou change them, and they shall pass away;
But Thou art the selfsame,
And Thy years shall have no end.
The children of Thy servants shall dwell securely,
And their seed shall be established before Thee.

תְּפִלָּה לְעָנִי כִי־יַעֲטֹף וְלִפְנֵי יְהֹוָה יִשְׁפֹּךְ שִׂיחוֹ:

יְהֹוָה שִׁמְעָה תְפִלָּתִי וְשַׁוְעָתִי אֵלֶיךָ תָבוֹא:

אַל־תַּסְתֵּר פָּנֶיךָ מִמֶּנִּי בְּיוֹם צַר לִי הַטֵּה־אֵלַי אָזְנֶךָ בְּיוֹם אֶקְרָא מַהֵר עֲנֵנִי:

כִּי־כָלוּ בְעָשָׁן יָמָי וְעַצְמוֹתַי כְּמוֹקֵד נִחָרוּ:

הוּכָּה כָעֵשֶׂב וַיִּבַשׁ לִבִּי כִּי־שָׁכַחְתִּי מֵאֲכֹל לַחְמִי:

מִקּוֹל אַנְחָתִי דָּבְקָה עַצְמִי לִבְשָׂרִי:

דָּמִיתִי לִקְאַת מִדְבָּר הָיִיתִי כְּכוֹס חֳרָבוֹת: שָׁקַדְתִּי וָאֶהְיֶה כְּצִפּוֹר בּוֹדֵד עַל־גָּג:

כָּל־הַיּוֹם חֵרְפוּנִי אוֹיְבָי מְהוֹלָלַי בִּי נִשְׁבָּעוּ:

כִּי־אֵפֶר כַּלֶּחֶם אָכָלְתִּי וְשִׁקֻּוַי בִּבְכִי מָסָכְתִּי:

מִפְּנֵי־זַעַמְךָ וְקִצְפֶּךָ כִּי נְשָׂאתַנִי וַתַּשְׁלִיכֵנִי:

יָמַי כְּצֵל נָטוּי וַאֲנִי כָּעֵשֶׂב אִיבָשׁ:

וְאַתָּה יְהֹוָה לְעוֹלָם תֵּשֵׁב וְזִכְרְךָ לְדֹר וָדֹר:

אַתָּה תָקוּם תְּרַחֵם צִיּוֹן כִּי־עֵת לְחֶנְנָהּ כִּי־בָא מוֹעֵד:

כִּי־רָצוּ עֲבָדֶיךָ אֶת־אֲבָנֶיהָ וְאֶת־עֲפָרָהּ יְחֹנֵנוּ:

וְיִירְאוּ גוֹיִם אֶת־שֵׁם יְהֹוָה וְכָל־מַלְכֵי הָאָרֶץ אֶת־כְּבוֹדֶךָ:

כִּי־בָנָה יְהֹוָה צִיּוֹן נִרְאָה בִּכְבוֹדוֹ:

פָּנָה אֶל־תְּפִלַּת הָעַרְעָר וְלֹא־בָזָה אֶת־תְּפִלָּתָם:

תִּכָּתֶב זֹאת לְדוֹר אַחֲרוֹן וְעַם נִבְרָא יְהַלֶּל־יָהּ:

כִּי־הִשְׁקִיף מִמְּרוֹם קָדְשׁוֹ יְהֹוָה מִשָּׁמַיִם אֶל־אֶרֶץ הִבִּיט:

לִשְׁמֹעַ אֶנְקַת אָסִיר לְפַתֵּחַ בְּנֵי תְמוּתָה:

לְסַפֵּר בְּצִיּוֹן שֵׁם יְהֹוָה וּתְהִלָּתוֹ בִּירוּשָׁלָ‍ִם:

בְּהִקָּבֵץ עַמִּים יַחְדָּו וּמַמְלָכוֹת לַעֲבֹד אֶת־יְהֹוָה:

עִנָּה בַדֶּרֶךְ כֹּחִי קִצַּר יָמָי:

אֹמַר אֵלִי אַל־תַּעֲלֵנִי בַּחֲצִי יָמָי בְּדוֹר דּוֹרִים שְׁנוֹתֶיךָ:

לְפָנִים הָאָרֶץ יָסַדְתָּ וּמַעֲשֵׂה יָדֶיךָ שָׁמָיִם:

הֵמָּה יֹאבֵדוּ וְאַתָּה תַעֲמֹד וְכֻלָּם כַּבֶּגֶד יִבְלוּ כַּלְּבוּשׁ תַּחֲלִיפֵם וְיַחֲלֹפוּ:

וְאַתָּה־הוּא וּשְׁנוֹתֶיךָ לֹא יִתָּמּוּ:

בְּנֵי־עֲבָדֶיךָ יִשְׁכּוֹנוּ וְזַרְעָם לְפָנֶיךָ יִכּוֹן:

Psalm 103

Bless the Lord, O my soul; and all that is within me, bless His holy
name. Bless the Lord, O my soul, and forget not all His benefits:
who forgiveth all thine iniquity; who healeth all thy diseases; who
redeemeth thy life from the pit; who crowneth thee with loving-

kindness and tender mercies: who satisfieth thy years with good things; so that thy youth is renewed like the eagle's. The Lord executeth righteous acts, and judgments for all that are oppressed. He made known His ways unto Moses, His doings unto the children of Israel. The Lord is merciful and gracious, slow to anger, and abounding in loving-kindness. He will not always contend; neither will He keep his anger for ever. He hath not dealt with us after our sins, nor requited us after our iniquities. For as the heaven is high above the earth, so mighty is his loving-kindness over them that fear Him. As far as the east is from the west, so far hath He removed our transgressions from us. Like a father hath mercy upon his children, so the Lord hath mercy upon them that fear Him. For He knoweth our frame; He remembereth that we are dust. As for man, his days are as grass; as the flower of the field, so he flourisheth. For the wind passeth over it, and it is gone; and the place thereof shall know it no more. But the loving-kindness of the Lord is from everlasting to everlasting upon them that fear Him, and His righteousness unto children's children, to such as keep His covenant, and to those that remember His precepts to do them. The Lord hath established His throne in the heavens; and His kingdom ruleth over all. Bless the Lord, ye His angels: ye mighty in strength, that fulfill His word, hearkening unto the voice of His word. Bless the Lord, all ye His hosts; ye ministers of His, that do His will. Bless the Lord, all ye His works, in all places of His dominion: bless the Lord, O my soul.

לְדָוִד בָּרְכִי נַפְשִׁי אֶת־יְהֹוָה וְכָל־קְרָבַי אֶת־שֵׁם קָדְשׁוֹ: בָּרְכִי נַפְשִׁי אֶת־יְהֹוָה וְאַל־תִּשְׁכְּחִי כָּל־גְּמוּלָיו: הַסֹּלֵחַ לְכָל־עֲוֹנֵכִי הָרֹפֵא לְכָל־תַּחֲלוּאָיְכִי: הַגּוֹאֵל מִשַּׁחַת חַיָּיְכִי הַמְעַטְּרֵכִי חֶסֶד וְרַחֲמִים: הַמַּשְׂבִּיעַ בַּטּוֹב עֶדְיֵךְ תִּתְחַדֵּשׁ כַּנֶּשֶׁר נְעוּרָיְכִי: עֹשֵׂה צְדָקוֹת יְהֹוָה וּמִשְׁפָּטִים לְכָל־עֲשׁוּקִים: יוֹדִיעַ דְּרָכָיו לְמֹשֶׁה לִבְנֵי יִשְׂרָאֵל עֲלִילוֹתָיו: רַחוּם וְחַנּוּן יְהֹוָה אֶרֶךְ אַפַּיִם וְרַב־חָסֶד: לֹא־לָנֶצַח יָרִיב וְלֹא לְעוֹלָם יִטּוֹר: לֹא כַחֲטָאֵינוּ עָשָׂה לָנוּ וְלֹא כַעֲוֹנֹתֵינוּ גָּמַל עָלֵינוּ: כִּי כִגְבֹהַּ שָׁמַיִם עַל־הָאָרֶץ גָּבַר חַסְדּוֹ עַל־יְרֵאָיו: כִּרְחֹק מִזְרָח מִמַּעֲרָב הִרְחִיק מִמֶּנּוּ אֶת־פְּשָׁעֵינוּ: כְּרַחֵם אָב עַל־בָּנִים רִחַם יְהֹוָה עַל־יְרֵאָיו: כִּי־הוּא יָדַע יִצְרֵנוּ זָכוּר כִּי־עָפָר אֲנָחְנוּ: אֱנוֹשׁ כֶּחָצִיר יָמָיו כְּצִיץ הַשָּׂדֶה כֵּן יָצִיץ: כִּי רוּחַ עָבְרָה־בּוֹ וְאֵינֶנּוּ וְלֹא־יַכִּירֶנּוּ עוֹד מְקוֹמוֹ: וְחֶסֶד יְהֹוָה מֵעוֹלָם וְעַד־עוֹלָם עַל־יְרֵאָיו וְצִדְקָתוֹ לִבְנֵי בָנִים: לְשֹׁמְרֵי בְרִיתוֹ וּלְזֹכְרֵי פִקֻּדָיו לַעֲשׂוֹתָם: יְהֹוָה בַּשָּׁמַיִם הֵכִין כִּסְאוֹ וּמַלְכוּתוֹ בַּכֹּל מָשָׁלָה: בָּרְכוּ יְהֹוָה מַלְאָכָיו גִּבֹּרֵי כֹחַ עֹשֵׂי דְבָרוֹ לִשְׁמֹעַ בְּקוֹל דְּבָרוֹ: בָּרְכוּ יְהֹוָה כָּל־צְבָאָיו מְשָׁרְתָיו עֹשֵׂי רְצוֹנוֹ: בָּרְכוּ יְהֹוָה כָּל־מַעֲשָׂיו בְּכָל־מְקֹמוֹת מֶמְשַׁלְתּוֹ בָּרְכִי נַפְשִׁי אֶת־יְהֹוָה:

THE PROCESSIONAL

The participants march around the cemetery seven times, starting at the northeast corner. While doing so, they recite the following Psalms and prayers.

Psalm 90:16–17

And let the pleasantness of the Lord our God be upon us: and establish thou the work of our hands upon us; yea, the work of our hands establish thou it.

וִיהִי נְעַם אֲדֹנָי אֱלֹהֵינוּ עָלֵינוּ וּמַעֲשֵׂה יָדֵינוּ כּוֹנְנָה עָלֵינוּ וּמַעֲשֵׂה יָדֵינוּ כּוֹנְנֵהוּ׃

Psalm 104

Bless the Lord, O my soul: O Lord my God, thou art very great; Thou hast robed Thee in splendour and majesty, He covereth Himself with light as with a garment; He stretcheth out the heavens like a curtain: He layeth the beams of His upper chambers in the waters; He maketh the clouds His chariot; He walketh upon the wings of the wind. He maketh winds His messengers; His ministers flaming fire: He founded the earth upon its bases, that it might not be moved for ever. Thou didst cover it with the deep as with a vesture; the waters stood above the mountains. At Thy rebuke they fled; at the voice of Thy thunder they hasted away. The mountains rose, the valleys sank into the place which Thou hadst founded for them. Thou hast set a bound that they may not pass over; that they turn not again to cover the earth. He sendeth forth springs into the valleys; they run among the mountains. They give drink to every beast of the plain; the wild asses quench their thirst. By them the birds of the heaven have their dwelling, they utter their voice from among the branches. He giveth drink to the mountains from his upper chambers: the earth is satisfied with the fruit of Thy works. He causeth grass to grow for the cattle, and herbs for the service of man; that he may bring forth bread from the earth; and wine that maketh glad the heart of man, and oil to make his face to shine, and bread that strengtheneth man's heart. The trees of the Lord are satisfied; the cedars of Lebanon which He hath planted; where the birds make their nests: as for the stork, the fir trees are her house. The high mountains are for the wild goats; the rocks are a refuge for the conies. He made the moon for seasons; the sun knoweth its going down. Thou makest darkness, and it is night; wherein all the beasts of the forest do move. The young lions roar after their prey, and seek their food from God. The sun ariseth, they get them away, and lay them down in their dens. Man goeth forth unto his work and to his labour until the evening. How manifold are thy works, O Lord! In wisdom hast Thou made them all: the earth is full of Thy possessions. Yonder is the sea, great and of wide extent; therein are moving things innumerable, living creatures both small and great. There the ships make their course; there is leviathan whom Thou hast formed to sport therein. These all wait upon Thee, that Thou mayest give them their food in due season. Thou givest unto them, they gather; Thou openest Thine hand, they are satisfied with good. Thou hidest Thy face, they are confounded; Thou gatherest in their breath, they die, and return to their dust. Thou sendest forth Thy spirit, they are created; and Thou renewest the face of the ground. Let the glory of the Lord endure for ever; let the Lord rejoice in His works. He looketh on the earth, and it trembleth; He toucheth the mountains and they smoke. I will sing unto the Lord as long as I live: I will sing praise to my God while I have my being. May my meditation be sweet unto Him: as for me, I will rejoice in the Lord. Sinners shall be consumed out of the earth, and the wicked shall be no more. Bless the Lord, O my soul: praise ye the Lord.

בָּרְכִי נַפְשִׁי אֶת־יְהֹוָה. יְהֹוָה אֱלֹהַי גָּדַלְתָּ מְּאֹד הוֹד וְהָדָר לָבָשְׁתָּ: עֹטֶה־אוֹר כַּשַּׂלְמָה נוֹטֶה שָׁמַיִם כַּיְרִיעָה: הַמְקָרֶה בַמַּיִם עֲלִיּוֹתָיו הַשָּׂם־עָבִים רְכוּבוֹ הַמְהַלֵּךְ עַל־כַּנְפֵי־רוּחַ: עֹשֶׂה מַלְאָכָיו רוּחוֹת מְשָׁרְתָיו אֵשׁ לֹהֵט: יָסַד־אֶרֶץ עַל־מְכוֹנֶיהָ בַּל־תִּמּוֹט עוֹלָם וָעֶד: תְּהוֹם כַּלְּבוּשׁ כִּסִּיתוֹ עַל־הָרִים יַעַמְדוּ־מָיִם: מִן־גַּעֲרָתְךָ יְנוּסוּן מִן־קוֹל רַעַמְךָ יֵחָפֵזוּן: יַעֲלוּ הָרִים יֵרְדוּ בְקָעוֹת אֶל־מְקוֹם זֶה יָסַדְתָּ לָהֶם: גְּבוּל־שַׂמְתָּ בַּל־יַעֲבֹרוּן בַּל־יְשֻׁבוּן לְכַסּוֹת הָאָרֶץ: הַמְשַׁלֵּחַ מַעְיָנִים בַּנְּחָלִים בֵּין הָרִים יְהַלֵּכוּן: יַשְׁקוּ כָּל־חַיְתוֹ שָׂדָי יִשְׁבְּרוּ פְרָאִים צְמָאָם: עֲלֵיהֶם עוֹף־הַשָּׁמַיִם יִשְׁכּוֹן מִבֵּין עֳפָאיִם יִתְּנוּ־קוֹל: מַשְׁקֶה הָרִים מֵעֲלִיּוֹתָיו מִפְּרִי מַעֲשֶׂיךָ תִּשְׂבַּע הָאָרֶץ: מַצְמִיחַ חָצִיר לַבְּהֵמָה וְעֵשֶׂב לַעֲבֹדַת הָאָדָם לְהוֹצִיא לֶחֶם מִן־הָאָרֶץ: וְיַיִן יְשַׂמַּח לְבַב־אֱנוֹשׁ לְהַצְהִיל פָּנִים מִשָּׁמֶן וְלֶחֶם לְבַב־אֱנוֹשׁ יִסְעָד: יִשְׂבְּעוּ עֲצֵי יְהֹוָה אַרְזֵי לְבָנוֹן אֲשֶׁר נָטָע: אֲשֶׁר־שָׁם צִפֳּרִים יְקַנֵּנוּ חֲסִידָה בְּרוֹשִׁים

בֵּיתָהּ: הָרִים הַגְּבֹהִים לַיְּעֵלִים סְלָעִים מַחְסֶה לַשְׁפַנִּים: עָשָׂה יָרֵחַ לְמוֹעֲדִים שֶׁמֶשׁ יָדַע
מְבוֹאוֹ: תָּשֶׁת־חֹשֶׁךְ וִיהִי לָיְלָה בּוֹ־תִרְמֹשׂ כָּל־חַיְתוֹ־יָעַר: הַכְּפִירִים שֹׁאֲגִים לַטָּרֶף וּלְבַקֵּשׁ
מֵאֵל אָכְלָם: תִּזְרַח הַשֶּׁמֶשׁ יֵאָסֵפוּן וְאֶל־מְעוֹנֹתָם יִרְבָּצוּן: יֵצֵא אָדָם לְפָעֳלוֹ וְלַעֲבֹדָתוֹ
עֲדֵי־עָרֶב: מָה־רַבּוּ מַעֲשֶׂיךָ יְהֹוָה כֻּלָּם בְּחָכְמָה עָשִׂיתָ מָלְאָה הָאָרֶץ קִנְיָנֶךָ: זֶה הַיָּם גָּדוֹל
וּרְחַב יָדָיִם שָׁם־רֶמֶשׂ וְאֵין מִסְפָּר חַיּוֹת קְטַנּוֹת עִם־גְּדֹלוֹת: שָׁם אֳנִיּוֹת יְהַלֵּכוּן לִוְיָתָן זֶה־
יָצַרְתָּ לְשַׂחֶק־בּוֹ: כֻּלָּם אֵלֶיךָ יְשַׂבֵּרוּן לָתֵת אָכְלָם בְּעִתּוֹ: תִּתֵּן לָהֶם יִלְקֹטוּן תִּפְתַּח יָדְךָ
יִשְׂבְּעוּן טוֹב: תַּסְתִּיר פָּנֶיךָ יִבָּהֵלוּן תֹּסֵף רוּחָם יִגְוָעוּן וְאֶל־עֲפָרָם יְשׁוּבוּן: תְּשַׁלַּח רוּחֲךָ
יִבָּרֵאוּן וּתְחַדֵּשׁ פְּנֵי אֲדָמָה: יְהִי כְבוֹד יְהֹוָה לְעוֹלָם יִשְׂמַח יְהֹוָה בְּמַעֲשָׂיו: הַמַּבִּיט לָאָרֶץ
וַתִּרְעָד יִגַּע בֶּהָרִים וְיֶעֱשָׁנוּ: אָשִׁירָה לַיהֹוָה בְּחַיָּי אֲזַמְּרָה לֵאלֹהַי בְּעוֹדִי: יֶעֱרַב עָלָיו שִׂיחִי
אָנֹכִי אֶשְׂמַח בַּיהֹוָה: יִתַּמּוּ חַטָּאִים מִן־הָאָרֶץ וּרְשָׁעִים עוֹד אֵינָם בָּרְכִי נַפְשִׁי אֶת־יְהֹוָה
הַלְלוּיָהּ:

Isaiah 42:10-21

Sing unto the Lord a new song, and His praise from the end of
earth; ye that go down to the sea, and all that is therein, the isles,
and the inhabitants thereof.

Let the wilderness and the cities thereof lift up their voice, the
villages that Kedar doth inhabit; let the inhabitants of Sela exult,
let them shout from the top of the mountains.

Let them give glory unto the Lord, and declare His praise in the
islands.

The Lord will go forth as a mighty man, He will stir up jealousy
like a man of war; He will cry, yea, He will shout aloud, He will
prove Himself mighty against His enemies.

I have a long time held my peace, I have been still and refrained
Myself; now I will cry like a travailing woman, gasping and panting
at once.

I will make waste mountains and hills, and dry up all their herbs;
and I will make the rivers islands, and will dry up the pools.

And I will bring the blind by a way they knew not, in paths that
they knew not will I lead them; I will make darkness light before
them, and rugged places plain. These things will I do, and I will not
leave them undone.

They shall be turned back, greatly ashamed, that trust in graven
images, that say unto molten images: "Ye are our gods."

Hear, ye deaf, and look, ye blind, that ye may see.

Who is blind, but My servant? Or deaf, as My messenger that I send? Who is blind as he that is wholehearted, and blind as the Lord's servant?

Seeing many things, thou observest not; opening the ears, he heareth not.

The Lord was pleased, for His righteousness' sake, to make the teaching great and glorious.

שִׁירוּ לַיהוָה שִׁיר חָדָשׁ, תְּהִלָּתוֹ מִקְצֵה הָאָרֶץ, יוֹרְדֵי הַיָּם וּמְלֹאוֹ, אִיִּים וְיֹשְׁבֵיהֶם.

יִשְׂאוּ מִדְבָּר וְעָרָיו חֲצֵרִים תֵּשֵׁב קֵדָר, יָרֹנּוּ יֹשְׁבֵי סֶלַע מֵרֹאשׁ הָרִים יִצְוָחוּ.

יָשִׂימוּ לַיהוָה כָּבוֹד, וּתְהִלָּתוֹ בָּאִיִּים יַגִּידוּ.

יְיָ כַּגִּבּוֹר יֵצֵא, כְּאִישׁ מִלְחָמוֹת יָעִיר קִנְאָה, יָרִיעַ אַף יַצְרִיחַ, עַל אֹיְבָיו יִתְגַּבָּר.

הֶחֱשֵׁיתִי מֵעוֹלָם אַחֲרִישׁ אֶתְאַפָּק, כַּיּוֹלֵדָה, אֶשֹּׁם וְאֶשְׁאַף יָחַד.

אַחֲרִיב הָרִים וּגְבָעוֹת וְכָל עֶשְׂבָּם אוֹבִישׁ, וְשַׂמְתִּי נְהָרוֹת לָאִיִּים וַאֲגַמִּים אוֹבִישׁ.

וְהוֹלַכְתִּי עִוְרִים בְּדֶרֶךְ לֹא יָדָעוּ, בִּנְתִיבוֹת לֹא יָדְעוּ אַדְרִיכֵם, אָשִׂים מַחְשָׁךְ לִפְנֵיהֶם לָאוֹר וּמַעֲקַשִּׁים לְמִישׁוֹר, אֵלֶּה הַדְּבָרִים עֲשִׂיתִים וְלֹא עֲזַבְתִּים.

נָסֹגוּ אָחוֹר יֵבֹשׁוּ בֹשֶׁת הַבֹּטְחִים בַּפָּסֶל, הָאוֹמְרִים לְמַסֵּכָה אַתֶּם אֱלֹהֵינוּ.

הַחֵרְשִׁים שְׁמָעוּ, וְהַעִוְרִים הַבִּיטוּ לִרְאוֹת:

מִי עִוֵּר כִּי אִם עַבְדִּי וְחֵרֵשׁ כְּמַלְאָכִי אֶשְׁלָח, מִי עִוֵּר כִּמְשֻׁלָּם וְעִוֵּר כְּעֶבֶד יְיָ.

רָאוֹת רַבּוֹת וְלֹא תִשְׁמֹר, פָּקוֹחַ אָזְנַיִם וְלֹא יִשְׁמָע. יְיָ חָפֵץ לְמַעַן צִדְקוֹ, יַגְדִּיל תּוֹרָה וְיַאְדִּיר.

Recitation

We beseech Thee, release Thy captive nation by the mighty strength of Thy right hand. Accept the joyful chant of Thy people, lift us and purify us, O revered God. O Thou mighty One, guard as the apple of Thine eye them that meditate upon Thy unity. Bless them, purify them, have mercy upon them, ever bestow Thy charity unto them. O powerful and holy Being, in Thine abounding goodness lead Thy congregation. Turn, Thou who art the only and exalted God, unto Thy people, who are mindful of Thy holiness. Accept our prayer and hearken unto our cry, Thou who knowest all secrets. Blessed be His name, whose glorious kingdom is for ever and ever.

אָנָּא. בְּכֹחַ גְּדֻלַּת יְמִינְךָ תַּתִּיר צְרוּרָה. קַבֵּל רִנַּת עַמְּךָ שַׂגְּבֵנוּ טַהֲרֵנוּ נוֹרָא. נָא גִבּוֹר דּוֹרְשֵׁי יִחוּדְךָ כְּבָבַת שָׁמְרֵם. בָּרְכֵם טַהֲרֵם רַחֲמֵם צִדְקָתְךָ תָּמִיד גָּמְלֵם. חֲסִין קָדוֹשׁ בְּרֹב טוּבְךָ נַהֵל עֲדָתֶךָ. יָחִיד גֵּאֶה לְעַמְּךָ פְּנֵה זוֹכְרֵי קְדֻשָּׁתֶךָ. שַׁוְעָתֵנוּ קַבֵּל וּשְׁמַע צַעֲקָתֵנוּ יוֹדֵעַ תַּעֲלוּמוֹת. בָּרוּךְ שֵׁם כְּבוֹד מַלְכוּתוֹ לְעוֹלָם וָעֶד:

Sermon Or Address

Concluding Prayer

O Lord, may it be Thy will to remove from us and from all Thy people, the house of Israel, all kinds of disease, destruction, and disastrous plagues. Deliver us from unmerciful, evil decrees that visit and afflict this world. As for him that trusteth in God, let loving-kindness surround him. Amen.

He will destroy death for ever; the Lord God will wipe away tears from all faces, and He will remove from all the earth the rebuke of His people; for the Lord hath spoken it.

יְהִי רָצוֹן, שֶׁתָּסִיר מֵעָלֵינוּ וּמֵעַל כָּל עַמְּךָ בֵּית יִשְׂרָאֵל כָּל מִינֵי חֳלִי וּמַשְׁחִית וּמַגֵּפָה וּפֶגַע רָע, וְתַצִּילֵנוּ מִגְּזֵרוֹת קָשׁוֹת וְרָעוֹת הַמִּתְרַגְּשׁוֹת לָבֹא בָּעוֹלָם, וְהַבּוֹטֵחַ בַּייָ חֶסֶד יְסוֹבְבֶנּוּ, אָמֵן.

בִּלַּע הַמָּוֶת לָנֶצַח, וּמָחָה אֲדֹנָי אֱלֹהִים דִּמְעָה מֵעַל כָּל פָּנִים, וְחֶרְפַּת עַמּוֹ יָסִיר מֵעַל כָּל הָאָרֶץ, כִּי יְהֹוָה דִּבֵּר.

Grace After Meals
for the Bereaved

In the house of a mourner the following Introductory Form is used:

He who says Grace proceeds: "With the sanction of those present"

בִּרְשׁוּת רַבּוֹתַי

We will bless Him that comforteth the mourners, and of whose bounty we have partaken.

נְבָרֵךְ מְנַחֵם אֲבֵלִים שֶׁאָכַלְנוּ מִשֶּׁלּוֹ:

The others respond:

Blessed be He that comforteth the mourners, of whose bounty we have partaken, and through whose goodness we live.

בָּרוּךְ מְנַחֵם אֲבֵלִים שֶׁאָכַלְנוּ מִשֶּׁלּוֹ וּבְטוּבוֹ חָיִינוּ:

He who says Grace repeats the last sentence. Persons present who have not partaken of the meal, say the following:

Blessed be His name, yea, continually to be blessed for ever and ever.

בָּרוּךְ וּמְבוֹרָךְ שְׁמוֹ תָּמִיד לְעוֹלָם וָעֶד:

269

If less than three males above the age of thirteen be present, begin here:

Blessed art Thou, O Lord our God, King of the universe, who feedest the whole world with Thy goodness, with grace, with loving-kindness and tender mercy; Thou givest food to all creatures, for thy loving-kindness endureth for ever. Through Thy great goodness food hath never failed us: O may it not fail us for ever and ever for Thy great name's sake, since Thou nourishest and sustainest all beings, and doest good unto all, and providest food for all Thy creatures whom Thou hast created. Blessed art Thou, O Lord, who givest food unto all.

We thank Thee, O Lord our God, because Thou didst give as an heritage unto our fathers a desirable, good and ample land, and because Thou didst bring us forth, O Lord our God, from the land of Egypt, and didst deliver us from the house of bondage; as well as for Thy covenant which Thou hast sealed in our flesh, Thy Law which Thou hast taught us, Thy statutes which Thou hast made known unto us, the life, grace and loving-kindness which Thou hast bestowed upon us, and for the food wherewith Thou dost constantly feed and sustain us on every day, in every season, at every hour.

On Chanukah and Purim add, "We thank Thee also for the miracles," etc., p. 271

For all this, O Lord our God, we thank and bless Thee, blessed be Thy name by the mouth of all living continually and for ever, even as it is written, And thou shalt eat and be satisfied, and thou shalt bless the Lord thy God for the good land which He hath given thee. Blessed art Thou, O Lord, for the land and for the food.

Have mercy, O Lord our God, upon Israel Thy people, upon Jerusalem Thy city, upon Zion the abiding place of Thy glory, upon the kingdom of the house of David Thine anointed, and upon the great and holy house that was called by Thy name. O our God, our

בָּרוּךְ אַתָּה יְהֹוָה אֱלֹהֵינוּ מֶלֶךְ הָעוֹלָם. הַזָּן אֶת הָעוֹלָם כֻּלּוֹ. בְּטוּבוֹ בְּחֵן בְּחֶסֶד וּבְרַחֲמִים. הוּא נוֹתֵן לֶחֶם לְכָל בָּשָׂר. כִּי לְעוֹלָם חַסְדּוֹ: וּבְטוּבוֹ הַגָּדוֹל תָּמִיד לֹא חָסַר לָנוּ וְאַל יֶחְסַר לָנוּ מָזוֹן לְעוֹלָם וָעֶד בַּעֲבוּר שְׁמוֹ הַגָּדוֹל. כִּי הוּא אֵל זָן וּמְפַרְנֵס לַכֹּל וּמֵטִיב לַכֹּל וּמֵכִין מָזוֹן לְכָל בְּרִיּוֹתָיו אֲשֶׁר בָּרָא. בָּרוּךְ אַתָּה יְהֹוָה. הַזָּן אֶת הַכֹּל:

נוֹדֶה לְךָ יְהֹוָה אֱלֹהֵינוּ עַל שֶׁהִנְחַלְתָּ לַאֲבוֹתֵינוּ אֶרֶץ חֶמְדָּה טוֹבָה וּרְחָבָה. וְעַל שֶׁהוֹצֵאתָנוּ יְהֹוָה אֱלֹהֵינוּ מֵאֶרֶץ מִצְרַיִם. וּפְדִיתָנוּ מִבֵּית עֲבָדִים. וְעַל בְּרִיתְךָ שֶׁחָתַמְתָּ בִּבְשָׂרֵנוּ. וְעַל תּוֹרָתְךָ שֶׁלִּמַּדְתָּנוּ. וְעַל חֻקֶּיךָ שֶׁהוֹדַעְתָּנוּ. וְעַל חַיִּים חֵן וָחֶסֶד שֶׁחוֹנַנְתָּנוּ. וְעַל אֲכִילַת מָזוֹן שָׁאַתָּה זָן וּמְפַרְנֵס אוֹתָנוּ תָּמִיד בְּכָל יוֹם וּבְכָל עֵת וּבְכָל שָׁעָה:

On Chanukah and Purim add, "We thank Thee also for the miracles," etc.

וְעַל הַנִּסִּים וְעַל הַפֻּרְקָן וְעַל הַגְּבוּרוֹת וְעַל הַתְּשׁוּעוֹת וְעַל הַמִּלְחָמוֹת שֶׁעָשִׂיתָ לַאֲבוֹתֵינוּ בַּיָּמִים הָהֵם בַּזְּמַן הַזֶּה:

לחנוכה

בִּימֵי מַתִּתְיָהוּ בֶּן יוֹחָנָן כֹּהֵן גָּדוֹל חַשְׁמוֹנָאִי וּבָנָיו כְּשֶׁעָמְדָה מַלְכוּת יָוָן הָרְשָׁעָה עַל עַמְּךָ יִשְׂרָאֵל לְהַשְׁכִּיחָם תּוֹרָתֶךָ וּלְהַעֲבִירָם מֵחֻקֵּי רְצוֹנֶךָ, וְאַתָּה בְּרַחֲמֶיךָ הָרַבִּים עָמַדְתָּ לָהֶם בְּעֵת צָרָתָם רַבְתָּ אֶת רִיבָם דַּנְתָּ אֶת דִּינָם נָקַמְתָּ אֶת נִקְמָתָם מָסַרְתָּ גִבּוֹרִים בְּיַד חַלָּשִׁים וְרַבִּים בְּיַד מְעַטִּים וּטְמֵאִים בְּיַד טְהוֹרִים וּרְשָׁעִים בְּיַד צַדִּיקִים וְזֵדִים בְּיַד עוֹסְקֵי תוֹרָתֶךָ וּלְךָ עָשִׂיתָ שֵׁם גָּדוֹל וְקָדוֹשׁ בְּעוֹלָמֶךָ וּלְעַמְּךָ יִשְׂרָאֵל עָשִׂיתָ תְּשׁוּעָה גְדוֹלָה וּפֻרְקָן כְּהַיּוֹם הַזֶּה וְאַחַר כַּךְ בָּאוּ בָנֶיךָ לִדְבִיר בֵּיתֶךָ וּפִנּוּ אֶת הֵיכָלֶךָ וְטִהֲרוּ אֶת מִקְדָּשֶׁךָ וְהִדְלִיקוּ נֵרוֹת בְּחַצְרוֹת קָדְשֶׁךָ וְקָבְעוּ שְׁמוֹנַת יְמֵי חֲנֻכָּה אֵלּוּ לְהוֹדוֹת וּלְהַלֵּל לְשִׁמְךָ הַגָּדוֹל:

לפורים

בִּימֵי מָרְדְּכַי וְאֶסְתֵּר בְּשׁוּשַׁן הַבִּירָה כְּשֶׁעָמַד עֲלֵיהֶם הָמָן הָרְשָׁע בִּקֵּשׁ לְהַשְׁמִיד לַהֲרוֹג וּלְאַבֵּד אֶת כָּל הַיְּהוּדִים מִנַּעַר וְעַד זָקֵן טַף וְנָשִׁים בְּיוֹם אֶחָד בִּשְׁלוֹשָׁה עָשָׂר לְחֹדֶשׁ שְׁנֵים עָשָׂר הוּא חֹדֶשׁ אֲדָר וּשְׁלָלָם לָבוֹז: וְאַתָּה בְּרַחֲמֶיךָ הָרַבִּים הֵפַרְתָּ אֶת עֲצָתוֹ וְקִלְקַלְתָּ אֶת מַחֲשַׁבְתּוֹ וַהֲשֵׁבוֹתָ לּוֹ גְּמוּלוֹ בְּרֹאשׁוֹ וְתָלוּ אוֹתוֹ וְאֶת בָּנָיו עַל הָעֵץ:

וְעַל הַכֹּל יְהֹוָה אֱלֹהֵינוּ אֲנַחְנוּ מוֹדִים לָךְ וּמְבָרְכִים אוֹתָךְ. יִתְבָּרַךְ שִׁמְךָ בְּפִי כָּל חַי תָּמִיד לְעוֹלָם וָעֶד: כַּכָּתוּב. וְאָכַלְתָּ וְשָׂבָעְתָּ וּבֵרַכְתָּ אֶת יְהֹוָה אֱלֹהֶיךָ עַל הָאָרֶץ הַטּוֹבָה אֲשֶׁר נָתַן לָךְ. בָּרוּךְ אַתָּה יְהֹוָה. עַל הָאָרֶץ וְעַל הַמָּזוֹן:

רַחֵם יְהֹוָה אֱלֹהֵינוּ עַל יִשְׂרָאֵל עַמֶּךָ. וְעַל יְרוּשָׁלַיִם עִירֶךָ. וְעַל צִיּוֹן מִשְׁכַּן כְּבוֹדֶךָ. וְעַל מַלְכוּת בֵּית דָּוִד מְשִׁיחֶךָ. וְעַל הַבַּיִת הַגָּדוֹל וְהַקָּדוֹשׁ שֶׁנִּקְרָא שִׁמְךָ עָלָיו: אֱלֹהֵינוּ

Father, feed us, nourish us, sustain, support and relieve us, and speedily, O Lord our God, grant us relief from all our troubles. We beseech Thee, O Lord our God, let us not be in need either of the gifts of men or of their loans, but only of Thy helping hand, which is full, open, holy and ample, so that we may not be ashamed nor confounded for ever and ever.

On Sabbath say:

Be pleased, O Lord our God, to fortify us by Thy commandments, and especially by the commandment of the seventh day, this great and holy Sabbath, since this day is great and holy before Thee, that we may rest and repose thereon in love in accordance with the precept of Thy will. In Thy favor, O Lord our God, grant us such repose that there be no trouble, grief or lamenting on the day of our rest. Let us, O Lord our God, behold the consolation of Zion Thy city, and the rebuilding of Jerusalem Thy holy city, for Thou art the Lord of salvation and of consolation.

On New Moons and Festivals add:

Our God and God of our fathers! May our remembrance rise and come and be accepted before Thee, with the remembrance of our fathers, of Messiah the son of David Thy servant, of Jerusalem Thy holy city, and of all Thy people the house of Israel, bringing deliverance and well-being, grace, loving-kindness and mercy, life and peace on this day of—
   On the New Moon say: The New Moon.
   On New Year: Memorial.
   On Tabernacles: The Feast of Tabernacles.
   On the Eighth Day of Solemn Assembly and on the Rejoicing of the Law: The Eighth-day Feast of Solemn Assembly.
   On Passover: The Feast of Unleavened Bread.
   On Pentecost: The Feast of Weeks.

Remember us, O Lord our God, thereon for our well-being; be mindful of us for blessing, and save us unto life: by Thy promise of salvation and mercy, spare us and be gracious unto us; have mercy upon us and save us; for our eyes are bent upon Thee, because Thou art a gracious and merciful God and King.

אָבִינוּ רְעֵנוּ זוּנֵנוּ פַּרְנְסֵנוּ וְכַלְכְּלֵנוּ וְהַרְוִיחֵנוּ. וְהַרְוַח לָנוּ יְהֹוָה אֱלֹהֵינוּ מְהֵרָה מִכָּל צָרוֹתֵינוּ: וְנָא אַל תַּצְרִיכֵנוּ יְהֹוָה אֱלֹהֵינוּ לֹא לִידֵי מַתְּנַת בָּשָׂר וָדָם וְלֹא לִידֵי הַלְוָאָתָם. כִּי אִם לְיָדְךָ הַמְּלֵאָה הַפְּתוּחָה הַקְּדוֹשָׁה וְהָרְחָבָה. שֶׁלֹּא נֵבוֹשׁ וְלֹא נִכָּלֵם לְעוֹלָם וָעֶד:

רְצֵה וְהַחֲלִיצֵנוּ יְהֹוָה אֱלֹהֵינוּ בְּמִצְוֹתֶיךָ וּבְמִצְוַת יוֹם הַשְּׁבִיעִי הַשַּׁבָּת הַגָּדוֹל וְהַקָּדוֹשׁ הַזֶּה. כִּי יוֹם זֶה גָּדוֹל וְקָדוֹשׁ הוּא לְפָנֶיךָ לִשְׁבָּת בּוֹ וְלָנוּחַ בּוֹ בְּאַהֲבָה כְּמִצְוַת רְצוֹנֶךָ. וּבִרְצוֹנְךָ הָנִיחַ לָנוּ יְהֹוָה אֱלֹהֵינוּ שֶׁלֹּא תְהֵא צָרָה וְיָגוֹן וַאֲנָחָה בְּיוֹם מְנוּחָתֵנוּ. וְהַרְאֵנוּ יְהֹוָה אֱלֹהֵינוּ בְּנֶחָמַת צִיּוֹן עִירֶךָ. וּבְבִנְיַן יְרוּשָׁלַיִם עִיר קָדְשֶׁךָ. כִּי אַתָּה הוּא בַּעַל הַיְשׁוּעוֹת וּבַעַל הַנֶּחָמוֹת:

אֱלֹהֵינוּ וֵאלֹהֵי אֲבוֹתֵינוּ יַעֲלֶה וְיָבֹא וְיַגִּיעַ וְיֵרָאֶה וְיֵרָצֶה וְיִשָּׁמַע וְיִפָּקֵד וְיִזָּכֵר זִכְרוֹנֵנוּ וּפִקְדוֹנֵנוּ. וְזִכְרוֹן אֲבוֹתֵינוּ וְזִכְרוֹן מָשִׁיחַ בֶּן דָּוִד עַבְדֶּךָ. וְזִכְרוֹן יְרוּשָׁלַיִם עִיר קָדְשֶׁךָ. וְזִכְרוֹן כָּל עַמְּךָ בֵּית יִשְׂרָאֵל לְפָנֶיךָ. לִפְלֵיטָה וּלְטוֹבָה לְחֵן וּלְחֶסֶד וּלְרַחֲמִים וּלְחַיִּים וּלְשָׁלוֹם בְּיוֹם

לראש חדש — רֹאשׁ הַחֹדֶשׁ

לראש השנה — הַזִּכָּרוֹן

לסכות — חַג הַסֻּכּוֹת

לשמיני עצרת ושמחת תורה — שְׁמִינִי חַג הָעֲצֶרֶת

לפסח חַג הַמַּצוֹת

לשבועות חַג הַשָּׁבֻעוֹת

הַזֶּה זָכְרֵנוּ יְהֹוָה אֱלֹהֵינוּ בּוֹ לְטוֹבָה. וּפָקְדֵנוּ בּוֹ לִבְרָכָה. וְהוֹשִׁיעֵנוּ בּוֹ לְחַיִּים. וּבִדְבַר יְשׁוּעָה וְרַחֲמִים חוּס וְחָנֵּנוּ. וְרַחֵם עָלֵינוּ וְהוֹשִׁיעֵנוּ. כִּי אֵלֶיךָ עֵינֵינוּ. כִּי אֵל מֶלֶךְ חַנּוּן וְרַחוּם אָתָּה:

Comfort, O Lord our God, the mourners of Jerusalem and those who share in this present mourning. Do Thou give them comfort in place of their mourning, and gladness instead of their grief, as it is said, As one whom his mother comforteth, so will I comfort you, and in Jerusalem shall ye be comforted. Blessed art Thou, O Lord, who comfortest Zion by the rebuilding of Jerusalem.

> Blessed art Thou, O Lord our God, King of the universe, O God, our Father, our King, our Creator, our Redeemer, our Holy One, the Holy One of Jacob, the living King, who art kind and dealest kindly with all, true God and Judge, who judgest with righteousness, and in judgment takest the souls of men unto Thyself, who rulest in Thy world, doing therein according to Thy will, for all Thy ways are judgment. We are Thy people and Thy servants, and for all things it is our duty to give thanks unto Thee and to bless Thee. O Thou who repairest the breaches in Israel, mayest Thou also repair this breach in us, granting us life and peace. Mayest Thou ever bestow upon us grace, loving-kindness, mercy and all good: of no manner of good let us be in want.

The All-merciful shall reign over us for ever and ever. The All-merciful shall be blessed in heaven and on earth. The All-merciful shall be praised throughout all generations, glorified amongst us to all eternity, and honored amongst us for everlasting. May the All-merciful grant us an honorable livelihood. May the All-merciful break the yoke from off our neck, and lead us upright to our land. May the All-merciful send a plentiful blessing upon this house, and upon this table at which we have eaten. May the All-merciful send us Elijah the prophet (let him be remembered for good), who shall give us good tidings, salvation, and consolation. May the All-merciful bless

A child at his parent's table says:°

my honored father, the master of this house, and my honored mother, the mistress of this house, them, their household, their children, and all that is theirs;

° The following has to be varied according to circumstances.

נַחֵם יְיָ אֱלֹהֵינוּ אֶת אֲבֵלֵי יְרוּשָׁלַיִם וְאֶת הָאֲבֵלִים הַמִּתְאַבְּלִים בָּאֵבֶל הַזֶּה. נַחֲמֵם
מֵאֶבְלָם וְשַׂמְּחֵם מִיגוֹנָם. כָּאָמוּר. כְּאִישׁ אֲשֶׁר אִמּוֹ תְּנַחֲמֶנּוּ כֵּן אָנֹכִי אֲנַחֶמְכֶם
וּבִירוּשָׁלַיִם תְּנֻחָמוּ. בָּרוּךְ אַתָּה יְיָ: מְנַחֵם צִיּוֹן בְּבִנְיַן יְרוּשָׁלָיִם:

בָּרוּךְ אַתָּה יְיָ אֱלֹהֵינוּ מֶלֶךְ הָעוֹלָם. הָאֵל אָבִינוּ מַלְכֵּנוּ בּוֹרְאֵנוּ גּוֹאֲלֵנוּ קְדוֹשֵׁנוּ
קְדוֹשׁ יַעֲקֹב. הַמֶּלֶךְ הַחַי הַטּוֹב וְהַמֵּטִיב. אֵל אֱמֶת. דַּיַּן אֱמֶת. שׁוֹפֵט צֶדֶק וְלֹקֵחַ נְפָשׁוֹת
בְּמִשְׁפָּט. וְשַׁלִּיט בְּעוֹלָמוֹ לַעֲשׂוֹת בּוֹ כִּרְצוֹנוֹ. כִּי כָל דְּרָכָיו מִשְׁפָּט. וַאֲנַחְנוּ עַמּוֹ וַעֲבָדָיו.
וְעַל הַכֹּל אֲנַחְנוּ חַיָּבִים לְהוֹדוֹת לוֹ וּלְבָרְכוֹ. גּוֹדֵר פְּרָצוֹת בְּיִשְׂרָאֵל הוּא יִגְדֹּר אֶת
הַפִּרְצָה הַזֹּאת מֵעָלֵינוּ לְחַיִּים וּלְשָׁלוֹם. הוּא יִגְמְלֵנוּ לָעַד חֵן חֶסֶד וְרַחֲמִים וְכָל טוֹב.
וּמִכָּל טוֹב אַל יְחַסְּרֵנוּ:

הָרַחֲמָן, הוּא יִמְלוֹךְ עָלֵינוּ לְעוֹלָם וָעֶד. הָרַחֲמָן, הוּא יִתְבָּרַךְ בַּשָּׁמַיִם וּבָאָרֶץ.
הָרַחֲמָן, הוּא יִשְׁתַּבַּח לְדוֹר דּוֹרִים, וְיִתְפָּאַר בָּנוּ לָעַד וּלְנֵצַח נְצָחִים, וְיִתְהַדַּר בָּנוּ לָעַד
וּלְעוֹלְמֵי עוֹלָמִים.

הָרַחֲמָן, הוּא יְפַרְנְסֵנוּ בְּכָבוֹד. הָרַחֲמָן הוּא יִשְׁבֹּר עֻלֵּנוּ מֵעַל צַוָּארֵנוּ וְהוּא יוֹלִיכֵנוּ
קוֹמְמִיּוּת לְאַרְצֵנוּ. הָרַחֲמָן, הוּא יִשְׁלַח לָנוּ בְּרָכָה מְרֻבָּה בַּבַּיִת הַזֶּה וְעַל שֻׁלְחָן זֶה
שֶׁאָכַלְנוּ עָלָיו. הָרַחֲמָן, הוּא יִשְׁלַח לָנוּ אֶת אֵלִיָּהוּ הַנָּבִיא זָכוּר לַטּוֹב, וִיבַשֶּׂר לָנוּ בְּשׂוֹרוֹת
טוֹבוֹת יְשׁוּעוֹת וְנֶחָמוֹת.

הָרַחֲמָן, הוּא יְבָרֵךְ אֶת אָבִי מוֹרִי בַּעַל הַבַּיִת הַזֶּה, וְאֶת אִמִּי מוֹרָתִי בַּעֲלַת הַבַּיִת
הַזֶּה, אוֹתָם וְאֶת בֵּיתָם וְאֶת זַרְעָם וְאֶת כָּל אֲשֶׁר לָהֶם

A master of the house says:°

me, (and my wife and my children) and all that is mine;

At a stranger's table say:°

the master of this house (and his wife and his children) and all that is his;

us also and all that is ours, as our fathers Abraham, Isaac, and Jacob were each blessed with his own comprehensive blessing; even thus may He bless all of us together with a perfect blessing, and let us say, Amen.

Both on their and on our behalf may there be such advocacy on high as shall lead to enduring peace; and may we receive a blessing from the Lord, and righteousness from the God of our salvation; and may we find grace and good understanding in the sight of God and man.

On Sabbath:

May the All-merciful let us inherit the day which shall be wholly a Sabbath and rest in the life everlasting.

On New Moon:

May the All-merciful renew unto us this month for good and for blessing.

On Festivals:

May the All-merciful let us inherit the day which is altogether good.

On New Year:

May the All-merciful renew unto us this year for good and for blessing.

°The following has to be varied according to circumstances.

הָרַחֲמָן, הוּא יְבָרֵךְ אוֹתִי וְאֶת אִשְׁתִּי וְאֶת זַרְעִי וְאֶת כָּל אֲשֶׁר לִי.

הָרַחֲמָן, הוּא יְבָרֵךְ אֶת בַּעַל הַבַּיִת הַזֶּה אוֹתוֹ(וְאֶת אִשְׁתּוֹ וְאֶת זַרְעוֹ) וְאֶת כָּל אֲשֶׁר לוֹ.

אוֹתָנוּ וְאֶת כָּל אֲשֶׁר לָנוּ, כְּמוֹ שֶׁנִּתְבָּרְכוּ אֲבוֹתֵינוּ, אַבְרָהָם יִצְחָק וְיַעֲקֹב: בַּכֹּל, מִכֹּל, כֹּל. כֵּן יְבָרֵךְ אוֹתָנוּ כֻּלָּנוּ יַחַד, בִּבְרָכָה שְׁלֵמָה, וְנֹאמַר אָמֵן:

בַּמָּרוֹם יְלַמְּדוּ עֲלֵיהֶם וְעָלֵינוּ זְכוּת, שֶׁתְּהֵא לְמִשְׁמֶרֶת שָׁלוֹם, וְנִשָּׂא בְרָכָה מֵאֵת יְהֹוָה וּצְדָקָה מֵאֱלֹהֵי יִשְׁעֵנוּ, וְנִמְצָא חֵן וְשֵׂכֶל טוֹב בְּעֵינֵי אֱלֹהִים וְאָדָם:

הָרַחֲמָן, הוּא יַנְחִילֵנוּ יוֹם שֶׁכֻּלּוֹ שַׁבָּת וּמְנוּחָה לְחַיֵּי הָעוֹלָמִים:

הָרַחֲמָן, הוּא יְחַדֵּשׁ עָלֵינוּ אֶת הַחֹדֶשׁ הַזֶּה לְטוֹבָה וְלִבְרָכָה:

הָרַחֲמָן, הוּא יַנְחִילֵנוּ יוֹם שֶׁכֻּלּוֹ טוֹב:

הָרַחֲמָן, הוּא יְחַדֵּשׁ עָלֵינוּ אֶת הַשָּׁנָה הַזֹּאת לְטוֹבָה וְלִבְרָכָה:

On the Intermediate Days of Tabernacles:

May the All-merciful raise up for us the fallen Tabernacle of David.

May the All-merciful make us worthy of the days of the Messiah, and of the life of the world-to-come.

On Weekdays:

Great salvation giveth he to his king.°

On Sabbaths, Festivals, and New Moons:

He is a tower of salvation to his king;° and showeth loving-kindness to His anointed, to David and to his seed, for evermore. He who maketh peace in His high places, may He make peace for us and for all Israel, and say ye, Amen.

O fear the Lord, ye His holy ones; for there is no want to them that fear Him. Young lions do lack and suffer hunger: but they that seek the Lord shall not want any good. O give thanks unto the Lord, for He is good: for His loving-kindness endureth for ever. Thou openest Thine hand, and satisfiest every living thing with favor. Blessed is the man that trusteth in the Lord, and whose trust the Lord is. I have been young and now I am old; yet have I not seen the righteous forsaken, nor his seed begging for bread. The Lord will give strength unto His people; the Lord will bless His people with peace.

° These changes are based upon the two readings of this verse in Psalm 18:51, and II Sam. 22:51 respectively.

הָרַחֲמָן הוּא יָקִים לָנוּ אֶת סֻכַּת דָּוִד הַנּוֹפֶלֶת:

הָרַחֲמָן, הוּא יְזַכֵּנוּ לִימוֹת הַמָּשִׁיחַ וּלְחַיֵּי הָעוֹלָם הַבָּא.

מַגְדִּיל

מִגְדּוֹל
יְשׁוּעוֹת מַלְכּוֹ, וְעֹשֶׂה חֶסֶד לִמְשִׁיחוֹ לְדָוִד וּלְזַרְעוֹ עַד עוֹלָם: עֹשֶׂה שָׁלוֹם בִּמְרוֹמָיו, הוּא
יַעֲשֶׂה שָׁלוֹם עָלֵינוּ וְעַל כָּל יִשְׂרָאֵל, וְאִמְרוּ אָמֵן:

יְראוּ אֶת יְהֹוָה קְדוֹשָׁיו, כִּי אֵין מַחְסוֹר לִירֵאָיו: כְּפִירִים רָשׁוּ וְרָעֵבוּ, וְדוֹרְשֵׁי יְהֹוָה
לֹא יַחְסְרוּ כָל טוֹב: הוֹדוּ לַיהֹוָה כִּי טוֹב, כִּי לְעוֹלָם חַסְדּוֹ: פּוֹתֵחַ אֶת יָדֶךָ, וּמַשְׂבִּיעַ לְכָל
חַי רָצוֹן: בָּרוּךְ הַגֶּבֶר אֲשֶׁר יִבְטַח בַּיהֹוָה, וְהָיָה יְהֹוָה מִבְטַחוֹ: נַעַר הָיִיתִי גַם זָקַנְתִּי וְלֹא
רָאִיתִי צַדִּיק נֶעֱזָב, וְזַרְעוֹ מְבַקֶּשׁ לָחֶם: יְהֹוָה עֹז לְעַמּוֹ יִתֵּן, יְהֹוָה יְבָרֵךְ אֶת עַמּוֹ בַשָּׁלוֹם:

Mishnah Study in
a House of Mourning

APPLICATION: GENERAL; at the start of the *shiv'ah*

MISHNAH: *Sanhedrin* 11:3

חֹמֶר בְּדִבְרֵי סוֹפְרִים מִדִּבְרֵי תוֹרָה, הָאוֹמֵר אֵין תְּפִלִּין, כְּדֵי לַעֲבֹר עַל דִּבְרֵי תוֹרָה,
פָּטוּר. חָמֵשׁ טוֹטָפוֹת, לְהוֹסִיף עַל דִּבְרֵי סוֹפְרִים, חַיָּב:

TRANSLATION

The words of the scribes carry a greater stringency than what is
[explicitly stated in the written] words of the Torah. [Thus] he who
says there is no religious imperative to wear phylacteries [*tefillin*],
with the aim of encouraging transgression of the Torah, is not liable
[to capital punishment]. He who declares that *tefillin* should con-
tain] five [rather than four] paragraphs from Scripture, with the
purpose of adding to the words of the scribes, *is* liable.

COMMENTARY

The two sources of the divine revelation are the Written Torah and
the Oral Tradition, which was revealed simultaneously. Without
the Oral Tradition the Written Torah is often quite incomprehensible. The Oral Tradition consists not only of what was revealed to
Moses with the Written Torah, but is also the result of the painstak-
ing study and research of the sages of later generations. Our sages—
referred to as scribes during a certain period of Jewish history—
uncovered layers of meaning in the Written Torah not readily
apparent to the untutored. Their study of the text yielded imperatives which might otherwise have remained hidden.

280

Our *mishnah* distinguishes between an assault on the Written Torah and an assault on the Oral Torah. A denial of the imperative to wear *tefillin* is an assault on the Written Torah. This assault is really harmless. Because the imperative is clearly spelled out in the written text, the credibility of a person who claims that the Torah does not oblige us to wear *tefillin* would be lost, and he would not be taken seriously. An assault on the Oral Tradition is more grave. The untutored cannot easily disprove the contention that there should be five, rather than four, scriptural passages in the *tefillin*, But because the Oral Torah is more vulnerable to assault than the Written Torah, an attack against the Oral Tradition is a far more serious offense than an attack on the Written Tradition.

APPLICATION

It is our custom to study a selection from the Oral Tradition after each worship service in a *shiv'ah* house. Our selection is usually made from the Mishnah, the basis of the Talmud. The contents of the Mishnah were originally transmitted orally. However, when the lives of its teachers were threatened, and the danger emerged that it would be forgotten with the demise of its teachers, the Mishnah was preserved in written form and edited by Rabbi Judah the Prince in the year 200 C.E.

The reason we study the Mishnah rather than other areas of the Oral Tradition in a house of mourning is that the word *mishnah* is an anagram for the word *neshamah* ("soul"). We study the Mishnah in the faith that by so doing we benefit the soul of the departed. We associate him/her with the endless tradition of our people. We assure him/her that his/her spiritual heritage is also our collective spiritual heritage. We justify his/her existence by showing that he/she lived meaningfully, loyal to the tradition of his/her forebears, and true to their charge of passing their tradition on to the next generation.

The passage from the Mishnah which we have just studied indicates how very vulnerable our tradition is. It can easily be assaulted and rapidly be forgotten. The tragic vulnerability of our tradition places a special burden of responsibility upon the bereaved family. Its members must do whatever they can to preserve it, by dedicating themselves to maintaining it, initially, at least, as they mourn their great loss. In this way, they convey real immortality upon beloved departed. They show that he/she was a real link in the chain of Jewish tradition. They refuse to allow him/her to become an unlamented "missing link."

Shiv'ah as an Affirmation of Life

APPLICATION: GENERAL

MISHNAH: *Berakhot* 3:1

מִי שֶׁמֵּתוֹ מוּטָל לְפָנָיו, פָּטוּר מִקְּרִיאַת שְׁמַע (וּמִן הַתְּפִלָּה) וּמִן הַתְּפִלִּין. נוֹשְׂאֵי הַמִּטָּה
וְחִלּוּפֵיהֶן וְחִלּוּפֵי חִלּוּפֵיהֶן, אֶת שֶׁלִּפְנֵי הַמִּטָּה וְאֶת שֶׁלְּאַחַר הַמִּטָּה, אֶת שֶׁלַּמִּטָּה צֹרֶךְ
בָּהֶן, פְּטוּרִים, וְאֶת שֶׁאֵין לַמִּטָּה צֹרֶךְ בָּהֶן, חַיָּבִין. אֵלּוּ וָאֵלּוּ פְּטוּרִין מִן הַתְּפִלָּה:

TRANSLATION

One whose dead lies unburied before him is exempt from the
obligation of reciting the *Shema*, from saying the [*Shemoneh Esrei*]
prayer, and from wearing *tefillin* (phylacteries). The successive
relays of pallbearers, as well as participants in the funeral procession, who precede and follow the bier, and who will become
involved in handling the bier, are exempt. Those who will not
become involved in handling the bier are obligated. Both [partici-
pants in the funeral procession who are pallbearers or otherwise
involved with handling the bier] and [participants in the funeral
procession who are not directly involved with handling the bier] are
alike exempted from the obligation of reciting the [*Shemoneh
Esrei*] prayer.

COMMENTARY

The general principle upon which this *mishnah* is based is that "a
person who is preoccupied with the performance of a *mitzvah*
(religious obligation) is exempted from the simultaneous performance of another *mitzvah*." The following *mitzvot* are mentioned
in our *mishnah*:

283

The Burial of the Dead.

Three classes of people are involved in the performance of this *mitzvah*. The first is made up of the seven closest kin of the deceased, (see above, p. 44), who are primarily preoccupied with the burial. The second consists of those participants in the funeral procession who will actually handle the bier. The third consists of participants in the funeral procession who will not come into direct contact with the bier, but whose participation in the funeral is an expression of their respect for the deceased.

The Recitation of the Shema

This *mitzvah* is the biblical requirement to recite Deuteronomy 6:5–9, Deuteronomy 11:13–21, and Numbers 15:37–49 in the morning and in the evening. These three paragraphs constitute the "recitation of the *Shema*." They include our affirmation of faith in the unity of God, and of our obligation to love Him, to study His Torah, to teach it to our children and children's children, and to perform His *mitzvot*. Three *mitzvot* which are specifically mentioned in the *Shema* are the wearing of *tefillin* by Jewish males, the fixing of *mezuzot* to the doorposts of one's house and place of business, and the attachment of *tzitziyot* (fringes) to the four-cornered garments which Jewish males wear. The recitation of the *Shema* also affirms our belief in individual providence and in reward and punishment.

The *Shemoneh Esrei* Prayer

This is *the* prayer par excellence of the Jewish people. Its weekday version consists of nineteen blessings. *Shemoneh Esrei* means "eighteen." That was the original number of blessings included in the prayer. It is the centerpiece of all Jewish public worship services. Its recitation is rabbinically ordained and requires a great deal of concentration.

The Wearing of *Tefillin*

This is one of the imperatives which is mentioned in the *Shema*. The imperative to bind the commandments of God "as a sign upon thy hands and as frontlets between thine eyes" appears four times in the Torah—in the first two paragraphs of the *Shema* and in Exodus 13. The passages containing the imperative are written by a qualified scribe upon parchment and placed in a specially constructed black leather box to be worn on one's forehead and on one's left upper arm. The four passages are written on a single scroll in the *tefillin* box to be bound to one's arm, and on four separate scrolls in the box to be worn upon one's forehead. Straps, knotted in a special way, are used to bind the boxes to one's arm and around one's head.

Our *mishnah* states that the seven closest kin of the deceased are exempted from the *mitzvot* of the recitation of the *shema*, the saying of the *Shemoneh Esrei* prayer, and the wearing of *tefillin* during their period of *aninut* (as explained above, p. 44). During this period, the seven closest kin are assumed to be preoccupied with the burial and funeral arrangements. Obviously, the successive relays of pallbearers who will be responsible for the actual handling of the bier are occupied with that act of loving-kindness and are, thus, exempted from performance of the *mitzvot* which are enumerated in our *mishnah*. Those who participate in the funeral procession, but have no specific role with regard to the handling of the bier, are obligated to perform the biblically ordained commandments—the recitation of the *Shema* and the wearing of *tefillin*—but are exempted from the recitation of the *Shemoneh Esrei* prayer, both because it is rabbinically rather than scripturally ordained, and because it requires a great deal of concentration and should not be said when one is walking.

APPLICATION

The significance of our *mishnah* far transcends the technical principle of the impossibility of the simultaneous performance of two different *mitzvot*. It reflects the profound insight of our sages into the emotional impact of the loss of a near and dear one. Rabbi Joseph B. Soloveitchik once declared that the loss of a loved one represents the defeat of the bereaved by the intrusion of death. It reminds the bereaved that death *does* have dominion. In a sense, it mocks at all of life's values. It suggests to us that our efforts and our hopes and our strivings are ultimately for naught, and that our destiny is death. It thus represents a negation of our self-worth.

Under such conditions, our sages understood that it is not possible for us to affirm our profoundest beliefs in a benevolent and loving deity; to turn to Him in prayer is to bind ourselves to do His will.

They understood, however, that prolonged self-negation is unhealthy and can become pathological. When the interment has taken place, therefore, one passes from the stage of self-negation to self-affirmation. This transformation is symbolized by our affirmation of faith, and by our acceptance of its imperatives. It is reflected in our heroic attempt to turn to God in prayer, notwithstanding our pain and sorrow.

Our *mishnah* reminds us that death is an inescapable part of life, and that it often provokes emotions of doubt and despair. It suggests to us that a loving God understands our pain and confusion; it also reminds us that we cannot allow ourselves to be enthralled by despair and to surrender to self-negation. It suggests that by turning to God at precisely that time when we often feel that we have been forsaken by Him, we will reestablish our sense of self-worth and our conviction that life is meaningful.

This is the beginning of the *shiv'ah* period for this family. We pray that the despair, the pain, the doubt, and the heartache will gradually be transformed into acceptance of the reality of death and of the value of the life of faith and commitment.

Intent and Deed:
New Commitments

APPLICATION: GENERAL

MISHNAH: *Kelim* 25:9(b)

כָּל הַכֵּלִים יוֹרְדִין לִידֵי טֻמְאָתָן בְּמַחֲשָׁבָה, וְאֵינָן עוֹלִים מִידֵי טֻמְאָתָן אֶלָּא בְּשִׁנּוּי
מַעֲשֶׂה, שֶׁהַמַּעֲשֶׂה מְבַטֵּל מִיַּד הַמַּעֲשֶׂה וּמִיַּד מַחֲשָׁבָה, וּמַחֲשָׁבָה אֵינָה מְבַטֶּלֶת לֹא מִיַּד
מַעֲשֶׂה וְלֹא מִיַּד מַחֲשָׁבָה:

TRANSLATION

All vessels become susceptible to ritual uncleanness through intention, but cannot be rendered unsusceptible except through a new
practical application; for a change of practical application undoes
the [effects of a previous] practical application and of [a previous]
intention, whereas [a change of] intention [alone] neither undoes
the [effects of a previous] practical application nor [of a previous]
intention.

COMMENTARY

The background to this *mishnah* derives from an earlier *mishnah*
(*Kelim* 12:1): "A *man's* ring is [susceptible to] ritual impurity. But a
ring [used as a decoration] for cattle or for utensils, and all other
rings, are not susceptible to ritual impurity." Thus, in *our* case, a
person's mere intention to himself to wear a decorative cattle ring
renders it immediately susceptible to ritual uncleanness. However,
the mere intent to use a human decorative ring for cattle does *not*
undo its susceptibility to uncleanness. An actual change of use is
required, for only an act can undo the effects of a previous act.
Indeed, a change of practical application can undo the effects of

287

both a previous practical application and the previous intent. Thus, the initial intent to apply the cattle ring to human use renders it susceptible to uncleanness. But an act indicating that it has reverted to its original application can undo the effects of that original intent. On the other hand, however, mere intent to apply a human ring to cattle use can undo neither the effects of the previous intent to apply it to human use, nor, if it had already been used as a human ring, its prior practical application.

APPLICATIONS

General

Our rather technical *mishnah* is of overarching general significance. It establishes the principle that intention alone is of great consequence—contradicting the popular proverb that "the road to hell is paved with good intentions." In the popular view, mere intention is useless. In the Jewish view, on the other hand, "the final act resides in the initial intent."

The atmosphere in *shiv'ah* houses is almost always charged with good intentions. Members of the bereaved family often resolve to make changes in their personal lifestyles as a result of the great loss they have suffered. Such resolutions run the gamut from a desire to adopt healthier habits, like giving up smoking and doing more exercise, to making better use of their own remaining years by spending more time with their families, by devoting themselves to communal work, through self-improvement, through study, to changing their religious and ideological lifestyles by attending synagogue more regularly—at least during the period of mourning.

Such intentions are valuable. They establish a mood for transformation, and effect attitudinal changes. But intent alone cannot undo the effects of previous action. Habits have to be broken by accepting new habits, in spite of the fact that it is not at all easy to change a comfortable lifestyle.

The habit of the regular recitation of *Kaddish* during public worship each morning and evening of the eleven-month mourning period has often transformed the lifestyle of an entire family. It has changed more Jewish lives than have all the techniques which are used by gifted teachers to attract the alienated back into the fold.

At this time, the intentions of the bereaved are wonderful. They wish to show love, honor, and respect to the deceased by making a commitment. Let me not pretend that this will be an easy commitment to keep. It will not. You will not feel like waking up early after a late-night meeting or working overtime. You will want to stay in bed a little longer on a cold, dark, winter morning. But remember, intent is not enough. Only action can undo the effects of previous inaction.

The deceased *deserves* commitment. Was not he/she committed to the bereaved when they needed him/her to wake up in the dead of night, to suffer winter's cold and summer's heat for their sakes? Let them reciprocate this love by turning the intent of the *shiv'ah* week into a year-long, perhaps lifelong, commitment. Anything else will not do full justice to the deceased.

In Praise of a Man of Action

Our *mishnah* establishes the general principle that deeds are far more important than intentions.

(The rabbi/study leader should speak of the deceased as a person of action, describing his/her numerous accomplishments in detail.)

Such a person of action can be shown respect only in the way he/she would appreciate—through reciprocal action.

(The rabbi/study leader should now continue with the general application above, beginning, "The atmosphere in *shiv'ah houses* . . .")

Challenge to the Mourners: Adding "Godness" to the World

APPLICATION Children of the Deceased

MISHNAH *Avot* 3:14

הוּא הָיָה אוֹמֵר, חָבִיב אָדָם שֶׁנִּבְרָא בְּצֶלֶם. חִבָּה יְתֵרָה נוֹדַעַת לוֹ שֶׁנִּבְרָא בְּצֶלֶם,
שֶׁנֶּאֱמַר, כִּי בְּצֶלֶם אֱלֹהִים עָשָׂה אֶת־הָאָדָם. חֲבִיבִין יִשְׂרָאֵל שֶׁנִּקְרְאוּ בָּנִים לַמָּקוֹם. חִבָּה
יְתֵרָה נוֹדַעַת לָהֶם שֶׁנִּקְרְאוּ בָּנִים לַמָּקוֹם, שֶׁנֶּאֱמַר, בָּנִים אַתֶּם לַה' אֱלֹהֵיכֶם. חֲבִיבִין
יִשְׂרָאֵל, שֶׁנִּתַּן לָהֶם כְּלִי חֶמְדָּה. חִבָּה יְתֵרָה נוֹדַעַת לָהֶם שֶׁנִּתַּן לָהֶם כְּלִי חֶמְדָּה שֶׁבּוֹ
נִבְרָא הָעוֹלָם, שֶׁנֶּאֱמַר כִּי לֶקַח טוֹב נָתַתִּי לָכֶם, תּוֹרָתִי אַל־תַּעֲזֹבוּ:

TRANSLATION

He [Rabbi Akiva] used to say: Beloved is man, for he was created in the divine image. By a special love it was made known to him that he was created in the divine image, as it is said: *In the image of God, He made man* (Genesis 9:6). Beloved are Israel for they have been called God's children. By a special love that was made known to them that they were called children of God, as it said: *You are the children of the Lord* (Deuteronomy 14:1). Beloved are Israel, for a special instrument was given to them. By a special love it was made known to them that a precious instrument was given to them, through which the world was created, as it is said: *For I gave them a good doctrine; forsake not my Torah* (Proverbs 4:2).

COMMENTARY

The Jerusalem Talmud (*Nedarim* 6:4) records the view of Rabbi Akiva that the verse *Thou shalt love thy neighbor as thyself* (Leviticus 19:18) is the most all-embracing principle of the Torah. Ben Azzai rejects this view, proposing, instead, the verse *This is the book of the generations of Adam; in the day that God created man, in the likeness of God made He him* (Genesis 5:1).

Ben Azzai rejects the notion that loving one's neighbor as oneself is the crowning principle of the Torah, because "as thyself" is made the determinant of love of others. This criterion would permit a masochist to become a sadist!

In our *mishnah*, Rabbi Akiva apparently embraces the view of Ben Azzai. Our love of neighbor is based upon the "godness" which he reflects, and is irrespective of what we think of ourselves. It is, therefore, absolute.

The notion of the divine image is widely misunderstood. It is, in fact, man's charismatic quality of autonomous creativity which is so designated. Gifted with will and with intellect, man, like God, can become an independent source of creativity and causality. Rabbi Akiva points out that the gift of this divine quality was granted by God to all His children. Israel, however, enjoys a unique filial relationship with God, and we are granted the special opportunity of actualizing our potential through the instrumentality of the Torah.

APPLICATION

Since man reflects "godness," the death of any human being means a diminution of "godness" in the world (*mi'ut ha-demut*). The challenge to the bereaved is to magnify the diminished divine image. This is why they say *Kaddish* for eleven months, with its opening stanza: "Magnified and sanctified be His great Name." This is why they lead the community in prayer. It is a public demonstration of the sanctification of the divine Name. This is why they behave as true children of God, by taking care of His other children—human beings in need who turn to them for assistance. This is why they study Torah in memory of the deceased, since the Torah is the instrument through which the potential for "godness" is actualized.

There is no need for me to dot my i's and to cross my t's. The message is quite clear. The bereaved have a special task during the coming twelve months. It is nothing more and nothing less than to restore the divinity which was diminished by the passing of the beloved deceased in the ways outlined above. Your beloved departed, and the Almighty, deserve no less!

Revival of the Dead:
A Challenge to the Living

APPLICATION: GENERAL

MISHNAH: *Sotah* 9:15(c)

רַבִּי פִּנְחָס בֶּן־יָאִיר אוֹמֵר, זְרִיזוּת מְבִיאָה לִידֵי נְקִיּוּת, וּנְקִיּוּת מְבִיאָה לִידֵי טָהֳרָה,
וְטָהֳרָה מְבִיאָה לִידֵי־פְּרִישׁוּת, וּפְרִישׁוּת מְבִיאָה לִידֵי קְדֻשָּׁה, וּקְדֻשָּׁה מְבִיאָה לִידֵי עֲנָוָה,
וַעֲנָוָה מְבִיאָה לִידֵי יִרְאַת־חֵטְא, וְיִרְאַת־חֵטְא מְבִיאָה לִידֵי חֲסִידוּת, וַחֲסִידוּת מְבִיאָה
לִידֵי רוּחַ־הַקֹּדֶשׁ. וְרוּחַ־הַקֹּדֶשׁ מְבִיאָה לִידֵי תְחִיַּת־הַמֵּתִים, וּתְחִיַּת־הַמֵּתִים בָּאָה עַל־יְדֵי
אֵלִיָּהוּ זָכוּר לַטּוֹב, אָמֵן:

TRANSLATION

Rabbi Pinchas ben Ya'ir said: Diligence leads to cleanliness, cleanliness to purity, purity to separateness, separateness to sanctity, sanctity to humility, humility to fear of sin, fear of sin to piety, piety to divine inspiration, divine inspiration to the revival of the dead, and the revival of the dead will be facilitated by Elijah the Prophet, may he be remembered for good. Amen.

COMMENTARY

This *mishnah* enumerates the steps on the ladder of spiritual perfection, each one of which precedes to the next. If we are not punctilious, we cannot be clean. A clean mind is dependent upon a clean body. Spiritual purity results in our separation from negative environmental influences. Such disciplined self-control and self-sacrifice reflect humility, and are its precondition. The truly humble person does not denigrate himself/herself. He/she merely attributes success to God-given opportunities. This attitude pre-

293

pares one for thoroughgoing reverence for God. Such reverence, in turn, transforms one's personality and enables one to become genuinely pious—a level we now see as higher even than holiness, in that the holy person simply does not transgress the divine will by sullying him/herself, whereas the truly pious individual is infused by the divine presence and radiates that presence in his/her life. Such a person opens him/herself to divine inspiration. The ultimate redemption, the fulfillment of history, will be the product of all these steps.

APPLICATION

In his hierarchy of values, Rabbi Pinchas ben Ya'ir gives pride of place to the revival of the dead. This miraculous event, however, is the culmination of a process. It will not occur automatically, but is the result of great effort on behalf of the living.

The bereaved are paralyzed by the passing of their loved one. They wish for nothing more than his/her restoration to life. Rabbi Pinchas ben Ya'ir makes this wish their challenge. The speed of the process depends upon their actions, upon the way in which *they* mount the steps to spiritual perfection. The faith of our loved ones is in our hands.

(The rabbi/study leader should speak of any of the attributes enumerated by Rabbi Pinchas ben Ya'ir which the deceased characterized, and call upon the bereaved to emulate those virtues and, hopefully, to add to them in order to hasten the process of salvation.)

A Lesson for the End
of the *Shiv'ah*

APPLICATION: GENERAL

MISHNAH: *Mo'ed Katan* 3:9

בְּרָאשֵׁי חֳדָשִׁים, בַּחֲנֻכָּה וּבְפוּרִים, מְעַנּוֹת וּמְטַפְּחוֹת, בָּזֶה וּבָזֶה (אֲבָל) לֹא מְקוֹנְנוֹת. נִקְבַּר הַמֵּת, לֹא מְעַנּוֹת וְלֹא מְטַפְּחוֹת. אֵיזֶהוּ עִנּוּי, שֶׁכֻּלָּן עוֹנוֹת כְּאֶחָת. קִינָה, שֶׁאַחַת מְדַבֶּרֶת וְכֻלָּן עוֹנוֹת אַחֲרֶיהָ, שֶׁנֶּאֱמַר, וְלַמֵּדְנָה בְנֹתֵיכֶם נֶהִי, וְאִשָּׁה רְעוּתָהּ קִינָה. אֲבָל לֶעָתִיד לָבוֹא הוּא אוֹמֵר, בִּלַּע הַמָּוֶת לָנֶצַח, וּמָחָה אֲדֹנָי יֱהוִה דִּמְעָה מֵעַל כָּל־פָּנִים וגו':

TRANSLATION

On New Moons, Chanukah, and Purim [the professional lamenters] both lament and clap their hands. They do not lead the responsive lament either on this [the intermediate days of festivals] or on that [New Moons, Chanukah, and Purim]. After the removal of the dead, [the lamenters] neither lament nor clap their hands. Which mode of lament is called *inuy* in Hebrew? When [the lamenters] all lament in unison. Which [mode of lament is called] *Kinah?* When one leads and the others answer responsively—as it is written (Jeremiah 9:19): "Let them teach their daughters lamentation (*nehi*), and one woman [shall lead] the other in *kinah*." However, concerning the [idyllic] time to come, he declares (Isaiah 25:8): "He shall swallow up death forever, and the Lord God shall wipe away tears of all faces, and the reproach of His people shall He remove from off all the earth."

COMMENTARY

This *mishnah* concludes Tractate *Mo'ed Katan*, the last chapter of which is the *locus classicus* for the talmudic discussion of mourning.

As we have seen in Part One of this volume, public mourning is inappropriate on festive occasions. Our *mishnah* deals with semi-festive occasions, like the intermediate days of Passover and Tabernacles, and the even less festive days of the New Moon, Chanukah, and Purim. The *mishnah* reflects a period when professional female lamenters were employed to help the mourners express their grief. They would lift the lid off repression by utilizing the techniques described in the *mishnah*—in a rhythmic, mesmerizing clapping of the hands, laments in unison, and responsive laments, which would involve all those who were present. It would appear that the clapping of the hands was singularly expressive of emotion and was, for this reason, forbidden on the intermediate days of Passover and Tabernacles, the most festive of the public half-holidays.

APPLICATION

This *mishnah* is particularly appropriate at the final service of the *shiv'ah* week, since it reflects the characteristic optimism of the sages. Having delineated the laws of mourning in all their detail, we are transported to a time when we shall not be in mourning. They remind us that "weeping may tarry in the night, but joy will come in the morning" (Psalm 30:6).

On one level, they remind us that death is not the putting out of the lamp because darkness has come, but because it heralds the dawn of life eternal. Death belongs only to the here and now, the temporal realm. In the perspective of eternal life, which God has promised, death will truly be swallowed up in life eternal. On this level, the mourners are comforted in the certainty that their loved ones are at peace.

On another level, the quotation at the end of the *mishnah* reminds us that "our days of mourning shall be ended" (Isaiah 25:8), that life must go on in its familiar routines, and that we give no dignity to the deceased by remaining paralyzed by grief, unable to live as fully as they taught us to do.

A traditional greeting at this time would have us declare to the mourners: "may you have no more *tza'ar* (upset and sorrow)." It is impossible to take this sentiment literally. Death is part of life—at least until that distant, idyllic future of which the prophet speaks. Joy is punctuated by sorrow, and happiness by despair.

What then can we wish the mourners as they prepare to rise from *shiv'ah?* That there shall be *much* more happiness than sadness, gladness than despair, joy than sorrow, triumph than tragedy—and that they may find fulfillment in and be fortified by their family and loyal friends.

The Promise of Life
Beyond the Grave

APPLICATION: GENERAL

MISHNAH: *Sanhedrin* 10:1

כָּל־יִשְׂרָאֵל יֵשׁ לָהֶם חֵלֶק לָעוֹלָם הַבָּא, שֶׁנֶּאֱמַר וְעַמֵּךְ כֻּלָּם צַדִּיקִים לְעוֹלָם יִירְשׁוּ אָרֶץ נֵצֶר מַטָּעַי מַעֲשֵׂה יָדַי לְהִתְפָּאֵר. וְאֵלּוּ שֶׁאֵין לָהֶם חֵלֶק לָעוֹלָם הַבָּא, הָאוֹמֵר אֵין תְּחִיַּת הַמֵּתִים מִן־הַתּוֹרָה, וְאֵין תּוֹרָה מִן־הַשָּׁמַיִם, וְאַפִּיקוֹרוֹס. רַבִּי עֲקִיבָא אוֹמֵר, אַף הַקּוֹרֵא בַּסְפָרִים הַחִיצוֹנִים, וְהַלּוֹחֵשׁ עַל הַמַּכָּה וְאוֹמֵר כָּל־הַמַּחֲלָה אֲשֶׁר־שַׂמְתִּי בְמִצְרַיִם לֹא אָשִׂים עָלֶיךָ כִּי אֲנִי ה' רֹפְאֶךָ. אַבָּא שָׁאוּל אוֹמֵר, אַף הַהוֹגֶה אֶת הַשֵּׁם בְּאוֹתִיּוֹתָיו:

TRANSLATION

All Jews have a share in the world-to-come, as it is said: *Your people shall all be righteous; they shall inherit the land forever; the branch of my planting, the work of my hands that I may be glorified* (Isaiah 60:21). And who are they who have no share in the world-to-come? He who denies biblical authority for [belief in] resurrection of the dead; and he who denies the divine origin of the Torah; and the Epicurean. Rabbi Akiva says: He [is also excluded] who studies sectarian writings, and he who pronounces an incantation over a wound, saying: *I will put none of the diseases upon you which I have put upon the Egyptians, for I am the Lord who heals you* (Exodus 15:26). Abba Sha'ul says: He [is also excluded] who pronounces the ineffable name of God as it is written.

COMMENTARY

This *mishnah* promises life beyond the grave to the vast majority of Jews. Only six classes of individuals are excluded.

1. He who denies that personal immortality is a biblical doctrine certainly does not deserve personal immortality.
2. He who denies the divine authorship of the Torah surely cannot merit the divine promise of life after death. If God could not effect the translation of the purely spiritual content of the divine mind into a material medium—the written Torah—He cannot be relied upon to translate physical beings—people—into a purely spiritual realm.
3. The Epicurean denies personal providence, the very basis of our expectation of life after death. Accordingly, he is excluded from its benefits.
4. Sectarian texts misapply biblical promises and distort the clear meaning of the text to suit their own propaganda purposes. He who studies these texts exchanges the inauthentic for the authentic, thus sacrificing the reward promised for authentic belief.
5. Incantations for healing are also an inappropriate use of the Scriptures. Historically, since the spell also involved spitting, it showed contempt for the divine name which was uttered as part of the magic formula. Contempt and superstition are certainly no foundations for the expectation of divine reward.
6. The objection of Abba Sha'ul was to the inappropriate invocation of the ineffable divine name in the marketplace, where it would not command awe and reverence. This cavalier attitude to God provokes an equally cavalier response from Him. If we don't take God seriously, He will not invite us into His presence in the realm of the spirit.

APPLICATION

Happily, the deceased did not fall into any of the six above-mentioned categories. He/she was a serious person, not a scoffer. He/she was not led astray by sectarian propaganda, believed in the power of God, and treated Him with reverence. Accordingly, he/she is now enjoying conscious existence beyond the grave. He/she is, to use the popular expression, "in heaven."

But what is the Jewish concept of heaven? Heaven is a state. It is not a place "somewhere up there." It is the invisible spiritual dimension which envelops and surrounds us.

Nor is heaven monolithic, it has many gradations, some more desirable than others. The desirability of these gradations is defined by their closeness to God. The closer they are to God, the more desirable they are, because God represents fully actualized existence. He *is* Being. Conversely, distance from God represents diminished existence. Indeed, hell is the state of being absolutely cut off from God, absolutely deprived of existence. This is why *karet* (cutting off) is the worst of all the biblical punishments, worse even than death itself.

If heaven has gradations, what most Jews are promised is at least a modest portion of the spiritual realm—a minimally fulfilled life beyond the grave. Happily, some of us merit a fuller life with God. We pray that this is the situation of the deceased. Happily, too, our location in heaven is not fixed. Jewish mystic sources inform us that we can advance to ever higher levels of heaven. But this advance depends upon those loved ones whom we leave behind. They justify us by sanctifying the name of God, by carrying on the tradition to which we should have showed loyalty, by studying the Torah, and by performing acts of loving-kindness.

The promise of heaven for the deceased is thus a challenge to the bereaved. To the extent that they will be true to the tradition of their ancestors, their dearly beloved departed will progress to an ever more fully realized life with God in the realm beyond the grave.

Conditions for
Entering Heaven

APPLICATION: GENERAL

MISHNAH: *Berakhot* 9:5

לֹא יָקֵל אָדָם אֶת רֹאשׁוֹ כְּנֶגֶד שַׁעַר הַמִּזְרָח, שֶׁהוּא מְכֻוָּן כְּנֶגֶד בֵּית קָדְשֵׁי הַקֳּדָשִׁים. לֹא
יִכָּנֵס לְהַר הַבַּיִת בְּמַקְלוֹ וּבְמִנְעָלוֹ וּבְפֻנְדָּתוֹ וּבְאָבָק שֶׁעַל־רַגְלָיו. וְלֹא יַעֲשֶׂנּוּ קַפַּנְדַּרְיָא.
וּרְקִיקָה — מִקַּל וָחֹמֶר.

TRANSLATION

A person should not behave in an unseemly fashion when facing
the eastern gate of the sanctuary, which is opposite the Holy of
Holies. He should not enter the Temple Mount carrying a staff,
wearing shoes, a money belt, and with dust upon his feet. Nor
should he make the Temple Mount a shortcut. [If all this is required
out of respect for the Sanctuary] how much more so is spitting forbidden [in its environs].

COMMENTARY

Scripture (Leviticus 19:30) commands reverence for the Sanctuary: "You shall respect My Sanctuary." Respect for God's Sanctuary reflects our reverence for Him. Dignified, modest, and
respectful behavior is required in its environs—from the time one
approaches the entrance, throughout the entire Temple Mount
area, and in one's deportment when one enters the Sanctuary.

The *staff* represents human power, which can be a weapon or a
support. In the Temple, neither is appropriate. Instruments of
destruction are taboo, for "they shall not hurt or destroy in all My
holy mountain" (Isaiah 11:9), and God is support enough.

301

The *money belt* represents materialism, also inappropriate in the Temple. *Clean, bare feet* reflect simplicity, modesty, and our awareness that we are on holy ground. *God* is to protect us from thorns and thistles—not our own inventions. Abuse of the holy for our personal purposes, taking a *shortcut* through the Sanctuary environment, perverts its sublime status. *Spitting* reflects contempt. Obviously, this is the very antithesis of reverence for the sacred.

APPLICATION

Personal immortality, life beyond the grave, is regarded as our spiritual mode of existence in the presence of the Lord, in the heavenly sanctuary. Our life on *this* side of the grave is our preparation for entering into His presence, for gaining permanent access to the heavenly sanctuary. Our *mishnah* details five preconditions for gaining access,

1. *We cannot use our staffs to enter the heavenly sanctuary.* (The rabbi/study leader should spell out the virtues of kindness and sensitivity of the deceased, how he/she did not abuse power nor abuse those who needed them. He should stress those significant personal accomplishments of the deceased which provide access into the heavenly sanctuary and which require no artificial support to help the deceased gain entry.)

2. *You cannot take it with you. Tickets to heaven are not for sale.* Some people tend to forget that shrouds have no pockets. They leave this world as tight-fisted as they entered it (The rabbi/study leader should show how *this* was not the case with the deceased.)

3. *Clean, bare feet.* (The rabbi/study leader should describe some hard times of the deceased, the thorns and thistles upon which he/she walked. Notwithstanding, he/she did not bemoan his/her fate. The deceased knew that the ground upon which he/she stood was holy, and accepted the difficulties with love and forbearance. He/she lived honorably. We are certain that he/she will bring no dirt with him/her, no traces of corruption, into the heavenly sanctuary.)

4. *No shortcuts.* People are often tempted to take shortcuts to success. They cheat in business. They exploit workers. They abuse their power. Not so the deceased. (The rabbi/study leader should

spell out how diligently and honestly he/she made a living, and discuss his/her reputation with colleagues, customers, clients, employers, and employees.)

5. *Respect, not contempt.* Many people hold those who achieve less than they do in contempt, and look down upon those who do not share their standards and ideals. Happily, the deceased did not belong in this category. (The rabbi/study leader should tell of his/her respect for others and illustrate with biographical examples.)

If these are the preconditions for gaining access to the heavenly sanctuary, we can be confident that the deceased has been admitted and trailing clouds of glory.

Earning Our Eternal Reward

APPLICATIONS: *THE BA'AL TESHUVAH* (PENITENT); GENERAL

The *Ba'al Teshuvah* (penitent); general

MISHNAH: *Avot* 4:16–17

רַבִּי יַעֲקֹב אוֹמֵר, הָעוֹלָם הַזֶּה דּוֹמֶה לַפְּרוֹזְדוֹר בִּפְנֵי הָעוֹלָם הַבָּא. הַתְקֵן עַצְמְךָ
בַּפְּרוֹזְדוֹר, כְּדֵי שֶׁתִּכָּנֵס לַטְּרַקְלִין:
הוּא הָיָה אוֹמֵר, יָפָה שָׁעָה אַחַת בִּתְשׁוּבָה וּמַעֲשִׂים טוֹבִים בָּעוֹלָם הַזֶּה, מִכָּל חַיֵּי הָעוֹלָם
הַבָּא. וְיָפָה שָׁעָה אַחַת שֶׁל קוֹרַת רוּחַ בָּעוֹלָם הַבָּא, מִכָּל חַיֵּי הָעוֹלָם הַזֶּה:

TRANSLATION

Rabbi Ya'akov said: This world is like a lobby before the world-to-come; prepare yourself in the lobby, so that you may enter the banquet area. He used to say: Better is one hour of repentance and good deeds in this world than the whole life of the world-to-come; and better is one hour of the blissfulness of tranquility of spirit in the world-to-come than the whole life of this world.

COMMENTARY

Our text makes two points:

1. *The world beyond the grave is incomparably superior to the world we know.* We cannot really be faulted for taking this statement "with a grain of salt." Our experience teaches us otherwise: Life in this world is real. Life is earnest. Death appears to be its cruel conclusion and its final frustration. However, the parable cited at the beginning of Part One of this volume will clarify the view of our sages, here articulated by Rabbi Ya'akov: Imagine that a child in its mother's womb were to be told of its impending birth. Imagine, also, that it had the ability to compare the safety and

304

security of life in the amniotic sac—its needs taken care of automatically, and seemingly permanently—with the terrifying reality of its painful passage through the narrow birth canal, and into the fearfully unfamiliar, buzzing, dazzling, dangerous, dry environment at the other end. Would it willingly exchange the womb for the world? Given its limited experience, surely not. However, notwithstanding its dangers, life lived outside the womb—without its previous limitations—soon comes to be preferred by all but the most neurotic of people. As birth is the frightening passage of the fetus into the terrifying unknown, so death too is the passage of the human into another unkown dimension. Both are stages in our development, part of God's plan for our personal evolution. The notion of life after *death* for those who have been born is no less rational and no less reasonable than the notion of life after *birth* for those who are yet to be born. Rabbi Ya'akov emphasizes not only the reality of life after death, but also its incomparable superiority to terrestrial life, limited as it is by the constraints of the material body.

2. *The world we know is a vital precondition for eternal bliss.* It is true that a single hour of tranquility in the world to come is greater than all the pleasures of this life—because, beyond the grave, even a moment is eternal. Still, the experience of that eternal bliss is conditional upon the way we live here on earth. This life is the school from which we graduate into the next. What we attain there depends upon how we live here. For this reason, Rabbi Ya'akov states that a moment of repentance and good deeds in this world is better than all of life in the world-to-come if it is unenhanced by meaningful, spiritual experiences in the earthly school from which the deceased has graduated.

APPLICATIONS

The *Ba'al Teshuvah*

The deceased was not always a committed Jew. His/her early experience was devoid of real religious significance. The decision to make a religious commitment was an enormous step. It cast the deceased into a more restrictive existence. It forced him/her to swim against the social stream. Former friends and associates, and even family members, were resentful of the decision, hurt by their exclusion from pivotal areas of his/her life, and found the new commitment hard to understand.

But resentment mellowed into respect, and misunderstanding into admiration. Even those who would not walk his/her road admit, in the end, that his/hers was a life of meaningful significance.

Our *mishnah* assures us that it was of ultimate significance, that he/she prepared him/herself well in the lobby in order to gain entry into the banquet hall.

General

The life of the deceased was punctuated by *ma'asim tovim*—meritorious deeds. (The rabbi/study leader should speak in detail about the good deeds performed by the deceased in all areas of life.)

Our *mishnah* assures us that his/her life was of ultimate significance, that he/she prepared himself/herself well in the lobby of existence in order to achieve entry into the banquet hall.

We are comforted by the knowledge that he/she has merited a special portion in the world-to-come. May his/her memory be a blessing and an inspiration.

What We Owe Our Parents I

APPLICATION: BEREAVED CHILDREN

MISHNAH: *Kiddushin* 1:7

כָּל־מִצְוֹת הַבֵּן עַל־הָאָב, אֲנָשִׁים חַיָּבִין וְנָשִׁים פְּטוּרוֹת. וְכָל־מִצְוֹת הָאָב עַל־הַבֵּן, אֶחָד אֲנָשִׁים וְאֶחָד נָשִׁים חַיָּבִין.

TRANSLATION

Men are obligated to perform, and women are exempted from performing, all those religious imperatives (*mitzvot*) which a father owes his son. But men and women are alike obliged to perform those *mitzvot* which a son owes his father.

COMMENTARY

The Talmud spells out the obligations of a Jewish father to his son. They include the covenantal circumcision of the lad on the eighth day of his life, his redemption as soon as possible after the thirtieth day of life if he is firstborn, the obligation to teach him Torah, to train him for a worldly occupation, to marry him off and, according to another opinion, to teach him to swim (that is, life-preserving strategies in dangerous situations). Women are exempted (but not precluded) from these obligations, since, unlike all men, they are not themselves obligated in all these areas.

In return, all children, male and female, owe their parents reverence—expressed by not sitting in their usual place and by not contradicting them when they speak, etc., etc.—and honor—expressed by clothing them, feeding them, helping them get about etc., etc.

307

APPLICATION

A cynic remarked that one parent can take care of a dozen children, whereas a dozen children cannot take care of a single dependent parent. (The rabbi/study leader should expand upon this point.)

The talmudic elaboration of our *mishnah* cites six general areas of parental responsibility. Parents introduce their children into the covenantal community. The act of redemption transforms a biological event, the birth of a baby, often unplanned, into an act of deliberate choice. The father states that his child is more valuable to him than money, and establishes parenting as his primary commitment. Jewish parents make their children citizens of two civilizations—the Jewish and the general—and train them for participation in both. They teach them survival strategies, and strive to make them independent, autonomous links in the chain of Jewish generations. In return for all this, children owe their parents minimal gestures of respect and are responsible for satisfying their minimal physical needs.

We show our final respect to our parents and our gratitude for all that they have done by the seriousness with which we take our mourning practices and by striving to emulate them in our own lives. It is the least we can do for them in light of what they have done for us.

(The rabbi/study leader should spell out in some detail what the deceased did for his/her children. In this way, it should be clear to the children what they owe to their parents, even posthumously.)

What We Owe Our Parents II

MISHNAH: *Eduyot* 2:9

הוּא הָיָה אוֹמֵר, הָאָב זוֹכֶה לַבֵּן, בַּנּוֹי, וּבַכֹּחַ, וּבָעשֶׁר, וּבַחָכְמָה, וּבַשָּׁנִים, וּבְמִסְפַּר
הַדּוֹרוֹת לְפָנָיו וְהוּא הַקֵּץ, שֶׁנֶּאֱמַר קֹרֵא הַדֹּרוֹת מֵראשׁ, אַף עַל פִּי שֶׁנֶּאֱמַר וַעֲבָדוּם וְעִנּוּ
אֹתָם אַרְבַּע מֵאוֹת שָׁנָה, שֶׁנֶּאֱמַר וְדוֹר רְבִיעִי יָשׁוּבוּ הֵנָּה:

TRANSLATION

He [Rabbi Akiba] used to say: A father endows his son with beauty, strength, wealth, wisdom, years, and [with the merits of] the number of generations before him, of which he is the last, as it is said: *He calls the generations from the head* (Isaiah 41:4). Although it was said: *And they shall serve them and they shall afflict them for 400 years* (Genesis 15:13), it was [also] said: *And the fourth generation will return here* (Genesis 15:16).

COMMENTARY

Rabbi Akiba elaborates the genetic, moral, cultural, and material endowments transmitted to children by their parents, specifying physical appearance, physical prowess, intellectual heritage, financial support, wealth, and longevity. Also included with beauty and strength are the intangible attributes of grace or inner beauty and courage. Rabbi Akiba stresses that the parental endowment of children does not begin with the parent him/herself. He/she is merely the last link in a long chain of generations, and transmits the merits of earlier generations to his/her descendants. Thus, according to the proof-text, the lengthy enslavement predicted for Israel in Egypt was abbreviated through the merit of the patriarch Abraham.

309

APPLICATION

The deceased, too, was the final link in a long chain of generations. (The rabbi/study leader should describe his/her origins.) Accordingly, the values which he/she bestowed upon his/her children are the endowments of many wonderful people living in different places and at different times.

However, the most obvious endowments of the children derive directly from their parents, and it is for these that the bereaved need to be particularly grateful.

We shall not discuss physical endowments, since the transmission of a genetic code is both unconscious and effortless. The transmission of moral values, on the other hand, requires conscious effort and great perseverance. Our *mishnah* cites four of these intangible endowments, each of which deserves fuller elaboration.

Grace and Inner Beauty

The English language distinguishes between the beautiful and the beauteous. The former describes one's outward appearance. The latter defines the spiritual beauty which radiates from the soul of a person. This inner beauty expresses itself in generosity of spirit, in loving, caring, and giving. (The rabbi/spiritual leader should now show how the deceased was beauteous, and how that grace was transmitted to his/her children.)

Inner Strength

The sages defined inner strength as self-control (*Avot* 4:1). This is *true* heroism. It demands the imposition of will upon instinct. It is one of the most difficult of the virtues which we are asked to cultivate, because it always involves self-denial and self-sacrifice for the sake of the achievement of a greater ideal, such as the needs of our children. In this respect, the deceased was a true Jewish hero, and for this his/her children owe him/her more than they can ever repay. (The rabbi/study leader should elaborate on the self-sacrifice and self-denial of the deceased and attempt to show how this virtue is reflected in his/her family.)

Wealth

This, too, is redefined by our sages to mean satisfaction with one's lot (*Avot* 4:1). Irrespective of our actual material endowments, we are only truly rich when we are satisfied with what we have. (The rabbi/study leader should attempt to apply this virtue to the deceased and to his/her family.)

Wisdom

There are two types of wisdom. One is gained from formal study. (If applicable, the rabbi/study leader should speak of the Torah and general intellectual background of the deceased, and of the efforts he/she made to grant his/her children the best possible opportunities. If the background was limited, the emphasis should be made upon the sacrifices the deceased endured in order to give his/her children much more than he/she ever had.) The other type of wisdom is defined by our sages as the ability to see the future (*Avot* 1:4). (The rabbi/study leader should speak about the native intelligence and the perspicacity of the deceased, and emphasize how important an endowment this is to his/her children.)

Our *mishnah* has a "sting in its tail." It refuses to permit us to rest on our laurels. It reminds us that the transmission of special endowments is transgenerational. The heritage of the grandparents belongs to their grandchildren. The deceased will have lived in vain if he/she is really what our *mishnah* calls the *ketz*—the end—of a glorious tradition.

It is the solemn duty of the bereaved to emulate the deceased by transmitting his/her grace and inner beauty, courage and inner strength, spiritual wealth and wisdom to *their children* and to their children's children.

In this way, the memory of the deceased will truly be a blessing.

Living on Credit

APPLICATION: A PARENT

MISHNAH: *Avot* 3:16

הוּא הָיָה אוֹמֵר, הַכֹּל נָתוּן בָּעֵרָבוֹן, וּמְצוּדָה פְרוּסָה עַל כָּל הַחַיִּים, הַחֲנוּת פְּתוּחָה,
וְהַחֶנְוָנִי מַקִּיף, וְהַפִּנְקָס פָּתוּחַ, וְהַיָּד כּוֹתֶבֶת, וְכָל הָרוֹצֶה לִלְווֹת יָבוֹא וְיִלְוֶה, וְהַגַּבָּאִים
מַחֲזִירִים תָּדִיר בְּכָל יוֹם, וְנִפְרָעִין מִן הָאָדָם מִדַּעְתּוֹ וְשֶׁלֹּא מִדַּעְתּוֹ, וְיֵשׁ לָהֶם עַל מַה
שֶׁיִּסְמֹכוּ, וְהַדִּין דִּין אֱמֶת, וְהַכֹּל מְתֻקָּן לַסְּעוּדָה:

TRANSLATION

He [Rabbi Akiva] used to say: Everything is given on credit, and
the net is spread for all the living. The shop is open; and the dealer
gives credit; and the ledger lies open; and the hand writes; and
whosoever wishes to borrow may come and borrow; but the collectors regularly make their daily rounds, and exact payment from
man whether he is content or not; and they back up their demand
for payment; and the judgment is a judgment of truth; and everything is prepared for the feast.

COMMENTARY

In this *mishnah*, Rabbi Akiva employs the notion of buying on
credit as his metaphor of life. Life is a loan. Everything is given to
us on credit. The storekeeper is generous. He places no ceiling on
our credit-line. However, He keeps the ledger carefully. No entry is
omitted, we cannot escape our obligation to render payment. The
collectors are diligent and they have incontestable proof of their
claims against us. There is simply no getting away with it. The net
is spread wide—as it is written: *For also man too will not know his
appointed time, like fish trapped in an evil net. . . when it suddenly
falls on them (Ecclesiastes* 9:12). Characteristically, however, Rabbi

Akiva ends on a note of optimism. When all is said and done, and the accounting has been completed, all are invited to the feast—a portion in the world-to-come awaits each and every one of us.

APPLICATION

Many of us take life's blessings for granted, believing that they are ours of right. Because they are so freely given, they are not properly appreciated. Because of our perception of personal proprietary rights to these blessings, we often misuse them and abuse them.

The deceased received many real choice blessings from the Divine Storekeeper—good health, a wonderful wife/husband, lovely children, doting grandchildren, loyal friends, a caring community, and an honorable livelihood, a beautiful home, precious possessions. (The rabbi/study leader is to elaborate on these blessings where they are applicable, and others also.)

Unlike so many of us, though, the deceased did not take his/her blessings for granted. He/she understood that they were not absolute gifts, but that he/she might have to return them to their real Owner in the event of default on payment. He/she knew, indeed, how to appreciate, preserve, value, and protect his/her special precious treasures.

It can be said that parents are the covers of life's Ledger. Their children and their accomplishments are its pages. The covers hold the pages in place. When a cover is removed, however, the pages come apart more easily. This is an ofttimes tragic consequence of the passing of a parent.

The deceased valued the togetherness and closeness of the family above all else. Its continued cohesion even in the absence of its cover would be the ultimate blessing and the answer to the ultimate prayer of the deceased.

May the mourners make this wish come true—even as they continue to add pages to the ledger of this wonderful family, and may they all be comforted together with the other mourners in Zion and Jerusalem.

In Praise of a Retiree
Who Continued to Serve.
In Praise of
a Devoted Daughter.
In Praise of a Son-in-Law
or Daughter-in-Law.

APPLICATIONS: A RETIREE WHO DID COMMUNITY SERVICE; A DEVOTED DAUGHTER, SON-IN-LAW, OR DAUGHTER-IN-LAW

MISHNAH: *Terumot* 11:10

מַדְלִיקִין שֶׁמֶן שְׂרֵפָה בְּבָתֵּי כְנֵסִיּוֹת, וּבְבָתֵּי מִדְרָשׁוֹת, וּבַמְּבוֹאוֹת הָאֲפֵלִין, וְעַל גַּבֵּי הַחוֹלִין בִּרְשׁוּת כֹּהֵן. בַּת יִשְׂרָאֵל שֶׁנִּשֵּׂאת לַכֹּהֵן, וְהִיא לְמוּדָה אֵצֶל אָבִיהָ, אָבִיהָ מַדְלִיק בִּרְשׁוּתָהּ. מַדְלִיקִין בְּבֵית הַמִּשְׁתֶּה, אֲבָל לֹא בְּבֵית הָאֵבֶל, דִּבְרֵי רַבִּי יְהוּדָה. וְרַבִּי יוֹסֵי אוֹמֵר בְּבֵית הָאֵבֶל, אֲבָל לֹא בְּבֵית הַמִּשְׁתֶּה. רַבִּי מֵאִיר אוֹסֵר כָּאן וְכָאן. רַבִּי שִׁמְעוֹן מַתִּיר כָּאן וְכָאן:

TRANSLATION

The oil of [heave offerings which has become defiled and must be] burned, may be kindled in synagogues, houses of study, dark alleys, and in the presence of the sick—if the priest (*kohen*) gives permission. [In the case of] the daughter of an Israelite who was married to a *kohen,* her father may kindle [such oil] with her permission, if she is accustomed to visit him regularly. According to Rabbi Judah, [such oil] may be kindled at a festive gathering, but not in a house of mourning. But Rabbi Yossi declares that [such oil may be kindled] in the house of mourning, but not at a festive gathering. Rabbi Meir forbids [its kindling] in either situation, and Rabbi Shim'on permits in both.

COMMENTARY

In ancient times, *kohanim* were entitled to a gift from the produce of the land, which the sages ruled should average two percent of the harvest. They were also entitled to a tithe of the tithe which was given to Levites. These priestly entitlements were known as heave offerings (*terumot*).

A heave offering which had become defiled had outlived its utility, and had to be destroyed. However, should it be put to public service, the sages permitted its use. Thus it could be kindled in synagogues, schools, and dark alleys. Its use for private purposes required the consent (and, according to some, the physical presence) of a *kohen* or his wife (who was also entitled to the heave offering).

The debate about its use at festive gatherings and in houses of mourning relates to its use in the absence of a *kohen*.

The view which precludes its use in a house of mourning is based upon the fear that the lamp might be removed to another place where a *kohen* was not present, since visitors at a *shiv'ah* house do not "dress up" and will not mind risking oil stains on their garments—which "dressed up" party-goers will avoid.

The view which precludes the use of heave-offering oil at festive gatherings is based upon the fear that the party-goers may forget themselves and carry the lamp to another place where there are no *kohanim*—oblivious of the possibility of soiling their garments with oil stains.

Rabbi Meir is fearful that the lamp will be removed both in the house of mourning and at the party—for the reasons given.

Rabbi Shim'on holds that the lamp will be removed in neither case—because of the solemnity of the house of mourning, and the fear of soiling party clothes at a celebration. The Halakhah came to follow the view of Rabbi Shim'on.

APPLICATIONS

A Retiree Who Continues to Serve

In a society where people are long-lived, retirees are often made to feel that they have outlived their usefulness. They are like the tainted heave-offering oil—considered to be burned out and useless. Some retirees refuse to accept this condition. Like the oil of the heave offering, they can become devoted to other noble and public purposes. They can bring light to synagogue, school, and the general population, the "man in the street." They can light up a house of mourning and brighten a *simchah* (joyful gathering).

(The rabbi/study leader should talk about the preretirement career of the deceased. He can then elaborate on his/her postretirement period of service—to the Jewish community, if applicable [synagogues, schools, organizations, projects], the general community [lighting the way in dark streets], and the weak and weary [the sick, the mourners]. His/her zest for life, celebration and joy in family celebrations should be described.)

A Devoted Daughter

The rabbi/study leader should indicate that only a *kohen* or his wife could benefit from the heave-offering oil. This would include the daughter of an Israelite who was married to a *kohen*, but not her Israelite father. In extraordinary circumstances, however, even the Israelite father could be granted the special privilege of the use of the heave-offering oil. If his daughter visited him regularly, and cared for him, her light would become his light.

(The rabbi/study leader should tell of the devotion of the daughter, describe how she brought light to her parents' home and enabled them to brighten their lives.)

It is not by mere chance that the law of the devoted daughter is included in a *mishnah* which deals with other unusual uses of the sacred oil. (This daughter, the rabbi/study leader can point out, brought light not only to her parents' home, but to the Jewish and general communities, to the weak and the vulnerable, as illustrated in the first part of the application of this *mishnah*. He can also describe her zest for life and her joy in family celebrations.)

A Son-in-Law or Daughter-in-Law

The rabbi/study leader should indicate that only a *kohen* or his wife could derive benefit from the heave-offering oil. This would include the daughter of an Israelite who was married to a *kohen* but not an Israelite father. In extraordinary circumstances, however, even the Israelite father could be granted the special privilege of the use of the heave-offering oil. If his daughter regularly visited him and cared for him, her husband's light would become his light. This is a clear case of a father-in-law deriving benefit from his relationship with his son-in-law. (The rabbi/study leader should describe the special relationship between the parents-in-law and the son-in-law. He should point out how the son-in-law not only enabled his wife to continue to serve her parents with love and devotion, but how he made it possible for her to do so. The rabbi/study leader may use this text as a springboard for speaking about a devoted daughter-in-law. He can point out how the *mishnah* highlights the role of "children-in-law" for their parents-in-law, and generalize from son-in-law to daughter-in-law.

He should then go on to point out that it is by no means accidental that the law of the devoted "child-in-law" is included in a *mishnah* which deals with other uses of the sacred oil. *This* son-in-law/daughter-in-law, the rabbi/study leader could point out, brought light not only to the home of his/her in-laws, but to the Jewish and general community, to the weak and vulnerable. He can point out how he/she comforted the mourners and took joy in family celebrations—as above.)

The Jewish Mother

APPLICATION: A DEVOTED MOTHER

MISHNAYOT: *Avot* 2:10–16

חֲמִשָּׁה תַלְמִידִים הָיוּ לוֹ לְרַבָּן יוֹחָנָן בֶּן זַכַּאי וְאֵלּוּ הֵן רַבִּי אֱלִיעֶזֶר בֶּן הוֹרְקָנוֹס רַבִּי יְהוֹשֻׁעַ בֶּן חֲנַנְיָא רַבִּי יוֹסֵי הַכֹּהֵן רַבִּי שִׁמְעוֹן בֶּן נְתַנְאֵל וְרַבִּי אֶלְעָזָר בֶּן עֲרָךְ. הוּא הָיָה מוֹנֶה שְׁבָחָם רַבִּי אֱלִיעֶזֶר בֶּן הוֹרְקָנוֹס בּוֹר סוּד שֶׁאֵינוֹ מְאַבֵּד טִפָּה רַבִּי יְהוֹשֻׁעַ בֶּן חֲנַנְיָא אַשְׁרֵי יוֹלַדְתּוֹ רַבִּי יוֹסֵי הַכֹּהֵן חָסִיד רַבִּי שִׁמְעוֹן בֶּן נְתַנְאֵל יְרֵא חֵטְא רַבִּי אֶלְעָזָר בֶּן עֲרָךְ כְּמַעְיָן הַמִּתְגַּבֵּר. . . . אָמַר לָהֶם צְאוּ וּרְאוּ אֵיזוֹ הִיא דֶרֶךְ טוֹבָה שֶׁיִּדְבַּק בָּהּ הָאָדָם. רַבִּי אֱלִיעֶזֶר אוֹמֵר עַיִן טוֹבָה רַבִּי יְהוֹשֻׁעַ אוֹמֵר חָבֵר טוֹב. . . . אָמַר לָהֶם צְאוּ וּרְאוּ אֵיזוֹ הִיא דֶרֶךְ רָעָה שֶׁיִּתְרַחֵק מִמֶּנָּה הָאָדָם. רַבִּי אֱלִיעֶזֶר אוֹמֵר עַיִן רָעָה. . . . הֵם אָמְרוּ שְׁלֹשָׁה דְבָרִים. . . . רַבִּי יְהוֹשֻׁעַ אוֹמֵר, עַיִן הָרָע, וְיֵצֶר הָרָע, וְשִׂנְאַת הַבְּרִיּוֹת, מוֹצִיאִים אֶת־הָאָדָם מִן־הָעוֹלָם:

TRANSLATION

Rabban Yochanan ben Zakkai had five disciples, and these are they: Rabbi Eliezer ben Hyrcanus, Rabbi Yehoshua ben Chananya, Rabbi Yossi the Priest, Rabbi Shimon ben Nataniel, and Rabbi Elazar ben Arakh. He used to recount their praise: Eliezer ben Hyrcanus is [like] a cemented cistern which loses not a drop [of what he has studied]; Rabbi Yehoshua ben Chananya—happy is she that gave birth to him; Rabbi Yossi ha-Kohen is a pious man; Rabbi Shim'on ben Nataniel is a fearer of sin; Rabbi Elazar ben Arakh is like a spring flowing with ever-sustained vigor. . . . He said to them: Go forth and see which is the good way to which a man should attach himself. Rabbi Eliezer said: A good eye; Rabbi Yehoshua said: A good friend. . . . He said to them: Go forth and see which is the evil way that a man should shun. Rabbi Eliezer said: An evil eye; Rabbi Yehoshua said: An evil companion. . . . They each said three things. . . . Rabbi Yehoshua said: The evil eye, the evil inclination, and hatred of his fellow men put a man out of the world.

318

COMMENTARY

Rabban Yochanan ben Zakkai's description of the special virtue of Rabbi Yehoshua is strikingly different from his description of the special virtues of his four other most outstanding disciples. In their case, a special attribute of the disciple is singled out for praise. In the case of Rabbi Yehoshua, his personal attributes are ignored and his mother is singled out for praise.

Some of the classical commentators on the Mishnah have suggested that Rabbi Yehoshua was so graced with extraordinarily lofty virtues that his behavior reflected gloriously upon his mother, who could bask in his reflected glory. The Jerusalem Talmud, however, rejects this explanation, holding not that Rabbi Yehoshua's mother *benefited* from her son's glory, but that her son's glory was the *result* of her influence and her efforts. The talmudic sages point out that she conditioned him to Torah study and to Torah values from his earliest infancy, taking his baby carriage to the study-hall in order to accustom his ears to the sweet sounds of the dialogue of Torah study. The Jerusalem Talmud suggests, in short, that whatever her famous son became was owing to his extraordinary mother, and that his values were simply a reflection of her's.

What were these values? Our *mishnayot* emphasize five.

The Importance of Suitable Companionship

A companion is not identical with a neighbor. A *chaver* ("companion") is literally the person to whom one becomes *mechubar* ("attached"), the extension of oneself, one's alter ego, a sounding board for one's ideas, and a source of one's intellectual growth. Clearly, Rabbi Yeshoshua's mother understood the importance of a good *chaver* and carefully chose the people with whom her son should become closely associated.

The Dangers of Corrupting Companionship

Because the influence of a *chaver* can be positive or negative, depending upon his character, Rabbi Yehoshua's mother not only actively selected positive role-models for her son, but filtered negative role-models from his life. Her role in her son's social life was thus simultaneously affirming and negating, since both attitudes are demanded in creating an optimal spiritual milieu.

The Dangers of a Begrudging Nature

Rabbi Yehoshua's mother taught her son the value of generosity, conveying to him the importance of rejoicing at the successes, attainments, and possessions of others, and warning him that to begrudge others the fruits of their labors would cause the fabric of society to unravel.

The Dangers of the Inclination to Evil

Rabbi Yehoshua's mother understood that begrudging others their attainments and possessions would lead to envy, to the temptation to deprive them of these possessions and attainments. This attitude, in turn, would ultimately result in—

The Evil of the Hatred of One's Fellow Man

Resentment and envy often lead to hatred. This is the death knell of a harmonious society.

APPLICATION

The bereaved are/is people/a person of significant accomplishment. He/she/they are beloved by his/her/their fellow human beings because he/she/they love their fellow human beings. As in the case of Rabbi Yehoshua, this is a reflection of the influence of the wonderful Jewish mother for whom we mourn at this time. (The rabbi/study leader should dwell upon the loving and beloved nature of the deceased.)

The bereaved is/are dedicated to helping fellow human beings by planning for their welfare rather than their undoing. As in Rabbi Yehoshua's case, this, too, reflects the attributes of the mother for whom we mourn. (The rabbi/study leader should give examples of the dedication of the deceased to her fellow human beings.)

The bereaved is/are of generous disposition. He/she/they does/do not begrudge anybody his possessions or accomplishments. In this respect, too, he/she/they reflects/reflect the value system of his/her/their mother, who was without an envious bone in her entire body.

The bereaved is/are what he/she/they have become because of the environment created by the mother whom we mourn today, because of the schools, the organizations, and close friends she chose for them. (The rabbi/study leader may well describe the educational and social institutions which the bereaved selected for her children, and the sacrifices these entailed for her.)

Like Rabbi Yehoshua, the bereaved have/has achieved enviable reputations. Like Rabbi Yehoshua, too, the bereaved are/is what they/he/she are/is today because of the influence of a wonderful Jewish mother of yesterday.

We can truly say with Rabban Yochanan ben Zakkai: Happy is she who gave birth to him/her/them. She is reflected in his/her/their virtues. She is immortalized in his/her/their lives. She continues to be a source of blessing through the blessings he/she/they bestowed.

May her memory always be a source of blessing and inspiration.

On the Loss of a Husband

MISHNAH: *Kiddushin* 3:6 (a)

הָאוֹמֵר לְאִשָּׁה הֲרֵי־אַתְּ מְקֻדֶּשֶׁת לִי עַל־מְנָת שֶׁאֲדַבֵּר עָלַיִךְ לַשִּׁלְטוֹן וְאֶעֱשֶׂה עִמָּךְ
כְּפוֹעֵל, דִּבֶּר עָלֶיהָ לַשִּׁלְטוֹן וְעָשָׂה עִמָּהּ כַּפּוֹעֵל, מְקֻדֶּשֶׁת, וְאִם לָאו, אֵינָהּ מְקֻדֶּשֶׁת.

TRANSLATION

If one says to a woman: "Behold, you are betrothed unto me on condition that I intervene on your behalf with the government," or "on condition that I shall serve you as a laborer," once he has intervened with the government on her behalf or served her as a laborer, she is betrothed unto him.

COMMENTARY

The talmudic exposition of this passage makes it clear that the betrothal is effected with a *perutah* (coin)—a gift of indisputable value. This is usually a sufficient method of betrothal. The additional conditions are not essential to the normal process of betrothal. Notwithstanding, should they be added to the gift of the *perutah*, the nonfulfillment of the additional conditions invalidates the entire betrothal.

APPLICATION

There are various types of marriage relationships. Some are merely formal, with a husband doing nothing more for his wife than is minimally required by Jewish law. Others go far beyond these minimal requirements. A husband becomes his wife's protector and sponsor, intervening for her protection and for the advancement of her interests and career, rendering himself vulnerable to rebuff from those who exercise power, in the hope that she will be helped. Often the husband will serve his wife hand and foot, providing for her needs as would a common laborer. He will consider no task too demeaning. Her every wish will be his command. And she will become so accustomed to his doing everything for her that she will consider such loving, lavish attention as a normal condition of the marital relationship.

This was certainly the case in this instance. (The rabbi/study leader should elaborate on the giving personality of the deceased and of his efforts, above and beyond the norm, on her behalf. He should illustrate this life of service and devotion with examples provided by family and friends.)

Of course, the marital covenant is not one-sided. As he loved her, so she loved him; as he cared for her, so she cared for him. They became an extension each of the other, a single caring, indivisible organism.

And now the organism is cut asunder. A part of her has been buried, and she feels abandoned and alone. Fortunately, she has a loving family and devoted friends to help her learn to cope with her loss and with her life. Fortunately, too, she has a caring community which will not abandon her in her time of need. Most of all, she has an endless store of precious memories of an extraordinary relationship to fortify her in her crisis and in the future.

The memory of his lifelong dedication is an abiding inspiration to all who knew him. It is surely a comfort to her whom he loved so much and who loved him so deeply in return.

The Loss of Little Children/
The Value of Human Life

APPLICATION: PARENTS BEREAVED OF CHILDREN; GENERAL

MISHNAH: *Ta'anit* 3:6

מַעֲשֶׂה שֶׁיָּרְדוּ זְקֵנִים מִירוּשָׁלַיִם לְעָרֵיהֶם, וְגָזְרוּ תַעֲנִית עַל שֶׁנִּרְאָה כִּמְלֹא פִי תַנּוּר שֶׁל דֶּפוֹן בְּאַשְׁקְלוֹן. וְעוֹד גָּזְרוּ תַעֲנִית עַל שֶׁאָכְלוּ זְאֵבִים שְׁנֵי תִינוֹקוֹת בְּעֵבֶר הַיַּרְדֵּן. רַבִּי יוֹסֵי אוֹמֵר, לֹא עַל שֶׁאָכְלוּ אֶלָּא עַל שֶׁנִּרְאָה:

TRANSLATION

The sages once went down from Jerusalem to their own towns and declared a public fast because blight the size of a loaf of bread whose dimensions might fill an oven's mouth was seen in [the produce of] Ashkelon. They also decreed a public fast because wolves had consumed two children beyond the Jordan. Rabbi Yossi said: Not because they consumed [the children], but because they were seen.

COMMENTARY

A public fast was declared in response to a public calamity, such as drought, flood, pestilence, disease, or invasion by foreign troops. Our *mishnah* is unusual in that the calamity was limited. Ashkelon was on the borders of the Holy Land, almost peripheral to it, and the blight was of rather limited extent. Transjordan was sparsely populated, not fully pacified, and a region of wild animals. Why, then, was a fast decreed for a minor outbreak of blight in a border town and for the loss of two children in "the wilds"—or, according

324

to Rabbi Yossi, for the mere sighting of wolves in untamed territory, far from the major areas of settlement?

The lesson of our sages is clear: human life is so valuable that a relatively minor loss of life is a public calamity. Indeed, even a potential loss of life—as signaled by the appearance of blight in Ashkelon or a wolf beyond the Jordan—is a public calamity.

APPLICATIONS

Parents Bereaved of a Child

There is surely no loss greater than the death of a child. The loss of an elderly parent is traumatic, but follows the natural order of things. The loss of a child is devastating. His/her parents mourn not only for the precious life of which they have been deprived, but also for the unspeakable potential which was not yet realized. (The rabbi/study leader should describe this potential, based upon the special characteristics manifested by the child in his/her all-too-brief existence.)

The authors of our *mishnah* offer some comfort to grieving parents. They assure them that the loss of children is not a private tragedy. It is shared by the entire community. It is considered to be a public catastrophe. We are all involved. We are all bereaved. The grieving parents must know that we walk with them as they travel through the valley of the shadow of death, and that we shall do everything within our power to help them.

In General

Our *mishnah* emphasizes the infinite value of *all* life. The population of a border town braces itself for trouble, and we all share the pain. Children in a faraway place are in jeopardy, and we all recoil in horror. Jewish losses are not private. They are felt throughout the community.

This is particularly true in this instance. The entire community is impoverished by the loss of the deceased.

(The rabbi/study leader should elaborate on the record of service and of the special contributions of the deceased to the community, and then spell out the public loss.

The rabbi/study leader should call upon members of the family to take the place of their departed loved ones and upon members of the community to emulate the departed by filling the void created by their passing.)

In Praise of a Deceased *Kohen* and His Family

APPLICATION: *KOHEN*; FAMILY WHO CARED
PERSONALLY FOR THE AGED

MISHNAH: *Terumot* 11:5

גַּרְעִינֵי תְרוּמָה, בִּזְמַן שֶׁהוּא מְכַנְּסָן, אֲסוּרוֹת. וְאִם הִשְׁלִיכָן, מֻתָּרוֹת. וְכֵן עַצְמוֹת
הַקֳּדָשִׁים, בִּזְמַן שֶׁהוּא מְכַנְּסָן, אֲסוּרִין. וְאִם הִשְׁלִיכָן, מֻתָּרִין. הַמֻּרְסָן מֻתָּר. סֻבִּין שֶׁל
חֲדָשׁוֹת אֲסוּרוֹת. וְשֶׁל יְשָׁנוֹת מֻתָּרוֹת. וְנוֹהֵג בַּתְּרוּמָה כְּדֶרֶךְ שֶׁהוּא נוֹהֵג בַּחֻלִּין. הַמְסַלֵּת
קַב אוֹ קַבַּיִם לִסְאָה, לֹא יְאַבֵּד אֶת הַשְּׁאָר, אֶלָּא יַנִּיחֵנּוּ בְּמָקוֹם הַמֻּצְנָע:

TRANSLATION

The kernels of the fruit of heave offerings are forbidden [to non-priests (non-*kohanim*)] if the priest (*kohen*) collects them. They are permitted to non-*kohanim* if [the *kohen*] casts them away. Similarly, the bones of sacrificial animals are forbidden to non-*kohanim* if the *kohen* collects them. They are permitted to non-*kohanim* if the *kohen* casts them away. Coarse bran [derived from heave offerings] is permitted [to non-*kohanim*]. The fine bran of very fresh [heave offering] produce is forbidden [to non-*kohanim*], but the fine bran of old produce is permitted. [The *kohen*] treats the heave offering as he does unconsecrated products . . .

COMMENTARY

Jewish males are divided into three categories. *Kohanim* [priests] are the descendants of Aaron, the brother of Moses. They have some privileges and many obligations and limitations. *Levi'im* [Levites] are descendants of the tribe of Levi. Nowadays, they have very few privileges and obligations. All other Jewish males are Israelites.

In ancient times, *kohanim* were entitled to a gift from the produce of the land, which the sages ruled should average two percent of the harvest. This was the heave offering (*terumah*). This offering was made by Israelites. Levites were entitled to a tithe (ten percent) of the produce, from which they gave *kohanim* a tithe as *their* heave offering. *Kohanim* were also entitled to eat some of the meat of most sacrificial animals.

Our *mishnah* establishes the rule that what some may consider to be edible, such as fruit kernels to which some fruit is attached, or bones not entirely stripped of meat, may be discarded by the *kohen* if he would discard similar unconsecrated products (*chullin*). His discarding of them removes their sanctity, and permits their use by non-*kohanim*. Coarse bran, bones, and kernels come under this rubric. The fine bran of fresh produce is forbidden to non-*kohanim* because it cannot be easily separated from the flour of the heave offering, which the *kohen* would clearly *not* discard.

APPLICATION

In Praise of a Deceased *Kohen*

Our *mishnah* states that a *kohen* treats consecrated objects as he does unconsecrated objects. Although the context of this rule is strictly technical, its symbolic application is marvelously moral. Some people treat only special classes of individuals with respect. They show deference to those they consider important, but ignore or show contempt to others. They pander to the rich, the powerful, the successful, and the prestigious. But they pay scant attention to the dependent, the humble, the poor, and the unsuccessful. The deceased was a *kohen* in the noblest, loftiest, classical sense. He made no distinction between *kodashim* (the consecrated) and *chullin* (unconsecrated). (The rabbi/study leader should elaborate on his concerned, sensitive, loving attitude to both "beautiful" and "ordinary" people.)

In Praise of His Loving Family

Our *mishnah* makes the point that *kohanim* may legitimately discard items of former value which have lost their usefulness. The pit of the fruit was its very kernel. Stripped of its nourishing quality, it may simply be cast aside. Bones are the foundation of the body. Stripped of the flesh, they too may be discarded. On the other hand, a *kohen* may hold onto these items, and as long as he does so, they retain their sanctity.

In an age of increasing longevity, old people, no longer useful to society, are ignored, neglected, warehoused, or discarded like old bones. They are too much bother to visit, to tend to, to talk to, to take out, to give a warm home to. (The rabbi/study leader should detail the loving care lavished on the deceased by his/her children and contrast this with the prevailing norm.)

A Premature Loss

APPLICATION: A PREMATURE LOSS

MISHNAH: *Avot* 2:15

רַבִּי טַרְפוֹן אוֹמֵר, הַיּוֹם קָצָר וְהַמְּלָאכָה מְרֻבָּה, וְהַפּוֹעֲלִים עֲצֵלִים, וְהַשָּׂכָר הַרְבֵּה, וּבַעַל
הַבַּיִת דּוֹחֵק:

הוּא הָיָה אוֹמֵר, לֹא עָלֶיךָ הַמְּלָאכָה לִגְמֹר, וְלֹא אַתָּה בֶּן חוֹרִין לִבָּטֵל מִמֶּנָּה. אִם לָמַדְתָּ
תּוֹרָה הַרְבֵּה, נוֹתְנִים לְךָ שָׂכָר הַרְבֵּה. וְנֶאֱמָן הוּא בַּעַל מְלַאכְתְּךָ שֶׁיְשַׁלֶּם־לְךָ שְׂכַר־
פְּעֻלָּתֶךָ. וְדַע, מַתַּן שְׂכָרָן שֶׁל צַדִּיקִים לֶעָתִיד לָבוֹא:

TRANSLATION

Rabbi Tarfon said: The day is short, and the work is great, and the
laborers are sluggish, and the reward is abundant, and the Master
of the house is urgent. He also used to say: It is not your duty to
complete the work, but neither are you free to desist from it. . . .
And faithful is your Employer to pay you the reward of your labor;
and know that the grant of reward unto the righteous will be in the
time to come.

COMMENTARY

This *mishnah* is a marvelous parable of life's challenges and frus-
trations. It suggests that life's abundant tasks are never completed,
notwithstanding the reward we can expect for their successful
accomplishment, despite the urging of our Maker. We are simply
too sluggish. However, Rabbi Tarfon offers a comforting thought.
We cannot really ever expect to complete all our projects. They are
too numerous, and life is necessarily too short. What matters, finally, is that we did not give up, that we did our very best. In the last
analysis, the reward is for our effort.

330

APPLICATION

We are met today to mourn the loss of a young life. Its potential unrealized, its promise unfulfilled, its dreams not translated into reality, its visions not yet all transformed into accomplishments, its hopes crushed, its beauty brought down, its blessings abbreviated, its years truncated.

What words of comfort can we offer? Is there balm enough in Gilead to soothe the wounds of his/her shattered, battered, grieving loved ones, still numb with shock, still paralyzed with grief, still immobilized by incomprehension?

May I tell you a story told to me by my teacher, guide, and mentor, the former Chief Rabbi of South Africa, the late Professor Louis I. Rabinowitz? His younger colleague, Rabbi Koppel Rosen, was unexpectedly informed that he was suffering from leukemia. Rabbi Rosen was shattered by the news. At a relatively young age he had achieved international recognition. He was the head of the most successful Jewish school in England. It was confidently predicted that his pedagogic ability and his oratorical powers would propel him into even greater prominence. Some even suggested that he would become the next Chief Rabbi of the British Commonwealth.

Rabbi Rosen was, initially, almost inconsolable at his condition. On the advice of friends, he journeyed to New York to consult with a charismatic rabbinic leader. When he returned to England, Rabbi Rabinowitz noticed a complete transformation. "What happened?" he asked his younger colleague. "Are you in remission?" Rabbi Rosen answered that the course of his illness had not been altered, that, on the contrary, it had become more serious. "Why, then," asked Rabbi Rabinowitz, "is your attitude so very different now, so much more positive than before?"

Rabbi Rosen's reply is worth recording. He said: "A life consists of quality and of quantity. The quality of our lives depends upon us. The quantity depends upon our Creator. I have done my part to the best of my ability. I know that He will do His in accordance with His infinite wisdom."

The quantity of the life for which we mourn was far too small. That, however, was God's ineffable decision. The quality, however, was unspeakably great. In so short a time, so very much was accomplished. So many people were touched. So many friends were made. So many wonderful deeds were performed. So much kindness was demonstrated. So much sensitivity was shown. (Rabbi/ study leader should provide details.)

It is sad that the labors of this brief life were unrewarded. It is comforting that Rabbi Tarfon assures us that the reward will be granted in the world-to-come, the realm beyond the grave.

At times such as this, we naturally dwell upon our loss. We fixate upon what it is that God has taken away. Perhaps like Job, we shall learn to declare, "The Lord has given, the Lord has also taken away. May the name of the Lord be praised." In remembering the treasure that God gave us, there is, perhaps, after all, balm to soothe our wounds.

May his/her pure soul be bound up in the bond of eternal life, and may the bereaved be comforted with all the other mourners in Zion and Jerusalem.

Accepting the Bad
with the Good

APPLICATION: GENERAL; ALSO IN THE CASE OF A
PERSON WHO HAS SUCCUMBED AFTER SERIOUS,
PROLONGED ILLNESS

MISHNAH: *Berakhot* 9:5

חַיָּב אָדָם לְבָרֵךְ עַל־הָרָעָה כְּשֵׁם שֶׁהוּא מְבָרֵךְ עַל־הַטּוֹבָה, שֶׁנֶּאֱמַר „וְאָהַבְתָּ אֵת יְיָ
אֱלֹהֶיךָ בְּכָל־לְבָבְךָ וּבְכָל־נַפְשְׁךָ וּבְכָל־מְאֹדֶךָ". „בְּכָל־לְבָבְךָ" — בִּשְׁנֵי יְצָרֶיךָ, בְּיֵצֶר טוֹב
וּבְיֵצֶר רָע. „וּבְכָל־נַפְשְׁךָ" — אֲפִלּוּ הוּא נוֹטֵל אֶת נַפְשֶׁךָ. „וּבְכָל־מְאֹדֶךָ" — בְּכָל־
מָמוֹנֶךָ. דָּבָר אַחֵר: „בְּכָל־מְאֹדֶךָ" — בְּכָל־מִדָּה וּמִדָּה שֶׁהוּא מוֹדֵד לְךָ, הֱוֵי מוֹדֶה לוֹ
בִּמְאֹד מְאֹד.

TRANSLATION

A person should bless [God] for that which is bad, just as he blesses
[God] for that which is good, as it is said: *And you shall love the
Lord your God with all your heart and with all your soul and with
all your might* (Deuteronomy 6:5). *With all your heart*—with both
inclinations, the inclination to good and the inclination to evil. *And
with all your soul*—even if He takes your soul. *And with all your
might*—with all your wealth or, alternatively, *and with all your
might* for whatever measure [God] metes out to you, offer abundant
thanks.

COMMENTARY

When one suffers a serious setback, such as the loss of a loved one,
one should recite the blessing: "Blessed are You, O Lord our God,
the true Judge," just as we respond to happy circumstances with a
blessing: "Blessed are You, O Lord our God, who is good and does

good." Good and bad are only such from the limited human perspective. From the divine perspective, the darkest cloud has a silver lining. Blessing is most strikingly concealed by death. But what appears to be bad today will, in the course of time, be seen in a brighter, more positive light. The *mishnah* illustrates this insight with a scriptural passage upon which it comments in detail, "And you shall love . . . with all your heart." The Hebrew word for "heart" is either *lev* or *levav*. *Levav* is a double form of the word *lev*. The use of this form suggests the simultaneous and contradictory inclinations of the heart—to good and to evil. The *mishnah* teaches that even purely visceral motivations can be sublimated and transformed. The sex urge, for example, can be sanctified by becoming the vehicle for the building of a committed, devoted, and loving family.

Nothing is more precious than life itself. We lament the loss of life. But when life is offered for a great cause, in an act of martyrdom, or in a war against tyranny, the negative aspect of the loss of life is transformed into a positive virtue. This is how we can love God "with all our soul"—*even if He takes it from us.*

We work hard for our wealth. It represents our independence and gives us dignity and status. In a real sense, it is "our might." For this reason, forced deprivation of our wealth is a great evil. However, when we donate our wealth to worthy causes, we transform this evil into an extraordinary act of goodness.

The *mishnah* offers a general interpretation of our response to good and evil by making a double play on the Hebrew word for "your might"—*me'odekha*. It resembles both the word *middah* ("measure") and *me'od* ("abundant"). Thus, "With all your *me'odekha*" can be made to mean: "For all and any *measures* that God metes out to you, be *abundantly* grateful." In short, when you see the silver lining behind the clouds, the good behind the bad, you can accept, and even come to terms with, the evil fact of death.

APPLICATION

In General

Death is perceived as the greatest of all evils (—for the obvious reasons which the rabbi/study leader can elaborate.) *This* death is a case in point for the grieving family (further elaboration.)

However, the pain can be eased by three considerations.

1. The rabbi/study leader should describe the ability of the deceased himself/herself to transform evil into good in the course of his/her life. The virtue of the deceased as a role-model should be elaborated.
2. The contribution of the "might" of the deceased should be discussed. This is an opportunity for the rabbi/study leader to speak about the charitable nature of the deceased.
3. The example of the deceased in appreciating life, notwithstanding its difficulties and its setbacks, should be elaborated on and discussed.

Remembering the quality of the life of the deceased transforms and relieves the agony of his/her death.

Death Following Debilitating Illness

Mourning is often a selfish act of self-pity. We perceive death as an evil because we bemoan our loss. Our agony would be eased if only we would contemplate death from the point of view of the deceased. (The rabbi/study leader should discuss the illness, pain, and suffering of the deceased, and point out that he/she is now at peace, without pain, in the company of departed loved ones. He should show that what is an evil for the grieving family is a blessing for the deceased, and ask the family to attempt to give thanks for that blessing. The ability to do so is the ultimate act of loving concern and altruistic, selfless devotion.)

Community Leadership

APPLICATION: COMMUNITY LEADERS

MISHNAH: *Avot* 2:2

רַבָּן גַּמְלִיאֵל בְּנוֹ שֶׁל רַבִּי יְהוּדָה הַנָּשִׂיא אוֹמֵר, וְכָל־הָעֲמֵלִים עִם הַצִּבּוּר, יִהְיוּ עֲמֵלִים
עִמָּהֶם לְשֵׁם שָׁמַיִם, שֶׁזְּכוּת אֲבוֹתָם מְסַיַּעְתָּן וְצִדְקָתָם עוֹמֶדֶת לָעַד. וְאַתֶּם, מַעֲלֶה אֲנִי
עֲלֵיכֶם שָׂכָר הַרְבֵּה כְּאִלּוּ עֲשִׂיתֶם:

TRANSLATION

[Rabban Gamliel, the son of Rabbi Judah the Prince, declared:] Let all who preoccupy themselves with the community be pre-occupied with them for the sake of heaven, for then the merit of their fathers sustains them, and their righteousness endures forever. And as for you, [God will then say,] I account you worthy of great reward, as if you did it all yourselves.

COMMENTARY

In this dictum, Rabban Gamliel discusses the correct motivation for community involvement. Most people are motivated to strive for positions of leadership on account of their self-interest. They perceive, correctly, that such positions will bring them high visibility, honor, influence, and power. Rabban Gamliel rejects these motives as being unworthy. Involvement with and leadership of the Jewish community should be disinterested, completely altruistic.

On the basis of the well-known principle that "one who comes to perform an act in purity is granted special assistance" (B.T. *Shabbat* 104a), Rabban Gamliel assures the idealistic, selfless leader that he/she will be assisted by the merit of the fathers. It should be pointed out that the association of altruistic leadership of the community with the merit of the fathers is based upon the notion that "the community" is an abstract idea, and that, therefore, "the community does not die." In a real sense, then, the legendary leaders of generations and even centuries past still live on within "the community." Leadership of the community is thus the cooperative enterprise of the generations. It is in this sense that the righteous work of the leaders of this generation will stand future generations of leaders in good stead.

The final point which Rabban Gamliel makes is that great leaders are, ultimately, great motivators. They simply cannot do everything alone. The work must be done through those who are motivated by their leaders. Notwithstanding, the efforts of those they motivate are attributed to the leaders, thus benefiting both the recipients of the services they provide, the direct providers of these services, and the leaders who motivate the providers.

APPLICATION

The deceased was a gifted and devoted community leader. He/she served the community in many ways. (The rabbi/study leader should elaborate upon these various areas of service and of leadership.)

The deceased not only did good deeds in abundance, but also motivated others to follow suit. (The rabbi/study leader should speak about those who came to serve the community in consequence of the leadership of the deceased, and of his/her role in producing new cadres of leadership.)

It is impossible to be certain of a person's motives for becoming involved in the community and for accepting leadership responsibilities. The degree of self-sacrifice and self-denial which these roles impose is, perhaps, the only real barometer of sincerity. By these standards alone the deceased *must* be presumed to have offered a lifetime of service and leadership strictly "for the sake of heaven." The demands of office were costly rather than materially rewarding, and the psychic rewards were more than minimally offset by frustration.

Rabban Gamliel assures us that the righteous acts of the leader will endure forever, that he/she has long been in the sublime company of the immortals of our people. May his/her memory be a blessing and an inspiration.

Who Will Follow the Leader?

APPLICATION: THE PASSING OF A COMMUNITY LEADER

MISHNAH: *Menachot* 4:5

חֲבִתֵּי כֹהֵן גָּדוֹל, לֹא הָיוּ בָאוֹת חֲצָיִים, אֶלָּא מֵבִיא עִשָּׂרוֹן שָׁלֵם, וְחוֹצֵהוּ, וּמַקְרִיב מֶחֱצָה בַבֹּקֶר, וּמֶחֱצָה בֵּין הָעַרְבָּיִם. וְכֹהֵן שֶׁהִקְרִיב מֶחֱצָה בַּשַּׁחֲרִית וּמֵת וּמִנּוּ כֹהֵן אַחֵר תַּחְתָּיו, לֹא יָבִיא חֲצִי עִשָּׂרוֹן מִבֵּיתוֹ, וְלֹא חֲצִי עֶשְׂרוֹנוֹ שֶׁל רִאשׁוֹן, אֶלָּא מֵבִיא עִשָּׂרוֹן שָׁלֵם, וְחוֹצֵהוּ, וּמַקְרִיב מֶחֱצָה, וּמֶחֱצָה אָבֵד. נִמְצְאוּ שְׁנֵי חֲצָיִים קְרֵבִין, וּשְׁנֵי חֲצָיִים אוֹבְדִין. לֹא מִנּוּ כֹהֵן אַחֵר, מִשֶּׁל מִי הָיְתָה קְרֵבָה. רַבִּי שִׁמְעוֹן אוֹמֵר, מִשֶּׁל צִבּוּר. רַבִּי יְהוּדָה אוֹמֵר, מִשֶּׁל יוֹרְשִׁים. וּשְׁלֵמָה הָיְתָה קְרֵבָה:

HEBREW TEXT

TRANSLATION

The baked cakes of unleavened bread [which made up the daily meal offering] of the high priest, [half of which were brought in the morning, and half in the evening,] were not brought half [of a tenth of an *ephah*] at a time. Rather, a whole tenth of an *ephah* [of fine flour] was brought [in the morning]. [The high priest] would divide it [and knead from each half of the tenth of an *ephah* six unleavened loaves] and offer half [i.e., six loaves] in the morning, and half [i.e., six loaves] in the evening.

If the high priest offered half [of his daily meal offering] in the morning and then died, and they appointed another [high] priest in his place, the [successor] priest shall not bring half of a tenth [of an *ephah*] from his own home [for the evening meal offering] nor half of the half [of the *ephah* which had been prepared that morning by] the first [i.e., deceased high priest]. He should, instead, bring a whole tenth [of an *ephah*] and offer half of it [in the evening]. The other half would be destroyed. Accordingly, two halves would be offered and two halves would be destroyed.

If they did not appoint a successor high priest, whose [baked

338

cakes of unleavened bread] should be offered [as the high priest's meal offering]? Rabbi Shimon said: Those belonging to the community. Rabbi Yehudah said: Those belonging to his heirs. And a whole tenth [of an *ephah*—not a half] must be offered [both in the morning and in the evening].

COMMENTARY

Our *mishnah* is a functional exposition of the scriptural imperative: *This is the offering of Aaron and his sons . . . one tenth of an ephah of fine flour for a meal offering, perpetually, half of it in the morning, and half of it in the evening. It shall be made in a pan with oil. You shall offer it baked* (Leviticus 6:13–14). The *mishnah* explains that the cakes must be baked from fine flour *belonging* to the high priest, that an entire tenth part of an *ephah* (about four liters) of fine flour must be brought by the high priest in the morning, and then divided and baked into two lots of six loaves each, one lot to be offered by him as the morning meal offering and the second as the evening meal offering.

The second half of our *mishnah* deals with the responsibility for bringing the meal offering of the high priest in the event of his death following the morning offering. The principle is established that whoever is responsible must bring an entire tenth of an *ephah* of his own. If it is his successor high priest, he must utilize half of that tenth for the offering and destroy the other half. If no successor is appointed, either the community (according to Rabbi Shimon) or the heirs of the deceased high priest (according to Rabbi Yehudah) must bring the daily meal offering—in this case, a full tenth of an *ephah* both morning and evening.

APPLICATION

We are gathered here to mourn the loss of a community leader of distinction. (The rabbi/study leader should describe the leadership role and reputation of the deceased.)

Like the high priest of old, he/she brought a continual daily offering. (The rabbi/study leader should describe his/her special contributions.)

This offering was made from the bounty of his/her own talent and wealth. He/she was not the type of leader who claimed the privileges of office for him/herself and delegated the reponsibility to others. Nor was he/she the exponent of only a single cause. Like the high priest of old, the offering consisted of many loaves, and was well divided. (The rabbi/study leader should detail the causes which the deceased supported.)

Alas, the great leader is no more. He/she has been called away in the midst of the continual offering. No successor has been appointed, for, in a real sense, he/she is really irreplaceable. Who is to be responsible for the completion of his/her work? Two opinions are offered in our *mishnah*.

It is the opinion of Rabbi Shimon that the entire community is charged with the tasks. He/she represented and even personified the community. He/she took its load upon his/her shoulders. It is only proper that the community reclaim the collective responsibility. After all, what he/she did is beyond the ability of most other individuals. Only the community as a whole is capable of shouldering the enormous burden which he/she bore alone.

Rabbi Yehudah disagrees. The deceased was not childless. He/she did leave heirs. His/her children grew up in an environment of selfless devotion and unstinting service. They had the best role-models that were available. They were trained by the deceased. Surely they must be ready to assume the mantle and to accept the responsibility.

Significantly, the law was fixed according to Rabbi Yehudah. The Halakhah is that the heirs assume the responsibility. This is the extraordinary challenge which flows from the unusual privilege of having had so great a parent.

(The rabbi/study leader should now speak about the endowments of the heirs.)

If the children shoulder the burden, they will continue a wonderful tradition and they will grant the deceased tangible immortality in our community.

We pray that they *will* assume the mantle, grow into the role, and be worthy successors of their dearly beloved. Even as the memory of the deceased is an inspiration to them, it remains forever an inspiration to all those in the community who knew, loved, and respected him/her.

Torah and Worldly Occupation

APPLICATION: A BUSINESSMAN/PROFESSIONAL WHO CONTINUES TO STUDY TORAH

MISHNAH: *Avot* 2:2

רַבָּן גַּמְלִיאֵל בְּנוֹ שֶׁל רַבִּי יְהוּדָה הַנָּשִׂיא אוֹמֵר, יָפֶה תַלְמוּד תּוֹרָה עִם דֶּרֶךְ אֶרֶץ,
שֶׁיְּגִיעַת שְׁנֵיהֶם מְשַׁכַּחַת עָוֹן. וְכָל־תּוֹרָה שֶׁאֵין עִמָּהּ מְלָאכָה, סוֹפָהּ בְּטֵלָה וְגוֹרֶרֶת עָוֹן.

TRANSLATION

Rabban Gamliel, the son of Rabbi Judah the Prince, said: The study of the Torah combined with some worldly occupation is excellent, for the labor demanded by them both makes sin to be forgotten. All study of the Torah without work must, in the end, be futile and become the cause of sin.

COMMENTARY

This *mishnah* articulates the Jewish ideal that the study of Torah should be combined with the pursuit of a worldly occupation. Rabban Gamliel motivates this ideal by using the simple argument that full-time, permanent, exclusive devotion to the study of Torah will lead to idleness; and idleness, in turn, will lead to sin.

His dictum can be understood on a higher level also. A worldly occupation which is unconstrained by ethical principles is potentially corrupt and sinful. The moral principles which derive from the study of Torah should transform society. The student of Torah should not be isolated in an ivory tower. Torah should be removed from the tower and taken into the town, into the marketplace, into the factory, into the workplace, into the research laboratory, into the hospital, and into the office. Its principles should determine the conduct of our worldly occupations—which, in turn, should allow us "to sanctify the Name of God" by becoming living examples of commitment to His will.

APPLICATION

Unhappily, contemporary Jewish society is attracted to extremes. On the one hand, students of Torah who demonstrate special abilities are often encouraged to find personal spiritual fulfillment by becoming permanent, full-time students, without having to make a commitment to share their knowledge with others after a defined period of study. On the other hand, many *yeshiva* graduates abandon their regular study of the Torah when they are sucked into the vortex of a competitive society. They simply begrudge themselves the time for regular, routine study of the Torah—either because they are too preoccupied with the pressures of their livelihood, or because they are simply too exhausted at the end of a day's work to turn their attention to the Torah. Their preoccupation with making a living leads them to forget how to live meaningfully.

Fortunately, the deceased was an exception to these rules. He/she graduated from *yeshiva,* but remained committed to the regular study of Torah. His/hers was a synthesizing personality, which integrated the world of Torah into the secular world in which we all live.

(The rabbi/study leader should describe the Torah background of the deceased, his/her worldly occupation, and show how he/she synthesized Torah with his/her worldly occupation.)

As Rabban Gamliel foretold, the deceased's combination of Torah with his/her occupation *did* keep him/her far from sin. In reward of his/her commitment and righteousness, we pray that his/her soul will be bound up in the bond of eternal life. We pray, also, that he/she will be a role-model for others to follow.

A Conduit of Tradition

APPLICATION: RABBI, TEACHER

MISHNAH: *Avot* 1:1

מֹשֶׁה קִבֵּל תּוֹרָה מִסִּינַי, וּמְסָרָהּ לִיהוֹשֻׁעַ, וִיהוֹשֻׁעַ לִזְקֵנִים, וּזְקֵנִים לִנְבִיאִים, וּנְבִיאִים מְסָרוּהָ לְאַנְשֵׁי כְנֶסֶת הַגְּדוֹלָה. הֵם אָמְרוּ שְׁלֹשָׁה דְבָרִים, הֱווּ מְתוּנִים בַּדִּין, וְהַעֲמִידוּ תַלְמִידִים הַרְבֵּה, וַעֲשׂוּ סְיָג לַתּוֹרָה:

TRANSLATION

Moses received the Torah from Sinai. He passed it on to Joshua, Joshua to the Elders, the Elders to the Prophets, and the Prophets passed it on to the men of the Great Assembly. The men of the Great Assembly established three principles: be deliberate in judgment; raise up many disciples; make a fence around the Torah.

COMMENTARY

The first *mishnah* of Tractate *Avot* refers to the transmission of the Oral Tradition which was revealed to Moses simultaneously with the Written Torah. This Oral Tradition renders the Written Torah intelligible. It is enlarged and developed by succeeding generations of scholars. The work of the men of the Great Assembly was crucial to its development and popularization.

The Great Assembly was active for just over one hundred years (ca. 444–333 B.C.E.). It was a watershed period in Jewish history. The years following the return from the Babylonian exile and the rebuilding of the Temple witnessed the unraveling of the social and religious fabric of Jewish society in the Holy land.

The Great Assembly was called into session by Ezra the Scribe in order to reverse this process by establishing the Torah as the *de facto* constitution of the Jewish people. The attainment of this goal was based upon the threefold strategy of our *mishnah*.

343

Deliberation in Judgment

The law of the Torah was in competition with the legal system of Persia. Litigants could opt for judgment under either system. If the law of the Torah was to become the legal system of choice, the judges who rendered opinions according to its precepts would have to win the confidence of the populace by their fairness and wisdom in applying Torah to contemporary litigation.

Democratization of Torah

If the Torah were to become the foundation of society, it would have to win the adherence of the masses, because knowledge of the Torah leads to the love of Torah and loyalty to its precepts. A far-flung network of schools and academies would have to be established, in which the masses would study its law and lore, and become conditioned to its observance.

Preservation of its Imperatives

To ensure that the precepts of Torah were not undermined, a defensive strategy was devised. The precepts of the Torah were surrounded by a perimeter of rabbinic decrees, a "fence" devised by the sages. Thus, for example, writing on the Sabbath is forbidden by the Torah. By going further, and decreeing that even touching the writing instrument is forbidden, the sages created an effective fence around the Torah. If one could not handle a pen on the Sabbath, it is unlikely that one would actually come to write on the holy day.

APPLICATION

Like the men of the Great Assembly, the deceased worked during a watershed period of Jewish history—after the Holocaust and the establishment of the State of Israel. Like them, he functioned at a time when competing values vied for Jewish loyalty—hedonism, secularism, and the proliferation of cults.

The Tradition which had come down to his generation from Sinai was in danger of being abandoned. Like the men of the Great

Assembly, he devoted a lifetime to its preservation, renascence, and dissemination. The strategies he adopted were those of our *mishnah.*

He won adherence by personal example. As the personification of the Torah, he taught generations of admirers how its wisdom and fairness could illuminate contemporary problems, not taking second place to any alternative system and worldview. (Rabbi/ study leader should elaborate in some detail.)

He was primarily a teacher. He taught Torah on many levels, and raised up disciples in abundance, a significant number of whom were introduced to, and captivated by, Torah study through his patient insistence and pedagogic skills. (Rabbi/study leader to supply details.)

He was a leader of great personal integrity and courage. He did not flinch at making decrees whose purpose was the preservation of Tradition.

He became synonymous with the Torah wherever he was located, the personification of its principles and the advocate of its dissemination. He was a bridge between the generations.

His memory is a blessing to those to whom he handed on the Tradition of his fathers. May his soul be bound up in the bond of eternal life.

The Crown of a Good Name

MISHNAH: *Avot* 4:13

רַבִּי שִׁמְעוֹן אוֹמֵר, שְׁלֹשָׁה כְתָרִים הֵם, כֶּתֶר תּוֹרָה וְכֶתֶר כְּהֻנָּה וְכֶתֶר מַלְכוּת, וְכֶתֶר שֵׁם
טוֹב עוֹלֶה עַל גַּבֵּיהֶן

TRANSLATION

Rabbi Shim'on said: There are three crowns—the crown of Torah,
the crown of priesthood, and the crown of kingship; but the crown
of a good name excels them all.

COMMENTARY

On the face of it, Rabbi Shim'on's statement is inconsistent. He
informs us that there are three crowns—the crowns of Torah,
priesthood, and kingship. However, he then mentions a fourth—
the crown of a good name.

The great Rabbi Loew, the legendary Maharal of Prague,
resolves this inconsistency. There is a fundamental distinction
between the first three crowns, on the one hand, and the crown of a
good name, on the other. Because they are qualitatively different,
they are not grouped together.

The crowns of Torah, the priesthood, and kingship are linked
together by a common characteristic. In each case, the wearer may
claim the right to put the crown upon his own head. Anybody who
devotes himself/herself to the study of Torah and masters its
methodology, wisdom, and secrets may place that crown upon his/
her head. Any male descendant of Aaron may place the crown of

346

priesthood upon his head. It is nothing more nor nothing less than his birthright. Any male descendant of the house of David may wear the crown of kingship. It is simply the product of his lineage.

The crown of a good name, however, is totally different. Nobody can place it on his/her own head. Our sages tell us that we have all been given three names. The first is the name which our parents call us. We are usually named for someone they love and respect. The naming ritual conveys the prayer that we should live up to our given name and personify what it represents. The second is the name we give ourselves. This is the mask we wear in public, the impression we wish to make on friends and colleagues, how we wish to be known. The third is the name which others call us when we are not around to object or to intimidate them and to repress their honesty with our presence. Ultimately, when we are dead, this last name is the crown which others place upon our head. This is the crown which the *mishnah* rules surpasses all other crowns.

APPLICATION

All Decent People

The deceased is no longer physically present. He/she cannot dictate what it is we shall call him/her. The crown of a good name is in our hands. We can bestow it or withhold it. The choice is ours.

In this case the decision is clear. The deceased did live up to the meaning of his/her given name. (The rabbi/study leader can, if applicable, speak about the symbolism of the Hebrew name of the deceased.)

It is clear how the deceased wished us to see him/her. (The rabbi/study leader should speak about the strivings and the goals of the individual and of how these translated themselves into action.)

He/she deserves our ultimate recognition. We can, in absolute good conscience, place the crown upon his/her head. In a sense, however, we do not have to do so. He/she has long worn the crown of a good name with pride and with honor.

A Scholar, *Kohen,* or Leader

Our *mishnah* can be translated differently: "There are three crowns—the crown of Torah, the crown of priesthood, and the crown of kingship. But the crown of a good name is elevated through them." Thus understood, each of the first-mentioned three crowns is a stepping-stone to the ultimate crown, that of a good name.

(The rabbi/study leader should elaborate on the special crown to which the deceased can lay claim. If the deceased was a scholar, his/her scholarship should be described. If the deceased was either an actual *kohen* or a devoted servant of the community, this attribute should be spelled out. If the deceased was a community leader or a leader in business, he/she should be compared to a king and his/her accomplishments spelled out.)

The deceased clearly deserves the ultimate recognition. We can, in absolute good conscience, place the crown upon his/her head. In a sense, however, we do not have to do so. He/she has manifestly earned it himself/herself.

The Fully Accomplished Individual

Our *mishnah* can be translated differently: "There are three crowns—the crown of Torah, the crown of priesthood, and the crown of kingship; but the crown of a good name is elevated through them all." Thus understood, all three of the first-mentioned three crowns are stepping-stones and preconditions to the ultimate attainment, the achievement of the crown of a good name.

Seen in this light, a good name is attained only by rare individuals who are fully accomplished.

The deceased was clearly such an individual. His/her reputation for scholarship is well known and requires little elaboration. (The rabbi/study leader should, nevertheless, detail the scholarly component of the deceased's life.)

The deceased, moreover, like Aaron the priest, was a true servant of his/her people. He/she dedicated himself/herself to the common good. Few sacrifices were too great for the benefit of the community. He/she gave unstintingly of his/her time. Evenings were spent in meetings, and free time in devising strategies for communal advancement. The deceased was like Aaron in another respect as well. He/she "loved peace and pursued peace," loved his/her fellow man and made every effort to bring them close to the Torah.

The deceased was clearly a leader in Israel. (The rabbi/study leader should spell out his/her accomplishments as a community leader.)

It can be said without fear of contradiction that the deceased was a fully accomplished Jew. He/she crowned himself/herself with the first three crowns, and wore them with distinction. Through them, he/she won the most precious crown of all, the crown of a good name. The deceased cannot take their wealth with them; a good name, however, will accompany them through all eternity.

Withstanding Winds
of Change

APPLICATION: A PERSON OF ACTION

MISHNAH: *Avot* 3:17 (b)

הוּא הָיָה אוֹמֵר, כֹּל שֶׁחָכְמָתוֹ מְרֻבָּה מִמַּעֲשָׂיו, לְמָה הוּא דוֹמֶה, לְאִילָן שֶׁעֲנָפָיו מְרֻבִּין
וְשָׁרָשָׁיו מֻעָטִין, וְהָרוּחַ בָּאָה וְעוֹקַרְתּוֹ וְהוֹפַכְתּוֹ עַל פָּנָיו, שֶׁנֶּאֱמַר, וְהָיָה כְּעַרְעָר בָּעֲרָבָה
וְלֹא יִרְאֶה כִּי־יָבוֹא טוֹב וְשָׁכַן חֲרֵרִים בַּמִּדְבָּר אֶרֶץ מְלֵחָה וְלֹא תֵשֵׁב. אֲבָל כֹּל שֶׁמַּעֲשָׂיו
מְרֻבִּין מֵחָכְמָתוֹ, לְמָה הוּא דוֹמֶה, לְאִילָן שֶׁעֲנָפָיו מֻעָטִין וְשָׁרָשָׁיו מְרֻבִּין, שֶׁאֲפִלּוּ כָּל
הָרוּחוֹת שֶׁבָּעוֹלָם בָּאוֹת וְנוֹשְׁבוֹת בּוֹ אֵין מְזִיזוֹת אוֹתוֹ מִמְּקוֹמוֹ, שֶׁנֶּאֱמַר, וְהָיָה כְּעֵץ
שָׁתוּל עַל־מַיִם וְעַל־יוּבַל יְשַׁלַּח שָׁרָשָׁיו וְלֹא יִרְאֶה כִּי־יָבֹא חֹם, וְהָיָה עָלֵהוּ רַעֲנָן, וּבִשְׁנַת
בַּצֹּרֶת לֹא יִדְאָג, וְלֹא יָמִישׁ מֵעֲשׂוֹת פֶּרִי:

TRANSLATION

He [Rabbi Elazar ben Azaryah] used to say: He whose wisdom
exceeds his works, to what is he to be compared? To a tree whose
branches are many but whose roots are few. The wind blows,
uproots it, and turns it over. As it is said: *For he shall be like a
tamarisk in the steppes, not seeing when good comes, but abiding
in the parched places of the wilderness, in a land that is salt and
uninhabited* (Jeremiah 17:6). But he whose works exceed his wisdom, to what is he compared? To a tree whose branches are few but
whose roots are many. Though all of the winds in the world come
and blow against it, they cannot move it from its place, as it is said:
*For he shall be as a tree planted by water, striking down its roots to
the river, and not feeling when heat comes, but its foliage remains
green, and in the year of drought it has no care, for it ceases not to
bear fruit* (Jeremiah 17:8).

350

COMMENTARY

Rabbi Judah the Prince, the editor of the Mishnah, compared Rabbi Elazar ben Azaryah to a richly stocked merchant: "When a sage came before him, should he ask a question relating to Scripture, he would answer him; to Mishnah, he would answer him; to Midrash, he would answer him; to Halakhah, he would answer him; to rabbinic lore (Aggadah), he would answer him. When he would leave [Rabbi Elazar's] company, he would be filled with goodness and blessing" (*Avot d'Rabbi Natan* 18). There was no aspect of Torah in which Rabbi Elazar was not well-versed, and which he did not have at his fingertips. He was, in other words, the quintessential Torah scholar.

Our text, therefore, is most significant. Notwithstanding his personal accomplishments as a Torah scholar, Rabbi Elazar was not impressed with scholarship for its own sake. The purpose of the study of Torah, he holds, is to produce a faith-commitment capable of withstanding even the strongest outside pressures. Purely theoretical study of the Torah will not achieve this purpose, because it represents form rather than substance. Personalities are transformed by behavior modification rather than by encountering new ideas. Accordingly, the study of Torah is centered on its behavioral component. It should lead to the performance of and habituation to *mitzvot*. Such a life-style alone will produce a stable, religious personality, deeply rooted in the principles of Torah, and capable of withstanding any outside onslaught.

APPLICATION

The deceased was deeply rooted in his/her principles, the epitome of a stable, Jewish personality. He/she was battered by many powerful winds of change but ... (rabbi/study leader to elaborate).

There were countless others, more learned than the deceased, who were buffeted by those same winds but could not withstand the pressures. They were plucked up and overturned. They abandoned the tradition in which they had been nurtured, and forsook the study in which they had so excelled.

The success of the deceased in dealing with pressure and with trauma was his/her habituation to good deeds. He/she was primarily a person of deeds rather than of words, of action rather than of theory. (Rabbi/study leader should dwell on the good deeds of the deceased—within the circle of the family, place of occupation, community, etc., etc.)

Alas, the deceased has finally succumbed. He/she has finally been uprooted by the one storm which no mortal can withstand, the ultimate wind of change, the onslaught of death. He/she has been plucked up. But he/she is, finally, undefeated. Like all goodly, well-rooted, well-tended trees, he/she has yielded healthy fruit. His/her children (and grandchildren) follow in his/her footsteps, inspired by his/her example, determined to emulate his/her life of action. (Rabbi/study leader to elaborate.)

May the Almighty comfort the mourners together with all the other mourners in Zion and Jerusalem.

In Praise of Popularity

MISHNAH: *Avot* 3:10

הוּא הָיָה אוֹמֵר, כָּל שֶׁרוּחַ הַבְּרִיּוֹת נוֹחָה הֵימֶנּוּ, רוּחַ הַמָּקוֹם נוֹחָה הֵימֶנּוּ. וְכֹל שֶׁאֵין רוּחַ הַבְּרִיּוֹת נוֹחָה הֵימֶנּוּ, אֵין רוּחַ הַמָּקוֹם נוֹחָה הֵימֶנּוּ. רַבִּי דוֹסָא בֶן־הַרְכִּינָס אוֹמֵר, שֵׁנָה שֶׁל שַׁחֲרִית, וְיַיִן שֶׁל צָהֳרַיִם, וְשִׂיחַת הַיְלָדִים, וִישִׁיבַת בָּתֵּי כְנֵסִיּוֹת שֶׁל עַמֵּי הָאָרֶץ, מוֹצִיאִין אֶת הָאָדָם מִן הָעוֹלָם:

TRANSLATION

He [Rabbi Chanina ben Dosa] used to say: He in whom the spirit of his fellow men take delight, in him the spirit of the Lord takes delight; and he in whom the spirit of his fellow creatures does not take delight, in him does the spirit of the All-present not take delight.

COMMENTARY

This dictum of Rabbi Chanina ben Dosa is astonishing. He was known for his miraculous powers. The Mishnah (*Berakhot* 5:5) records his successful prayerful intervention to save the life of the ailing son of Rabban Yochanan ben Zakkai, the President of the Sanhedrin, whose wife, according to the talmudic commentary on the incident, asked him: "Is Chanina greater than you?" "No," he answered. "He is like the servant of the king [who enjoys familiarity with him and has access to his most private quarters], while I am like one of the king's ministers, [whose relation with him is formal, respectful, honorable, but somewhat distant]." Apparently, therefore, Rabbi Chanina had a special connection with God. He might thus have been expected to place acceptability to God higher on the scale of spiritual value than acceptability to his fellow man.

353

The entire point of our *mishnah* is that Rabbi Chanina does not do so. Acceptability to God is *conditional* upon acceptability to man. Being well-liked by one's peers is thus a Jewish ethical imperative of the highest order.

APPLICATION

Judged by this criterion, the deceased can be said to have found favor in the sight both of man and of God. He/she was an individual of great popularity, a person in whom a whole wide circle of people took enormous delight.

(The rabbi/study leader should describe the popularity of the deceased in the various contexts in which he/she was active— occupational, organizational, communal, and family.)

If a portion in the world-to-come is granted to those in whom their fellow man delight, the deceased is assured of pride of place, for God surely has taken great delight in him/her. He/she is a wonderful role-model to all who knew and loved him/her. His/her memory is already a blessing.

Works Rather Than Wisdom

APPLICATION: THE UNLEARNED

MISHNAH: *Avot* 3:9

רַבִּי חֲנִינָא בֶּן־דּוֹסָא אוֹמֵר, כֹּל שֶׁיִּרְאַת חֶטְאוֹ קוֹדֶמֶת לְחָכְמָתוֹ, חָכְמָתוֹ מִתְקַיֶּמֶת. וְכֹל שֶׁחָכְמָתוֹ קוֹדֶמֶת לְיִרְאַת חֶטְאוֹ, אֵין חָכְמָתוֹ מִתְקַיֶּמֶת. הוּא הָיָה אוֹמֵר, כֹּל שֶׁמַּעֲשָׂיו מְרֻבִּין מֵחָכְמָתוֹ, חָכְמָתוֹ מִתְקַיֶּמֶת. וְכֹל שֶׁחָכְמָתוֹ מְרֻבָּה מִמַּעֲשָׂיו, אֵין חָכְמָתוֹ מִתְקַיֶּמֶת:

TRANSLATION

Rabbi Chanina ben Dosa said: He in whom fear of sin comes before wisdom, his wisdom shall endure; but he in whom wisdom comes before fear of sin, his wisdom will not endure. He used to say: He whose works exceed his wisdom, his wisdom shall endure; but he whose wisdom exceeds his works, his wisdom will not endure.

COMMENTARY

Rabbi Chanina ben Dosa was one of the great charismatics of the Jewish tradition. He was known as a miracle worker and healer. The Mishnah (*Sotah* 9:15). refers to him as the last of the *anshei ha-ma'aseh*—people gifted with mystic powers. It is not surprising, therefore, that he should make wisdom, even the wisdom of the Torah, conditional upon piety and reverence for God. The study of the Torah as an empty intellectual exercise is of no greater value than is the study of any secular field. In order to endure and to be meaningful, it must be predicated upon awe, and backed by good deeds.

355

APPLICATION

The deceased was not a particularly learned Jew. He/she did not
have the opportunity of devoting him/herself to a thoroughgoing
study of the Torah. (The rabbi/study leader should speak about the
background of the deceased, and the reasons why he/she did not
become a scholar—a difficult childhood and his/her struggle for a
livelihood, for example.)

But he/she *was* a good person. He/she was genuinely pious.
His/her attitude was sincerely reverential. (The rabbi/study leader
should elaborate about his/her sincerity and native piety and goodness.)

Above all, he/she was a person of outstanding works. (The
rabbi/study leader should delineate the good works of the deceased
in detail, illustrating them anecdotally.)

The deceased may not have had formal Torah training, but
he/she was wise in another sense. Elsewhere in Tractate *Avot*, Ben
Zomah said, "Who is wise? He who learns from all men." The
deceased was humble. He/she possessed native curiosity and was
ready to learn from the school of life. This wisdom, backed by
his/her piety and his/her good deeds, will surely endure.

Unsung Heroes

APPLICATION: PRIVATE PEOPLE

MISHNAH: *Sanhedrin* 4:4 (b)

לְפִיכָךְ נִבְרָא אָדָם יְחִידִי, לְלַמֶּדְךָ שֶׁכָּל־הַמְאַבֵּד נֶפֶשׁ אַחַת מִיִּשְׂרָאֵל, מַעֲלֶה עָלָיו הַכָּתוּב
כְּאִלּוּ אִבֵּד עוֹלָם מָלֵא. וְכָל־הַמְקַיֵּם נֶפֶשׁ אַחַת מִיִּשְׂרָאֵל, מַעֲלֶה עָלָיו הַכָּתוּב כְּאִלּוּ קִיֵּם
עוֹלָם מָלֵא. וּמִפְּנֵי שְׁלוֹם הַבְּרִיּוֹת, שֶׁלֹּא יֹאמַר אָדָם לַחֲבֵרוֹ אַבָּא גָדוֹל מֵאָבִיךָ. וְשֶׁלֹּא יְהוּ
מִינִין אוֹמְרִים, הַרְבֵּה רְשׁוּיוֹת בַּשָּׁמָיִם. וּלְהַגִּיד גְּדֻלָּתוֹ שֶׁל הַקָּדוֹשׁ־בָּרוּךְ־הוּא, שֶׁאָדָם
טוֹבֵעַ כַּמָּה מַטְבְּעוֹת בְּחוֹתָם אֶחָד וְכֻלָּן דּוֹמִין זֶה לָזֶה, וּמֶלֶךְ מַלְכֵי הַמְּלָכִים הַקָּדוֹשׁ־בָּרוּךְ־
הוּא טָבַע כָּל־אָדָם בְּחוֹתָמוֹ שֶׁל אָדָם הָרִאשׁוֹן וְאֵין אֶחָד מֵהֶן דּוֹמֶה לַחֲבֵרוֹ. לְפִיכָךְ כָּל
אֶחָד וְאֶחָד חַיָּב לוֹמַר, בִּשְׁבִילִי נִבְרָא הָעוֹלָם.

TRANSLATION

For this reason was man created alone, to teach you that whosoever destroys a single Jewish life is considered by Scripture to have destroyed an entire universe; and whosoever preserves a single Jewish life is considered by Scripture to have preserved an entire universe. It is also for the sake of social harmony, so that none may say to his fellow: My original ancestor was greater than yours; and so that sectarians cannot claim the existence of two divinities; and to declare the greatness of the Holy One, blessed be He—since a man may make many coins from a single mold, and all will be identical, but the King of Kings, the Holy One, blessed be He, made all mankind from the mold of Adam, the first man, and none resembles any other completely. Accordingly, each and every one of us is obliged to say: For my sake was the world created.

COMMENTARY

The context of this extract from the Mishnah is a warning to those judging capital cases. Because the individual is of such infinite value, wrongful punishment must be avoided by any means. It is for this reason that the death sentence was so rare that Rabbi Akiva could declare that a Sanhedrin which executed one individual in seventy years was to be known as a murderous Sanhedrin.

On another level, this *mishnah* celebrates the essential equality of all people and their existential uniqueness.

APPLICATION

Our society is starved for super-heroes, for extraordinary personalities to admire and with whom to identify. These heroes are created by media managers and made larger than life. But our society has not yet learned to appreciate that *everyone* is really extraordinary, because everyone is unique. Super-heroes do not have to be created by media manipulators. They can be discovered behind the facades of ordinary faces in ordinary people.

The deceased may not be immediately recognizable as a super-hero. He/she did not develop a special facade. He/she did not crave national attention. His/her heroism was private, a product of his/her unique personality.

He/she would have been embarrassed to have his/her unsung heroism made public, because it consisted of so many little things, some of them apparently trivial. However, the time has now come to sing his/her praise, if only to present him/her as a role-model to be emulated and to make us aware that with his/her passing a whole universe has disappeared.

(The rabbi/study leader should describe the virtues, values, accomplishments, and special qualities of the deceased.)

May his/her memory be a blessing and an inspiration.

Simple Goodness Is Rewarded

APPLICATION: THOSE WHO HAVE ENJOYED NO GREAT MATERIAL SUCCESS

MISHNAH: *Avot 4:22*

הוּא הָיָה אוֹמֵר, הַיִּלּוֹדִים לָמוּת, וְהַמֵּתִים לְהֵחָיוֹת, וְהַחַיִּים לִדּוֹן. לֵידַע לְהוֹדִיעַ וּלְהִוָּדַע
שֶׁהוּא אֵל, הוּא הַיּוֹצֵר, הוּא הַבּוֹרֵא, הוּא הַמֵּבִין, הוּא הַדַּיָּן, הוּא עֵד, הוּא בַּעַל דִּין,
וְהוּא עָתִיד לָדוּן. בָּרוּךְ הוּא, שֶׁאֵין לְפָנָיו לֹא עַוְלָה וְלֹא שִׁכְחָה וְלֹא מַשּׂוֹא פָנִים וְלֹא
מִקַּח שׁוֹחַד, שֶׁהַכֹּל שֶׁלּוֹ. וְדַע שֶׁהַכֹּל לְפִי הַחֶשְׁבּוֹן. וְאַל יַבְטִיחֲךָ יִצְרֶךָ שֶׁהַשְּׁאוֹל בֵּית
מָנוֹס לָךְ, שֶׁעַל כָּרְחֲךָ אַתָּה נוֹצָר, (וְעַל כָּרְחֲךָ אַתָּה נוֹלָד), וְעַל כָּרְחֲךָ אַתָּה חַי, וְעַל
כָּרְחֲךָ אַתָּה מֵת, וְעַל כָּרְחֲךָ אַתָּה עָתִיד לִתֵּן דִּין וְחֶשְׁבּוֹן לִפְנֵי מֶלֶךְ מַלְכֵי הַמְּלָכִים
הַקָּדוֹשׁ בָּרוּךְ הוּא:

TRANSLATION

He [Rabbi Elazar ha-Kappar] used to say: Those who are born are destined to die; and the dead to be restored to life again; and the living to be judged, to know, to make known, and to be made conscious that He is God, He is the maker, He the creator, He the discerner, He the judge, He the witness, He the complainant; it is He who will judge in the future, blessed be He, with whom there is no unrighteousness, nor forgetfulness, nor respect of persons, nor taking of bribes; know also that everything is according to the reckoning; and let your imagination give you no hope that the grave will be a place of refuge for you; for you were given no option in your formation, in your birth, in your life, and in the fact that you will die and have to give future account and reckoning before the Supreme King of Kings, the Holy One, blessed be He.

COMMENTARY

Our *mishnah* makes two points:

1. *Death is not a state of unconscious oblivion.* Although our per-

359

sonal experience suggests that death is the final act of dissolution,
our *mishnah* assures us that it is a transition to a conscious state
beyond the grave.

2. *Death is never an escape from responsibility.* Although our
experience sometimes suggests that injustice prevails, that the righteous suffer and the wicked prosper, that virtue is often unrewarded
and vice is frequently unpunished—all this is true only in the world
of the here and the now—on this side of the grave. Our *mishnah*
assures us that in the world beyond, however, justice will be done.
Our righteous acts *will* be rewarded, and our wickedness recompensed. We are warned that our every act on earth is noted. We are
told that each virtuous deed is added to the others to enhance our
reward; each act of evil added to the others to magnify our retribution. We are reminded that the ultimate judgment is absolute. God
is a formidable litigant. Nothing is hidden from our omniscient
creator. He knows our every thought, and records our every deed.
He is a powerful prosecutor and an incorruptible judge.

APPLICATION

Our *mishnah* is distressing in that it teaches us that there is no
escape from responsibility, that even death is not a place of sanctuary from recompense for our actions. But our *mishnah* is also profoundly reassuring. It reminds us that a life of goodness, devotion,
commitment, and self-sacrifice—even at the expense of luxurious
self-indulgence—is anything but the folly which cynics are accustomed to suggest, that, on the contrary, our virtue will ultimately
be rewarded.

It is particularly comforting in this instance. The deceased was a
simple person and never succeeded in attaining great material success and prestige.

The materialist may have thought that his/her life was an existence of little accomplishment.

Our *mishnah* assures us otherwise. God has noted the things
which really count—his/her love of family, devotion to friends,
commitment to the work ethic, diligence, honesty, dependability,
self-denial and self-sacrifice. (The rabbi/study leader should
elaborate on these and other points.)

We cannot be confident that those who have attained great material success and status on this side of the grave have received significant recognition there, beyond the grave, where life is eternal. We are sure, however, that the deceased enjoys a special place there, where it really counts, with God, who has truly assessed the value of a simple, humble, unpretentious, devoted, and productive life.

May his/her memory be a blessing.

The Importance of
a Single Virtue

APPLICATION: MODEST, HUMBLE, PRIVATE PEOPLE

MISHNAYOT: *Avot* 4:3, 11

הוּא הָיָה אוֹמֵר, אַל תְּהִי בָז לְכָל אָדָם, וְאַל תְּהִי מַפְלִיג לְכָל דָּבָר, שֶׁאֵין לְךָ אָדָם שֶׁאֵין
לוֹ שָׁעָה וְאֵין לְךָ דָּבָר שֶׁאֵין לוֹ מָקוֹם:

רַבִּי אֱלִיעֶזֶר בֶּן־יַעֲקֹב אוֹמֵר, הָעוֹשֶׂה מִצְוָה אַחַת, קוֹנֶה לוֹ פְּרַקְלִיט אֶחָד. וְהָעוֹבֵר עֲבֵרָה
אַחַת, קוֹנֶה לוֹ קַטֵּיגוֹר אֶחָד. תְּשׁוּבָה וּמַעֲשִׂים טוֹבִים, כִּתְרִיס בִּפְנֵי הַפֻּרְעָנוּת.

TRANSLATION

He [Ben Azzai] used to say: Do not despise any man nor carp at
anything, for there is no man who does not have his hour, and there
is no thing which does not have its place.

Rabbi Eliezer ben Ya'akov said: He who carries out one religious
imperative (*mitzvah*) has acquired for himself an advocate; and he
who commits one transgression has acquired for himself an accuser.
Repentance and good deeds are a shield against punishment.

COMMENTARY

The meaning of these *mishnayot* is obvious. They require little
elaboration. Judaism is not an all-or-nothing commitment. One
does not have to be a fully accomplished individual to attain merit.
Each and every facet of one's life and character is intrinsically
important. No individual activity, no single accomplishment, no
isolated *mitzvah* can be regarded as trifling. Each by itself is a vehicle for eternal reward. No person, however humble, does not have
his/her special place in the divine economy.

APPLICATION

The deceased was a humble person. He/she led a private existence, content to devote himself/herself to the needs of a loving family and loyal circle of friends. Some might judge his/her modest existence as unspectacular and unglamorous. Not so Ben Azzai. He assures us that he/she has a special place in God's world, and will be rewarded accordingly. When we think back on the life of the deceased, we are struck by his/her special commitment to . . . (the rabbi/study leader should now elaborate on a special activity, a special cause, a special charity, or a special *mitzvah* to which the deceased was devoted).

Rabbi Eliezer's words are of great comfort to the bereaved. We are certain that the special quality/qualities of which we have spoken, will be effective advocates when he/she appears before God for his/her ultimate accounting and final judgment.

May his/her soul be bound up in the bond of eternal life.

Appearances Are Deceptive

APPLICATIONS: A PERSON FRAIL IN BODY; UNSPECTACULAR LIVES

MISHNAH: *Avot* 4:20

רַבִּי אוֹמֵר, אַל תִּסְתַּכֵּל בַּקַּנְקַן, אֶלָּא בַּמֶּה שֶׁיֶּשׁ בּוֹ. יֵשׁ קַנְקַן חָדָשׁ מָלֵא יָשָׁן, וְיָשָׁן שֶׁאֲפִלּוּ חָדָשׁ אֵין בּוֹ:

TRANSLATION

Rabbi [Judah the Prince] said: Look not at the flask, but at what it contains. There may be a new flask full of old wine, and an old flask that has not even new wine in it.

COMMENTARY

Rabbi Judah's statement is a reaction to the dictum of Rabbi Yossi bar Yehudah, which precedes it: "He who learns from the young, to what is he to be compared? To a person who eats unripe grapes and who drinks wine from his vat. And he who learns from the old, to what is he to be compared? To one who eats ripe grapes, and drinks old wine." According to Rabbi Yossi, wisdom is necessarily a product of age. Rabbi Judah disagrees. The content of a man's head does not depend upon his external appearance. The gray-haired eminence may be empty of wisdom, whereas a young head may be full of understanding, insight, and knowledge, since appearances are often deceptive.

APPLICATIONS

A Frail Body Can Envelop a Robust Spirit

The deceased was physically frail, the consequence of . . . (the rabbi/study leader should elaborate on the origin of the frailty, dwell upon the limitations that this frailty imposed upon the deceased, and describe the suffering and discomfort which the frailty caused).

However, this frail body contained a robust spirit, a lively intellect, and a generous heart. (The rabbi/study leader should expand upon these attributes, both conceptually and anecdotally.)

Scripture reminds us that "Man sees with his eyes, but God sees into the Heart" (I Samuel 16:7). We know that God has seen beyond his/her physical frailty, and will judge the flask by the fine wine it contains. As we contemplate his/her virtues, we shall surely do the same.

Unspectacular Lives Can Be Most Meaningful

Our hedonistic society idolizes the "beautiful people." They are rich, glamorous, popular, and successful. The world is their oyster. Members of the jet-set fly around the globe and attract sycophants and admirers who hope to benefit from their association. Our society disdains the materially unendowed and labels them as failures. Hedonists do not seek out their company and are contemptuous of their humble accomplishments.

Rabbi Judah has a different conception of "beautiful people." He refuses to judge a book by its unglamorous cover. Its contents are *all* important.

The cover of the deceased's Book of Life may not be immediately impressive. (The rabbi/study leader should discuss the outward appearance of his/her life—job, home, associates, etc.)

But the Book itself is rich in content. Every chapter is significant. The chapter entitled "Family," for example, should be required reading for all decent people. (The rabbi/study leader should elaborate on the deceased as a family man/woman.)

The chapter entitled "Occupation" is a model of integrity, diligence, and dependability. (The rabbi/study leader, should describe the work ethic and reputation of the deceased in some detail.)

The chapter entitled "Principles and Beliefs" demands our attention. (The rabbi/study leader should spell out the belief system of the deceased, as it expressed itself in his/her life and in the life of his/her family.)

The hedonists are wrong. Rabbi Judah is right. The deceased *was* a beautiful person. May we preserve the chapters of his/her life as a model for our own.

A Life Well-Lived

APPLICATION: GENERAL

MISHNAH: *Berakhot* 4:2

רַבִּי נְחוּנְיָא בֶּן־הַקָּנָה הָיָה מִתְפַּלֵּל בִּכְנִיסָתוֹ לְבֵית־הַמִּדְרָשׁ וּבִיצִיאָתוֹ תְּפִלָּה קְצָרָה. אָמְרוּ לוֹ: מַה־מָּקוֹם לִתְפִלָּה זוֹ? אָמַר לָהֶם: בִּכְנִיסָתִי־אֲנִי מִתְפַּלֵּל שֶׁלֹּא חֶאֱרַע תַּקָּלָה עַל־יָדִי, וּבִיצִיאָתִי־אֲנִי נוֹתֵן הוֹדָיָה עַל חֶלְקִי:

TRANSLATION

Rabbi Nechunya ben ha-Kanah used to utter a short prayer when he entered and when he departed from the House of Study. [His fellow students] said to him: What is the nature of this prayer? He said to them: When I enter, I pray that no harm be caused through me, and when I depart, I give thanks for my lot.

COMMENTARY

This *mishnah* refers to the House of Study (*Bet ha-Midrash*). Study in the *Bet ha-Midrash* was not merely theoretical. Binding decisions of halakhic [Torah law] imperatives arose out of the debates among the scholars, which would regulate the conduct of the Jewish community of that and of subsequent generations.

When Rabbi Nechunya ben ha-Kanah prepared himself for a period of Torah study, he would, according to the Talmud (*Berakhot* 28b), recite the following prayer: "May it be Your will, O Lord my God, that no harm be caused through me, in that I do not err in a halakhic decision, so that my colleagues will take delight in me; that I do not declare that which is impure to be pure, and that which is impure, pure; and that my colleagues do not err in a halakhic decision, so that I shall take delight in them." Upon conclusion of the study session, he would, according to the Talmud, declare: "I give thanks unto You, O Lord my God, that You have granted my portion among those that sit in the *Bet ha-Midrash* and not among those who idly while away their time in empty preoccupations. I arise early and they arise early. I arise early to study the Torah, and they arise early to empty preoccupations. I work hard and they work hard. I work hard and receive [divine] reward, and they work hard and receive no [divine] reward. I run and they run. I run to life eternal [beyond the grave], and they run [no further than] the grave."

APPLICATION

This *mishnah* can be seen as a metaphor of life's journey. Its two prayers consist of the following elements:

1. *The acceptance of responsibility for others.* We acknowledge that what we do in life will affect those around us, who rely upon our judgments and decisions.
2. *The desire for acceptability by those around us.* This is the wish both that we do not let down those for whom we care, and that they do not let *us* down. We have a deep need to be accepted and loved by those for whom we care, and to find dear ones whom we can accept as our closest friends.
3. *Gratitude for a meaningful, fruitful life.* The sense that our hard work has not been in vain.

(The rabbi/study leader can point out that all these elements of our *mishnah* have been satisfied in the life of the deceased. He can summarize the life and the accomplishments of the deceased under the above three headings and conclude that the deceased's journey on this earth is at an end.)

We are confident that he/she has been granted the reward of life eternal. May his/her memory be a blessing and an inspiration.

Against the Stream

APPLICATION: A PERSON OF INTEGRITY

MISHNAH: *Avot* 2:1

רַבִּי אוֹמֵר, אֵיזוֹהִי דֶרֶךְ יְשָׁרָה שֶׁיָּבוֹר לוֹ הָאָדָם, כֹּל שֶׁהִיא תִּפְאֶרֶת לְעוֹשֶׂיהָ וְתִפְאֶרֶת לוֹ מִן הָאָדָם. וֶהֱוֵי זָהִיר בְּמִצְוָה קַלָּה כְּבַחֲמוּרָה, שֶׁאֵין אַתָּה יוֹדֵעַ מַתַּן שְׂכָרָן שֶׁל מִצְוֹת.

TRANSLATION

Rabbi [Judah the Prince] said: Which is the right course that a man should choose for himself? That which he feels will bring honor to himself, and which also brings him honor from mankind. Be as careful [in the performance of an apparently] light religious precept (*mitzvah*) as of a grave one, for you do not know the reward which is granted for each precept.

COMMENTARY

Elsewhere in Tractate *Avot* (3:10), Rabbi Chanina ben Dosa had placed one's acceptability to one's fellow man on the highest moral plane. This dictum of Rabbi Judah the Prince goes much further. The achievement of popularity cannot be at the cost of personal integrity.

Social psychologists have described in great detail the dynamics of the human need for acceptance. To satisfy this need, well-intentioned people will do uncharacteristic and even bizarre things. They will sacrifice deeply held principles if they believe that their adherence to these principles will diminish their popularity. They will stifle the still small voice of conscience if their peers expect behavior patterns of them which are inconsistent with what they really believe.

"To thyself be true," demands Rabbi Judah the Prince. If per-

368

sonal beliefs place you beyond the social pale, so be it. If honesty and integrity demand that you resist the pressures of your peers, you must be prepared to do so. It is true that there is comfort in conforming; but conformity at the cost of conscience is simply unacceptable.

The next clause of our *mishnah* is consistent with Rabbi Judah's theme. Performance of religious precepts, too, must reflect our personal integrity. A Machiavellian approach to *mitzvot* is as unacceptable as a Machiavellian approach to society. Our performance of religious precepts cannot be motivated by a cost-benefit analysis. We perform *mitzvot* on the basis of honest religious commitment—not in the hope of personal recompense. We can no more be utilitarian and pragmatic in our attitudes to God than we can be in our conduct towards our fellow man.

APPLICATION

The deceased was scrupulously honest both in his/her attitudes to God and to his/her fellow man. He/she often took unpopular positions for the sake of principle, and willingly suffered the bitter criticism of his/her peers for what was considered to be negative ideological obstructionism. But, true to himself/herself, he/she resisted all the powerful pressures to conform. (The rabbi/study leader should give instances of the deceased's unswerving adherence to principle, spelling out the principle and making his point anecdotally.)

Our sages provide us with a fascinating test of the *kashrut* of a bird. If it has fallen into the water, we must suspect that skeletal trauma as a result of the impact may have rendered it unfit for consumption (*treif*), in that it will probably die as a result of the mishap. How do we determine the real state of its health? If it swims with the stream, it is *treif.* If it swims against the stream, it is strong, obviously healthy, and kosher.

The deceased was really kosher. He/she was prepared to be a loner, to go against the stream, to give principle priority over popularity. Paradoxically, this consistent honesty secured for him/her the real respect of his/her fellow men, and ultimately produced popularity of a more meaningful, more abiding kind.

May his/her soul be bound up in the bond of eternal life.

Doing Your Own Thing

APPLICATIONS: THE DESCENDANT OF A PRINCIPLED NONCONFORMIST; GENERAL

MISHNAH: *Eduyot* 5:7

בִּשְׁעַת מִיתָתוֹ אָמַר לִבְנוֹ, בְּנִי, חֲזֹר בְּךָ בְּאַרְבָּעָה דְבָרִים שֶׁהָיִיתִי אוֹמֵר. אָמַר לוֹ, וְלָמָּה לֹא חָזַרְתָּ בָּךְ? אָמַר לוֹ, אֲנִי שָׁמַעְתִּי מִפִּי הַמְרֻבִּים, וְהֵם שָׁמְעוּ מִפִּי הַמְרֻבִּים. אֲנִי עָמַדְתִּי בִּשְׁמוּעָתִי, וְהֵם עָמְדוּ בִּשְׁמוּעָתָן. אֲבָל אַתָּה שָׁמַעְתָּ מִפִּי הַיָּחִיד, וּמִפִּי הַמְרֻבִּין, מוּטָב לְהַנִּיחַ דִּבְרֵי הַיָּחִיד, וְלֶאֱחֹז בְּדִבְרֵי הַמְרֻבִּין. אָמַר לוֹ, אַבָּא, פְּקֹד עָלַי לַחֲבֵרֶיךָ. אָמַר לוֹ, אֵינִי מַפְקִיד. אָמַר לוֹ, שֶׁמָּא עַוְלָה מָצָאתָ בִי. אָמַר לוֹ, לָאו, מַעֲשֶׂיךָ יְקָרְבוּךָ וּמַעֲשֶׂיךָ יְרַחֲקוּךָ:

TRANSLATION

As he lay dying [Rabbi Akavya ben Mehalalel] said to his son: "My son, reverse yourself on the four matters on which I ruled [in opposition to the sages]." He said to him: "And why did *you* not reverse yourself [and abide by the decision of the majority]?" He said to him: "*I* received [these opinions] from the many, and they [my opponents claim to have] received theirs from the many. I adhered to my tradition, and they adhered to theirs. You, however, have heard [two different sets of opinions], one from a single authority, and the other from the many. It is better to abandon the opinion of the individual and to hold onto the opinion of the many." He said to him: "Father, recommend me to your colleagues." He said to him: "I shall give you no recommendation." He said to him: "Perhaps you have found some cause for complaint in me?" He said to him: "No! Your own deeds will either bring you near to the sages or alienate you [from them]."

COMMENTARY

The background to this remarkable dialogue between father and

370

son is to be found in the previous *mishnah* of the same chapter. There were four points of disagreement between Rabbi Akavya and the majority of his contemporaries, relating, respectively, to the identification of the symptoms of biblical leprosy, the determination of the color of a menstrual flow which would cause the ritual separation of a wife from her husband, the use of the hair of a blemished firstborn animal, and the applicability of the ordeal of jealousy to a convert and freed slave. Although the sages offered to elevate him to the rank of deputy to the president of the Sanhedrin if he retracted his minority opinion, Rabbi Akavya refused to sacrifice his integrity for the sake of high office.

The point of the dialogue in our *mishnah* is the insistence of the father that what was demanded by intellectual integrity in *his* case was not demanded in the case of his son. They simply were not coming from the same place. There is no virtue in opposing the sages without compelling cause. Opposition for the sake of opposition is without merit, and is nothing more than pure folly. Finally, Akavya's advice to his son is well taken. Career advancement should be *earned*. It is not secured by special "protektsia." Rabbi Akavya is consistent to the very end. Just as he had rejected the notion that elevation to the high office could be bought—in his case, by the abandonment of principle—he rejected it for his beloved son—in his case, through the influence of a famous father.

APPLICATIONS

To the Children of an Assimilated Family

The parallels are obvious: Children are not, under all circumstances, obliged to follow in the footsteps of their parents. Different generations are often products of different environments, value systems, ideologies, cultural backgrounds, and opportunities. Assimilated families may well have rejected the views of the sages for reasons which were valid for *them*. In their case, it may have been intellectually difficult for them to abandon the ideological positions and the habits to which they had become accustomed. But things *do* change. The emotional, spiritual, and ideological baggage of children is different from that of their parents. In fact, the parents would not resent a religious change on the part of their children. On the contrary, they would oppose rejection of the sages of

Judaism for no good cause, and would encourage their offspring to seek the truth for themselves. Like Akavya of the *mishnah*, they would declare: "*Chazor bakh*—retract, go back. Do not rely on influence. Your own deeds must draw you close to the sages."

(The rabbi/study leader should now personalize this comment and relate it to the reputation the deceased enjoyed for integrity and independence of thought, emphasizing the positive features of his/her worldview, while encouraging his/her children to return to the tradition.)

Like Rabbi Akavya, so extraordinary a parent would be pleased with a return to traditional values. On a level on which he/she would feel comfortable, he/she would regard such a return as an ultimately paradoxical triumph.

General

The rabbi/study leader should elaborate on the special accomplishments of the deceased and of the great distinction of which he/she was capable. Above all, the honesty and integrity of the deceased should be emphasized—his/her refusal to sell his/her soul for advancement. The special responsibilities of the children of such an extraordinary person should be dwelt upon. It should be pointed out to the children that they cannot depend upon the accomplishments of the deceased to ease them through life's crises. The deceased would, himself or herself, have rejected this approach and declared what Akavya did: "Your own deeds will either draw you near or alienate you."

In Praise of Flexibility

APPLICATION: A PERSON WHO HAS MADE MANY ADJUSTMENTS

MISHNAH: *Eduyot* 1:4

וְלָמָּה מַזְכִּירִין אֶת־דִּבְרֵי שַׁמַּאי וְהִלֵּל לְבַטָּלָה? לְלַמֵּד לַדּוֹרוֹת הַבָּאִים שֶׁלֹּא יְהֵא אָדָם עוֹמֵד עַל דְּבָרָיו, שֶׁהֲרֵי אֲבוֹת הָעוֹלָם לֹא עָמְדוּ עַל דִּבְרֵיהֶם:

TRANSLATION

Why are the opinions of Shammai and Hillel vainly recorded [in the Mishnah]? To teach future generations that a person should not obstinately assert his opinion, since the fathers of the world did not obstinately assert their opinions.

COMMENTARY

Of the 523 chapters of the Mishnah, only about five do not record a difference of opinion between the sages. Our *mishnah* asks why dissenting opinions are recorded even though the codifiers of the law reject them. It suggests the virtue of flexibility as an answer to the question. Even the great Hillel and Shammai were prepared to withdraw their opinions as soon as they were convinced of the merits of the opposing arguments. In their case, flexibility reflected their profound humility. For their part, on the other hand, the codifiers of the law were not overawed by the commanding stature of a Hillel or Shammai. They were sufficiently flexible to rule against these giants when logic and the situation so demanded. In their case, flexibility reflected great strength of character and conviction.

APPLICATION

One of the most striking characteristics of the deceased was his/her great flexibility. This attribute expressed itself in many ways.

373

It expressed itself, most obviously, in the many physical changes, moves, and adaptations which the deceased was required to make. (The rabbi/study leader should enumerate and describe these relocations and the circumstances which compelled them.)

The virtue of flexibility expressed itself also in successful changes made in the lifestyle, occupation, etc., of the deceased. These changes required both humility and enormous strength. (The rabbi/study leader should spell them out.)

The leadership (if applicable) of the deceased in his/her profession/trade/business/community is also a product of his/her great flexibility, openness, humility, strength, and tolerance. (The rabbi/study leader should expatiate on these activities.)

During the High Holy Days, we pray that we be inscribed in the Book of Life. The truth is that we ourselves make the various entries in our Book of Life. Our personal Book of Life, like the Mishnah, will record many discarded views and many changes. Like the Mishnah, also, the purpose of the preservation of these views is for the sake of future generations, so that they can learn the virtue of flexibility from us, which, more than any other virtue, reflects our attributes of humility and of strength. We pray that the lessons of the Book of Life of the deceasesd will not be lost on his/her descendants, that they will be an inspiration to coming generations to walk humbly with God and to show strength of conviction.

The Struggle for Survival

APPLICATION: A SURVIVOR; ONE WHO HAS SUFFERED MANY HARDSHIPS

MISHNAH: *Uktzin* 3:8

דָּגִים מֵאֵימָתַי מְקַבְּלִין טֻמְאָה, בֵּית שַׁמַּאי אוֹמְרִים, מִשֶּׁיִּצוֹדוּ. וּבֵית הִלֵּל אוֹמְרִים, מִשֶּׁיָּמוּתוּ. רַבִּי עֲקִיבָא אוֹמֵר, אִם יְכוֹלִין לִחְיוֹת.

TRANSLATION

When are fish susceptible to ritual impurity? The School of Shammai says: As soon as they have become entrapped. The School of Hillel says: Once they are dead. Rabbi Akiva says: If they can still live [if they get back into the water, they are not susceptible].

COMMENTARY

Fish become susceptible to ritual impurity when they are dead. Accordingly, the *mishnah* is asking when is a fish considered to be dead. Three opinions are offered, two of them extreme, and one an intermediate, compromise position.

The School of Shammai takes a position of extreme pessimism. The fish is considered to be dead as soon as it is entrapped, for it is unlikely that it will escape and return to the water alive.

The School of Hillel is wholly optimistic. Even if the fish is taken from its natural environment, so that death appears to be inevitable, it is not considered dead until it is actually dead. While there's life, there's hope—no matter how tenuous that life may be.

Rabbi Akiva suggests a compromise. He is a realist. If the fish is thrown back into the water, it will survive, notwithstanding the trauma it has suffered.

375

APPLICATION

Our *mishnah* can be taken as a parable of a life of hardship.

Like Shammai, some people give up the ghost as soon as they become entrapped in a situation from which they feel there is no escape—like the fish in the net, removed from their life-giving water. This is the unfortunate experience of Jews transplanted to an alien environment and out of contact with their life-sustaining origins. It was also the case with tens of thousands of Jews who found themselves in Nazi extermination centers. They were entrapped, and they knew it—and they resigned themselves to their inevitable extermination. Sadly, it is the experience of individuals who have fallen on hard times, who have suffered disastrous reversals in business. They are enmeshed by creditors, abandoned by friends, and crushed by failure. They all too often give up the struggle even before the inevitable collapse actually occurs.

Others, like Rabbi Akiva, are realists, but retain some optimism. They may be down and out, they may be beaten, they may be entrapped, but, given a chance by others, they will continue the struggle. If they are thrown back into the water, they will swim; they will give up hope only if they are totally abandoned.

A third type of individual, like Hillel, is totally, even irrationally, optimistic. These are the natural survivors. They may be in the very jaws of defeat. Escape may seem impossible. Death may seem inevitable. But they refuse to abandon hope and to renounce the struggle. While their heart beats ever so faintly, they seek a hole in the net. They devise means of escape. They search for a life-sustaining environment. They never say die.

The deceased is a disciple of Hillel in at least this striking respect. He/she is a classical survivor. His/her story is proof that optimism is never foolish, that the struggle can be crowned with victory. (The rabbi/study leader should tell the story of the survival of the deceased and of his/her subsequent success in detail.)

The deceased's long struggle is finally over. He/she has finally succumbed. But his/her life was a living lesson in courage, determination, inventiveness, faith, and optimism. May his/her memory be a blessing and an inspiration.

At the End of Life's Journey

APPLICATION: FOR HOLOCAUST SURVIVORS; FOR THOSE WHO HAVE TRANSCENDED LIFE'S EARLY DIFFICULTIES

MISHNAH: *Berakhot* 9:4

הַנִּכְנָס לַכְּרַךְ, מִתְפַּלֵּל שְׁתַּיִם, אַחַת בִּכְנִיסָתוֹ וְאַחַת בִּיצִיאָתוֹ. בֶּן עַזַּאי אוֹמֵר: אַרְבַּע,
שְׁתַּיִם בִּכְנִיסָתוֹ, וּשְׁתַּיִם בִּיצִיאָתוֹ. וְנוֹתֵן הוֹדָאָה לְשֶׁעָבַר וְצוֹעֵק לֶעָתִיד:

TRANSLATION

One who enters a large city should recite two prayers—one when he comes in, and the other when he departs. Ben Azzai says: Four [prayers]—two upon entering, and two upon departing. He should give thanks for what has passed, and cry out for what will happen in the future.

COMMENTARY

Because large cities were always perceived as dangerous, the sages instructed us to utter the following prayer before entering: "May it be Your will, O Lord my God, to cause me to enter this great city in peace." When leaving, one should say: "I give thanks unto You, O Lord my God, for having brought me from this great city in peace."

Ben Azzai was even more sensitive to the dangers of large cities. Before entering, therefore, he would have us pray for a safe entry, and when we are in the safety of a home or inn, he would have us give thanks for having been brought into the great city in peace. Similarly, upon leaving, he would have us give thanks for our safe departure and declare: "As You have brought me out in peace, so may You cause me to go in peace, lead me in peace, cause me to walk, step by step, in peace, and deliver me from the hand of any enemy who may lie in wait for me on the way" (*Berakhot* 60a).

These prayers established the general principle that one should give thanks for deliverance from the perils of the past and pray for safety in the uncertainty of the future.

APPLICATION

This *mishnah* can be used in the same general way as we used *Berakhot* 4:2, to convey the same kind of sentiments, but through the vehicle of a different text, to provide variety in different *shiv'ah* houses or at different funerals.

Its more specific application is as a tribute to survivors of the Holocaust and to those who have risen from adversity.

It can be interpreted as a metaphor of life's journey. It consists of two elements.

1. *It reminds us that we cannot take our survival in a dangerous world for granted.* It assumes our vulnerability and weakness in the face of life's dangers. As such, it is particularly applicable to survivors of the Holocaust and can be a springboard for a discussion of the deceased's journey through the Kingdon of Night and of the reasons for giving thanks for his/her personal resolution of the tragedy—family, business, community service, etc., etc. It can also be applied in tribute to anybody who has triumphed over despair or risen from adversity to success.

2. *It places our loss in perspective.* In a time of loss, we instinctively lament what has happened. This *mishnah* teaches us to be grateful for the gift of precious life. It demands that we examine and articulate the wonderful legacy of the departed (which the rabbi/study leader should summarize in some detail). It is a timely reminder that we do not really grieve for the departed, whose life was a triumph, and who is at peace in eternal closeness to God. When we lament, we cry out about the emptiness of *our* lives, deprived of the presence, comfort, and inspiration of the deceased.

We should learn to give thanks for the past and cry out for a future which will have to be mapped out without the guiding hand of the deceased, whose memory will always be a blessing and an inspiration.

The Uniqueness
of the Deceased

APPLICATION: GENERAL

MISHNAH: *Sotah* 9:15 (a)

מִשֶּׁמֵּת רַבִּי מֵאִיר, בָּטְלוּ מוֹשְׁלֵי מְשָׁלִים. מִשֶּׁמֵּת בֶּן־עַזַּאי, בָּטְלוּ הַשַּׁקְדָנִים. מִשֶּׁמֵּת בֶּן־
זוֹמָא, בָּטְלוּ הַדַּרְשָׁנִים. מִשֶּׁמֵּת רַבִּי יְהוֹשֻׁעַ, פָּסְקָה טוֹבָה מִן־הָעוֹלָם. מִשֶּׁמֵּת רַבָּן שִׁמְעוֹן
בֶּן־גַּמְלִיאֵל, בָּא גוֹבַי וְרַבּוּ צָרוֹת. מִשֶּׁמֵּת רַבִּי אֶלְעָזָר בֶּן־עֲזַרְיָה, פָּסַק הָעֹשֶׁר מִן־
הַחֲכָמִים. מִשֶּׁמֵּת רַבִּי עֲקִיבָא, בָּטַל כְּבוֹד הַתּוֹרָה. מִשֶּׁמֵּת רַבִּי חֲנִינָא בֶּן־דּוֹסָא, בָּטְלוּ
אַנְשֵׁי־מַעֲשֶׂה.

TRANSLATION

When Rabbi Meir died, the creators of parables were no more.
When Ben Azzai died, absolute diligence in study ceased. When
Ben Zoma died, expositors of the scriptural text were no more.
When Rabbi Joshua died, goodness departed from the world. When
Rabbi Shim'on ben Gamliel died, the locusts came and troubles
increased. When Rabbi Elazar ben Azariah died, wealth passed
away from the sages. When Rabbi Akiva died, the glory of the
Torah came to an end. When Rabbi Chanina ben Dosa died, men of
[miraculous] power were no more.

COMMENTARY

This *mishnah* describes the special characteristics of a number of
the greatest sages of the period of the Mishnah. Rabbi Meir was
known to have compiled as many as 300 parables and fables which
he used as a teaching device. Ben Azzai was so devoted to the study
of Torah that he refused to marry, lest family responsibilities deflect
him from his study. Ben Zoma was able to mine the hidden jewels

379

of the Torah text by his unique hermeneutical skills. The goodness and kindness of Rabbi Joshua were legendary, and were considered a shield against collective political calamity; immediately after his death a final calamitous revolt against Rome began, which was the beginning of the end of the Second Commonwealth. The personal virtue of Rabban Shim'on ben Gamliel shielded his generation from *natural* calamity. Rabbi Elazar ben Azariah was known not only for his wisdom but for his wealth also. The saintly, martyred Rabbi Akiva was one of the greatest Torah scholars of all time. Rabbi Chanina ben Dosa was a charismatic figure, known as a "miracle worker" and healer.

COMMENTARY

Our *mishnah* is not exhaustive. There were other great sages whose contributions were unique. Neither is it to be taken literally. There were others who later combined wealth and wisdom, whose dedication to Torah study was absolute, who could invoke the miraculous intervention of God, and so on. What the *mishnah* means to teach us is that everybody has at least one special characteristic for which he/she will be remembered. In his/her passing, a void is felt, and the feeling is experienced that that void will never be adequately filled.

(The rabbi/study leader should now elaborate on the special characteristics of the deceased, stressing how he/she shielded family and friends from trouble in much the same way as some of the sages of our *mishnah* did. He should list all special attributes, both material and spiritual. He should dwell on the special attributes, however.

The rabbi/study leader should talk of the void created by his/her passing, and challenge the mourners to try and fill that void by emulating the special characteristics of the deceased—just as each succeeding generation of our sages strove to fill the void left by *their* predecessors.)

Every Jew Can Be Righteous

APPLICATION: GENERAL

MISHNAH: *Sanhedrin* 8:5

בֶּן סוֹרֵר וּמוֹרֶה נִדּוֹן עַל שֵׁם סוֹפוֹ, יָמוּת זַכַּאי וְאַל יָמוּת חַיָּב, שֶׁמִּיתָתָן שֶׁל רְשָׁעִים הֲנָאָה לָהֶן וַהֲנָאָה לָעוֹלָם, וְלַצַּדִּיקִים, רַע לָהֶן וְרַע לָעוֹלָם. יַיִן וְשֵׁינָה לָרְשָׁעִים הֲנָאָה לָהֶן וַהֲנָאָה לָעוֹלָם, וְלַצַּדִּיקִים, רַע לָהֶן וְרַע לָעוֹלָם. פִּזּוּר לָרְשָׁעִים הֲנָאָה לָהֶן וַהֲנָאָה לָעוֹלָם, וְלַצַּדִּיקִים, רַע לָהֶן וְרַע לָעוֹלָם. כִּנּוּס לָרְשָׁעִים רַע לָהֶן וְרַע לָעוֹלָם, וְלַצַּדִּיקִים, הֲנָאָה לָהֶן וַהֲנָאָה לָעוֹלָם. שֶׁקֶט לָרְשָׁעִים רַע לָהֶן וְרַע לָעוֹלָם, וְלַצַּדִּיקִים, הֲנָאָה לָהֶן וַהֲנָאָה לָעוֹלָם:

TRANSLATION

The stubborn and rebellious son is judged by how [it is thought] his end will be. It is better that he die innocent than guilty, for the death of the wicked is a benefit to them and a benefit to the world. In the case of the righteous, however, [death] is a misfortune to them and to the world. Wine and sleep are a benefit to the wicked and a benefit to the world. In the case of the righteous, however, they are a misfortune for them and for the world. The dispersal of the wicked is a benefit to them and to the world. However, the dispersal of the righteous is a misfortune for them and for the world. A gathering of the wicked is bad for them and bad for the world. In the case of the righteous, however, it is a benefit for them and for the world. Quietude is bad for the wicked and bad for the world. In the case of the righteous, however, it is a benefit to them and to the world.

COMMENTARY

The scriptural passage relating to the stubborn and rebellious son (Deuteronomy 21:18–21) raises more questions than it answers.

381

The Jerusalem Talmud (*Sanhedrin* 8:1) elaborates on the para-doxical and apparently irrational nature of the subject. Indeed, in the Babylonian Talmud, Rabbi Shimon is of the opinion that the whole subject of the stubborn and rebellious son is purely theoreti-cal, and that no stubborn or rebellious son in the biblical sense ever existed or ever would exist. The inclusion of the passage in the Torah was merely to reward those who studied the Torah for their conceptual analysis of the passage (*Sanhedrin* 71a).

Be that as it may, the death of the stubborn and rebellious son is used by our *mishnah* as paradigmatic of the death of the wicked. Since he is judged (theoretically, at any rate) for crimes he will commit in the future, his death is beneficial to him, inasmuch as he comes before God untainted by any real crimes. Similarly, the wicked always benefit from their own death inasmuch as they are thus prevented from committing additional crimes and from further tainting themselves. It goes without saying that the death of the righteous is both a personal and a social disaster, because they are prevented from doing additional good deeds.

The drunken sleep of the wicked is of personal and social benefit, in that it keeps them out of trouble. In the case of the righteous, however, it prevents them from performing acts of benevolence.

The dispersal of the wicked is of personal and social benefit, since it prevents their collaboration with like-minded individuals. For this reason, a convention of the wicked is particularly dangerous. The opposite applies in the case of the righteous.

When the wicked enjoy tranquility, they can plot their nefarious schemes undisturbed—with obviously negative social con-sequences. When the righteous are at peace, however, they can pursue their conduct of kindness without distraction, with obvious social and personal benefit.

APPLICATION

A righteous person is one whose good deeds outweigh his bad. A wicked person simply has more demerits than merits. By this defini-tion, it is not difficult to be righteous. Righteousness is not the monopoly of the extraordinarily saintly. We can all be righteous, just as we can all too easily regress into wickedness.

(The rabbi/study leader should here spell out how the deceased fell within our definition of righteousness.)

The deceased was guilty neither of drunkenness nor of slumber. He was not asleep to opportunities of service. (The rabbi/study leader should elaborate on the service he performed.)

The deceased was not a misanthrope. He loved people and worked with many groups and organizations. (These should be detailed by the rabbi/study leader.)

His/her acts of benevolence were interrupted only by . . . (the rabbi/study leader should fill in this blank, referring, for example, to a Holocaust experience, sickness, a demanding business, etc., etc.).

It can truly be said that his/her death, like that of all the righteous, was a misfortune not only for the immediate family and friends, but for the community and for society as a whole.

May his/her soul be bound up in the bond of eternal life.

Every Jew Performs *Mitzvot*

APPLICATION: GENERAL

MISHNAH: *Makkot* 3:16

רַבִּי חֲנַנְיָא בֶּן־עֲקַשְׁיָא אוֹמֵר, רָצָה הַקָּדוֹשׁ־בָּרוּךְ־הוּא לְזַכּוֹת אֶת־יִשְׂרָאֵל, לְפִיכָךְ הִרְבָּה
לָהֶם תּוֹרָה וּמִצְוֹת, שֶׁנֶּאֱמַר יְיָ חָפֵץ לְמַעַן צִדְקוֹ יַגְדִּיל תּוֹרָה וְיַאְדִּיר:

TRANSLATION

Rabbi Chananya ben Akashya said: The Holy One, blessed be
He, desired to bestow merit upon Israel. Accordingly, He granted
them much Torah and many religious imperatives (*mitzvot*), as it is
said: *It pleased the Lord for the sake of His righteousness, to magnify the Torah and to make it honorable* (Isaiah 42:21).

COMMENTARY

The meaning of this *mishnah* is clear: The more *mitzvot* a person
performs, the greater will be his ultimate reward; the more Torah
he studies, the greater will be his spiritual recompense. The standard translation of the proof-text weakens its full impact. "For the
sake of His righteousness" should rather be rendered "To justify
him [i.e., Israel]." The meaning of the verse thus becomes: God
wished to justify the chosen status of the Jewish people. Accordingly, He enlarged His Torah and glorified it.

APPLICATION

In his commentary on this *mishnah*, the great Moses Maimonides
declares: "One of the fundamental principles of the Torah is that if
a person performs any one of the 613 commandments of the Torah
in a right and fitting manner . . . altruistically, and out of love, he

will merit life eternal. Accordingly, Rabbi Chananya declared that since there are so many *mitzvot*, it is impossible for a person not to have performed *one* of them perfectly during his entire lifetime and, by so doing, to have endowed his soul with eternity at that moment."

This comment must surely be of enormous comfort to the bereaved. Anybody who knew and loved the deceased is certain that he/she has indeed earned his/her eternal reward. He/she performed not one but many meritorious deeds in a life lived so very meaningfully.

Interestingly, Maimonides cites a striking support for his thesis. When the great martyr, Rabbi Chananya ben Teradyon, sought assurance from his colleagues that he was destined for life eternal, he was requested to single out an act of kindness which he had performed to perfection. (The rabbi/study leader should here elaborate on the kindnesses and acts of charity of the deceased.)

In another commentary on our *mishnah*, it is pointed out that every married person performs a *mitzvah* just by being married, and that God included the instinctive urge for companionship in the Torah merely in order to enable us to claim a reward for doing what comes naturally anyway. The relationship of the deceased with his/her spouse was far, far more than merely "being married." (The rabbi/study leader should discuss the special relationship in detail.) In terms of *this* criterion, too, the love and devotion of the deceased confers immortality upon him/her.

It has often been said that we achieve immortality through our children. This is true in a technical sense also. The man is commanded to be fruitful and multiply (Genesis 9:7). By merely having children a man earns his eternal reward. How much more so does this apply to the deceased. (The rabbi/study leader should speak about his/her parenting skills.)

It is possible to spend hours enumerating the *mitzvot* performed so beautifully by the deceased—honor of parents, sensitivity to the disadvantaged, etc., etc. (The rabbi/study leader can list and elaborate on a few.)

Indeed, we *are* certain that the deceased *has* merited life eternal. May his/her memory be a blessing, even as his/her soul is bound in the bond of eternal life.

The Children
and Grandchildren of
the Assimilated

APPLICATION: CHILDREN AND GRANDCHILDREN
OF AN ASSIMILATED FAMILY

MISHNAH: *Gittin* 4:9

הַמּוֹכֵר אֶת עַצְמוֹ וְאֶת־בָּנָיו לַגּוֹי, אֵין פּוֹדִין אוֹתוֹ, אֲבָל פּוֹדִין אֶת הַבָּנִים לְאַחַר מִיתַת־
אֲבִיהֶן. הַמּוֹכֵר שָׂדֵהוּ לַגּוֹי וְחָזַר וּלְקָחָהּ מִמֶּנּוּ (יִשְׂרָאֵל), הַלּוֹקֵחַ מֵבִיא מִמֶּנּוּ בִּכּוּרִים,
מִפְּנֵי תִקּוּן הָעוֹלָם:

TRANSLATION

There is no obligation to redeem a person who sells himself and his
son as slaves to a gentile. However, the children must be redeemed
after the death of their parents. If a person sells his field [in Israel]
to a gentile, he must take the first fruits and bring them [to Jerusalem each year] in order to enhance the general good.

COMMENTARY

Pidyon shevuyim, the redemption of captives, is accorded very
high priority in the Jewish scale of ethical imperatives. Scarcely any
price is too high for the ransom of Jewish captives. Since the situation of the captives is considered to be extremely perilous, the act of
redemption is regarded as life-saving (*piku'ach nefesh*).

The motivation for redemption is both physical and spiritual.
The life of the captive is imperiled. But even if it is spared, his soul
is at risk under the alien influence of his captors.

Accordingly, a person who deliberately courts this calamity, selling himself and his family into so hazardous a situation, places

himself beyond the pale. He cannot expect the community to ransom him. Not even his children are to be ransomed during his lifetime, for he cannot be relied upon not to sell them again. After his death, however, the community is obligated to ransom his children.

The second clause of the *mishnah* is translated according to the variant Hebrew version proposed by the classical commentators, Rabbi Shlomo Yitzchaki (Rashi) and Rabbi Ovadyah Bertinoro (the Rav). Its purpose was the prevention of the sale of real estate in Israel to gentiles. The annual obligation to purchase the first fruits from the buyer of the alienated property and to personally transport them to Jerusalem would discourage the alienation of Jewish property in the Holy Land.

APPLICATION

It has been noted that the discipline of *shiv'ah* observance and the eleven-month obligation to recite the *Kaddish* at the three daily public worship services yields a valuable "fringe benefit." The children from assimilated homes, who have been alienated from their traditions and taken captive by the allure of the gentile environment, reenter their communities, reclaim their heritage, and reaffiliate with the mainstream of Jewish commitment. In a sense, they ransom themselves from the clutches of the surrounding culture. In a still profounder sense, the act of redemption is the final, posthumous gesture of the deceased. His/her death becomes the occasion for the return of his/her descendants to the fold, to the world of his/her parents. In many cases, this gesture arches over several generations. The deceased may himself/herself have been "an infant captured by the pagans," may have become assimilated through no fault of his/her own, but as a result of prior neglect by a previous generation. The return of the second and third generations through observing the laws of mourning bestows a posthumous merit on the deceased, and is an ultimate Jewish justification of his/her life.

May the children and grandchildren make the effort and take the trouble to grant their forebears this special merit by means of their commitment to observe the period of mourning throughout the year as our tradition demands.

A House Divided

APPLICATION: A DISUNITED FAMILY

MISHNAH: *Uktzin* 3:12

אָמַר רַבִּי יְהוֹשֻׁעַ בֶּן לֵוִי עָתִיד הַקָּדוֹשׁ בָּרוּךְ הוּא לְהַנְחִיל לְכָל צַדִּיק וְצַדִּיק שְׁלֹשׁ מֵאוֹת וַעֲשָׂרָה עוֹלָמוֹת, שֶׁנֶּאֱמַר, לְהַנְחִיל אֹהֲבַי יֵשׁ וְאֹצְרֹתֵיהֶם אֲמַלֵּא . אָמַר רַבִּי שִׁמְעוֹן בֶּן חֲלַפְתָּא לֹא מָצָא הַקָּדוֹשׁ בָּרוּךְ הוּא כְּלִי מַחֲזִיק בְּרָכָה לְיִשְׂרָאֵל אֶלָּא הַשָּׁלוֹם, שֶׁנֶּאֱמַר יְיָ עֹז לְעַמּוֹ יִתֵּן יְיָ יְבָרֵךְ אֶת־עַמּוֹ בַשָּׁלוֹם:

TRANSLATION

Rabbi Yehoshua ben Levi said: The Holy One, blessed be He, will cause each and every righteous person to inherit 310 worlds, as it is said: *That I may cause those that love Me to inherit yesh, and that I may fill their treasuries* (Proverbs 8:21). Rabbi Shimon ben Chalafta said: The Holy One, blessed be He, could find no vessel that could contain Israel's blessing but Peace, as it is said: *The Lord will give strength unto His people. The Lord will bless His people with peace* (Psalm 29:11).

COMMENTARY

This is the very last *mishnah* in the entire Talmud. Significantly, it ends with the blessing of peace.

Its first clause deals with the ultimate reward of the righteous. According to Maimonides the word *yesh* of the proof-text means "unconditional existence." This is the promise of eternal life to those who have preoccupied themselves with the study of the Mishnah. The word *yesh* is also the numerical equivalent of the number 310. This is a poetic (but not literal) expression of the degree to which life beyond the grave is superior to life as we know it here on earth.

388

The final clause is in praise of peace. Aware that the Mishnah is characterized by divisions of opinion and by argumentation, Rabbi Shimon ben Chalafta urges that disputes be resolved in love, and that peace be established as the ultimate divine blessing.

APPLICATION

The two clauses of our *mishnah* are really interrelated. The phrase *kol tsaddik ve-tsaddik*, "each and every righteous person," hints at discord. Though differences of opinion abound in the Mishnah, proponents of different opinions should not denigrate their adversaries. Even opponents who take opposite sides in a conflict can each be righteous, and can each find justification for his/her position. Each can claim to be, and is, indeed, among those who love God and are loved by Him. If each protagonist is essentially a good person, the polarity of positions does not preclude the possibility of peace. However, the enterprise of peace-making requires great strength. Only strong people can hold such strong positions. Only strong people can accomplish the achievement of peace. Only the strong are secure enough to compromise. Only the strong can make gestures of rapprochement without loss of face. God gives the blessing of strength in order to allow us to attain the even greater blessing of peace. Let us dedicate ourselves to do His will, to find the strength which will bring us the blessing of peace.

Appearances are Deceptive

**APPLICATION: A PERSON FRAIL IN BODY:
UNSPECTACULAR LIVES**

MISHNAH: *Avot* 4:20

רַבִּי אוֹמֵר, אַל תִּסְתַּכֵּל בְּקַנְקַן, אֶלָּא, בְּמַה שֶׁיֵּשׁ בּוֹ; יֵשׁ קַנְקַן חָדָשׁ מָלֵא יָשָׁן, וְיָשָׁן,
שֶׁאֲפִילוּ חָדָשׁ אֵין בּוֹ:

TRANSLATION

Rabbi [Judah, the Prince] said: Look not at the flask, but at what it contains. There may be a new flask full of old wine, and an old flask that has not even new wine in it.

COMMENTARY

Rabbi Judah's statement is a reaction to the dictum of Rabbi Yossi bar Yehudah, which precedes it: "He who learns from the young, to what is he to be compared? To a person who eats unripe grapes and who drinks wine from his vat. And he who learns from the old, to what is he to be compared? To one who eats ripe grapes, and drinks old wine." According to Rabbi Yossi, wisdom is necessarily a product of age. Rabbi Judah disagrees. The content of a man's head does not depend upon his external appearance. The gray-haired eminence may be empty of wisdom, whereas a young head may be full of understanding, insight, and knowledge since appearances are often deceptive.

APPLICATIONS

A. *A frail body can envelop a robust spirit.* The deceased was physically frail, the consequence of . . . (the rabbi/study leader should elaborate on the origin of the frailty, dwell upon the

390

limitations that this frailty imposed upon the deceased, and describe the suffering and discomfort which the frailty caused).

However, this frail body contained a robust spirit, a lively intellect, and a generous heart. (The rabbi/study leader should expand upon thses attributes, both conceptually and anecdotally.)

Scripture reminds us that "Man sees with his eyes, but God sees into the heart (*I Sam.* 16:7)." We know that God has seen beyond his/her physical frailty, and will judge the flask by the fine wine it contains. As we contemplate his/her virtues, we shall surely do the same.

B. *Unspectacular lives can be most meaningful.* Our hedonistic society idolizes the "beautiful people." They are rich, glamorous, popular, and successful. The world is their oyster. Members of the jet-set fly around the globe and attract sycophants and admirers who hope to benefit from their association. Our society disdains the materially unendowed and labels them as failures. Hedonists do not seek out their company and are contemptuous of their humble accomplishments.

Rabbi Judah has a different conception of "beautiful people." He refuses to judge a book by its unglamourous covers. Its contents are *all* important.

The cover of the deceased's Book of Life may not be immediately impressive. (The rabbi/study leader should discuss the outward appearance of his/her life — job, home, associates, etc.)

But the Book itself is rich in content. Every chapter is significant. The chapter entitled "Family," for example, should be required reading for all decent people. (The rabbi/study leader should elaborate on the deceased as a family man/woman.)

The chapter entitled, "Occupation," is a model of integrity, diligence, and dependability. (The rabbi/study leader, should describe the work ethic and reputation of the deceased in some detail.)

The chapter entitled, "Principles and Beliefs," demands our attention. (The rabbi/study leader should spell out the belief system of the deceased, as it expressed itself in his/her life and in the life of his/her family.)

The hedonists are wrong. Rabbi Judah is right. The deceased *was* a beautiful person. May we preserve the chapters of his/her life as a model for our own.

Yahrzeit Record

Name of Deceased (English)	Date of Death (secular)	Day	Month	Year	Name of Deceased (Hebrew)

Index